Species Domain

スピーシーズドメイン

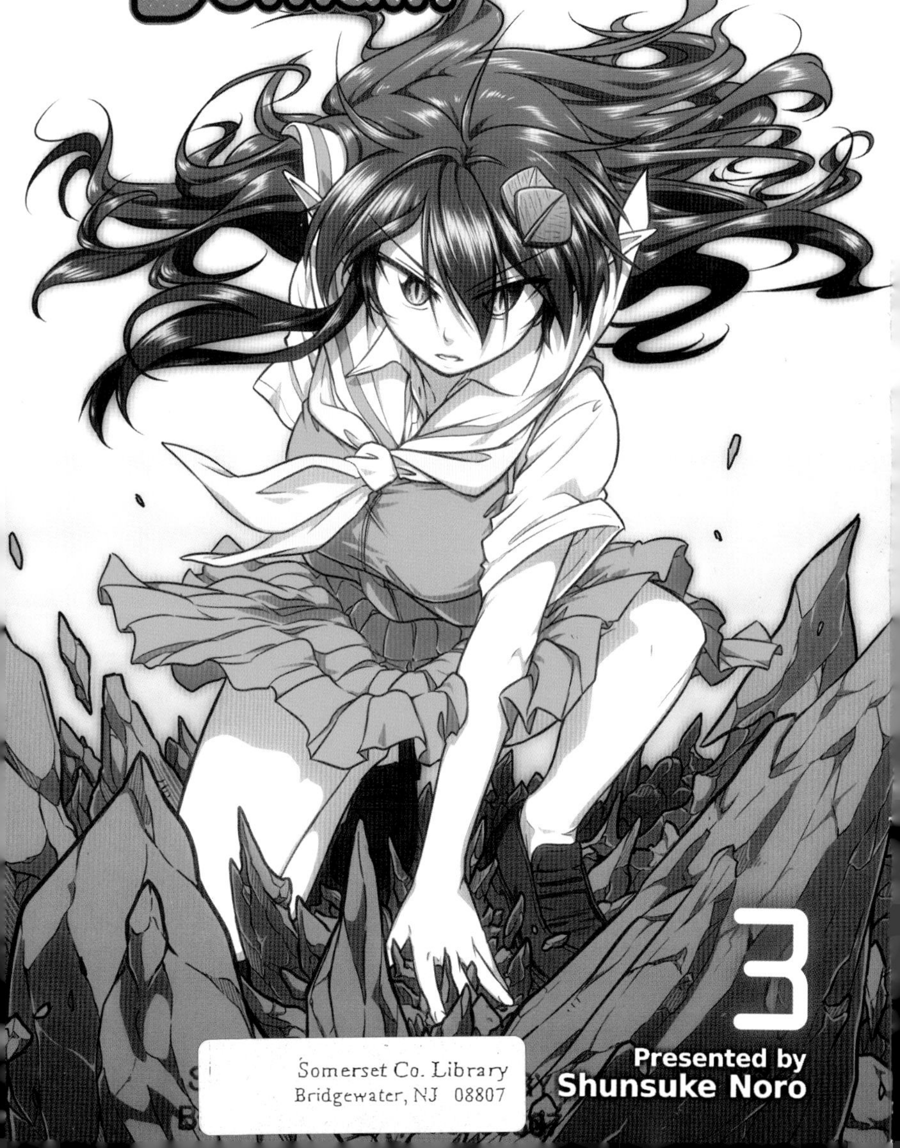

3

Presented by
Shunsuke Noro

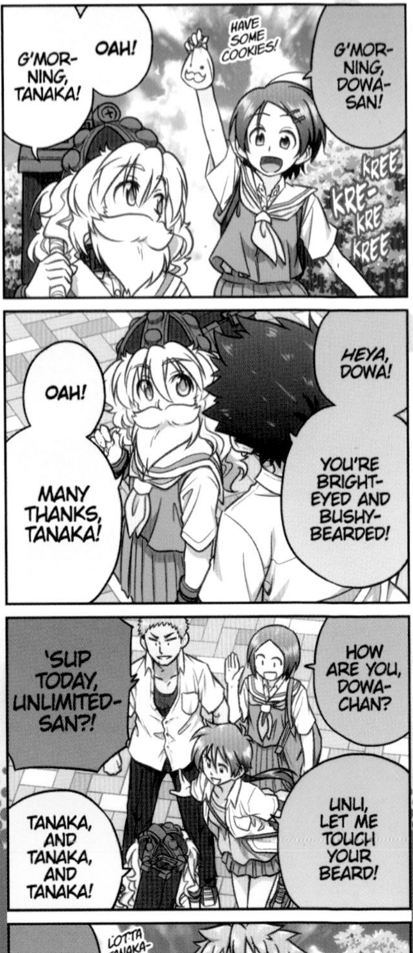
G'MOR-NING, DOWA-SAN!
HAVE SOME COOKIES!
OAH!
G'MOR-NING, TANAKA!
KREE KREE-KRE KREE
HEYA, DOWA!
YOU'RE BRIGHT-EYED AND BUSHY-BEARDED!
OAH!
MANY THANKS, TANAKA!
HOW ARE YOU, DOWA-CHAN?
'SUP TODAY, UNLIMITED-SAN?!
UNLI, LET ME TOUCH YOUR BEARD!
TANAKA, AND TANAKA, AND TANAKA!
WORD OF DOWA-CHAN MUST BE SPREADING TO MORE AND MORE TANAKA-SANS...
LOTTA TANAKA-SANS HERE...
SHE'S FORMING HER OWN TANAKA HAREM...
REERA REERA REE

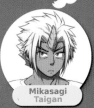

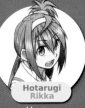

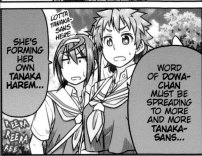

What will you do, Tanaka (Yoshi)-kun?

Species Domain 3

スピーシーズドメイン

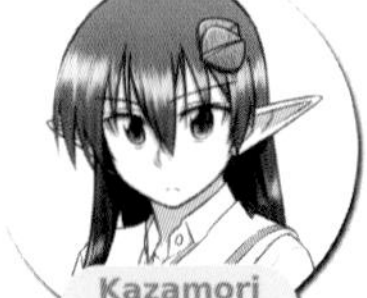

Kazamori Itoko

Elf. Wants to use magic but can't.

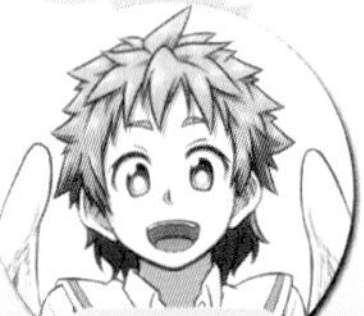

Hanei Miné

Icarus. Kind-hearted and large-breasted.

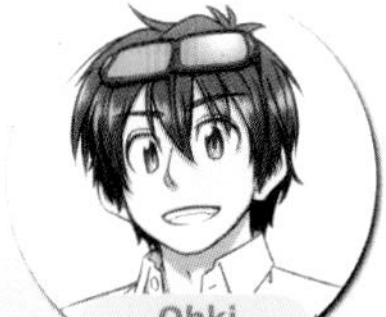

Ohki Hatsuhiko

Human. A science nut.

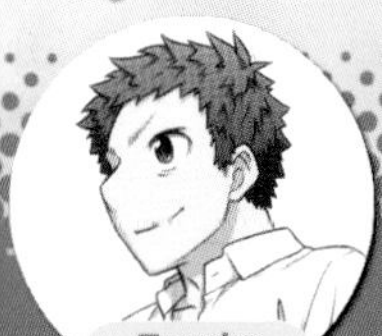

Tanaka Yoshirou

Human. Life of the party.

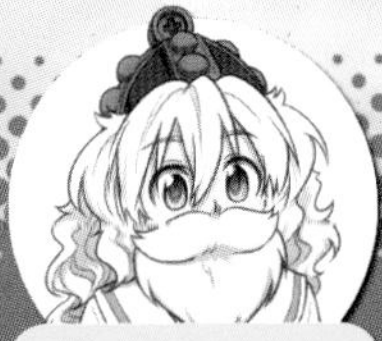

Dowa Unlimited

Dwarf. A girl with a beard.

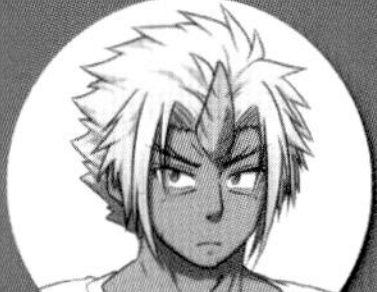

Mikasagi Taigan

Ogre. A young tough guy.

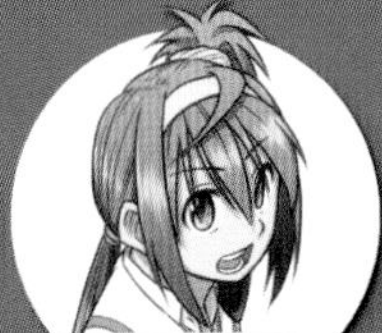

Hotarugi Rikka

Human. Tanaka's childhood friend.

Cover Design: 5Gas Design Studio

Chapter 15: Tanaka-kun Gushes

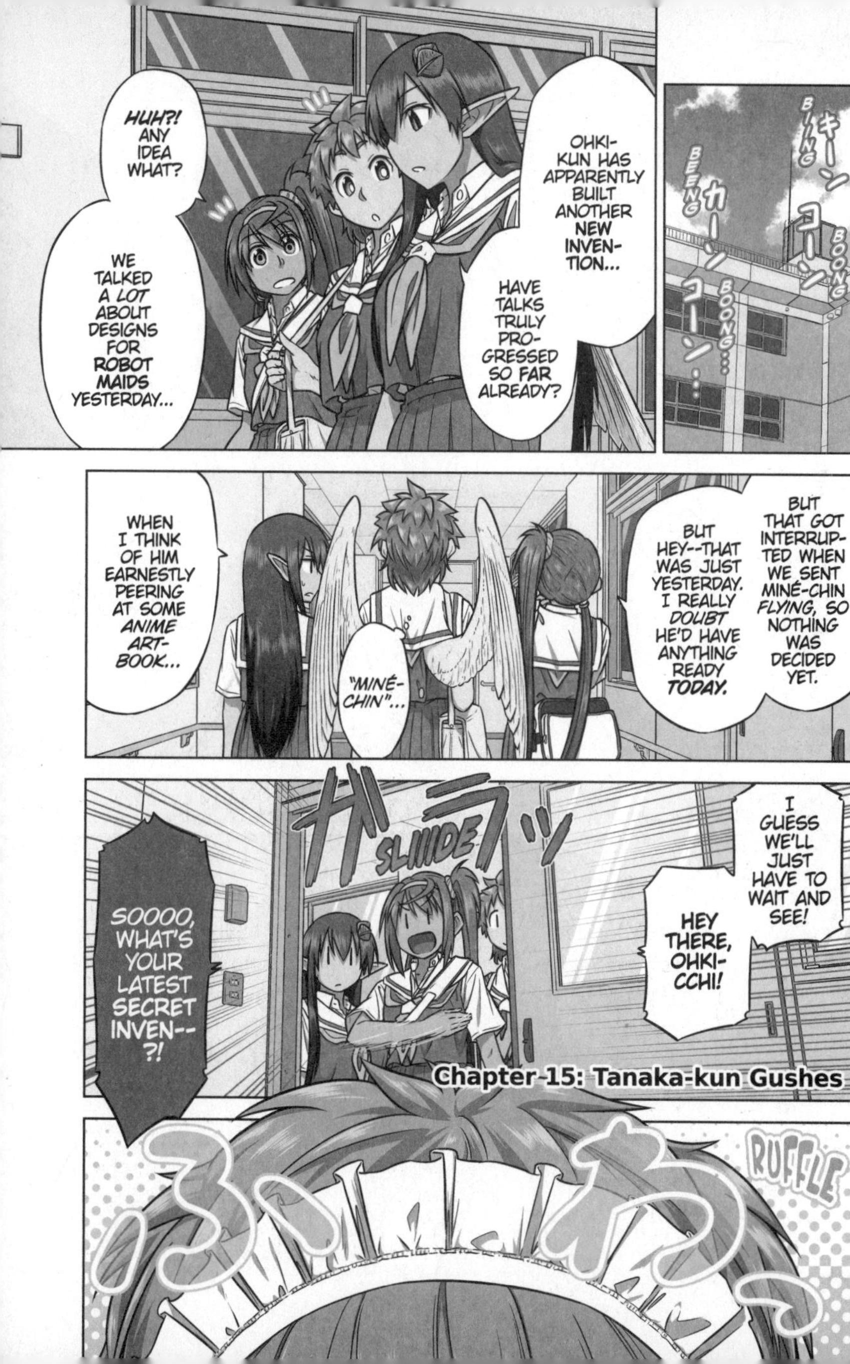
キーンコーンカーンコーン
BIIING BEEENG BOOONG BOOONG...
OHKI-KUN HAS APPARENTLY BUILT ANOTHER NEW INVENTION...
HAVE TALKS TRULY PROGRESSED SO FAR ALREADY?
HUH?! ANY IDEA WHAT?
WE TALKED A LOT ABOUT DESIGNS FOR ROBOT MAIDS YESTERDAY...
BUT THAT GOT INTERRUPTED WHEN WE SENT MINÉ-CHIN FLYING, SO NOTHING WAS DECIDED YET.
BUT HEY--THAT WAS JUST YESTERDAY. I REALLY DOUBT HE'D HAVE ANYTHING READY TODAY.
"MINÉ-CHIN"...
WHEN I THINK OF HIM EARNESTLY PEERING AT SOME ANIME ART-BOOK...
I GUESS WE'LL JUST HAVE TO WAIT AND SEE!
HEY THERE, OHKI-CCHI!
ガラッ
SLIIIDE
SOOOO, WHAT'S YOUR LATEST SECRET INVEN--?!
RUFFLE

Chapter 15: Tanaka-kun Gushes

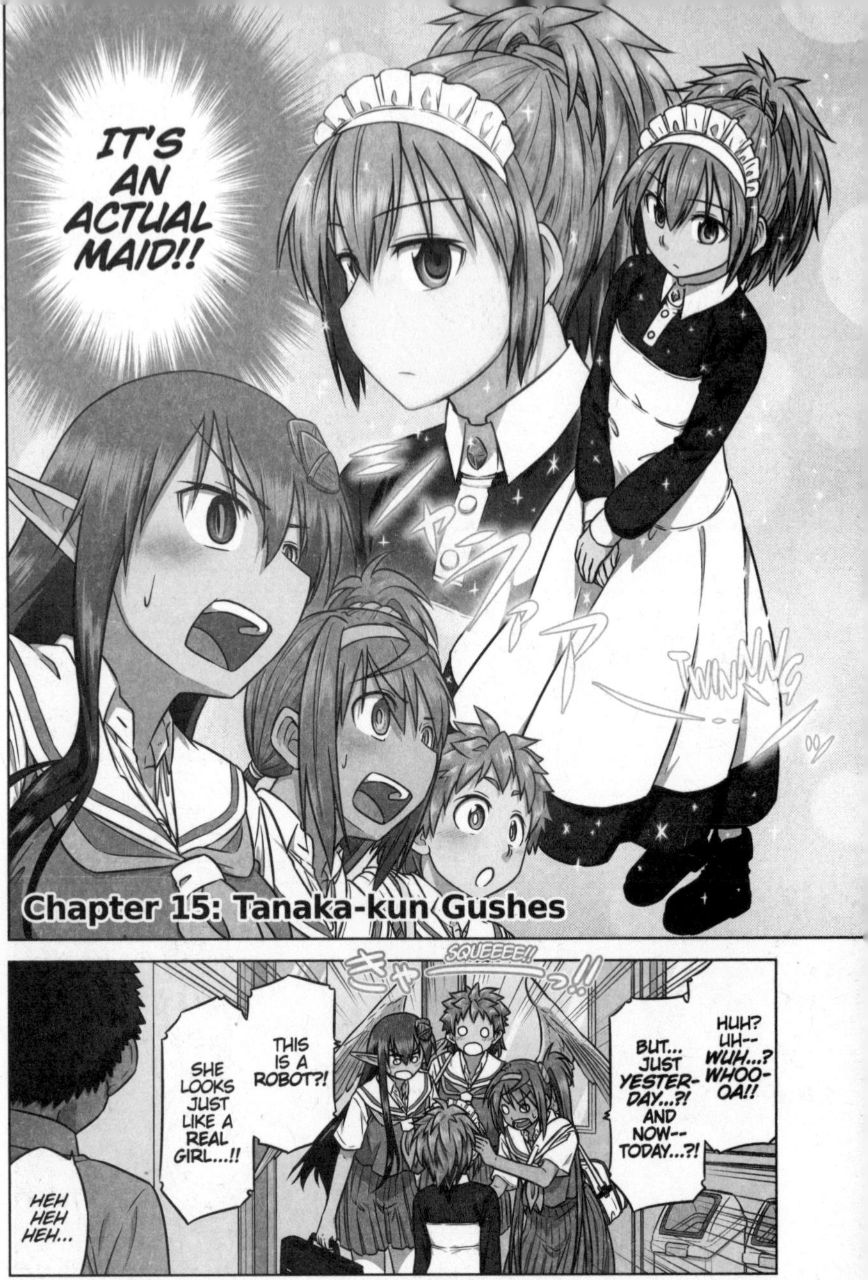
IT'S AN ACTUAL MAID!!
TWINNNG
きゃーーっ!!
SQUEEEE!!
HUH? UH-- WUH...? WHOOO-OA!!
BUT... JUST YESTER-DAY...?! AND NOW-- TODAY...?!
THIS IS A ROBOT?!
SHE LOOKS JUST LIKE A REAL GIRL...!!
HEH HEH HEH...

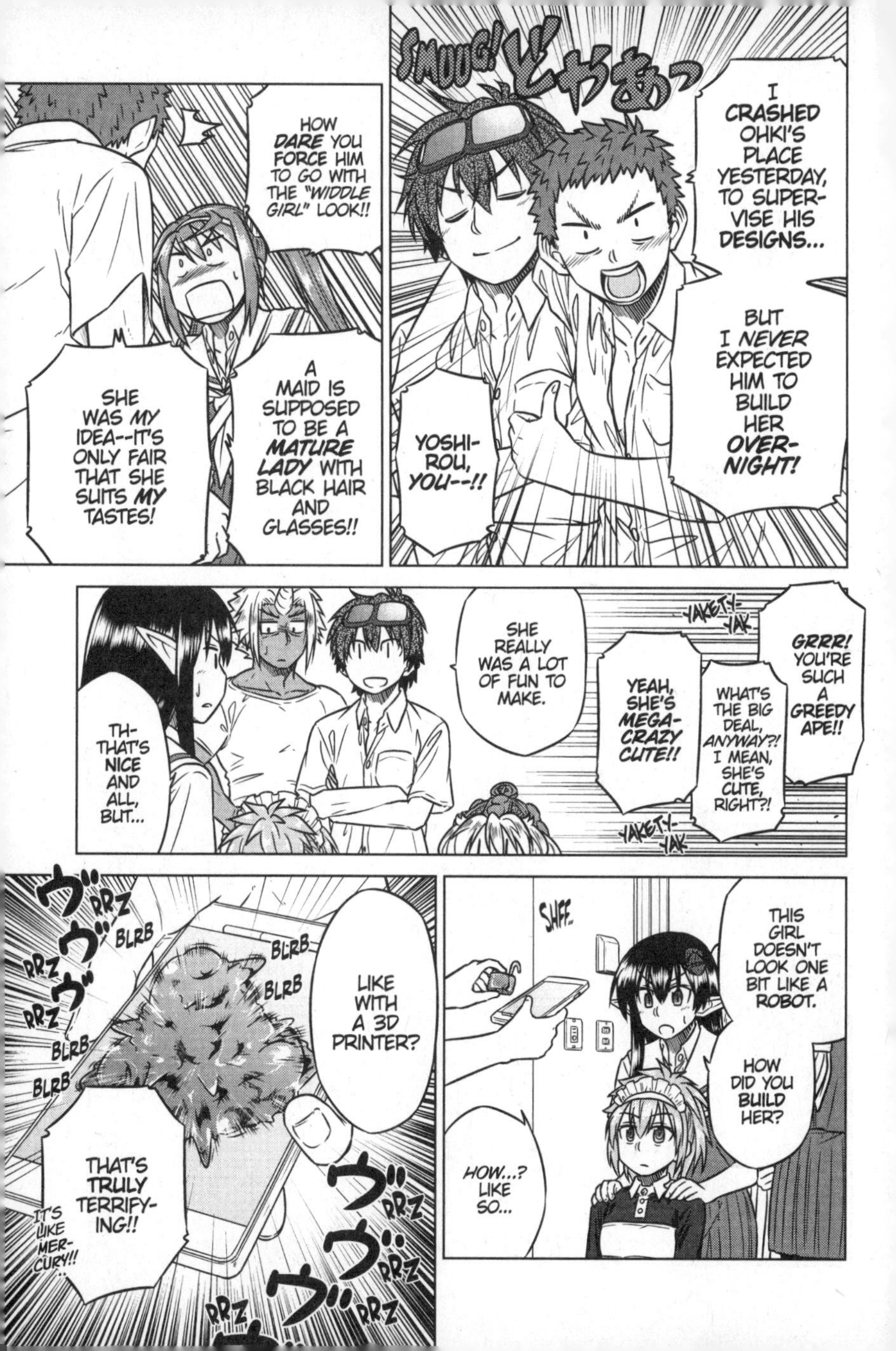
SMUUG! どやぁっ
I CRASHED OHKI'S PLACE YESTERDAY, TO SUPER-VISE HIS DESIGNS...
BUT I *NEVER* EXPECTED HIM TO BUILD HER *OVER-NIGHT!*
YOSHI-ROU, *YOU--!!*
HOW *DARE* YOU FORCE HIM TO GO WITH THE "*WIDDLE GIRL*" LOOK!!
A MAID IS SUPPOSED TO BE A *MATURE LADY* WITH BLACK HAIR AND GLASSES!!
SHE WAS *MY* IDEA--IT'S ONLY FAIR THAT SHE SUITS *MY* TASTES!
GRRR! YOU'RE SUCH A GREEDY APE!!
YAKETY-YAK
WHAT'S THE BIG DEAL, *ANYWAY?!* I MEAN, SHE'S CUTE, RIGHT?!
YAKETY-YAK
YEAH, SHE'S *MEGA-CRAZY CUTE!!*
SHE REALLY WAS A LOT OF FUN TO MAKE.
TH-THAT'S *NICE* AND ALL, BUT...
SHFF...
THIS GIRL DOESN'T LOOK ONE BIT LIKE A ROBOT.
HOW DID YOU *BUILD* HER?
HOW...? LIKE SO...
ヴ RRZ
BLRB
ヴ RRZ
ヴ RRZ
BLRB
BLRB
BLRB
BLRB
LIKE WITH A 3D PRINTER?
THAT'S *TRULY* TERRIFY-ING!!
IT'S LIKE MER-CURY!!...
ヴ RRZ
ヴ RRZ
ヴ RRZ
RRZ

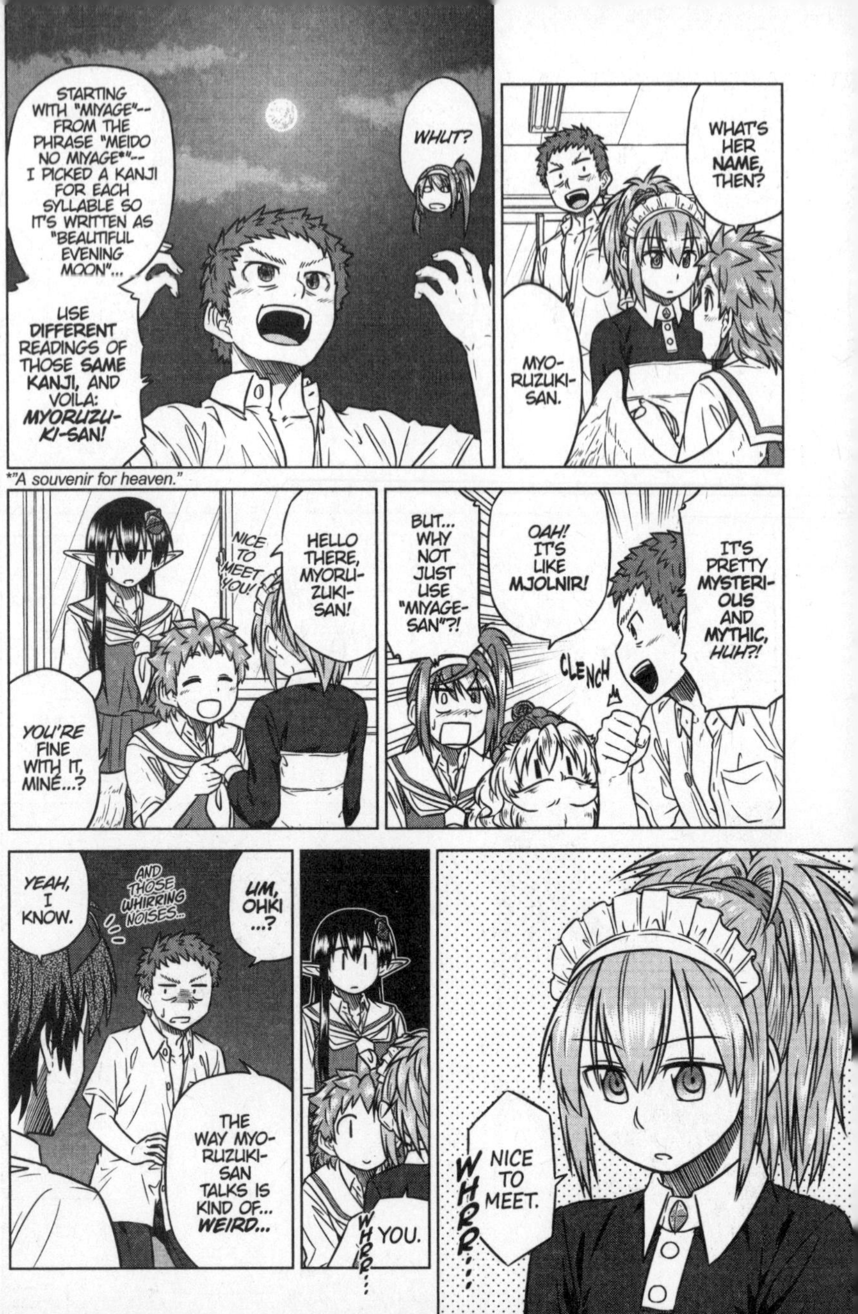
WHAT'S HER NAME, THEN?
MYO-RUZUKI-SAN.
WHUT?
STARTING WITH "MIYAGE"-- FROM THE PHRASE "MEIDO NO MIYAGE*"-- I PICKED A KANJI FOR EACH SYLLABLE SO IT'S WRITTEN AS "BEAUTIFUL EVENING MOON"...
USE DIFFERENT READINGS OF THOSE SAME KANJI, AND VOILA: MYORUZUKI-SAN!
IT'S PRETTY MYSTERIOUS AND MYTHIC, HUH?!
OAH! IT'S LIKE MJOLNIR!
CLENCH
BUT... WHY NOT JUST USE "MIYAGE-SAN"?!
HELLO THERE, MYORUZUKI-SAN!
NICE TO MEET YOU!
YOU'RE FINE WITH IT, MINE...?
NICE TO MEET.
WHRR...
UM, OHKI ...?
YOU.
WHRR...
YEAH, I KNOW.
AND THOSE WHIRRING NOISES...
THE WAY MYO-RUZUKI-SAN TALKS IS KIND OF... WEIRD...
*"A souvenir for heaven."

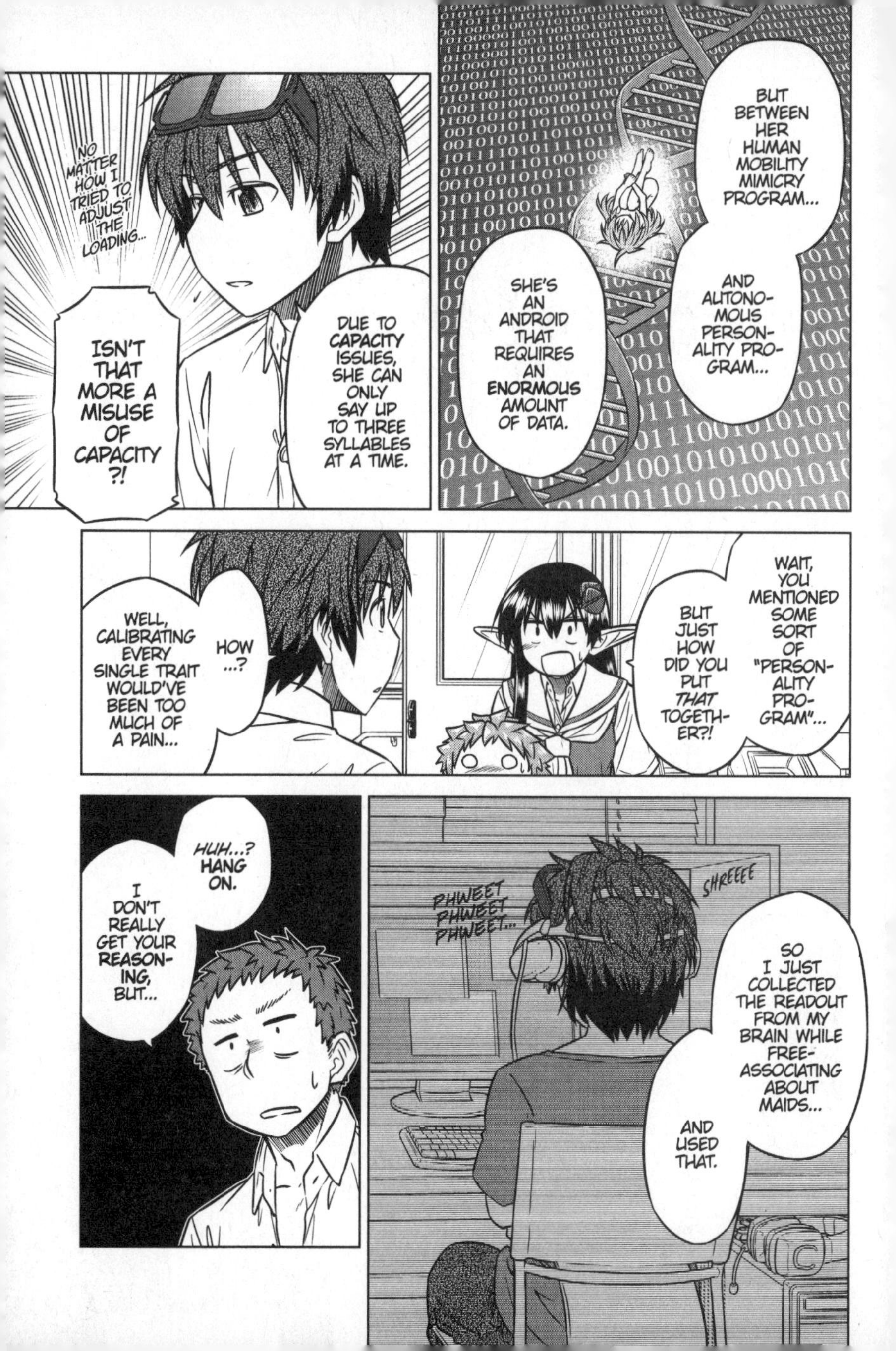

BUT BETWEEN HER HUMAN MOBILITY MIMICRY PROGRAM...
AND AUTONOMOUS PERSONALITY PROGRAM...
SHE'S AN ANDROID THAT REQUIRES AN ENORMOUS AMOUNT OF DATA.
DUE TO CAPACITY ISSUES, SHE CAN ONLY SAY UP TO THREE SYLLABLES AT A TIME.
NO MATTER HOW I TRIED TO ADJUST THE LOADING...
ISN'T THAT MORE A MISUSE OF CAPACITY?!
WAIT, YOU MENTIONED SOME SORT OF "PERSONALITY PROGRAM"...
BUT JUST HOW DID YOU PUT THAT TOGETHER?!
HOW...?
WELL, CALIBRATING EVERY SINGLE TRAIT WOULD'VE BEEN TOO MUCH OF A PAIN...
SHREEEE
PHWEET PHWEET PHWEET...
SO I JUST COLLECTED THE READOUT FROM MY BRAIN WHILE FREE-ASSOCIATING ABOUT MAIDS...
AND USED THAT.
HUH...? HANG ON.
I DON'T REALLY GET YOUR REASONING, BUT...

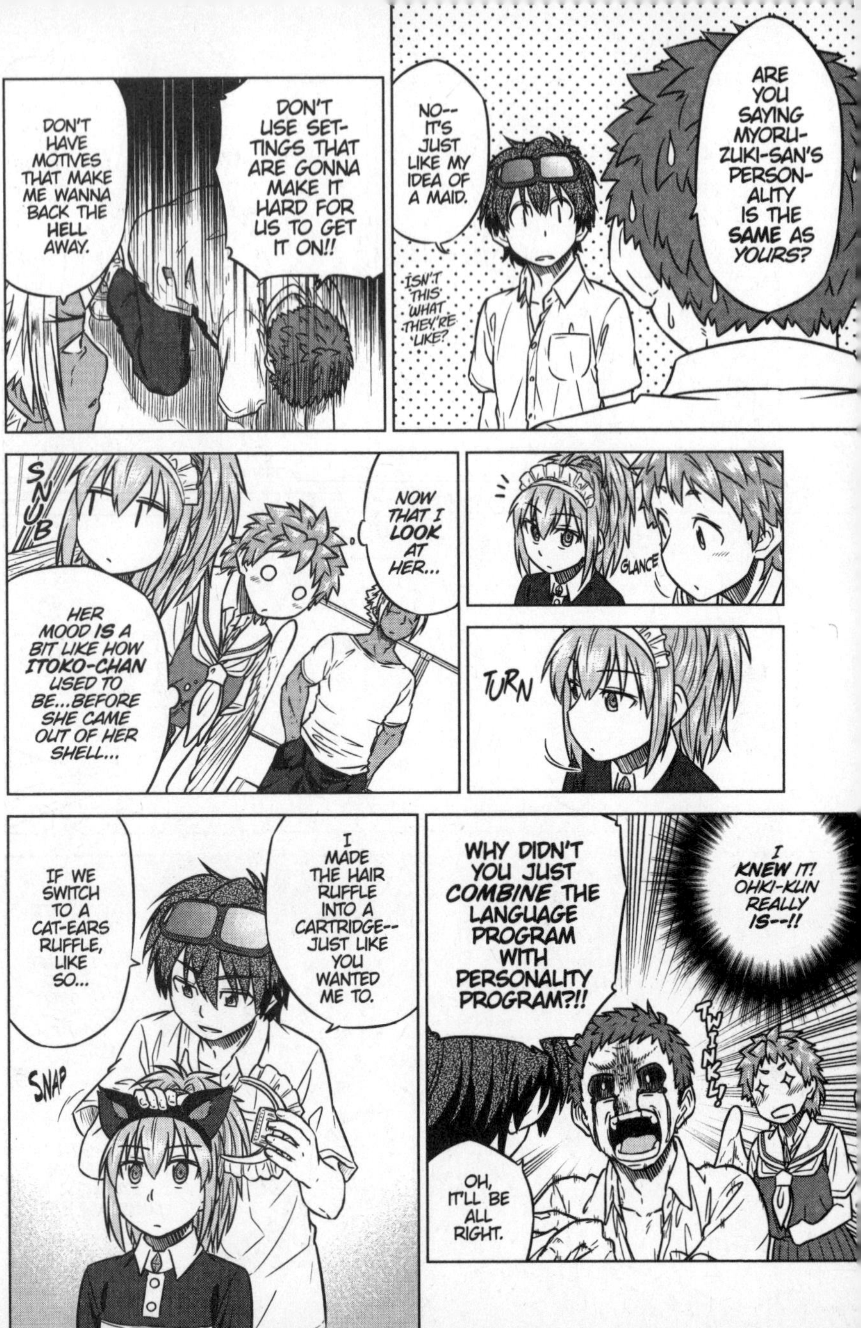
ARE YOU SAYING MYORUZUKI-SAN'S PERSONALITY IS THE SAME AS YOURS?
NO-- IT'S JUST LIKE MY IDEA OF A MAID.
ISN'T THIS WHAT THEY'RE LIKE?
DON'T USE SETTINGS THAT ARE GONNA MAKE IT HARD FOR US TO GET IT ON!!
DON'T HAVE MOTIVES THAT MAKE ME WANNA BACK THE HELL AWAY.
GLANCE
TURN
SNUB
NOW THAT I LOOK AT HER...
HER MOOD IS A BIT LIKE HOW ITOKO-CHAN USED TO BE...BEFORE SHE CAME OUT OF HER SHELL...
I KNEW IT! OHKI-KUN REALLY IS--!!
TWINKLE
WHY DIDN'T YOU JUST COMBINE THE LANGUAGE PROGRAM WITH PERSONALITY PROGRAM?!!
OH, IT'LL BE ALL RIGHT.
I MADE THE HAIR RUFFLE INTO A CARTRIDGE-- JUST LIKE YOU WANTED ME TO.
IF WE SWITCH TO A CAT-EARS RUFFLE, LIKE SO...
SNAP

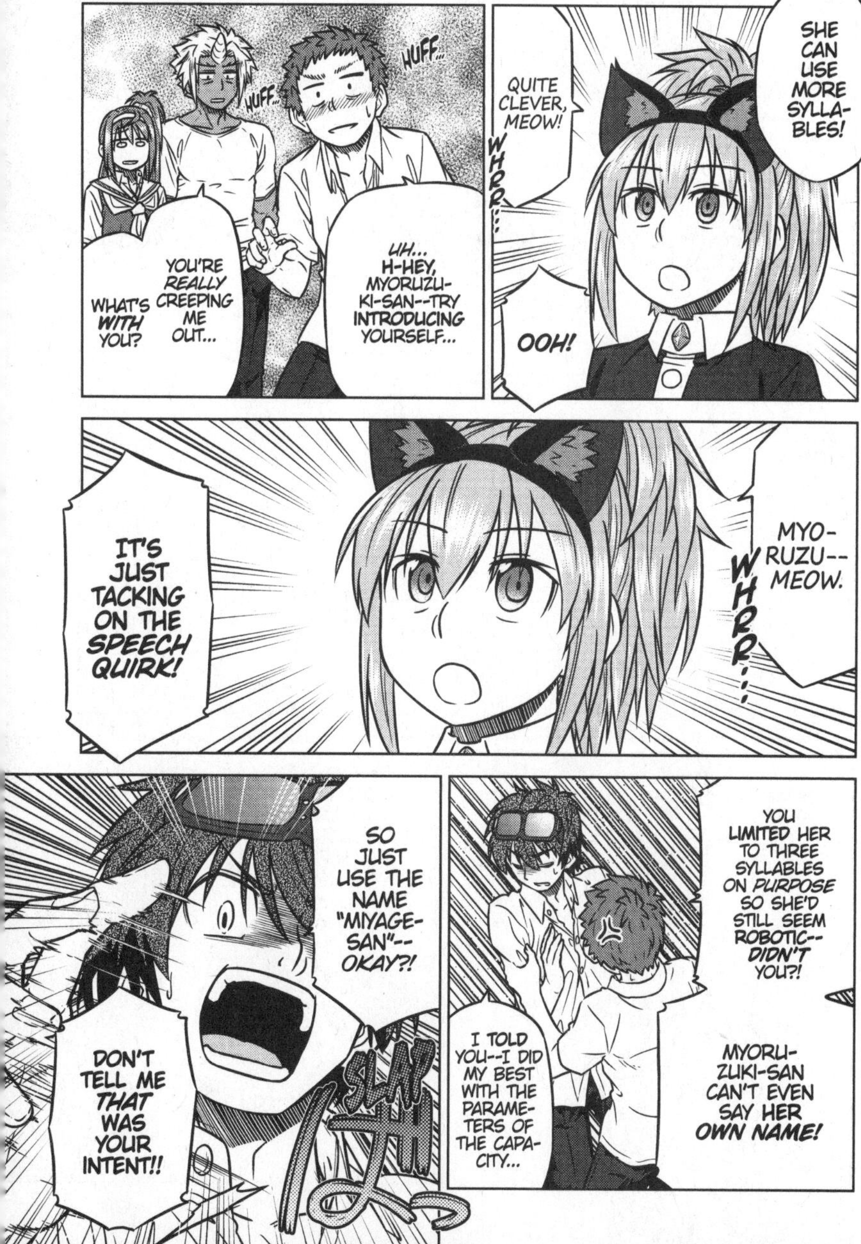
SHE CAN USE MORE SYLLABLES!
QUITE CLEVER, MEOW!
WHRR...
OOH!
HUFF...
HUFF...
UH... H-HEY, MYORUZUKI-SAN--TRY INTRODUCING YOURSELF...
YOU'RE *REALLY* CREEPING ME OUT...
WHAT'S *WITH* YOU?
MYO-RUZU--MEOW.
WHRR...
IT'S JUST TACKING ON THE *SPEECH QUIRK!*
YOU LIMITED HER TO THREE SYLLABLES ON *PURPOSE* SO SHE'D STILL SEEM ROBOTIC--*DIDN'T* YOU?!
MYORUZUKI-SAN CAN'T EVEN SAY HER *OWN NAME!*
I TOLD YOU--I DID MY BEST WITH THE PARAMETERS OF THE CAPACITY...
SO JUST USE THE NAME "MIYAGE-SAN"--*OKAY?!*
DON'T TELL ME *THAT* WAS YOUR INTENT!!
SLAP

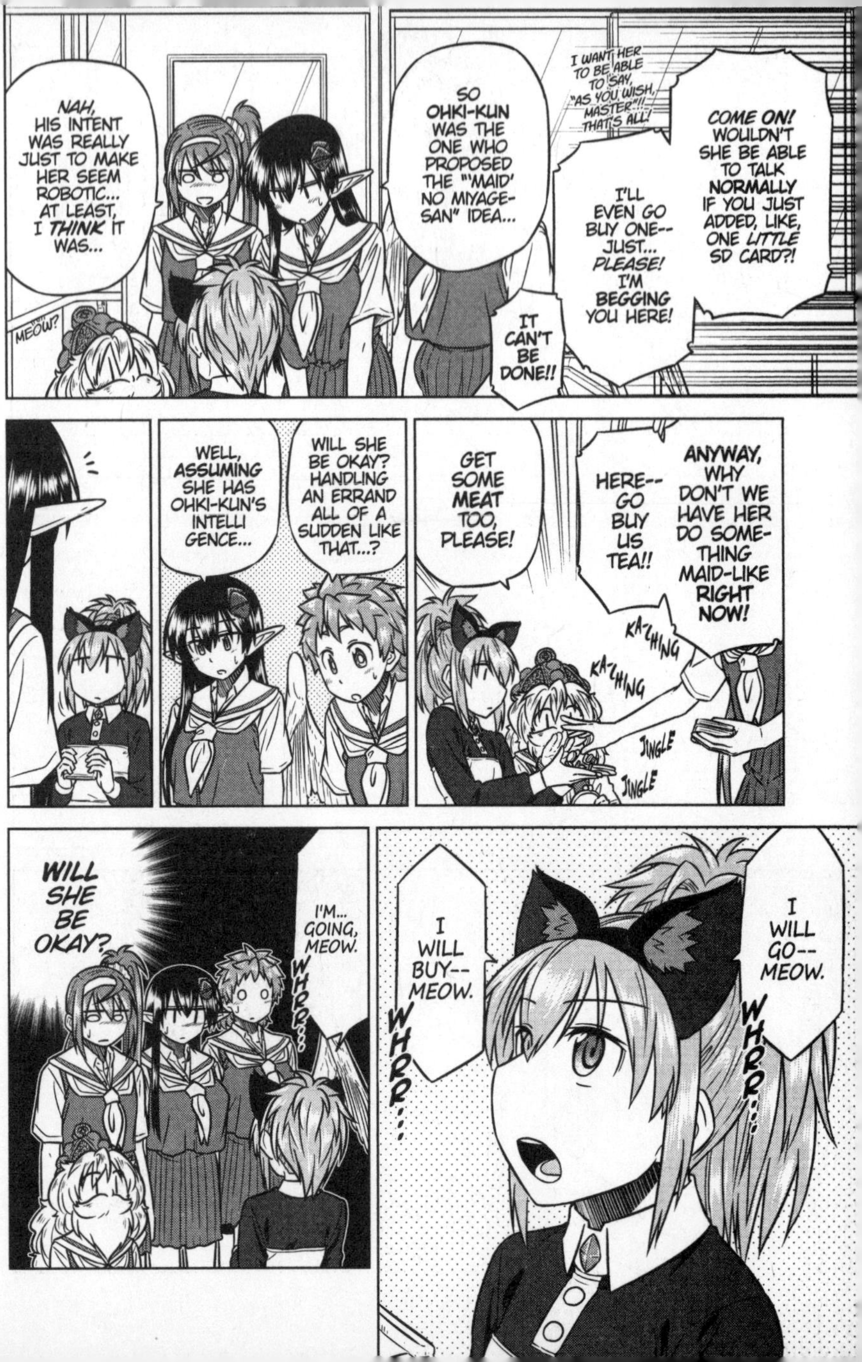
COME ON! WOULDN'T SHE BE ABLE TO TALK NORMALLY IF YOU JUST ADDED, LIKE, ONE LITTLE SD CARD?!
I WANT HER TO BE ABLE TO SAY, "AS YOU WISH, MASTER"!! THAT'S ALL!
I'LL EVEN GO BUY ONE-- JUST... PLEASE! I'M BEGGING YOU HERE!
IT CAN'T BE DONE!!
SO OHKI-KUN WAS THE ONE WHO PROPOSED THE "'MAID' NO MIYAGE-SAN" IDEA...
NAH, HIS INTENT WAS REALLY JUST TO MAKE HER SEEM ROBOTIC... AT LEAST, I THINK IT WAS...
MEOW?
ANYWAY, WHY DON'T WE HAVE HER DO SOME-THING MAID-LIKE RIGHT NOW!
HERE-- GO BUY US TEA!!
GET SOME MEAT TOO, PLEASE!
KA-CHING
KA-CHING
JINGLE
JINGLE
WILL SHE BE OKAY? HANDLING AN ERRAND ALL OF A SUDDEN LIKE THAT...?
WELL, ASSUMING SHE HAS OHKI-KUN'S INTELLI GENCE...
I WILL GO-- MEOW.
WHRR...
I WILL BUY-- MEOW.
WHRR...
I'M... GOING, MEOW.
WHRR...
WILL SHE BE OKAY?

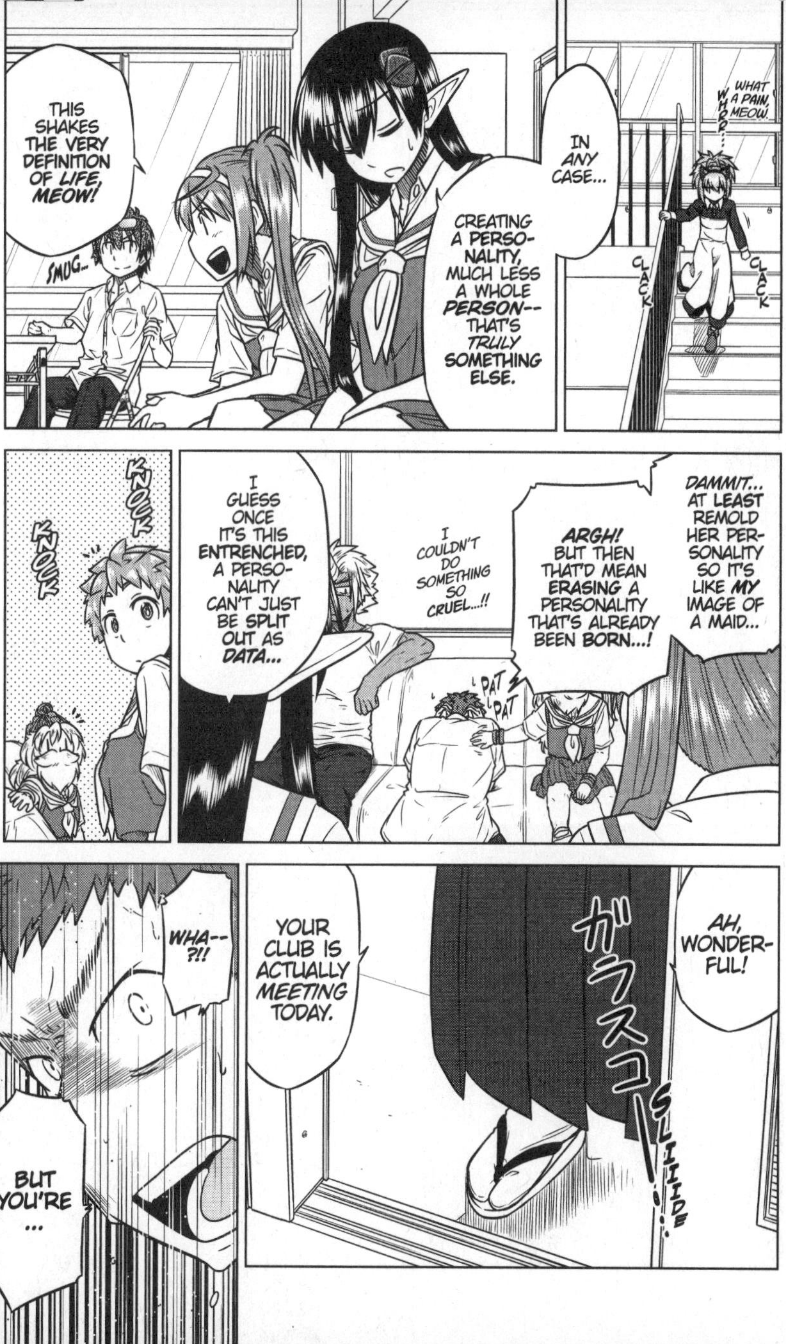
WHAT A PAIN, MEOW.
CLACK
CLACK
IN ANY CASE...
CREATING A PERSONALITY, MUCH LESS A WHOLE PERSON--THAT'S TRULY SOMETHING ELSE.
THIS SHAKES THE VERY DEFINITION OF LIFE, MEOW!
SMUG...
DAMMIT... AT LEAST REMOLD HER PERSONALITY SO IT'S LIKE MY IMAGE OF A MAID...
ARGH! BUT THEN THAT'D MEAN ERASING A PERSONALITY THAT'S ALREADY BEEN BORN...!
I COULDN'T DO SOMETHING SO CRUEL...!!
PAT PAT
I GUESS ONCE IT'S THIS ENTRENCHED, A PERSONALITY CAN'T JUST BE SPLIT OUT AS DATA...
KNOCK
KNOCK
AH, WONDERFUL!
ガラスコ
SLIIIDE...
YOUR CLUB IS ACTUALLY MEETING TODAY.
WHA--?!!
BUT YOU'RE...

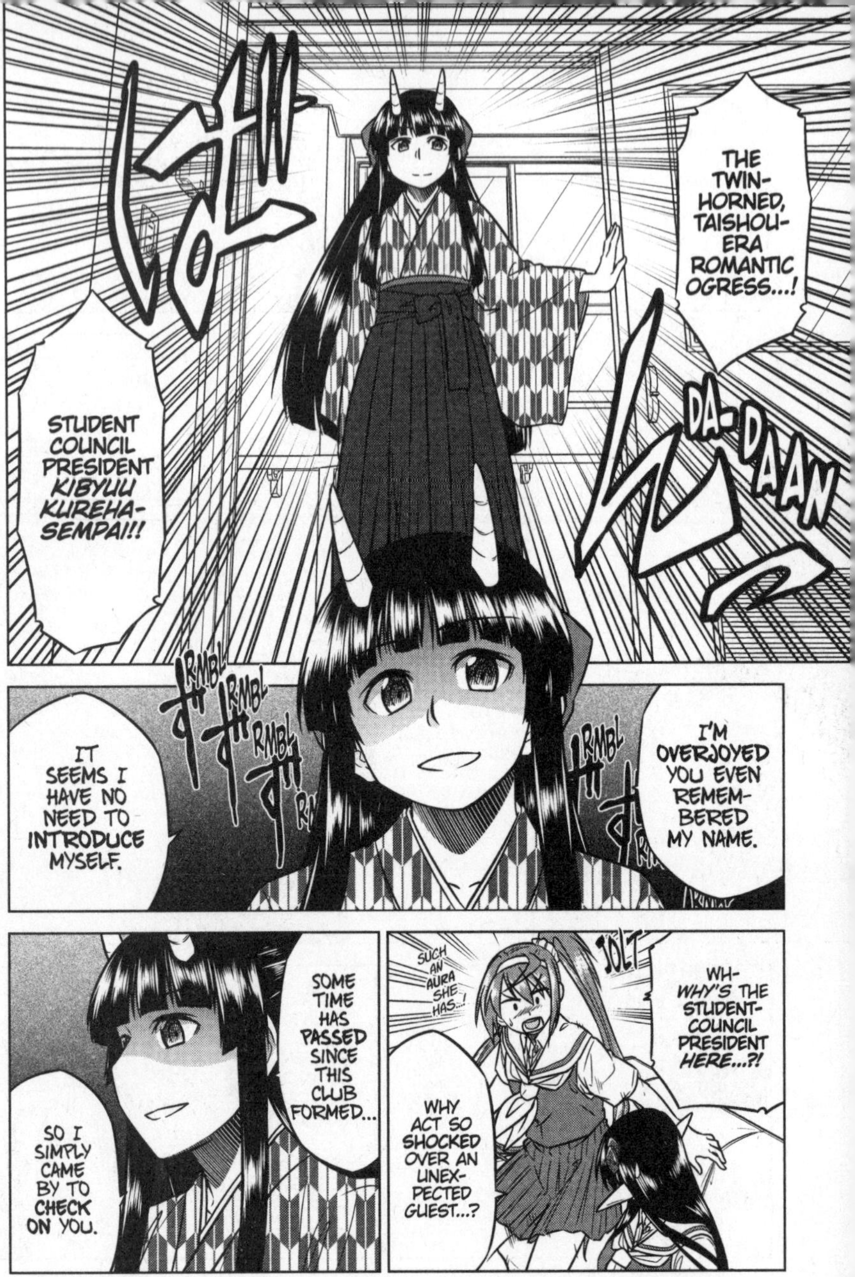
THE TWIN-HORNED, TAISHOU-ERA ROMANTIC OGRESS...!
DA-DAAN
STUDENT COUNCIL PRESIDENT KIBYUU KUREHA-SEMPAI!!
I'M OVERJOYED YOU EVEN REMEMBERED MY NAME.
RMBL RMBL RMBL RMBL
IT SEEMS I HAVE NO NEED TO INTRODUCE MYSELF.
WH- WHY'S THE STUDENT-COUNCIL PRESIDENT HERE...?!
JOLT
SUCH AN AURA SHE HAS...!
WHY ACT SO SHOCKED OVER AN UNEXPECTED GUEST...?
SOME TIME HAS PASSED SINCE THIS CLUB FORMED...
SO I SIMPLY CAME BY TO CHECK ON YOU.

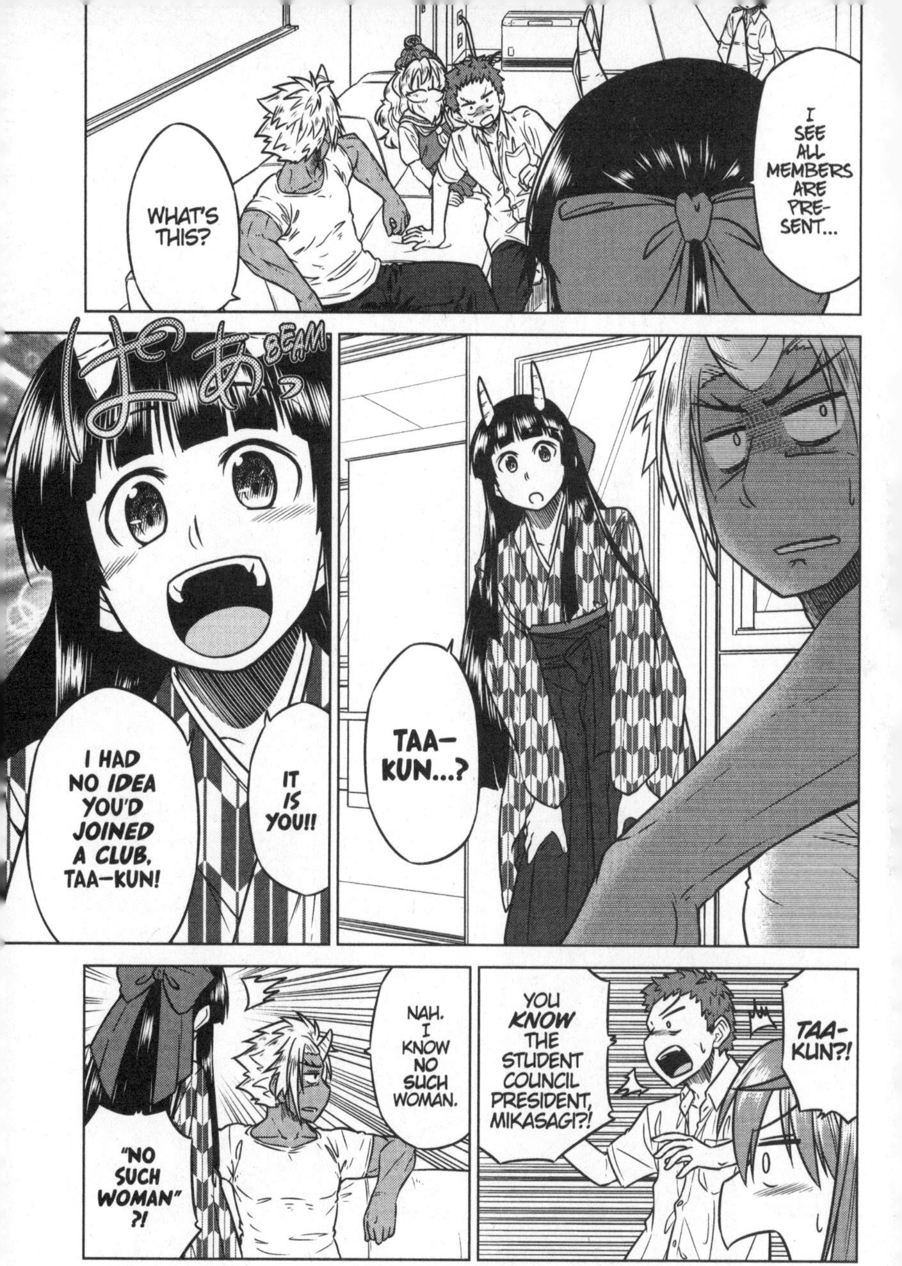
I SEE ALL MEMBERS ARE PRESENT...
WHAT'S THIS?
TAA-KUN...?
はあっ BEAM
IT IS YOU!!
I HAD NO IDEA YOU'D JOINED A CLUB, TAA-KUN!
TAA-KUN?!
YOU KNOW THE STUDENT COUNCIL PRESIDENT, MIKASAGI?!
NAH. I KNOW NO SUCH WOMAN.
"NO SUCH WOMAN"?!

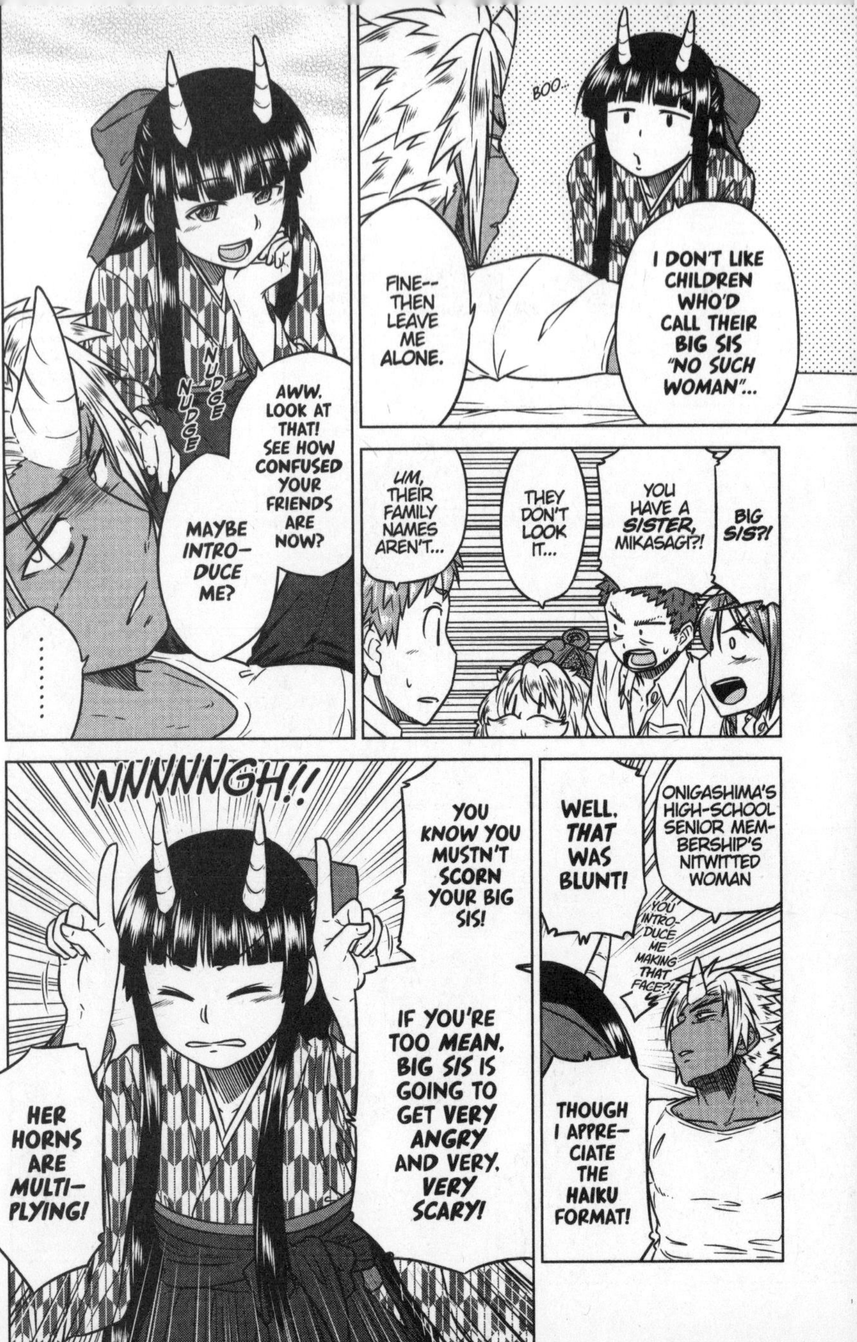

BOO...
I DON'T LIKE CHILDREN WHO'D CALL THEIR BIG SIS "NO SUCH WOMAN"...
FINE-- THEN LEAVE ME ALONE.
BIG SIS?!
YOU HAVE A SISTER, MIKASAGI?!
THEY DON'T LOOK IT...
UM, THEIR FAMILY NAMES AREN'T...
NUDGE NUDGE
AWW. LOOK AT THAT! SEE HOW CONFUSED YOUR FRIENDS ARE NOW?
MAYBE INTRO-DUCE ME?
......
ONIGASHIMA'S HIGH-SCHOOL SENIOR MEM-BERSHIP'S NITWITTED WOMAN
WELL. THAT WAS BLUNT!
YOU INTRO-DUCE ME MAKING THAT FACE?!
THOUGH I APPRE-CIATE THE HAIKU FORMAT!
NNNNNGH!!
YOU KNOW YOU MUSTN'T SCORN YOUR BIG SIS!
IF YOU'RE TOO MEAN, BIG SIS IS GOING TO GET VERY ANGRY AND VERY, VERY SCARY!
HER HORNS ARE MULTI-PLYING!

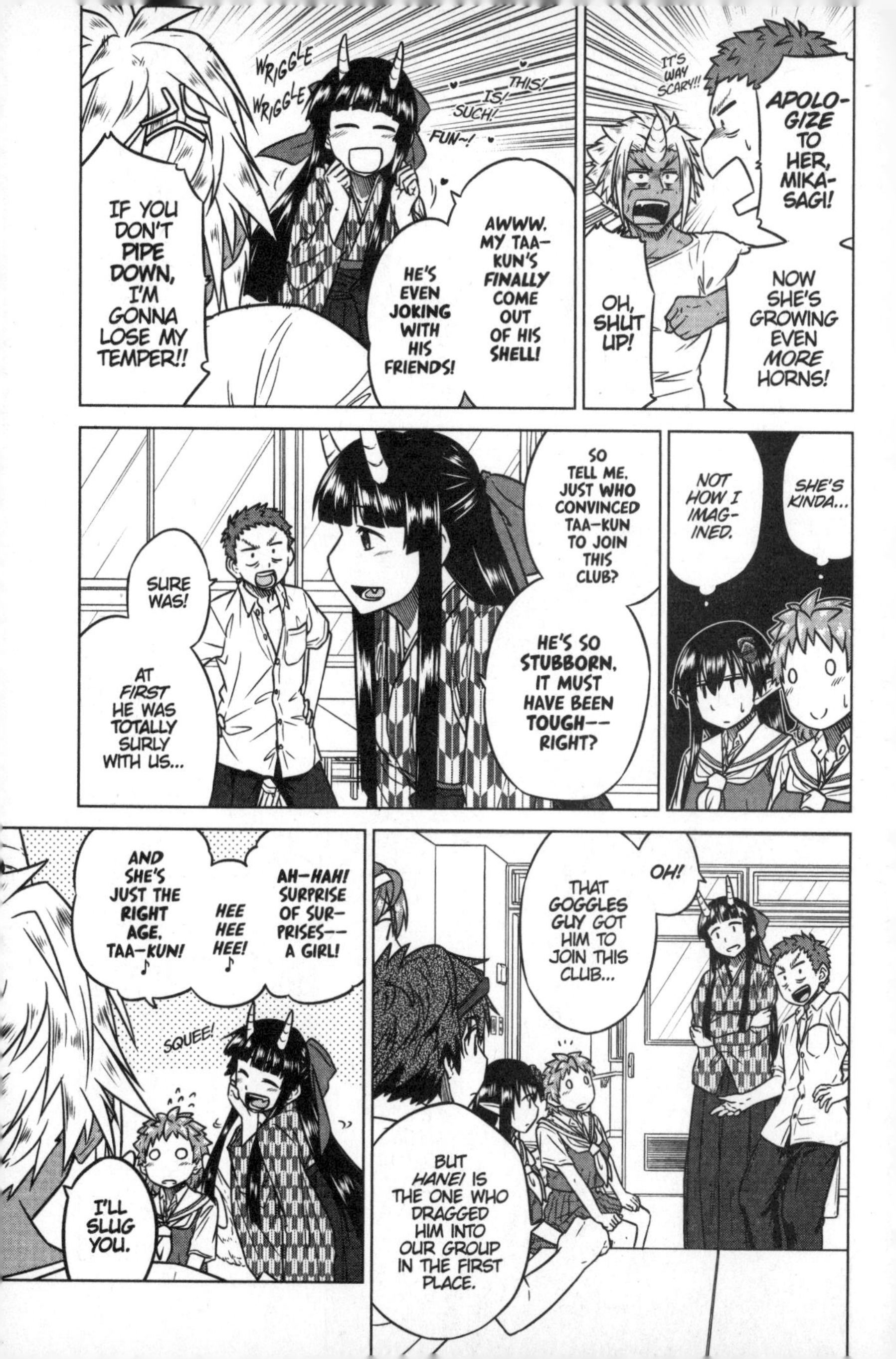
APOLOGIZE TO HER, MIKASAGI!
IT'S WAY SCARY!!
NOW SHE'S GROWING EVEN MORE HORNS!
OH, SHUT UP!
THIS! IS! SUCH! FUN~!
WRIGGLE WRIGGLE
AWWW. MY TAA-KUN'S FINALLY COME OUT OF HIS SHELL!
HE'S EVEN JOKING WITH HIS FRIENDS!
IF YOU DON'T PIPE DOWN, I'M GONNA LOSE MY TEMPER!!
SHE'S KINDA...
NOT HOW I IMAGINED.
SO TELL ME. JUST WHO CONVINCED TAA-KUN TO JOIN THIS CLUB?
HE'S SO STUBBORN, IT MUST HAVE BEEN TOUGH--RIGHT?
SURE WAS!
AT FIRST HE WAS TOTALLY SURLY WITH US...
OH!
THAT GOGGLES GUY GOT HIM TO JOIN THIS CLUB...
BUT HANEI IS THE ONE WHO DRAGGED HIM INTO OUR GROUP IN THE FIRST PLACE.
AH-HAH! SURPRISE OF SURPRISES--A GIRL!
HEE HEE HEE! ♪
AND SHE'S JUST THE RIGHT AGE, TAA-KUN! ♪
SQUEE!
I'LL SLUG YOU.

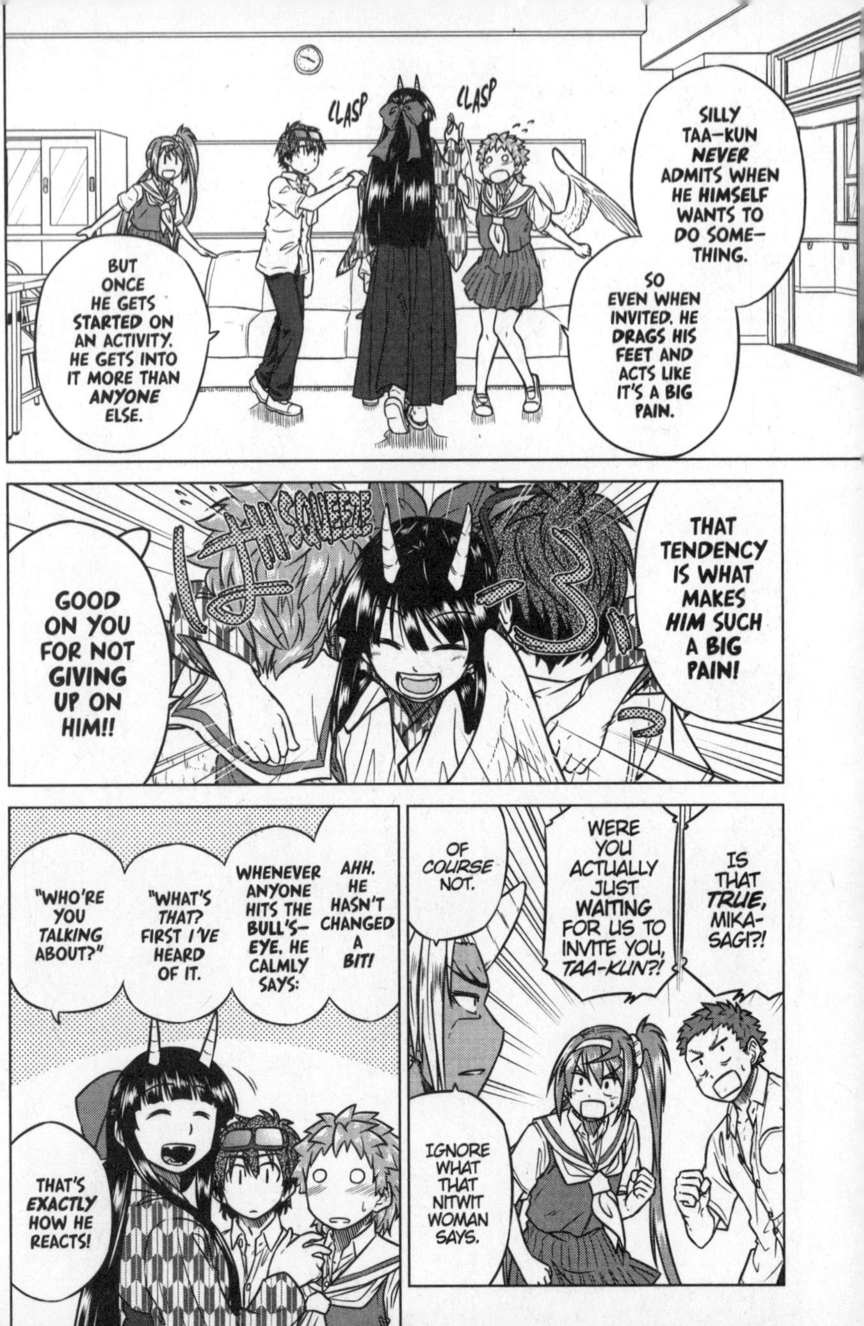
SILLY TAA-KUN NEVER ADMITS WHEN HE HIMSELF WANTS TO DO SOME-THING.
SO EVEN WHEN INVITED, HE DRAGS HIS FEET AND ACTS LIKE IT'S A BIG PAIN.
CLASP
CLASP
BUT ONCE HE GETS STARTED ON AN ACTIVITY, HE GETS INTO IT MORE THAN ANYONE ELSE.
THAT TENDENCY IS WHAT MAKES HIM SUCH A BIG PAIN!
SQUEEZE
GOOD ON YOU FOR NOT GIVING UP ON HIM!!
IS THAT TRUE, MIKA-SAGI?!
WERE YOU ACTUALLY JUST WAITING FOR US TO INVITE YOU, TAA-KUN?!
OF COURSE NOT.
IGNORE WHAT THAT NITWIT WOMAN SAYS.
AHH. HE HASN'T CHANGED A BIT!
WHENEVER ANYONE HITS THE BULL'S-EYE, HE CALMLY SAYS:
"WHAT'S THAT? FIRST I'VE HEARD OF IT.
"WHO'RE YOU TALKING ABOUT?"
THAT'S EXACTLY HOW HE REACTS!

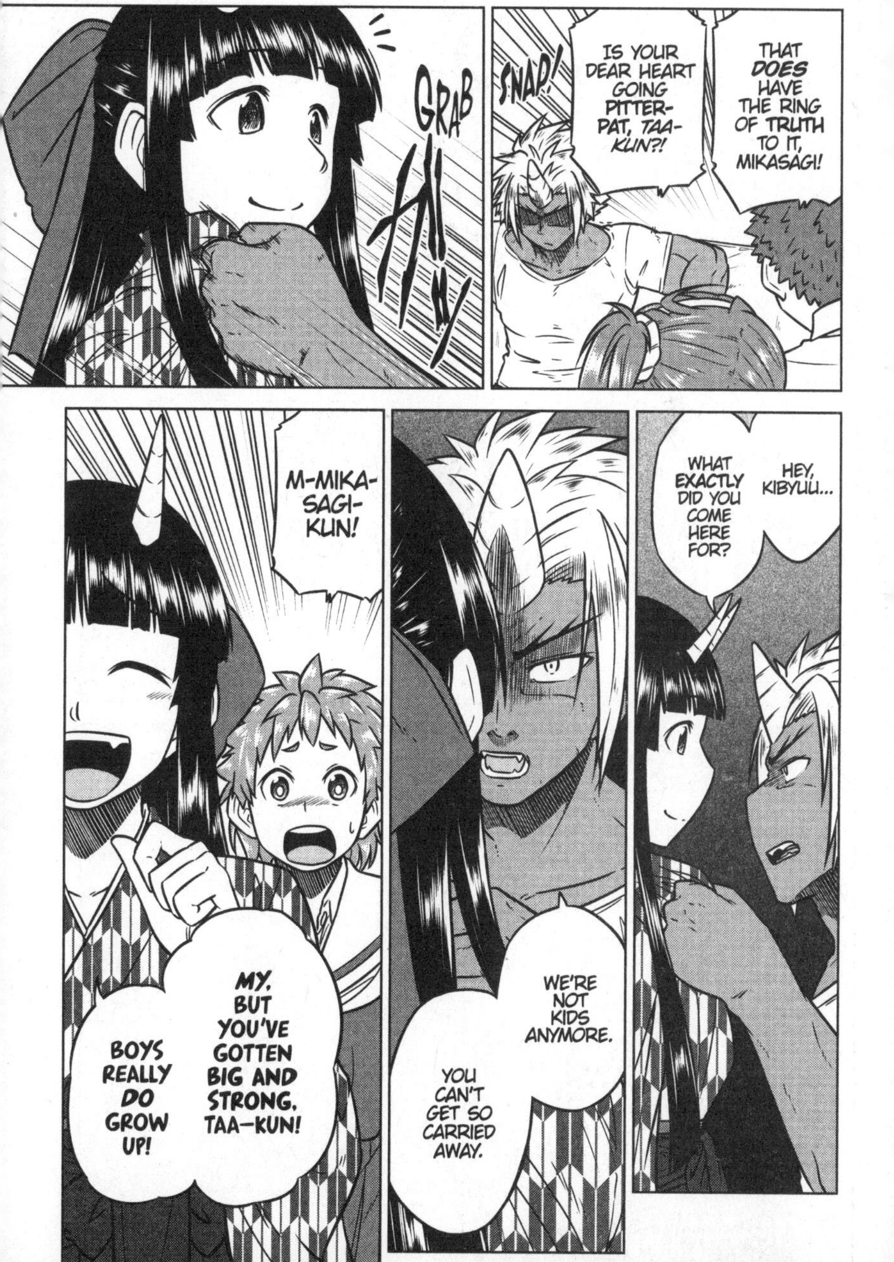
THAT DOES HAVE THE RING OF TRUTH TO IT, MIKASAGI!
IS YOUR DEAR HEART GOING PITTER-PAT, TAA-KUN?!
SNAP!
GRAB
HEY, KIBYUU...
WHAT EXACTLY DID YOU COME HERE FOR?
WE'RE NOT KIDS ANYMORE.
YOU CAN'T GET SO CARRIED AWAY.
M-MIKA-SAGI-KUN!
MY, BUT YOU'VE GOTTEN BIG AND STRONG, TAA-KUN!
BOYS REALLY DO GROW UP!

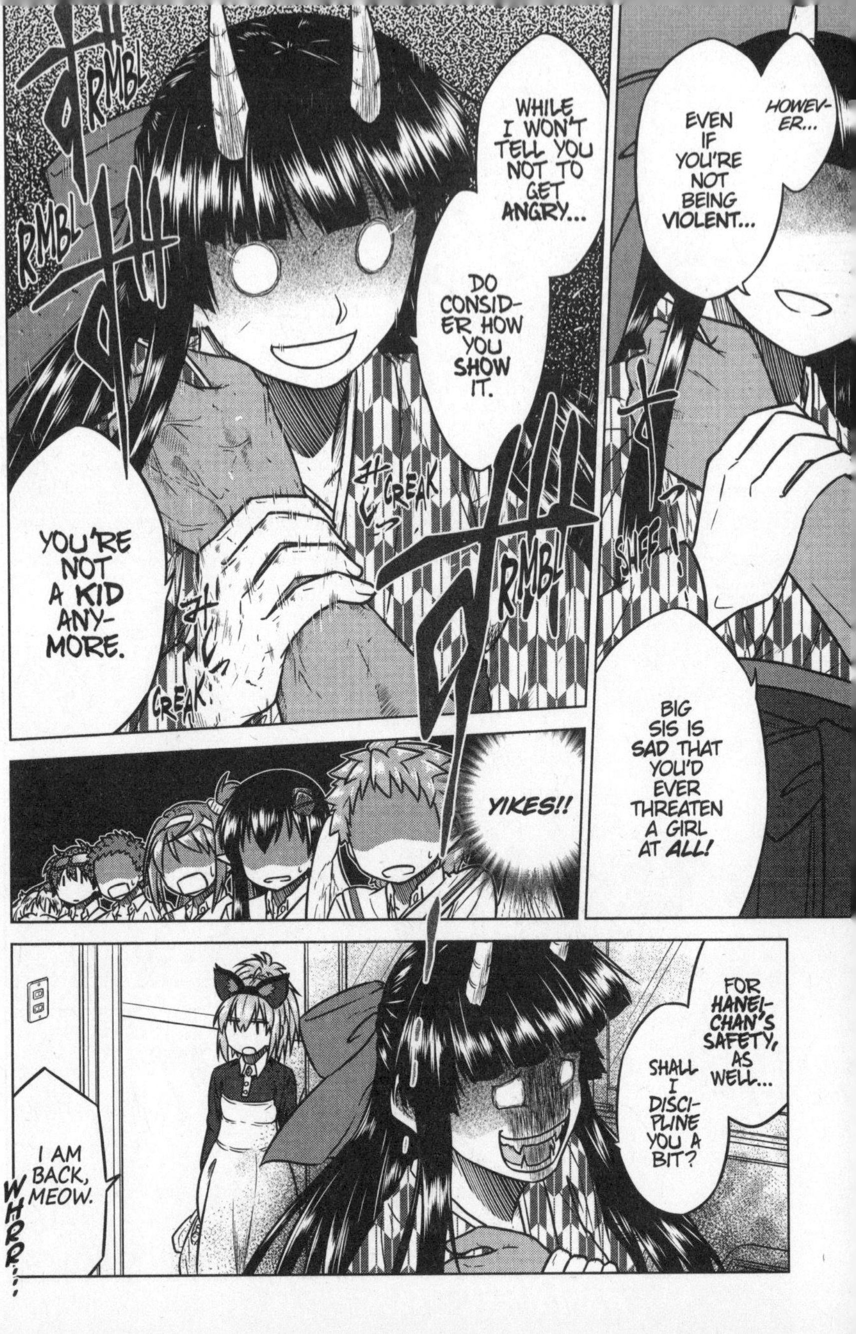
HOWEV-ER...
EVEN IF YOU'RE NOT BEING VIOLENT...
SHFF
RMBL
RMBL
WHILE I WON'T TELL YOU NOT TO GET ANGRY...
DO CONSID-ER HOW YOU SHOW IT.
YOU'RE NOT A KID ANY-MORE.
CREAK
CREAK
RMBL
BIG SIS IS SAD THAT YOU'D EVER THREATEN A GIRL AT ALL!
YIKES!!
FOR HANEI-CHAN'S SAFETY, AS WELL...
SHALL I DISCI-PLINE YOU A BIT?
I AM BACK, MEOW.
WHRRR...

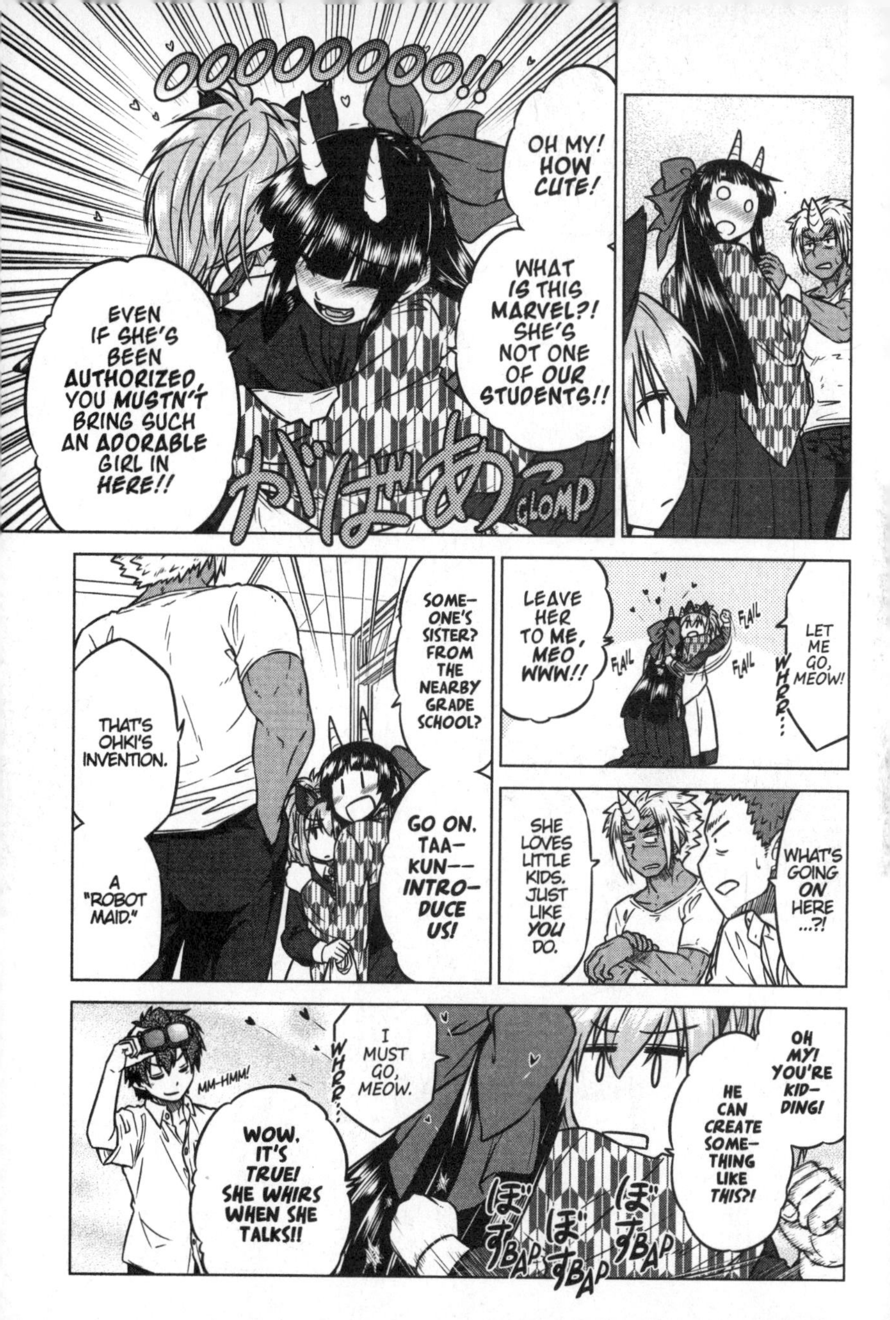
OOOOOOOO!!
OH MY! HOW CUTE!
WHAT IS THIS MARVEL?! SHE'S NOT ONE OF OUR STUDENTS!!
EVEN IF SHE'S BEEN AUTHORIZED, YOU MUSTN'T BRING SUCH AN ADORABLE GIRL IN HERE!!
がばぁっ GLOMP
LET ME GO, MEOW!
WHRR...
FLAIL
FLAIL
FLAIL
LEAVE HER TO ME, MEOWWW!!
WHAT'S GOING ON HERE...?!
SHE LOVES LITTLE KIDS. JUST LIKE YOU DO.
SOME-ONE'S SISTER? FROM THE NEARBY GRADE SCHOOL?
THAT'S OHKI'S INVENTION.
A "ROBOT MAID."
GO ON. TAA-KUN--INTRODUCE US!
OH MY! YOU'RE KID-DING!
HE CAN CREATE SOME-THING LIKE THIS?!
ぼす BAP
ぼす BAP
ぼす BAP
I MUST GO, MEOW.
WHRR...
MM-HMM!
WOW. IT'S TRUE! SHE WHIRS WHEN SHE TALKS!!

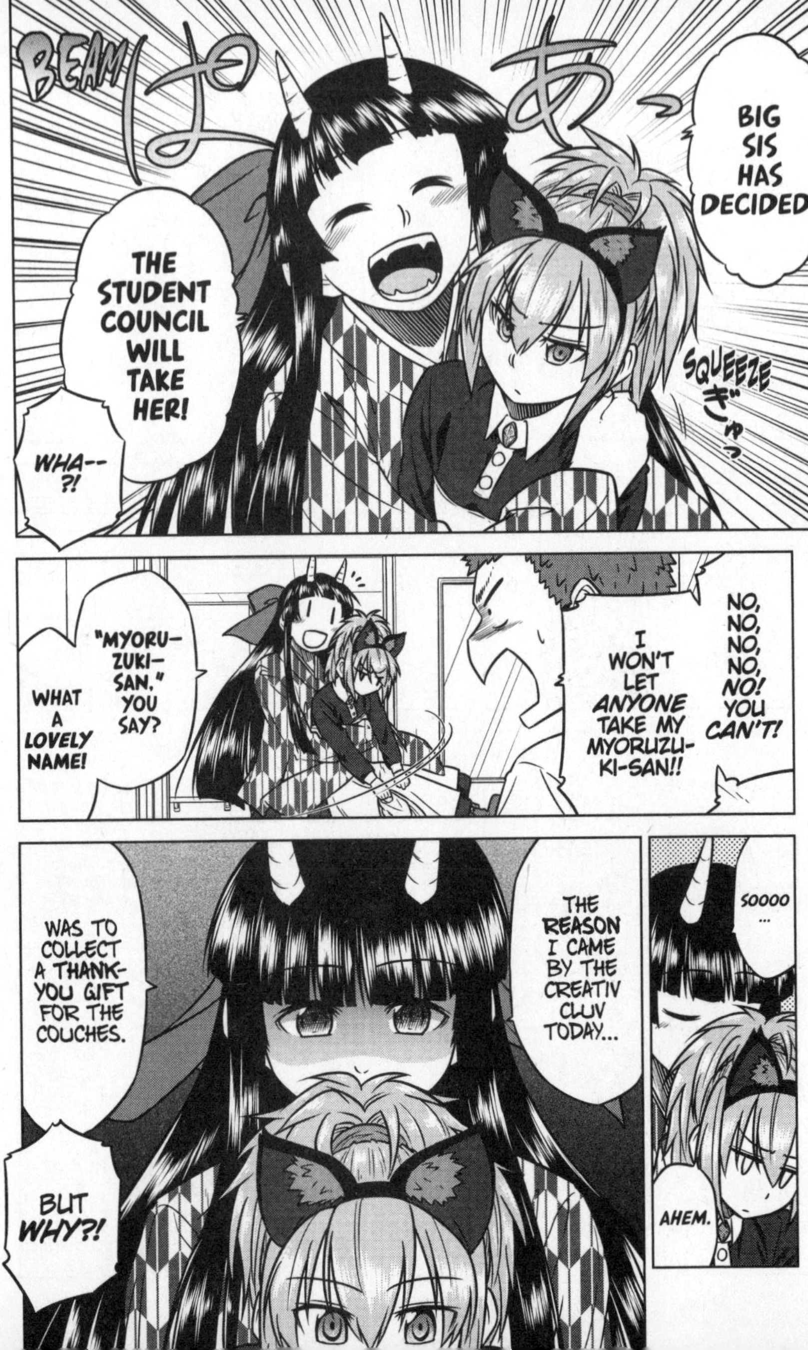
BIG SIS HAS DECIDED!
BEAM
THE STUDENT COUNCIL WILL TAKE HER!
SQUEEZE ぎゅっ
WHA--?!
NO, NO, NO, NO, NO! YOU CAN'T!
I WON'T LET ANYONE TAKE MY MYORUZUKI-SAN!!
"MYORUZUKI-SAN," YOU SAY?
WHAT A LOVELY NAME!
SOOOO...
AHEM.
THE REASON I CAME BY THE CREATIV CLUV TODAY...
WAS TO COLLECT A THANK-YOU GIFT FOR THE COUCHES.
BUT WHY?!

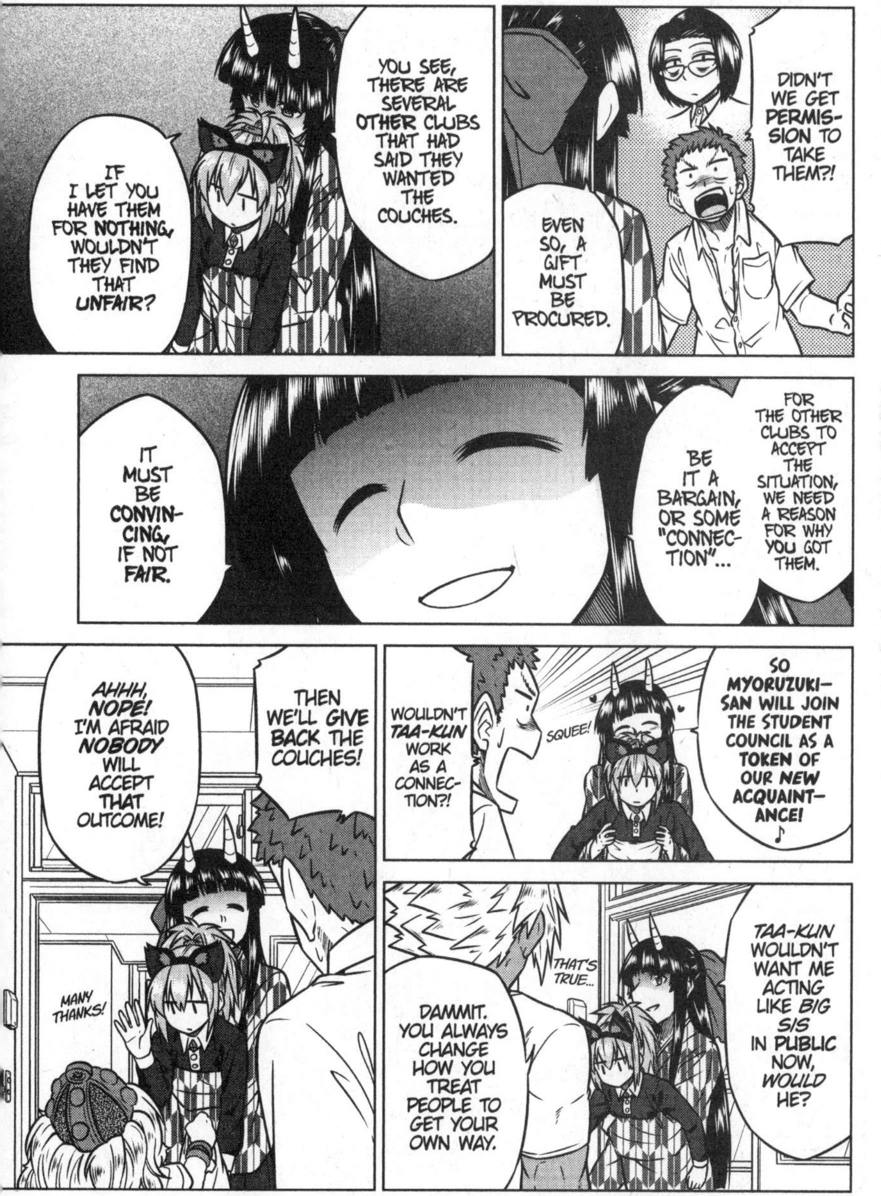
DIDN'T WE GET PERMISSION TO TAKE THEM?!
EVEN SO, A GIFT MUST BE PROCURED.
YOU SEE, THERE ARE SEVERAL OTHER CLUBS THAT HAD SAID THEY WANTED THE COUCHES.
IF I LET YOU HAVE THEM FOR NOTHING, WOULDN'T THEY FIND THAT UNFAIR?
FOR THE OTHER CLUBS TO ACCEPT THE SITUATION, WE NEED A REASON FOR WHY YOU GOT THEM.
BE IT A BARGAIN, OR SOME "CONNECTION"...
IT MUST BE CONVINCING, IF NOT FAIR.
SO MYORUZUKI-SAN WILL JOIN THE STUDENT COUNCIL AS A TOKEN OF OUR NEW ACQUAINTANCE! ♪
SQUEE!
WOULDN'T TAA-KUN WORK AS A CONNECTION?!
TAA-KUN WOULDN'T WANT ME ACTING LIKE BIG SIS IN PUBLIC NOW, WOULD HE?
THAT'S TRUE...
DAMMIT. YOU ALWAYS CHANGE HOW YOU TREAT PEOPLE TO GET YOUR OWN WAY.
THEN WE'LL GIVE BACK THE COUCHES!
AHHH, NOPE! I'M AFRAID NOBODY WILL ACCEPT THAT OUTCOME!
MANY THANKS!

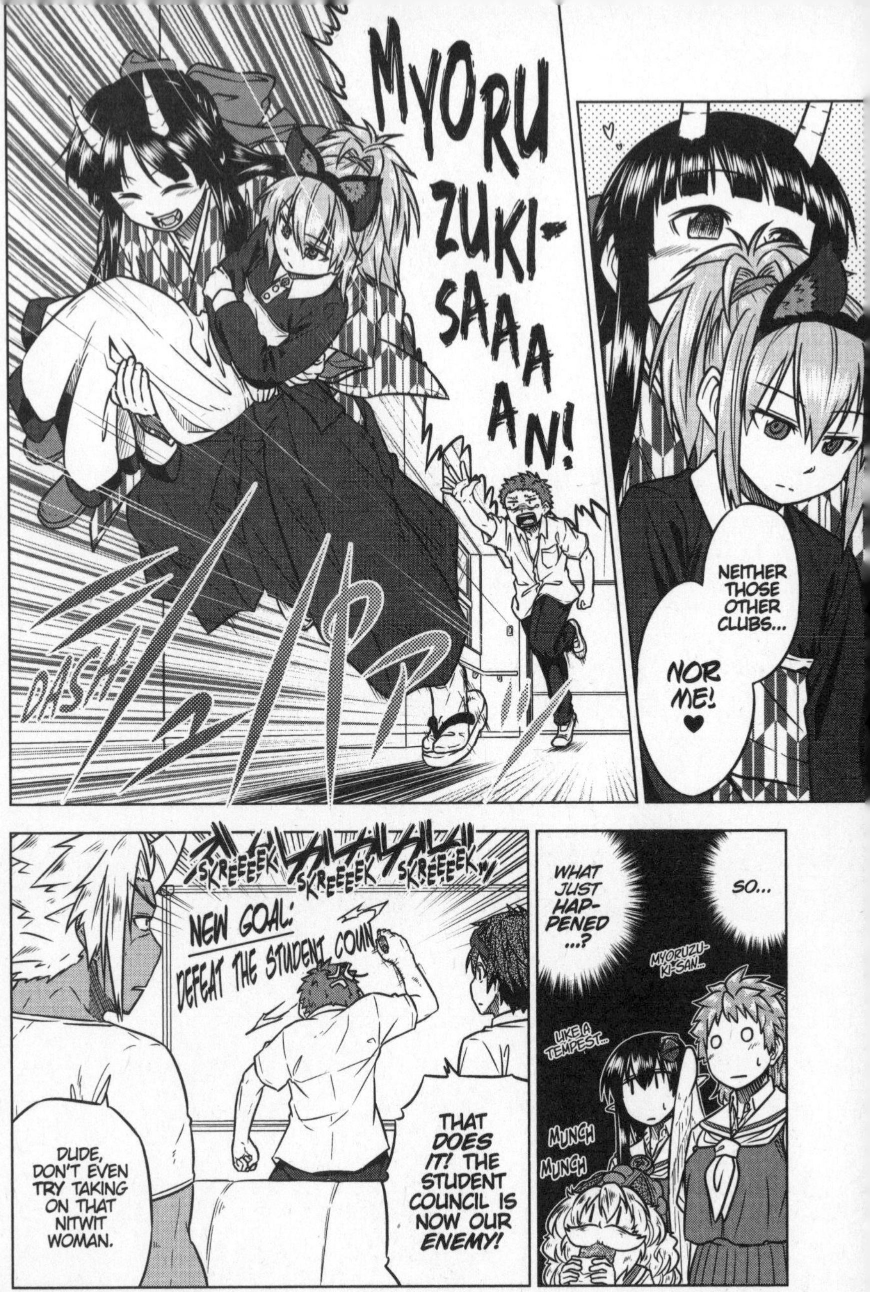
NEITHER THOSE OTHER CLUBS...
NOR ME! ♥
MYORUZUKI-SAAAAN!
DASH
SO...
WHAT JUST HAPPENED...?
MYORUZUKI-SAN...
LIKE A TEMPEST...
MUNCH
MUNCH
SKREEEEK SKREEEEK SKREEEEK
NEW GOAL:
DEFEAT THE STUDENT COUN
THAT DOES IT! THE STUDENT COUNCIL IS NOW OUR ENEMY!
DUDE, DON'T EVEN TRY TAKING ON THAT NITWIT WOMAN.

Chapter 15 • END

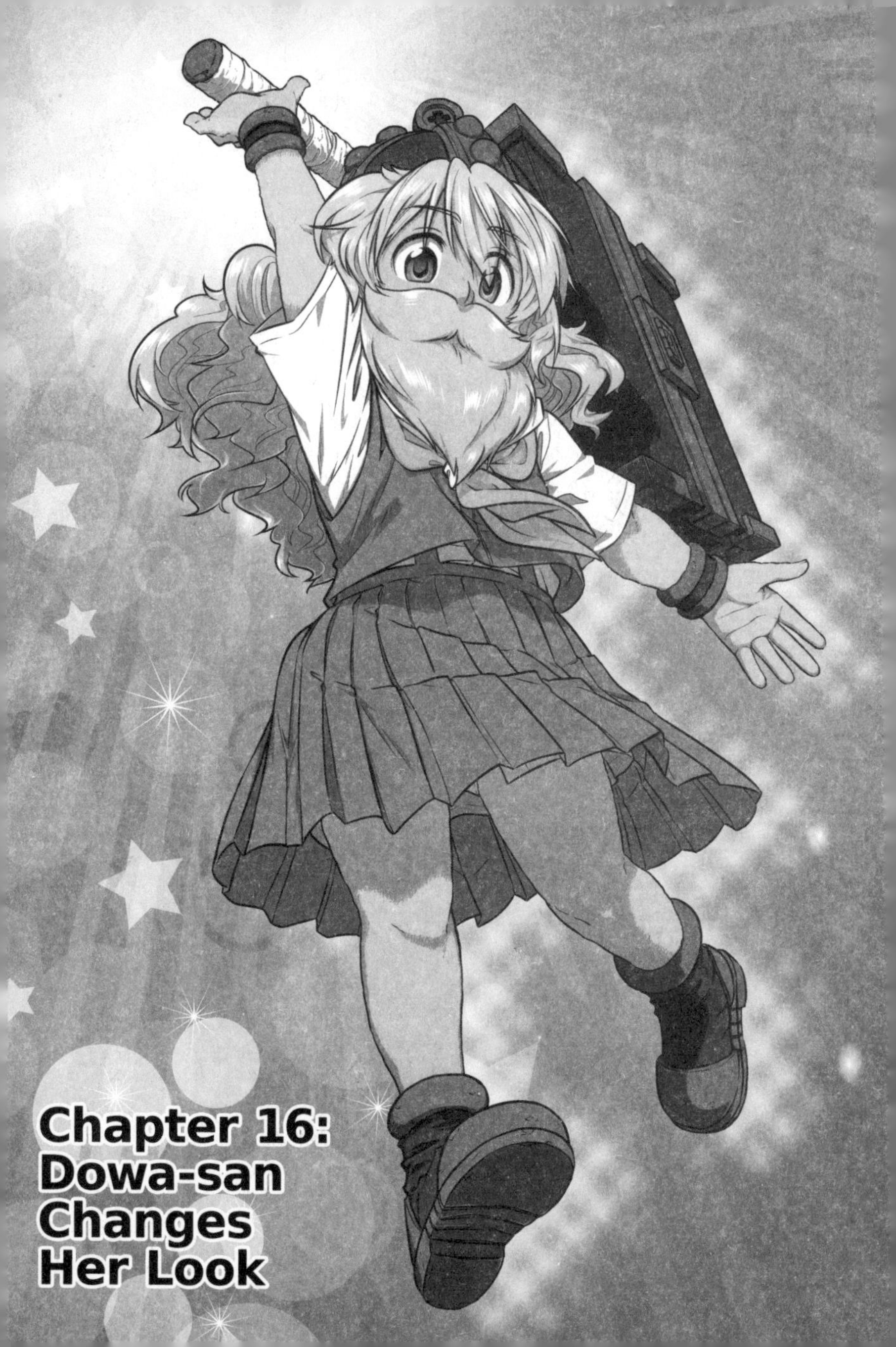
Chapter 16:
Dowa-san
Changes
Her Look

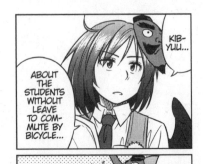

KIB- YUU...
ABOUT THE STUDENTS WITHOUT LEAVE TO COM- MUTE BY BICYCLE...
NUZZLE NUZZLE
HM...? WHO'S THAT GIRL?
TWINE TWINE
SHE'S MYORUZU- KI-SAN! I GOT HER FROM THE CREATIV CLUV AS THANKS FOR THE COUCHES!
HUMAN TRAF- FICKING?! WHAT ARE YOU THINK- ING?!
SHE'S AN AN- DROID, SO IT'S NO PROB- LEM!
BUT YOU CAN'T JUST TAKE SOMETHING LIKE THAT! IT'S WRONG!

Not to Mention *Incredibly* Costly!

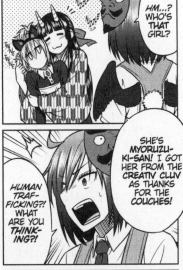

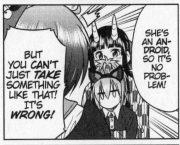

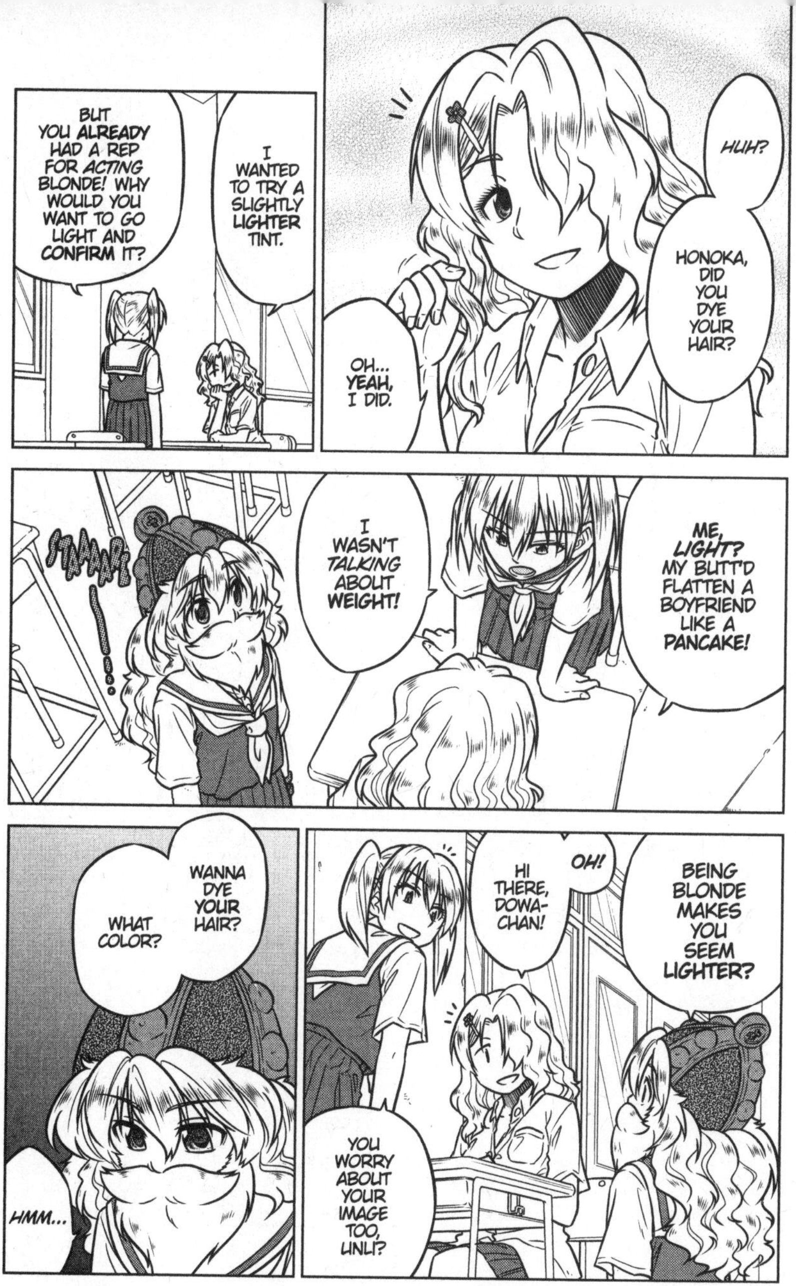
HUH?
HONOKA, DID YOU DYE YOUR HAIR?
OH... YEAH, I DID.
I WANTED TO TRY A SLIGHTLY LIGHTER TINT.
BUT YOU ALREADY HAD A REP FOR ACTING BLONDE! WHY WOULD YOU WANT TO GO LIGHT AND CONFIRM IT?
ME, LIGHT? MY BUTT'D FLATTEN A BOYFRIEND LIKE A PANCAKE!
I WASN'T TALKING ABOUT WEIGHT!
BEING BLONDE MAKES YOU SEEM LIGHTER?
OH!
HI THERE, DOWA-CHAN!
YOU WORRY ABOUT YOUR IMAGE TOO, UNUI?
WANNA DYE YOUR HAIR?
WHAT COLOR?
HMM...

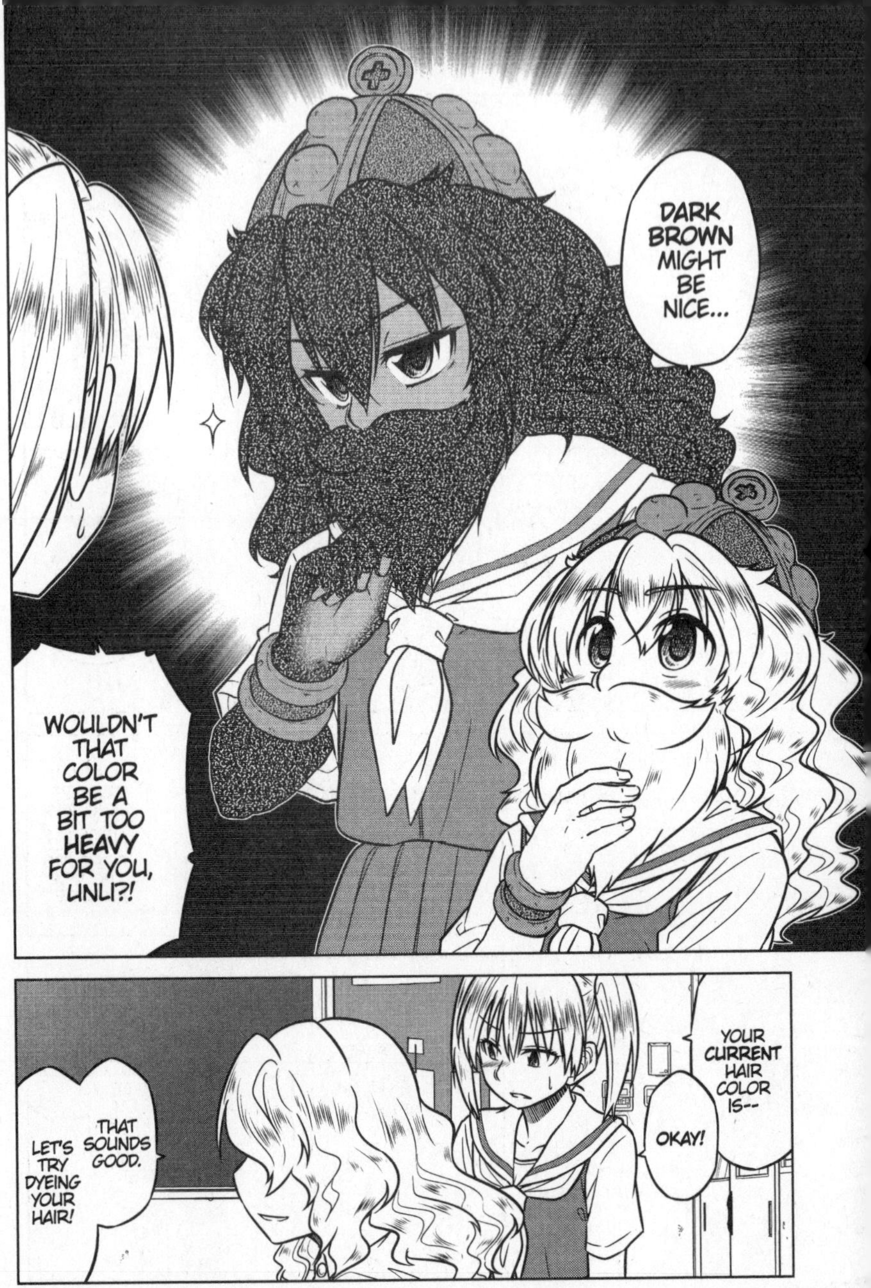
DARK BROWN MIGHT BE NICE...
WOULDN'T THAT COLOR BE A BIT TOO HEAVY FOR YOU, UNLI?!
YOUR CURRENT HAIR COLOR IS--
OKAY!
THAT SOUNDS GOOD.
LET'S TRY DYEING YOUR HAIR!

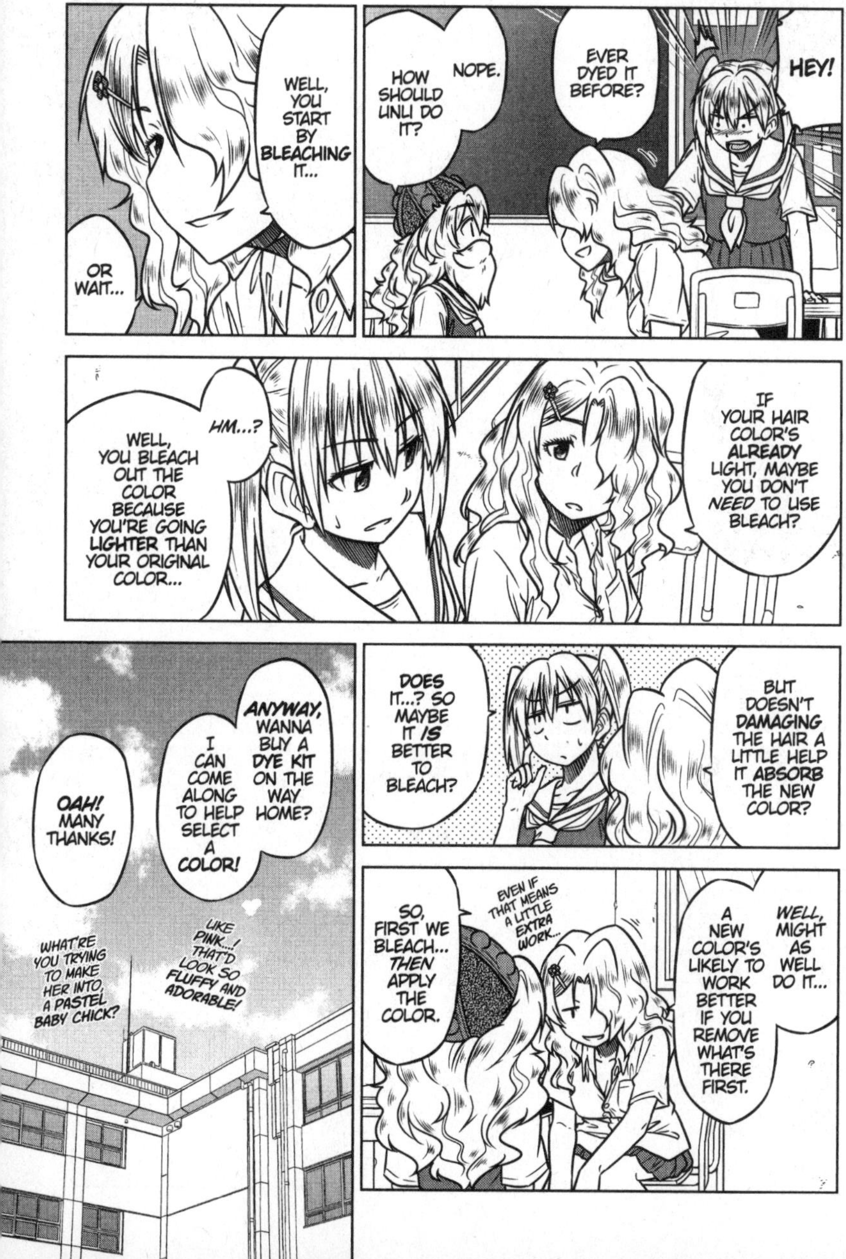
HEY!
EVER DYED IT BEFORE?
NOPE.
HOW SHOULD UNLI DO IT?
WELL, YOU START BY BLEACHING IT...
OR WAIT...
IF YOUR HAIR COLOR'S ALREADY LIGHT, MAYBE YOU DON'T NEED TO USE BLEACH?
HM...?
WELL, YOU BLEACH OUT THE COLOR BECAUSE YOU'RE GOING LIGHTER THAN YOUR ORIGINAL COLOR...
BUT DOESN'T DAMAGING THE HAIR A LITTLE HELP IT ABSORB THE NEW COLOR?
DOES IT...? SO MAYBE IT IS BETTER TO BLEACH?
WELL, MIGHT AS WELL DO IT...
A NEW COLOR'S LIKELY TO WORK BETTER IF YOU REMOVE WHAT'S THERE FIRST.
EVEN IF THAT MEANS A LITTLE EXTRA WORK...
SO, FIRST WE BLEACH... THEN APPLY THE COLOR.
ANYWAY, WANNA BUY A DYE KIT ON THE WAY HOME?
I CAN COME ALONG TO HELP SELECT A COLOR!
OAH! MANY THANKS!
LIKE PINK...! THAT'D LOOK SO FLUFFY AND ADORABLE!
WHAT'RE YOU TRYING TO MAKE HER INTO, A PASTEL BABY CHICK?

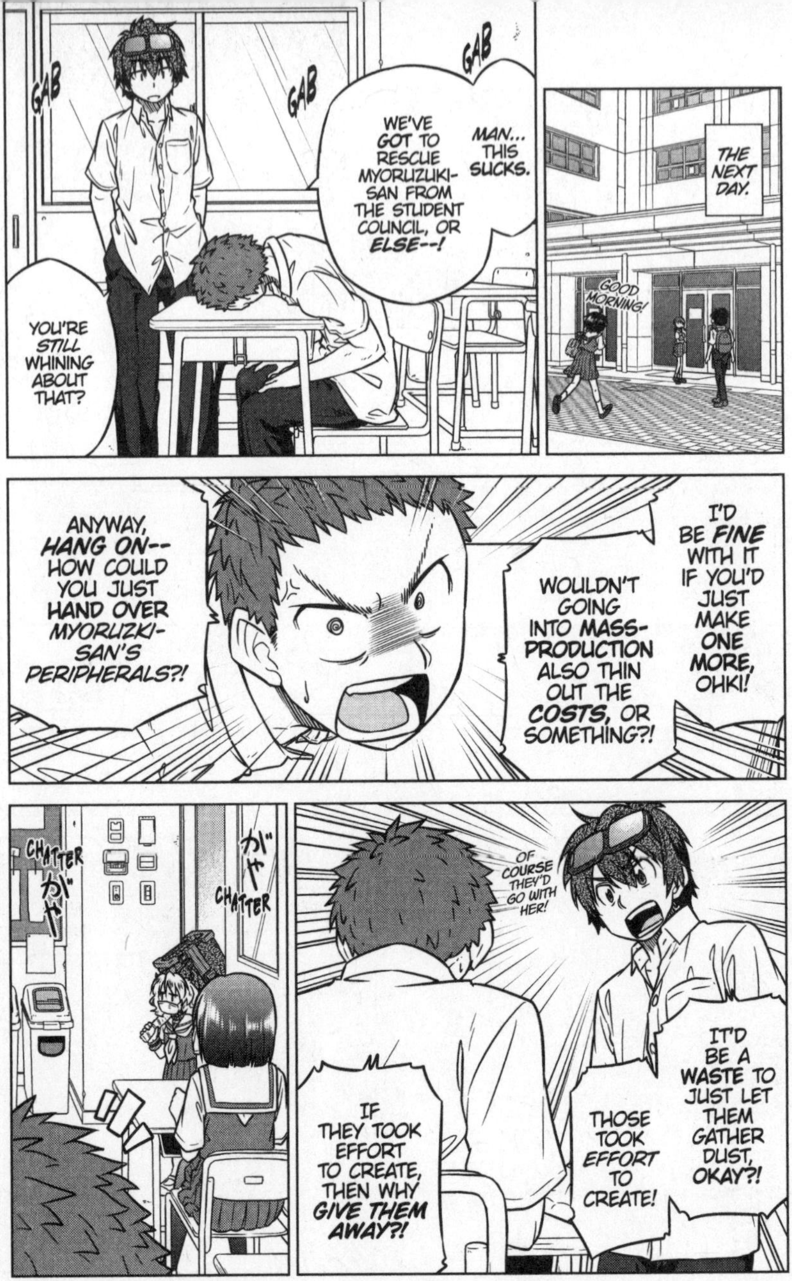
THE NEXT DAY.
GOOD MORNING!
GAB
GAB
GAB
MAN... THIS SUCKS.
WE'VE GOT TO RESCUE MYORUZUKI-SAN FROM THE STUDENT COUNCIL, OR ELSE--!
YOU'RE STILL WHINING ABOUT THAT?
I'D BE FINE WITH IT IF YOU'D JUST MAKE ONE MORE, OHKI!
WOULDN'T GOING INTO MASS-PRODUCTION ALSO THIN OUT THE COSTS, OR SOMETHING?!
ANYWAY, HANG ON-- HOW COULD YOU JUST HAND OVER MYORUZKI-SAN'S PERIPHERALS?!
OF COURSE THEY'D GO WITH HER!
IT'D BE A WASTE TO JUST LET THEM GATHER DUST, OKAY?!
THOSE TOOK EFFORT TO CREATE!
IF THEY TOOK EFFORT TO CREATE, THEN WHY GIVE THEM AWAY?!
がや
CHATTER
CHATTER
がや

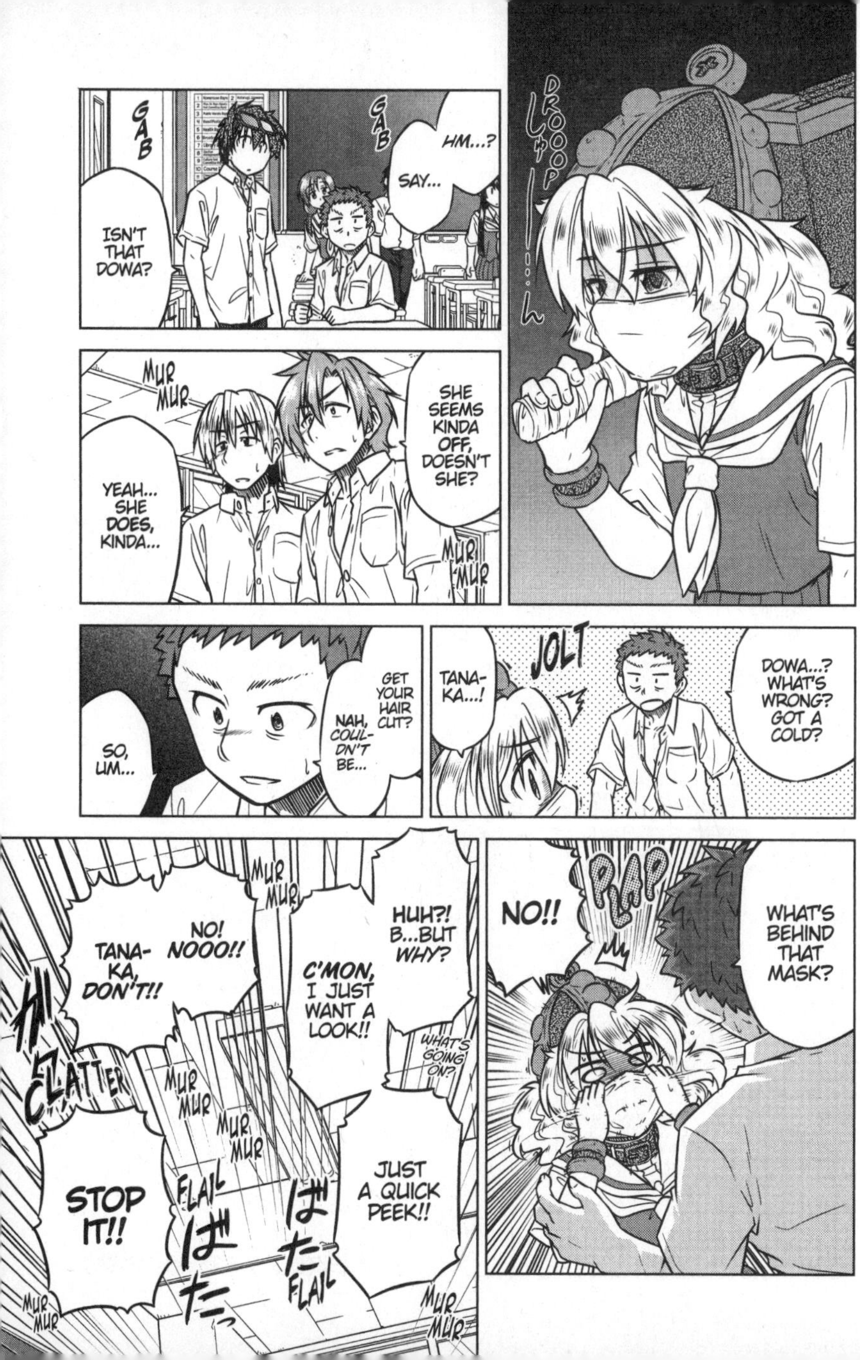
DROOOP
しゅーーん
GAB
HM...?
SAY...
GAB
ISN'T THAT DOWA?
MUR MUR
SHE SEEMS KINDA OFF, DOESN'T SHE?
YEAH... SHE DOES, KINDA...
MUR MUR
DOWA...? WHAT'S WRONG? GOT A COLD?
JOLT
TANA-KA...!
GET YOUR HAIR CUT?
NAH, COULDN'T BE...
SO, UM...
WHAT'S BEHIND THAT MASK?
PLAP
NO!!
HUH?! B...BUT WHY?
C'MON, I JUST WANT A LOOK!!
MUR MUR
NO! NOOO!!
TANA-KA, DON'T!!
WHAT'S GOING ON?
JUST A QUICK PEEK!!
MUR MUR
MUR MUR
FLAIL
ばたばたっ
FLAIL
STOP IT!!
CLATTER
MUR MUR
MUR MUR

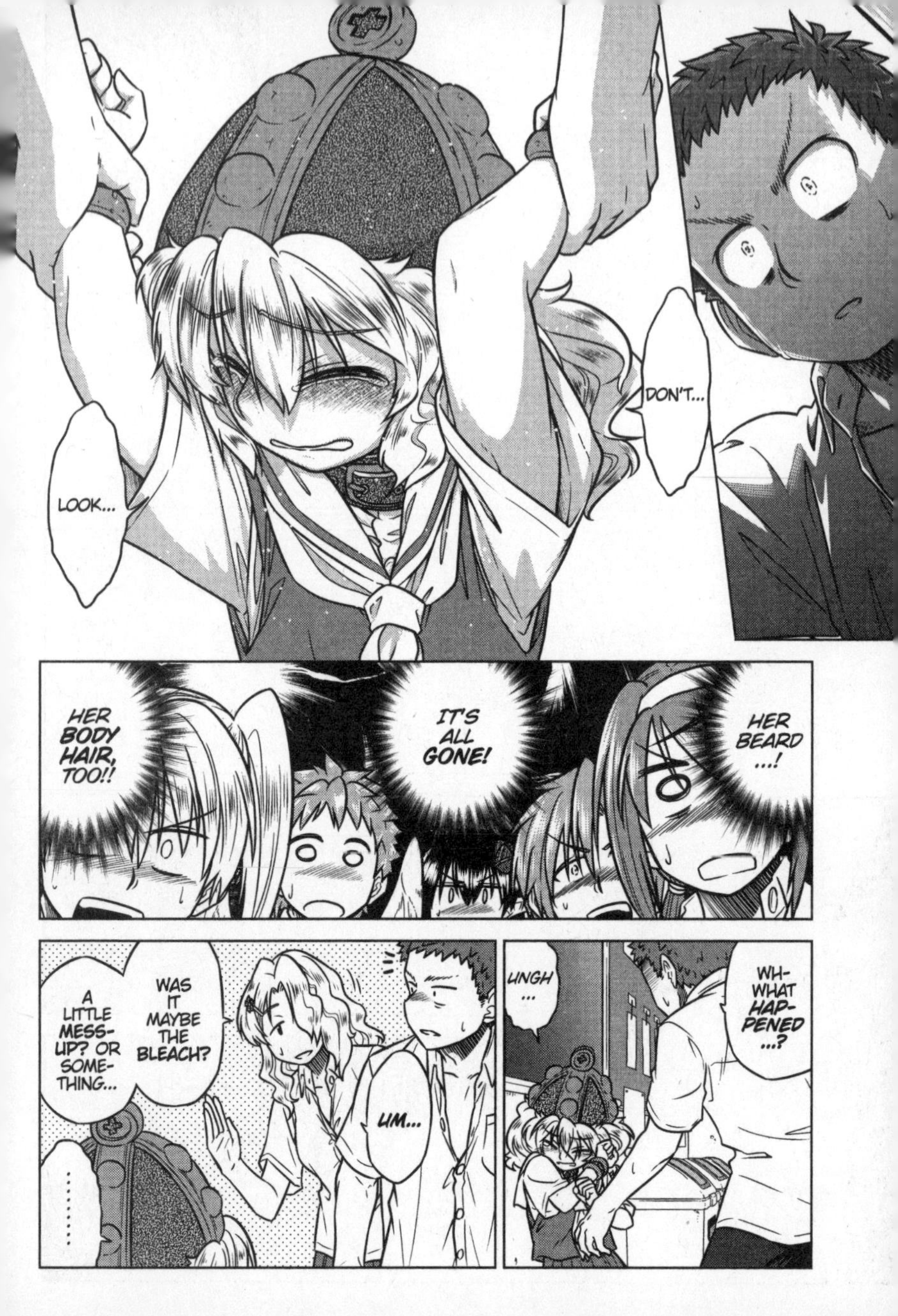

DON'T...
LOOK...
HER BEARD ...!
IT'S ALL GONE!
HER BODY HAIR, TOO!!
WH-WHAT HAP-PENED ...?
UNGH ...
WAS IT MAYBE THE BLEACH?
A LITTLE MESS-UP? OR SOME-THING...
UM...
......

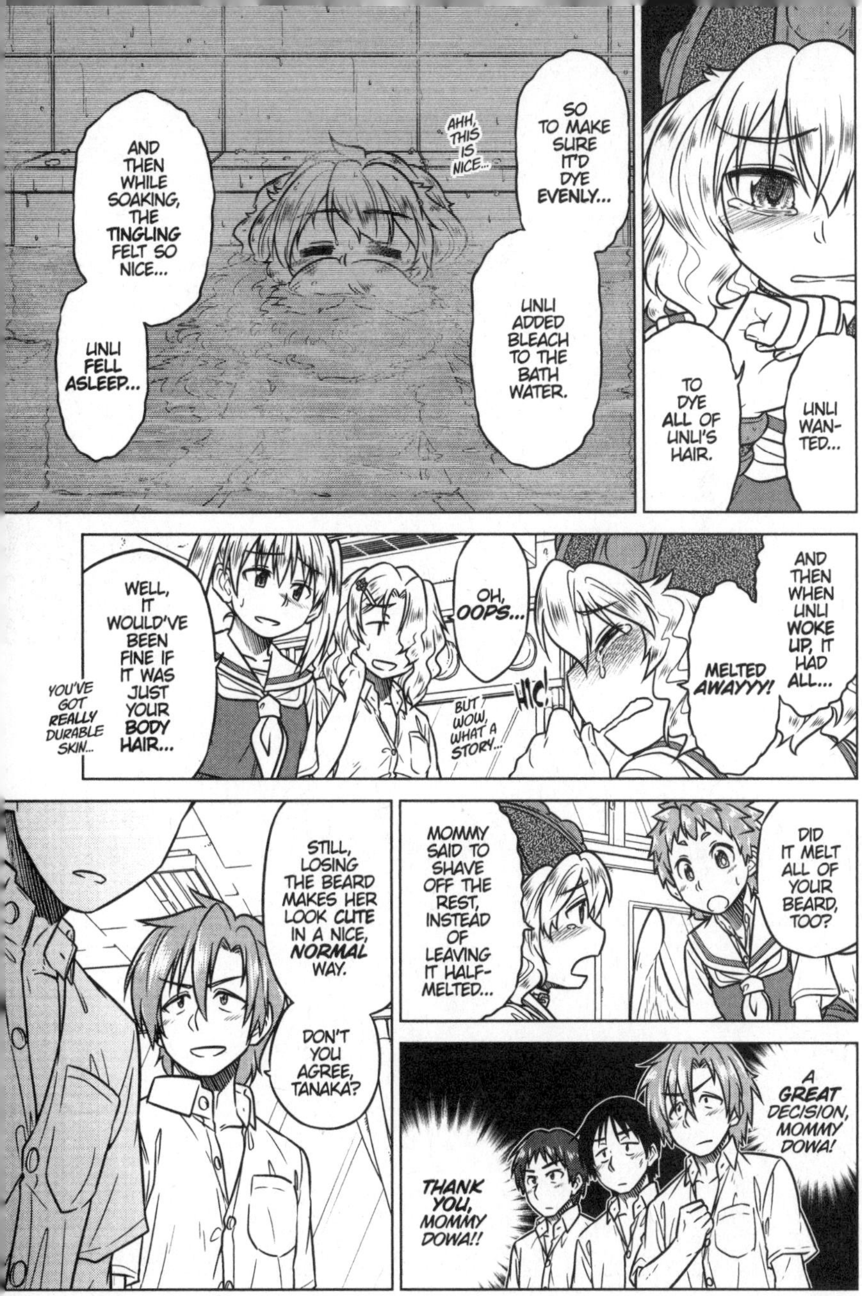
UNLI WANTED...
TO DYE ALL OF UNLI'S HAIR.
SO TO MAKE SURE IT'D DYE EVENLY...
UNLI ADDED BLEACH TO THE BATH WATER.
AHH, THIS IS NICE...
AND THEN WHILE SOAKING, THE TINGLING FELT SO NICE...
UNLI FELL ASLEEP...
AND THEN WHEN UNLI WOKE UP, IT HAD ALL...
MELTED AWAYYY!
HIC!
OH, OOPS...
BUT WOW, WHAT A STORY...
WELL, IT WOULD'VE BEEN FINE IF IT WAS JUST YOUR BODY HAIR...
YOU'VE GOT REALLY DURABLE SKIN...
DID IT MELT ALL OF YOUR BEARD, TOO?
MOMMY SAID TO SHAVE OFF THE REST, INSTEAD OF LEAVING IT HALF-MELTED...
A GREAT DECISION, MOMMY DOWA!
THANK YOU, MOMMY DOWA!!
STILL, LOSING THE BEARD MAKES HER LOOK CUTE IN A NICE, NORMAL WAY.
DON'T YOU AGREE, TANAKA?

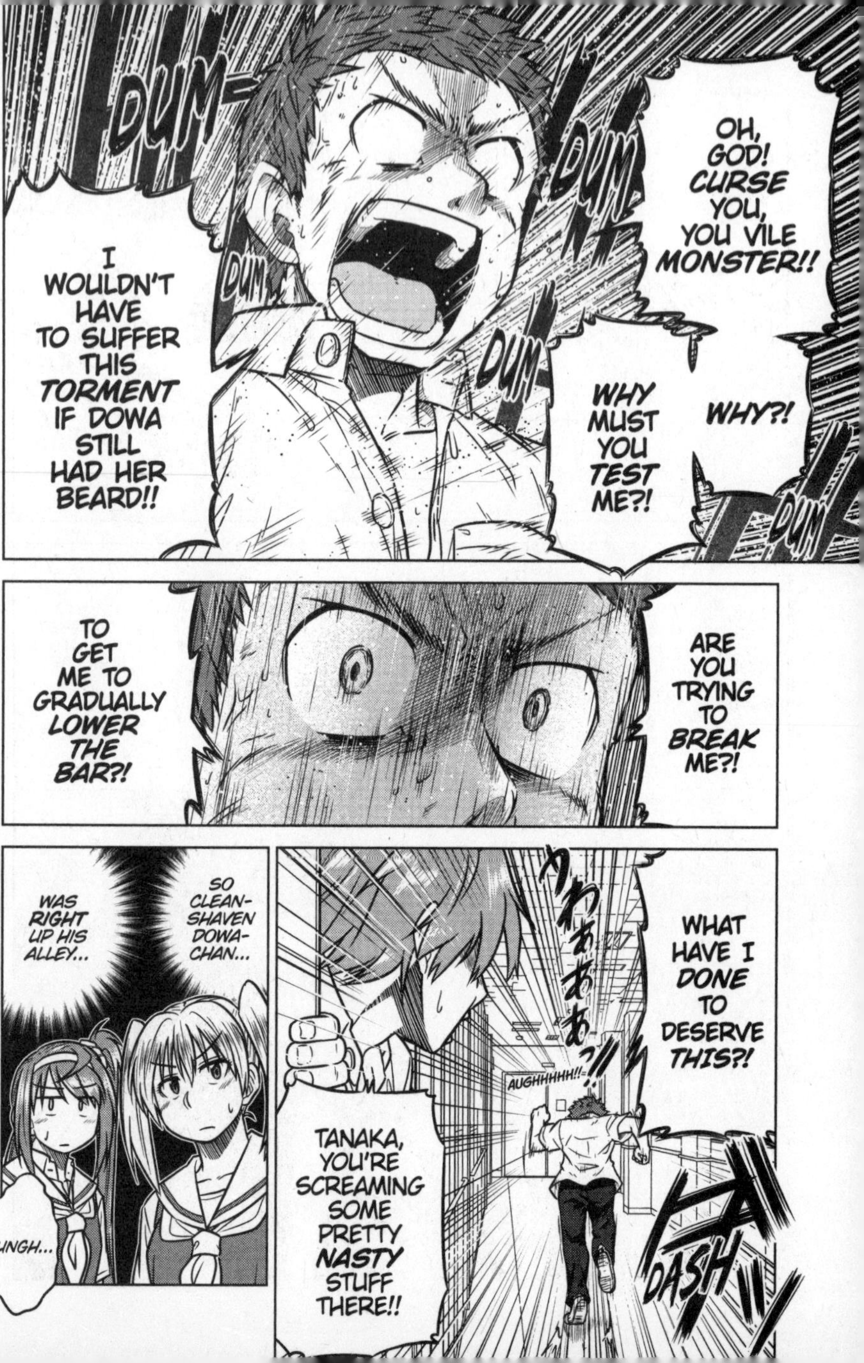
DUM-
OH, GOD! CURSE YOU, YOU VILE MONSTER!!
DUM
WHY?!
DUM
DUM
WHY MUST YOU TEST ME?!
DUM
DUM
I WOULDN'T HAVE TO SUFFER THIS TORMENT IF DOWA STILL HAD HER BEARD!!
ARE YOU TRYING TO BREAK ME?!
TO GET ME TO GRADUALLY LOWER THE BAR?!
WHAT HAVE I DONE TO DESERVE THIS?!
うわああああっ!!
AUGHHHHHH!!
DASH
TANAKA, YOU'RE SCREAMING SOME PRETTY NASTY STUFF THERE!!
SO CLEAN-SHAVEN DOWA-CHAN...
WAS RIGHT UP HIS ALLEY...
UNGH...

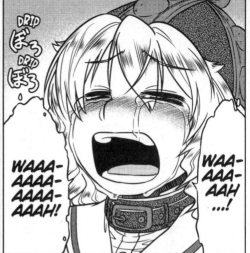

DRIP
ぼろ
DRIP
ぼろ
WAAA-AAA-AAH...!
WAAAA-AAAA-AAAA-AAAAH!
HUH...? UNLI?! WHAT'S--?!
SHE'S WAILING!!
NOW TANAKA... HATES UNLI...!
SOB SOB
TANAKA... PRAISED UNLI'S BEARD...
WEEP
WEEP
BUT NOW... NOW IT'S ALL GONE...!
WHAT SHOULD WE SAY...?!
WE CAN'T BEAR TO TELL HER HE ACTUALLY LIKES HER BETTER NOW!!
WAIT... DID HE PRAISE HER BEARD?
MAYBE IT WAS THAT ONE, "I JUST CAN'T GO FOR A GIRL WITH SUCH A SPLENDID KAISER BEARD!!" OUTBURST?
THAT'S SOME MAJORLY POSITIVE THINKING...
PSST PSST PSST PSST

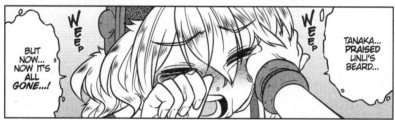

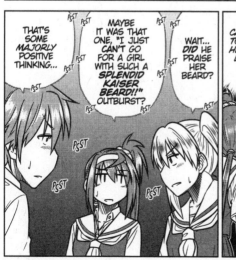

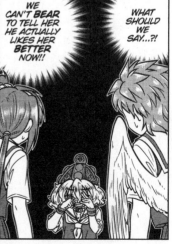

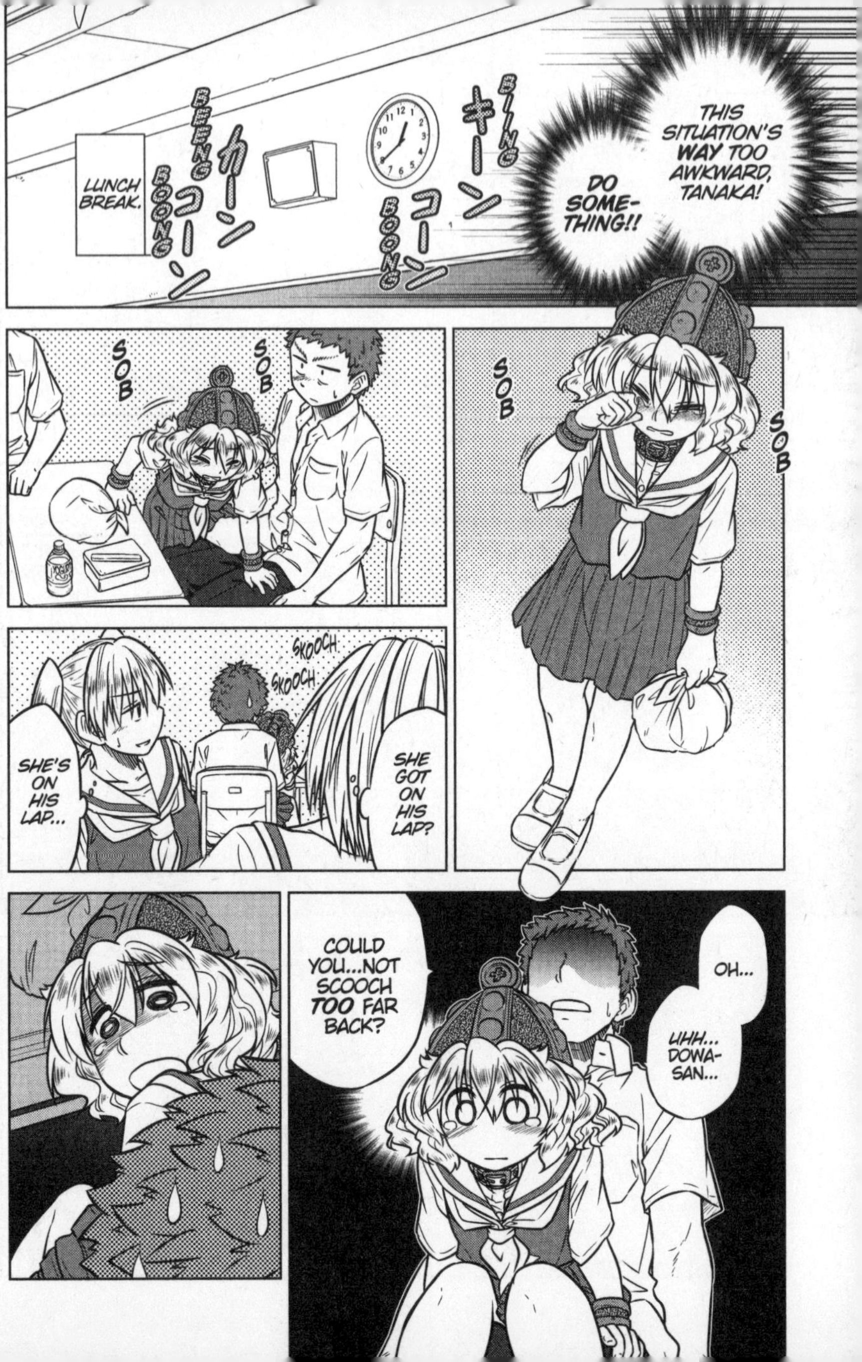
THIS SITUATION'S WAY TOO AWKWARD, TANAKA!
DO SOME-THING!!
BING
BOONG
BEENG
BOONG
LUNCH BREAK.
SOB
SOB
SOB
SOB
SKOOCH
SKOOCH
SHE GOT ON HIS LAP?
SHE'S ON HIS LAP...
OH...
UHH... DOWA-SAN...
COULD YOU...NOT SCOOCH TOO FAR BACK?

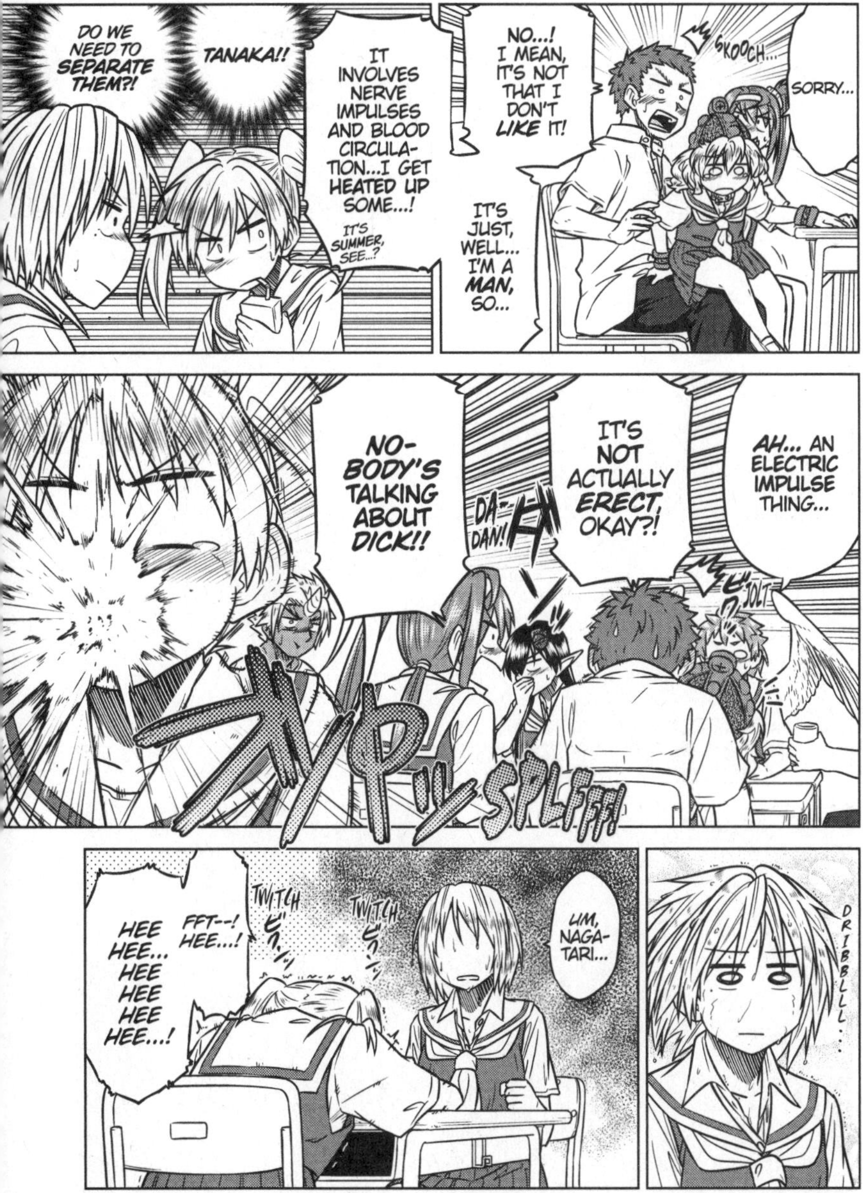
SKOOCH...
SORRY...
NO...! I MEAN, IT'S NOT THAT I DON'T LIKE IT!
IT'S JUST, WELL... I'M A MAN, SO...
IT INVOLVES NERVE IMPULSES AND BLOOD CIRCULATION...I GET HEATED UP SOME...!
IT'S SUMMER, SEE...?
TANAKA!!
DO WE NEED TO SEPARATE THEM?!
AH... AN ELECTRIC IMPULSE THING...
JOLT
IT'S NOT ACTUALLY ERECT, OKAY?!
DA-DAN!
NO-BODY'S TALKING ABOUT DICK!!
SPLFFFF!
DRIBBLLL...
UM, NAGATARI...
TWITCH
TWITCH
FFT--! HEE...!
HEE HEE... HEE HEE HEE HEE...!

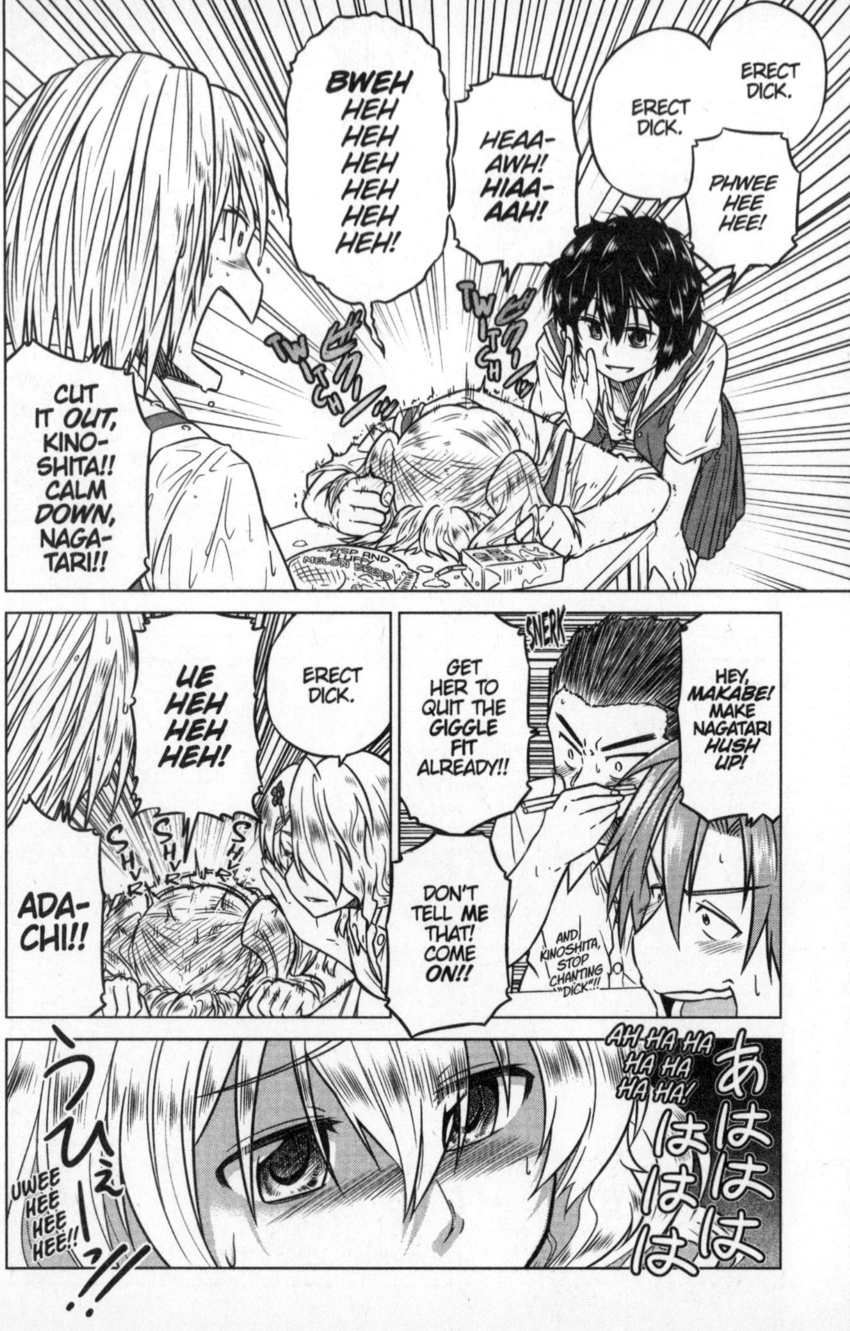
ERECT DICK.
ERECT DICK.
PHWEE HEE HEE!
HEAAA-AWH! HIAAA-AAH!
BWEH HEH HEH HEH HEH HEH HEH!
TWITCH
TWITCH
CUT IT OUT, KINOSHITA!! CALM DOWN, NAGATARI!!
CRISP AND FLUFFY MELON BREAD
SNERK
HEY, MAKABE! MAKE NAGATARI HUSH UP!
GET HER TO QUIT THE GIGGLE FIT ALREADY!!
AND KINOSHITA, STOP CHANTING "DICK"!!
DON'T TELL ME THAT! COME ON!!
ERECT DICK.
UE HEH HEH HEH!
SHVR SHVR SHVR
ADACHI!!
あははははは
AH HA HA HA HA HA HA!
うひぇーっ!!
UWEE HEE HEE HEE!!

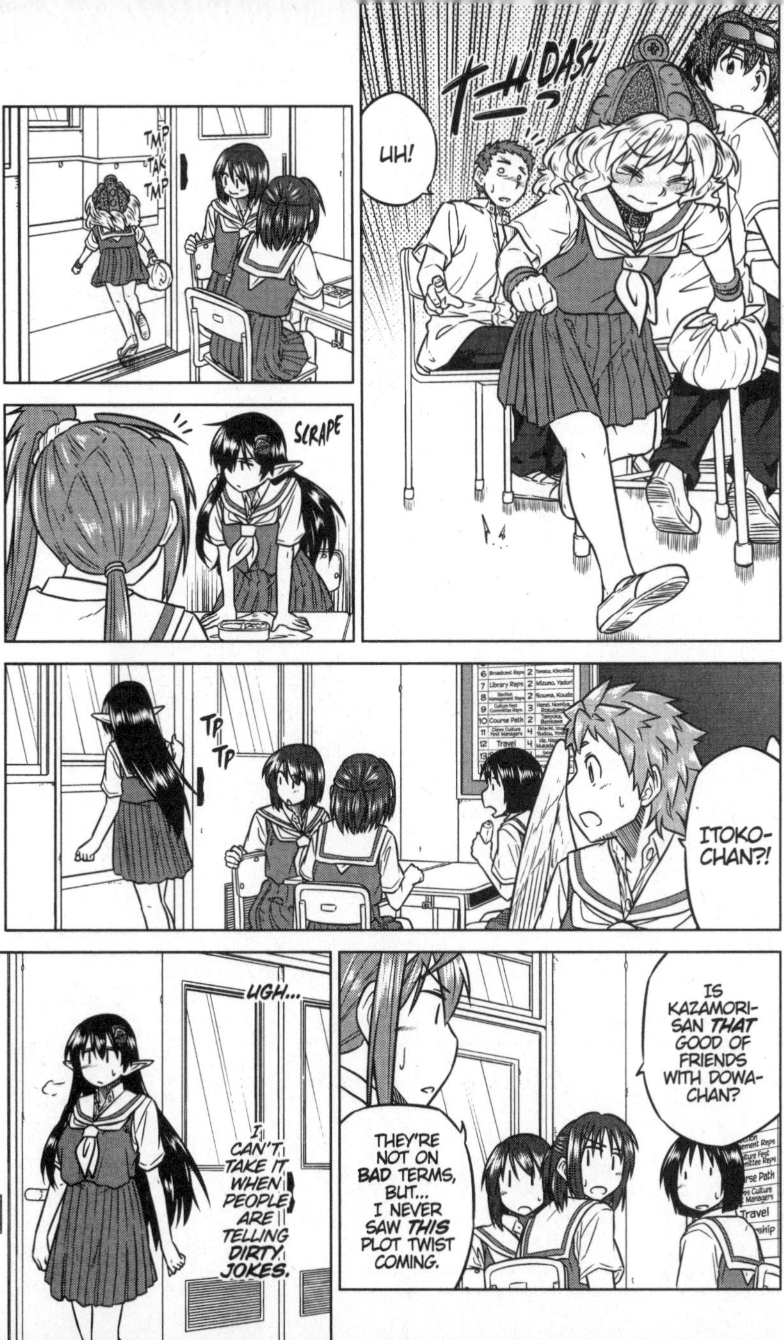
DASH
UH!
TMP
TAK
TMP
SCRAPE
ITOKO-CHAN?!
Tp
Tp
IS KAZAMORI-SAN THAT GOOD OF FRIENDS WITH DOWA-CHAN?
THEY'RE NOT ON BAD TERMS, BUT... I NEVER SAW THIS PLOT TWIST COMING.
UGH...
I CAN'T TAKE IT WHEN PEOPLE ARE TELLING DIRTY JOKES.

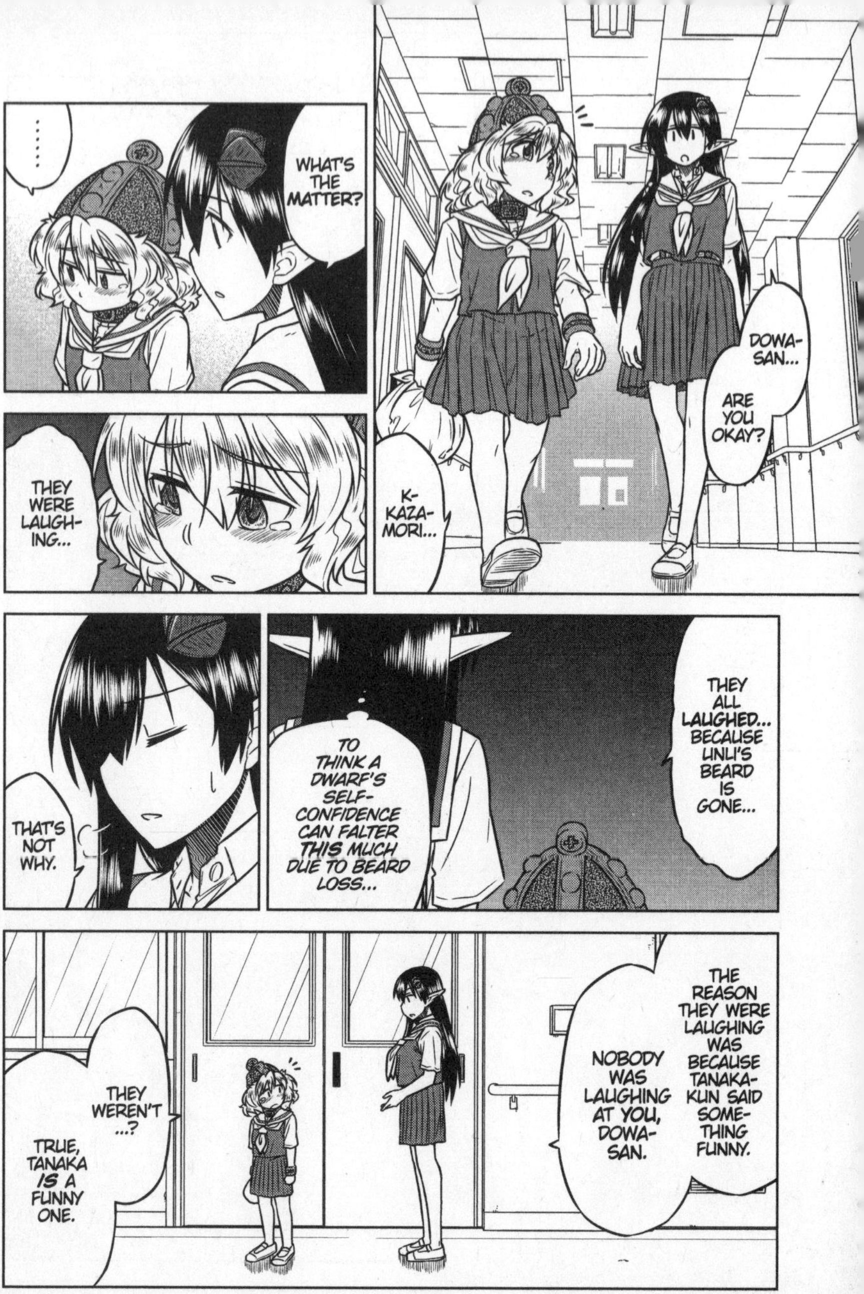
DOWA-SAN...
ARE YOU OKAY?
K-KAZAMORI...
WHAT'S THE MATTER?
......
THEY WERE LAUGHING...
THEY ALL LAUGHED... BECAUSE UNLI'S BEARD IS GONE...
TO THINK A DWARF'S SELF-CONFIDENCE CAN FALTER *THIS* MUCH DUE TO BEARD LOSS...
THAT'S NOT WHY.
THE REASON THEY WERE LAUGHING WAS BECAUSE TANAKA-KUN SAID SOMETHING FUNNY.
NOBODY WAS LAUGHING AT YOU, DOWA-SAN.
THEY WEREN'T ...?
TRUE, TANAKA *IS* A FUNNY ONE.

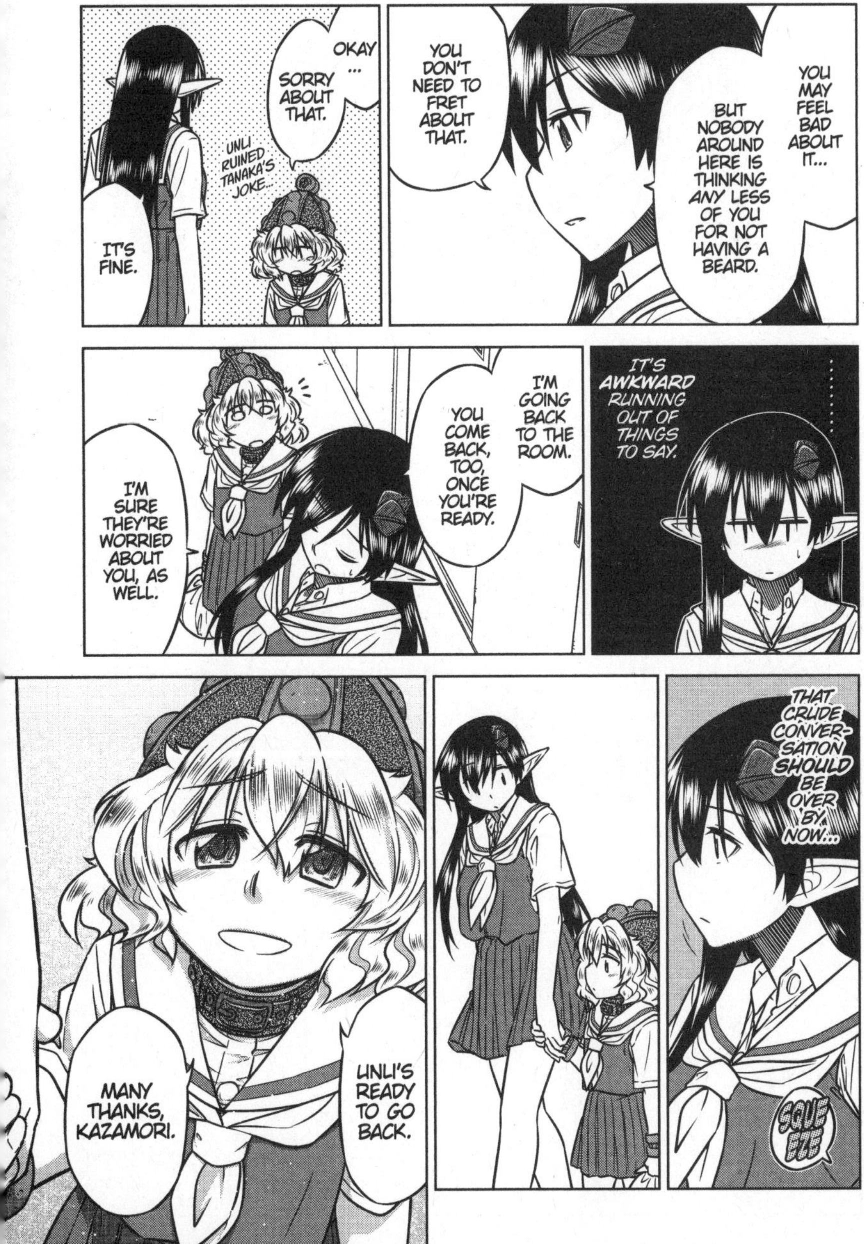
YOU MAY FEEL BAD ABOUT IT...
BUT NOBODY AROUND HERE IS THINKING ANY LESS OF YOU FOR NOT HAVING A BEARD.
YOU DON'T NEED TO FRET ABOUT THAT.
OKAY ...
SORRY ABOUT THAT.
UNLI RUINED TANAKA'S JOKE...
IT'S FINE.
IT'S AWKWARD RUNNING OUT OF THINGS TO SAY.
I'M GOING BACK TO THE ROOM.
YOU COME BACK, TOO, ONCE YOU'RE READY.
I'M SURE THEY'RE WORRIED ABOUT YOU, AS WELL.
THAT CRUDE CONVER-SATION SHOULD BE OVER BY NOW...
SQUE EZE
UNLI'S READY TO GO BACK.
MANY THANKS, KAZAMORI.

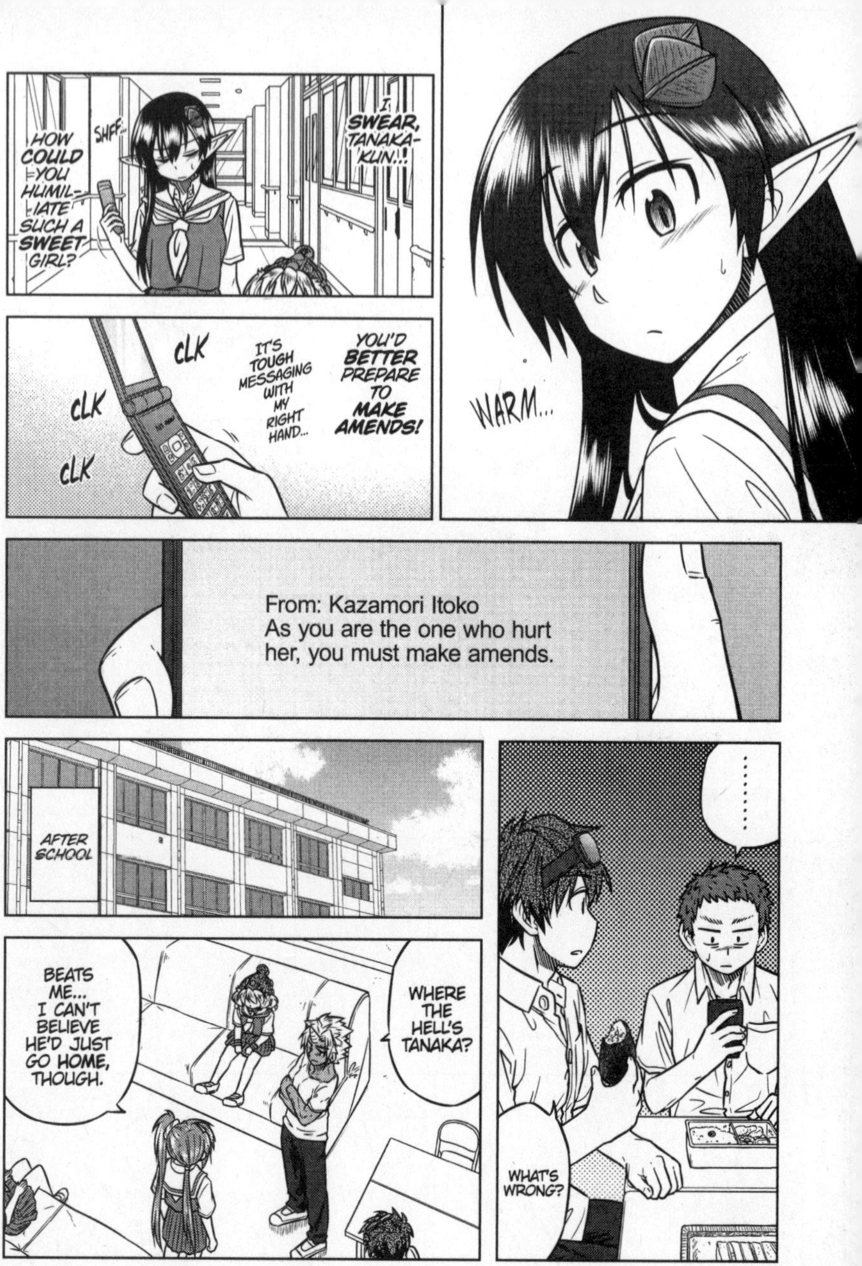
WARM...
I SWEAR, TANAKA-KUN...!
SHFF...
HOW COULD YOU HUMILIATE SUCH A SWEET GIRL?
YOU'D BETTER PREPARE TO MAKE AMENDS!
IT'S TOUGH MESSAGING WITH MY RIGHT HAND...
CLK
CLK
CLK
From: Kazamori Itoko
As you are the one who hurt her, you must make amends.
......
WHAT'S WRONG?
AFTER SCHOOL
WHERE THE HELL'S TANAKA?
BEATS ME... I CAN'T BELIEVE HE'D JUST GO HOME, THOUGH.

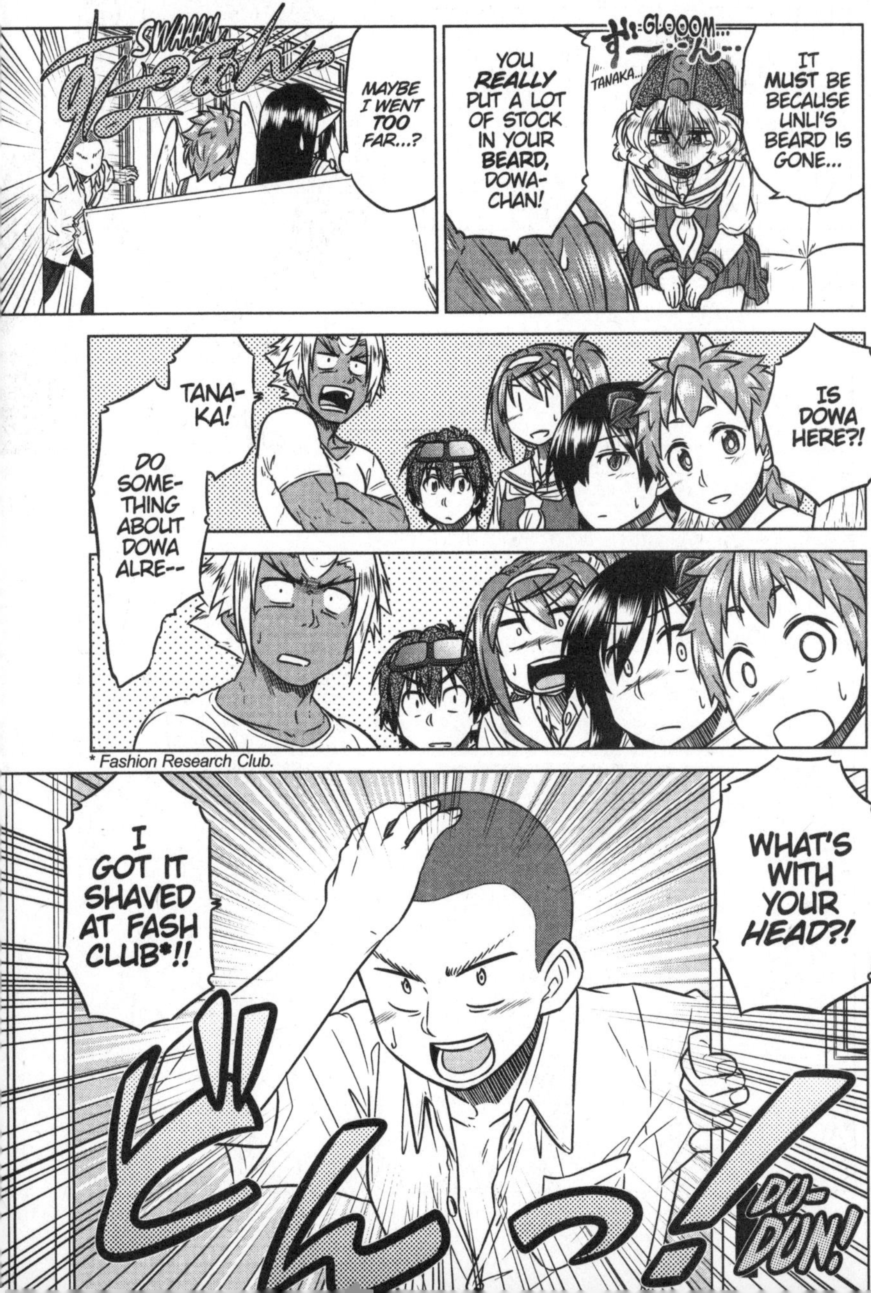
ずーーん…
Hi-GLOOOM...
IT MUST BE BECAUSE UNLI'S BEARD IS GONE...
TANAKA...
YOU REALLY PUT A LOT OF STOCK IN YOUR BEARD, DOWA-CHAN!
MAYBE I WENT TOO FAR...?
SWAAAM
IS DOWA HERE?!
TANA-KA!
DO SOME-THING ABOUT DOWA ALRE--
WHAT'S WITH YOUR HEAD?!
I GOT IT SHAVED AT FASH CLUB*!!
どんっ!
DU-DUN!

* Fashion Research Club.

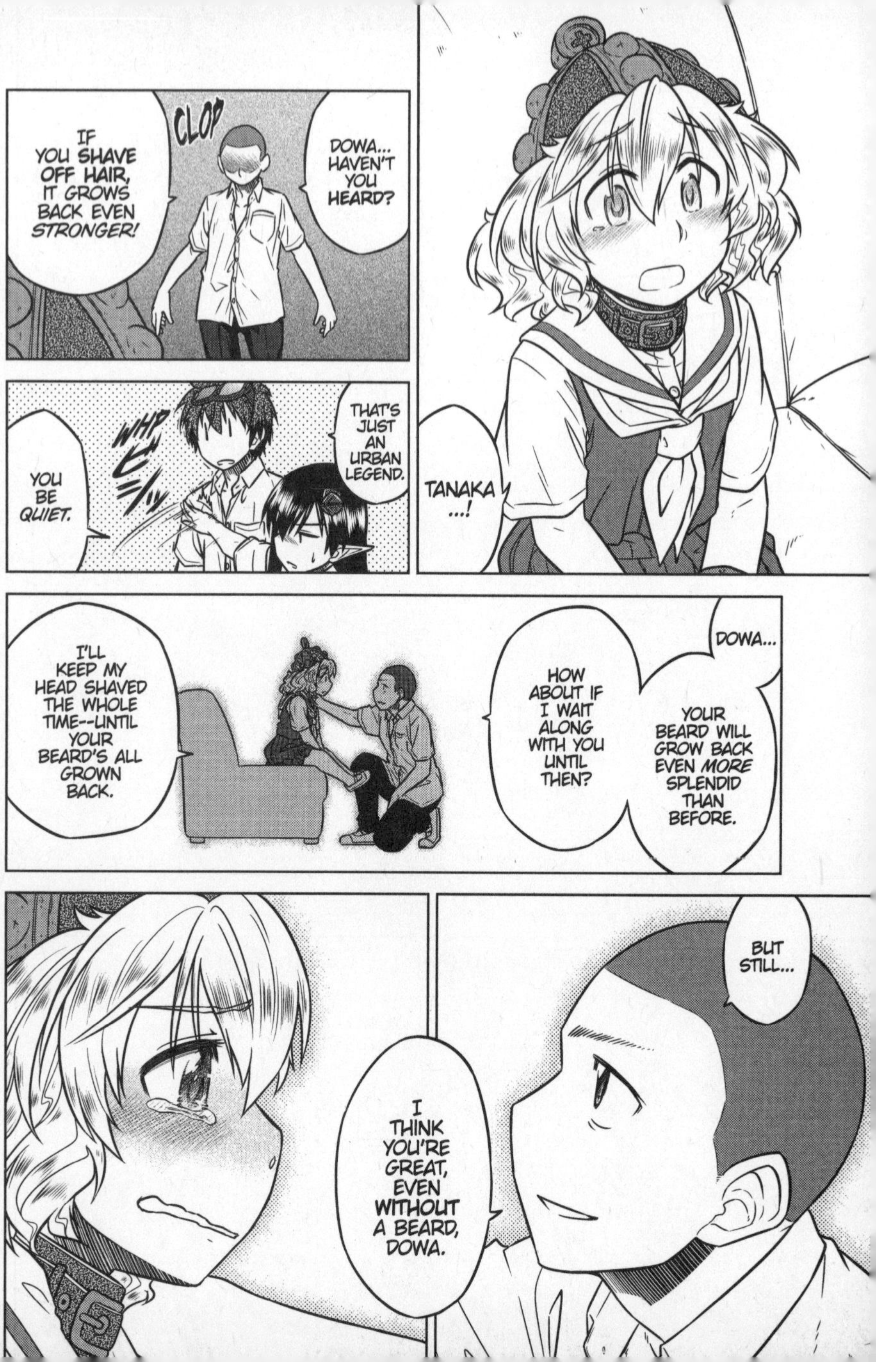
TANAKA ...!
DOWA... HAVEN'T YOU HEARD?
CLOP
IF YOU SHAVE OFF HAIR, IT GROWS BACK EVEN STRONGER!
THAT'S JUST AN URBAN LEGEND.
WHP
YOU BE QUIET.
DOWA...
YOUR BEARD WILL GROW BACK EVEN MORE SPLENDID THAN BEFORE.
HOW ABOUT IF I WAIT ALONG WITH YOU UNTIL THEN?
I'LL KEEP MY HEAD SHAVED THE WHOLE TIME--UNTIL YOUR BEARD'S ALL GROWN BACK.
BUT STILL...
I THINK YOU'RE GREAT, EVEN WITHOUT A BEARD, DOWA.

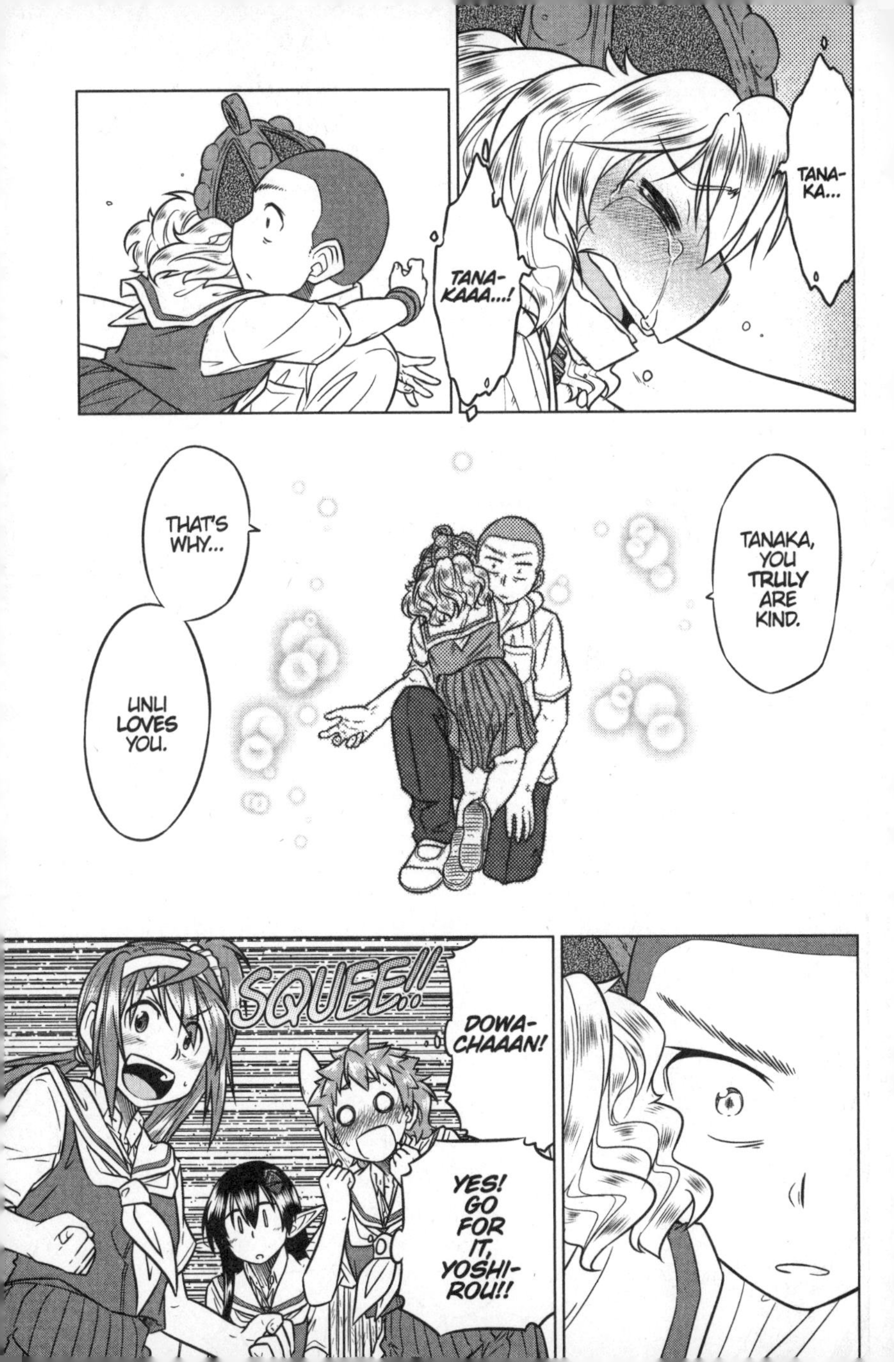
TANA-KA...
TANA-KAAA...!
TANAKA, YOU TRULY ARE KIND.
THAT'S WHY...
UNLI LOVES YOU.
DOWA-CHAAAN!
SQUEEE!!
YES! GO FOR IT, YOSHI-ROU!!

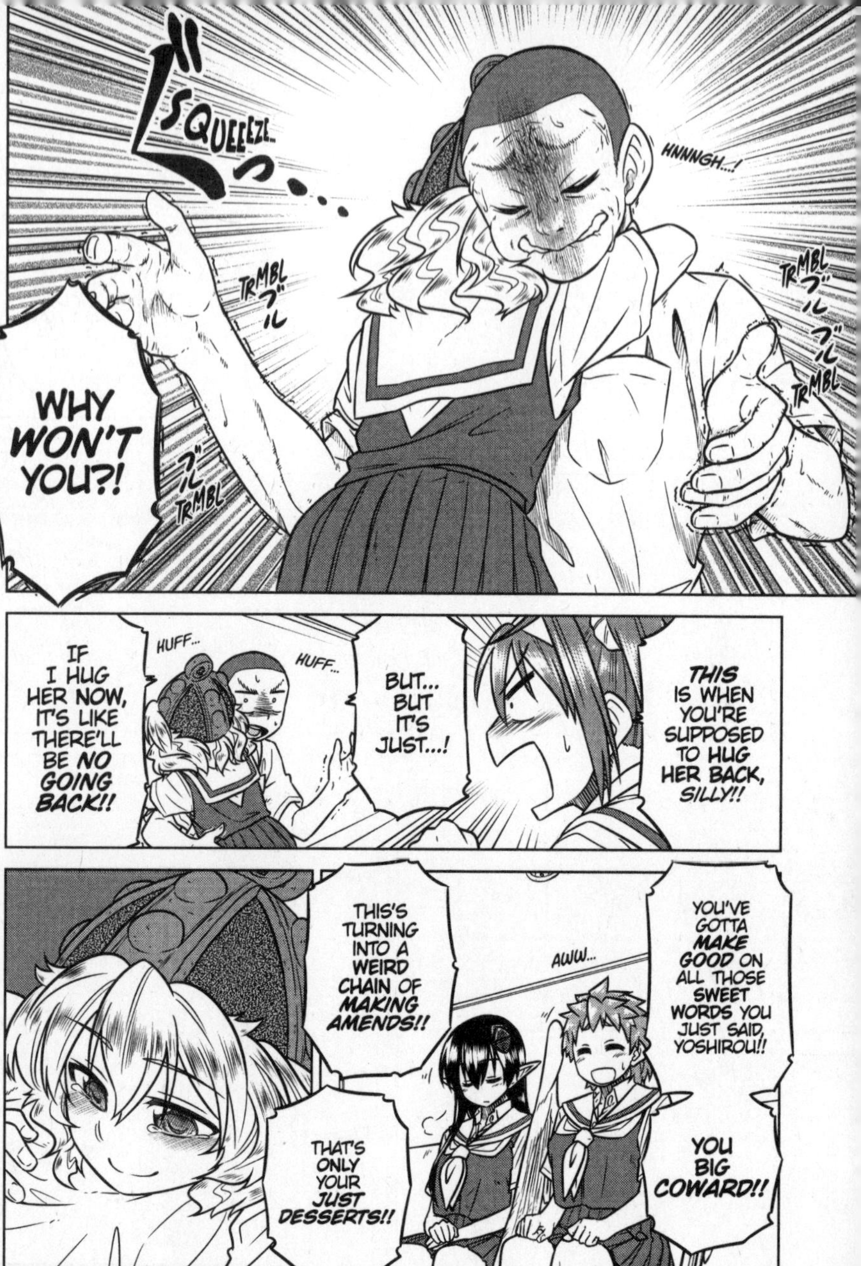
SQUEEEZE...
HNNNGH...!
TRMBL
TRMBL
TRMBL
TRMBL
WHY WON'T YOU?!
THIS IS WHEN YOU'RE SUPPOSED TO HUG HER BACK, SILLY!!
BUT... BUT IT'S JUST...!
HUFF...
HUFF...
IF I HUG HER NOW, IT'S LIKE THERE'LL BE NO GOING BACK!!
YOU'VE GOTTA MAKE GOOD ON ALL THOSE SWEET WORDS YOU JUST SAID, YOSHIROU!!
YOU BIG COWARD!!
AWW...
THIS'S TURNING INTO A WEIRD CHAIN OF MAKING AMENDS!!
THAT'S ONLY YOUR JUST DESSERTS!!

Chapter 16 • END

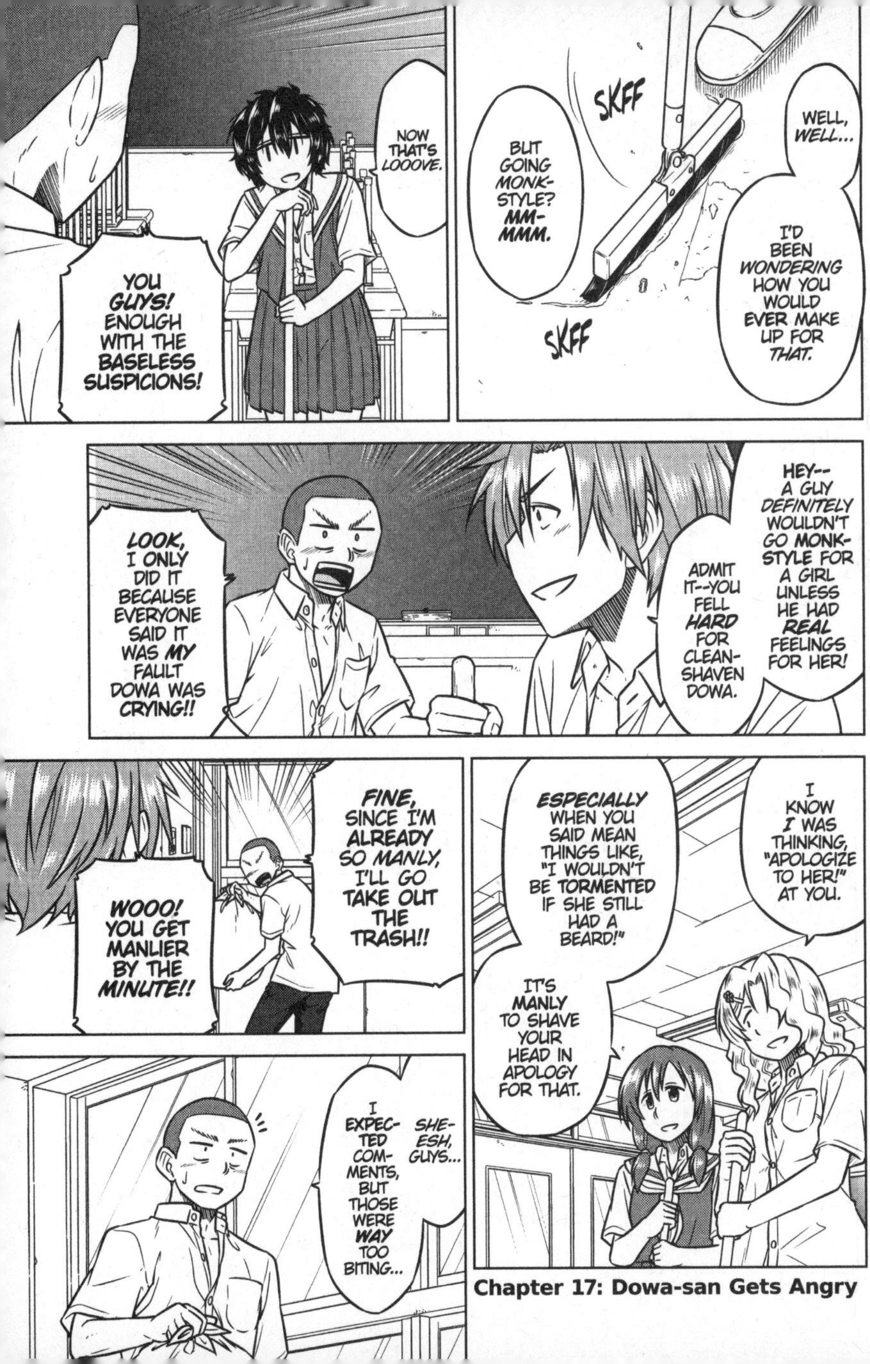
WELL, WELL...
I'D BEEN WONDERING HOW YOU WOULD EVER MAKE UP FOR THAT.
SKFF
SKFF
BUT GOING MONK-STYLE? MM-MMM.
NOW THAT'S LOOOVE.
YOU GUYS! ENOUGH WITH THE BASELESS SUSPICIONS!
HEY-- A GUY DEFINITELY WOULDN'T GO MONK-STYLE FOR A GIRL UNLESS HE HAD REAL FEELINGS FOR HER!
ADMIT IT--YOU FELL HARD FOR CLEAN-SHAVEN DOWA.
LOOK, I ONLY DID IT BECAUSE EVERYONE SAID IT WAS MY FAULT DOWA WAS CRYING!!
I KNOW I WAS THINKING, "APOLOGIZE TO HER!" AT YOU.
ESPECIALLY WHEN YOU SAID MEAN THINGS LIKE, "I WOULDN'T BE TORMENTED IF SHE STILL HAD A BEARD!"
IT'S MANLY TO SHAVE YOUR HEAD IN APOLOGY FOR THAT.
FINE, SINCE I'M ALREADY SO MANLY, I'LL GO TAKE OUT THE TRASH!!
WOOO! YOU GET MANLIER BY THE MINUTE!!
SHEESH, GUYS...
I EXPECTED COMMENTS, BUT THOSE WERE WAY TOO BITING...

Chapter 17: Dowa-san Gets Angry

Chapter 17: Dowa-san Gets Angry

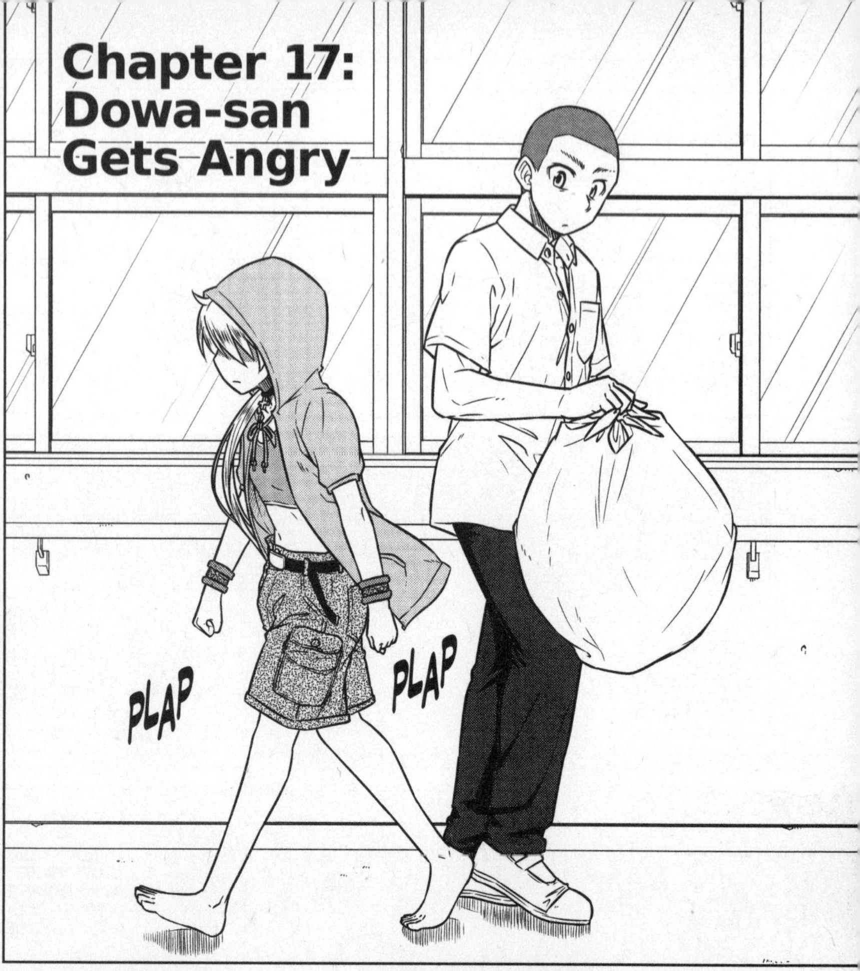
PLAP
PLAP

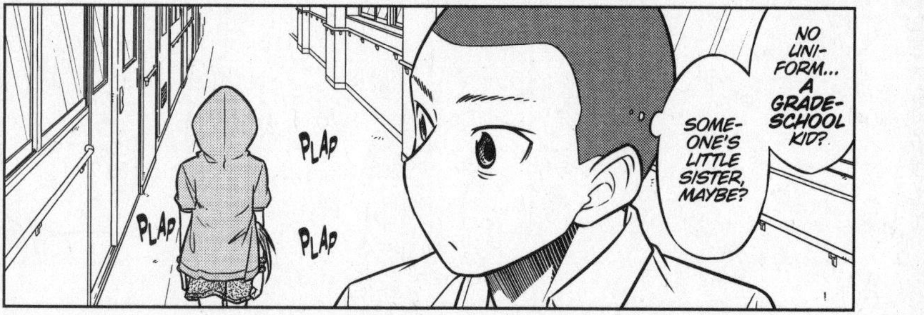
NO UNIFORM... A GRADE-SCHOOL KID?
SOMEONE'S LITTLE SISTER, MAYBE?
PLAP
PLAP
PLAP

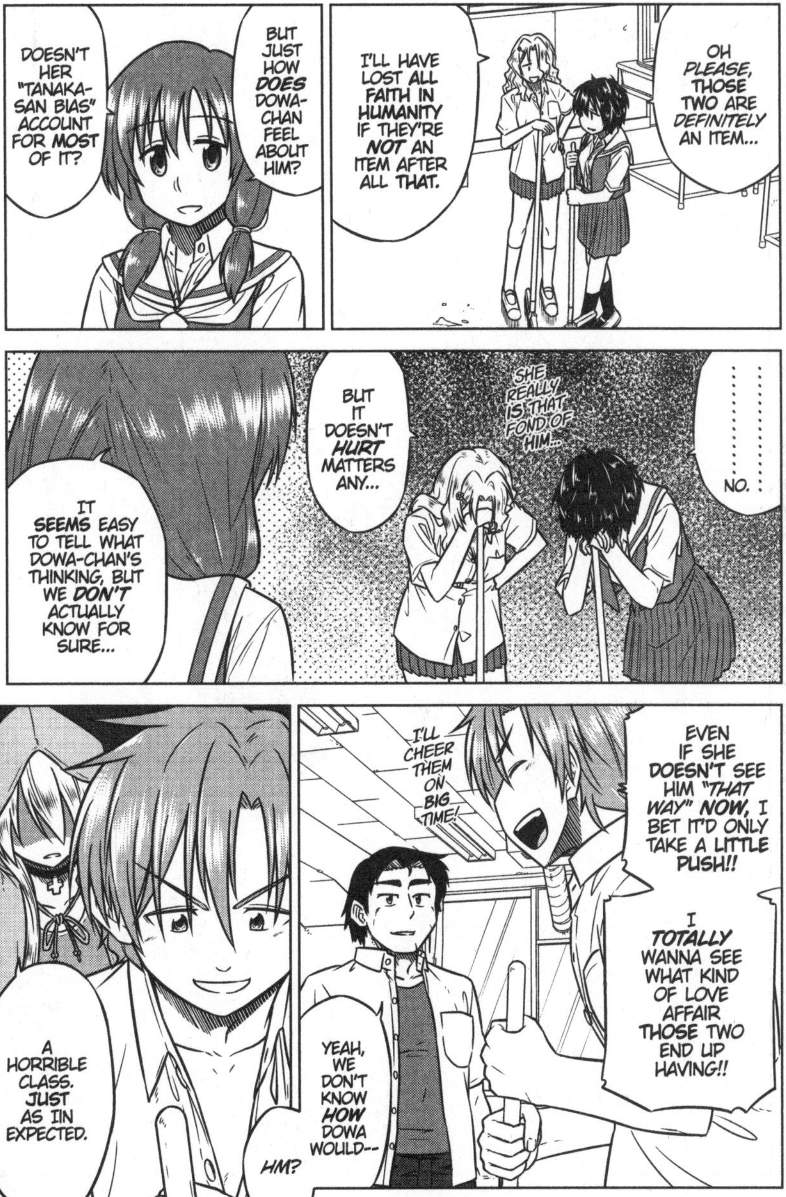

OH *PLEASE*, THOSE TWO ARE *DEFINITELY* AN ITEM...
I'LL HAVE LOST **ALL** FAITH IN **HUMANITY** IF THEY'RE ***NOT*** AN ITEM AFTER ALL THAT.
BUT JUST HOW ***DOES*** DOWA-CHAN FEEL ABOUT HIM?
DOESN'T HER "TANAKA-SAN BIAS" ACCOUNT FOR **MOST** OF IT?
...... NO.
SHE REALLY IS THAT FOND OF HIM...
BUT IT DOESN'T ***HURT*** MATTERS ANY...
IT **SEEMS** EASY TO TELL WHAT DOWA-CHAN'S THINKING, BUT WE ***DON'T*** ACTUALLY KNOW FOR SURE...
EVEN IF SHE **DOESN'T** SEE HIM "***THAT WAY***" ***NOW***, I BET IT'D ONLY TAKE A LITTLE **PUSH!!**
I'LL CHEER THEM ON BIG TIME!
I ***TOTALLY*** WANNA SEE WHAT KIND OF LOVE AFFAIR THOSE TWO END UP HAVING!!
YEAH, WE DON'T KNOW ***HOW*** DOWA WOULD--
HM?
A HORRIBLE CLASS. **JUST** AS IIN EXPECTED.

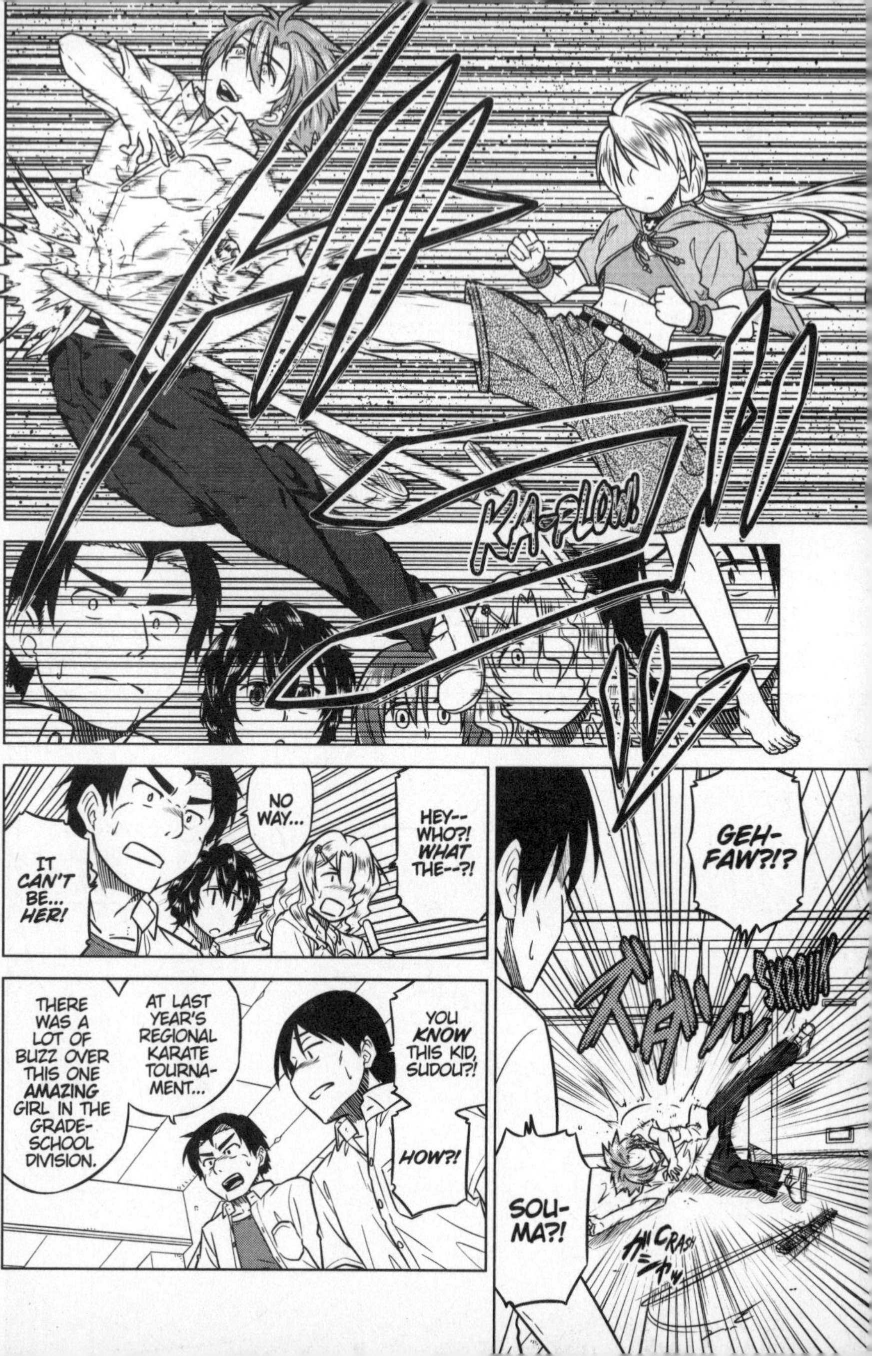
KA-FLOW!!
GEH-FAW?!?
SOU-MA?!
CRASH
HEY-- WHO?! WHAT THE--?!
NO WAY...
IT CAN'T BE... HER!
YOU KNOW THIS KID, SUDOU?!
HOW?!
AT LAST YEAR'S REGIONAL KARATE TOURNAMENT...
THERE WAS A LOT OF BUZZ OVER THIS ONE AMAZING GIRL IN THE GRADE-SCHOOL DIVISION.

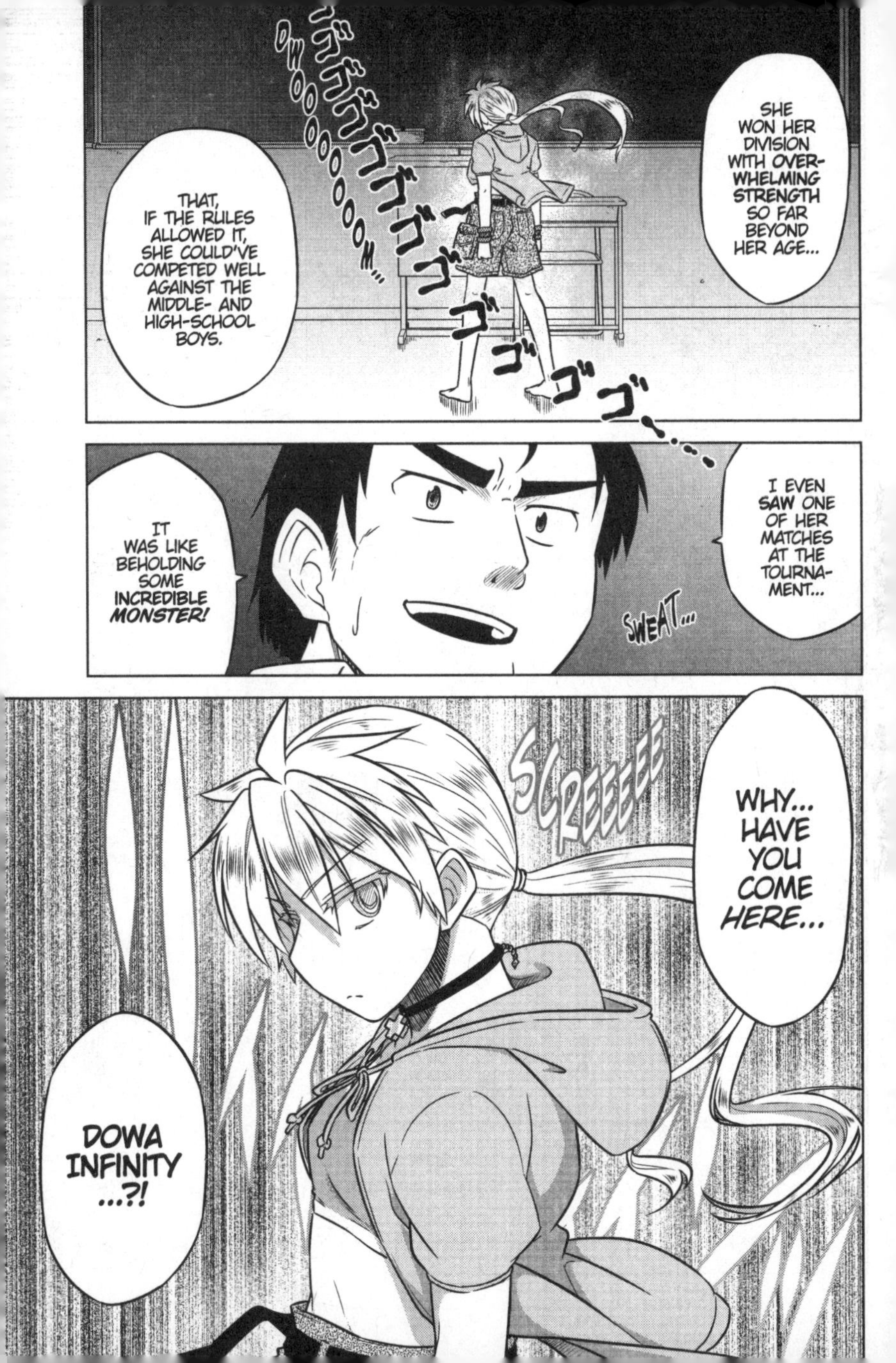
SHE WON HER DIVISION WITH OVER-WHELMING STRENGTH SO FAR BEYOND HER AGE...
DOWOOOOOOOOOOM...
THAT, IF THE RULES ALLOWED IT, SHE COULD'VE COMPETED WELL AGAINST THE MIDDLE- AND HIGH-SCHOOL BOYS.
I EVEN SAW ONE OF HER MATCHES AT THE TOURNA-MENT...
SWEAT...
IT WAS LIKE BEHOLDING SOME INCREDIBLE ***MONSTER!***
SCREEEEE
WHY... HAVE YOU COME ***HERE...***
DOWA INFINITY ...?!

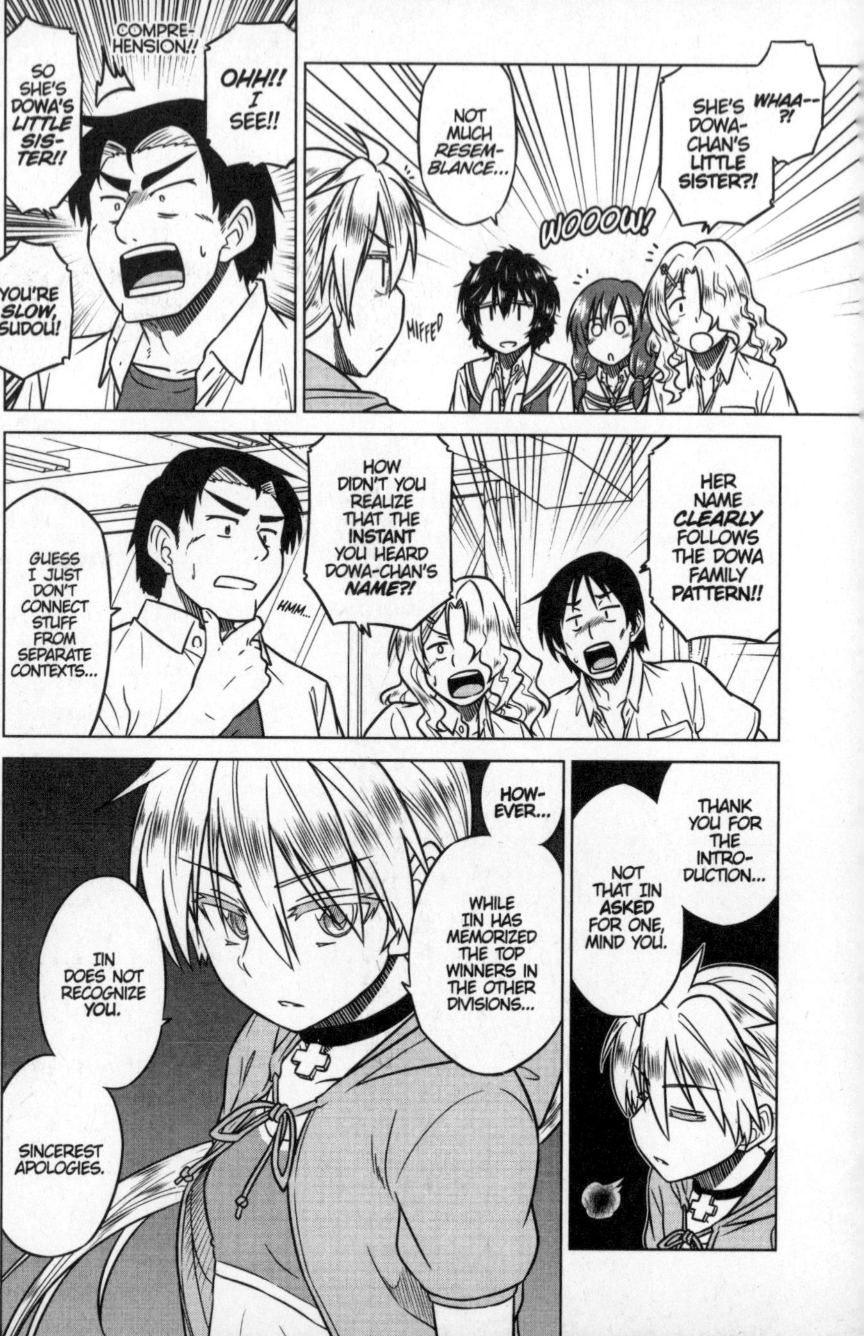

WHAA--?!
SHE'S DOWA-CHAN'S LITTLE SISTER?!
WOOOW!
NOT MUCH RESEMBLANCE...
MIFFED
COMPREHENSION!!
OHH!! I SEE!!
SO SHE'S DOWA'S LITTLE SISTER!!
YOU'RE SLOW, SUDOU!
HER NAME CLEARLY FOLLOWS THE DOWA FAMILY PATTERN!!
HOW DIDN'T YOU REALIZE THAT THE INSTANT YOU HEARD DOWA-CHAN'S NAME?!
HMM...
GUESS I JUST DON'T CONNECT STUFF FROM SEPARATE CONTEXTS...
THANK YOU FOR THE INTRODUCTION...
NOT THAT IIN ASKED FOR ONE, MIND YOU.
HOWEVER...
WHILE IIN HAS MEMORIZED THE TOP WINNERS IN THE OTHER DIVISIONS...
IIN DOES NOT RECOGNIZE YOU.
SINCEREST APOLOGIES.

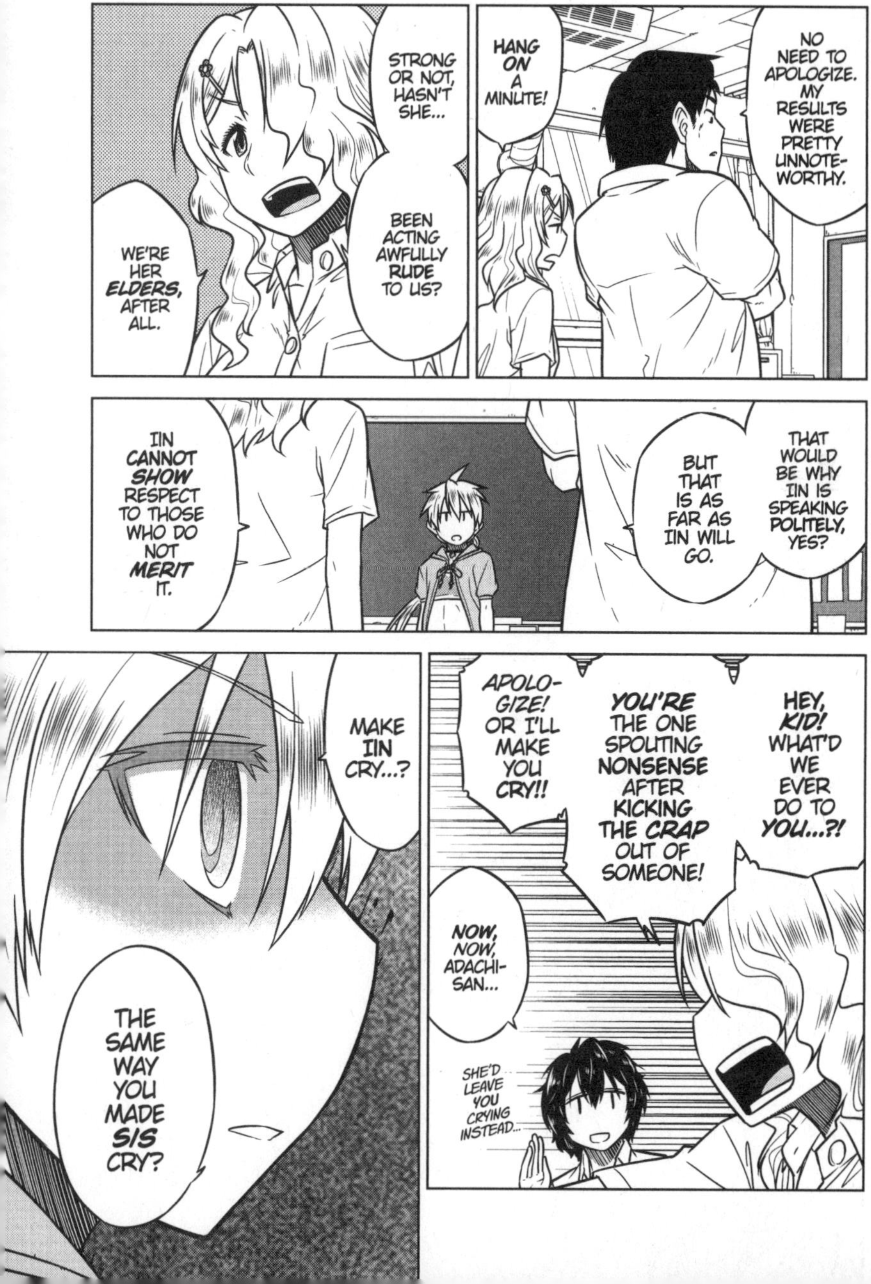
NO NEED TO APOLOGIZE. MY RESULTS WERE PRETTY UNNOTE-WORTHY.
HANG ON A MINUTE!
STRONG OR NOT, HASN'T SHE...
BEEN ACTING AWFULLY RUDE TO US?
WE'RE HER ELDERS, AFTER ALL.
THAT WOULD BE WHY IIN IS SPEAKING POLITELY, YES?
BUT THAT IS AS FAR AS IIN WILL GO.
IIN CANNOT SHOW RESPECT TO THOSE WHO DO NOT MERIT IT.
HEY, KID! WHAT'D WE EVER DO TO YOU...?!
YOU'RE THE ONE SPOUTING NONSENSE AFTER KICKING THE CRAP OUT OF SOMEONE!
APOLO-GIZE! OR I'LL MAKE YOU CRY!!
NOW, NOW, ADACHI-SAN...
SHE'D LEAVE YOU CRYING INSTEAD...
MAKE IIN CRY...?
THE SAME WAY YOU MADE SIS CRY?

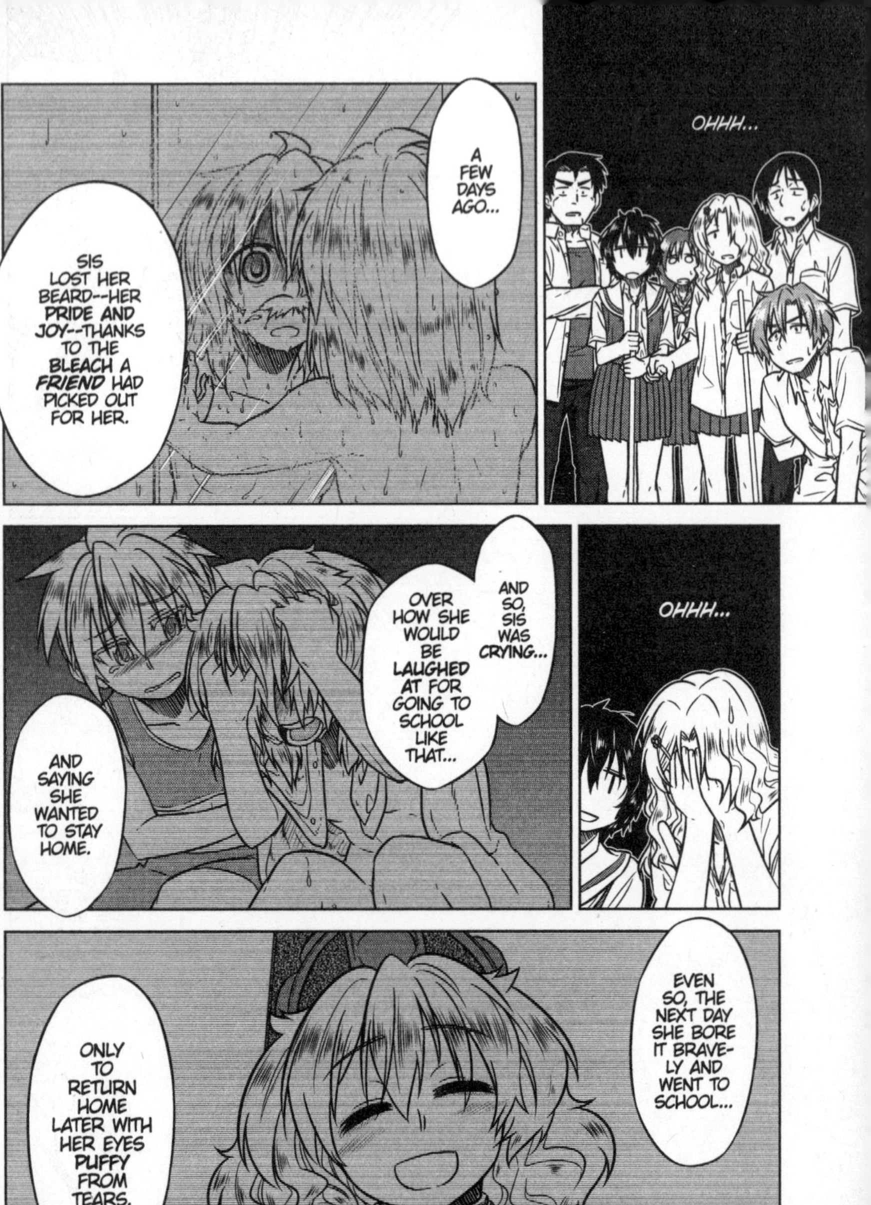
OHHH...
A FEW DAYS AGO...
SIS LOST HER BEARD--HER PRIDE AND JOY--THANKS TO THE BLEACH A FRIEND HAD PICKED OUT FOR HER.
OHHH...
AND SO, SIS WAS CRYING...
OVER HOW SHE WOULD BE LAUGHED AT FOR GOING TO SCHOOL LIKE THAT...
AND SAYING SHE WANTED TO STAY HOME.
EVEN SO, THE NEXT DAY SHE BORE IT BRAVELY AND WENT TO SCHOOL...
ONLY TO RETURN HOME LATER WITH HER EYES PUFFY FROM TEARS.

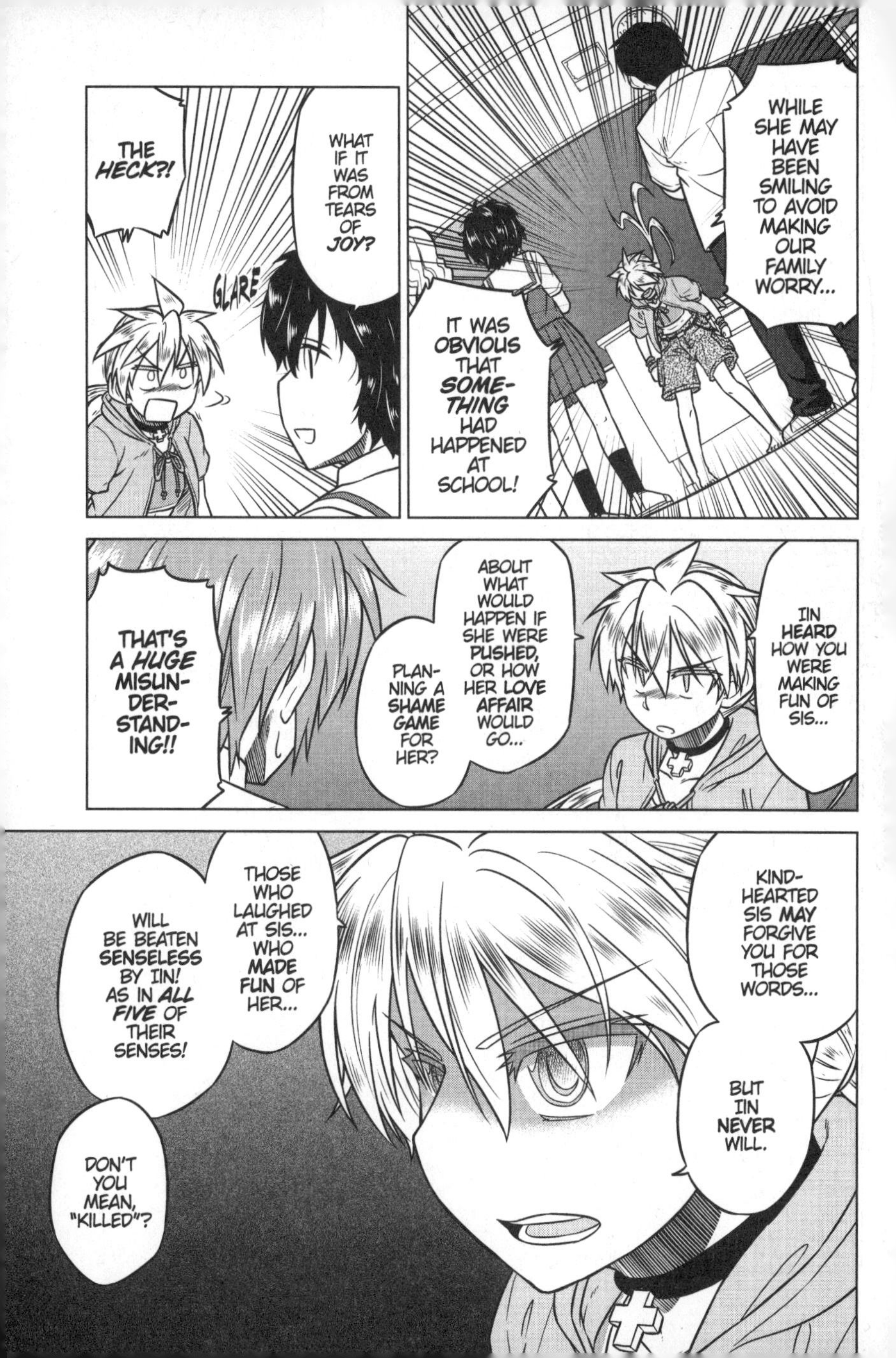
WHILE SHE MAY HAVE BEEN SMILING TO AVOID MAKING OUR FAMILY WORRY...
IT WAS OBVIOUS THAT SOMETHING HAD HAPPENED AT SCHOOL!
WHAT IF IT WAS FROM TEARS OF JOY?
GLARE
THE HECK?!
IIN HEARD HOW YOU WERE MAKING FUN OF SIS...
ABOUT WHAT WOULD HAPPEN IF SHE WERE PUSHED, OR HOW HER LOVE AFFAIR WOULD GO...
PLANNING A SHAME GAME FOR HER?
THAT'S A HUGE MISUNDERSTANDING!!
KIND-HEARTED SIS MAY FORGIVE YOU FOR THOSE WORDS...
BUT IIN NEVER WILL.
THOSE WHO LAUGHED AT SIS... WHO MADE FUN OF HER...
WILL BE BEATEN SENSELESS BY IIN! AS IN ALL FIVE OF THEIR SENSES!
DON'T YOU MEAN, "KILLED"?

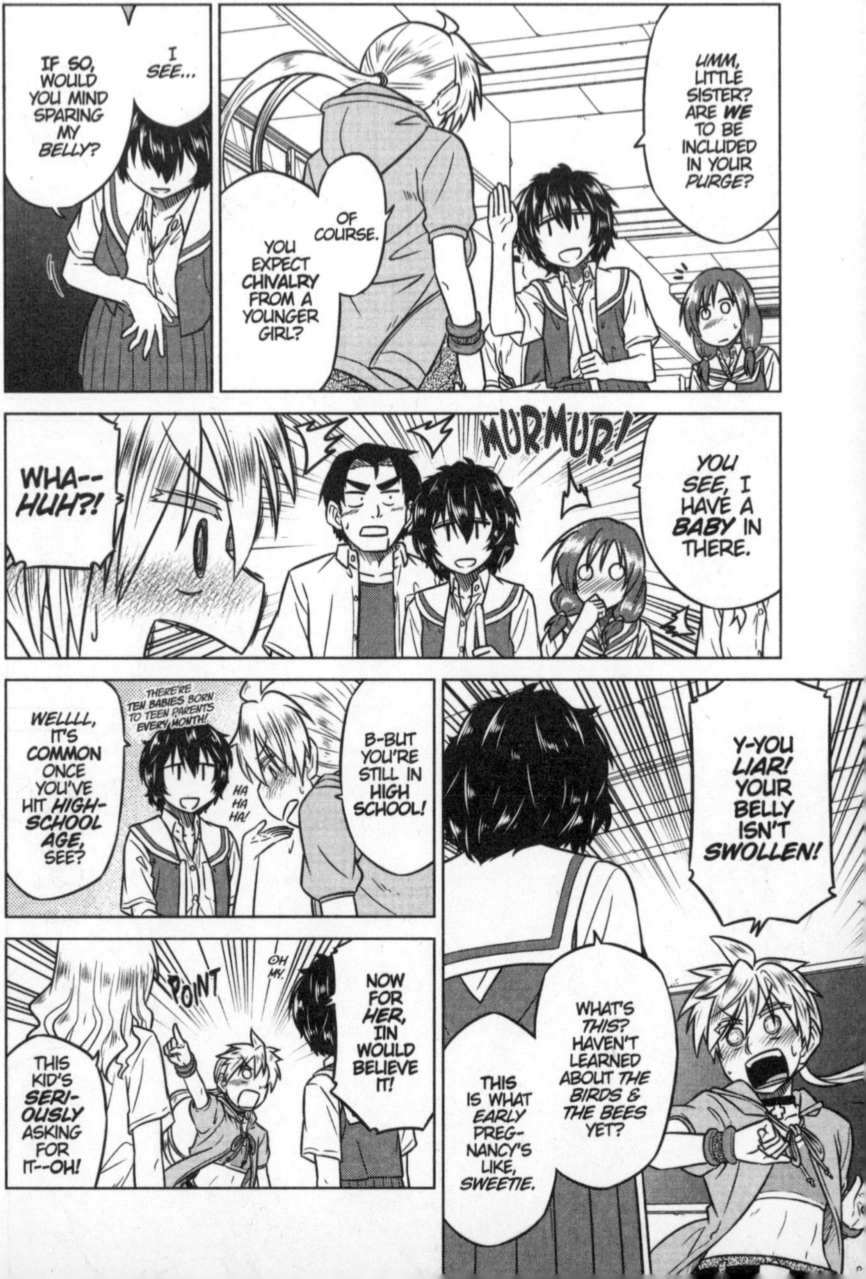
UMM, LITTLE SISTER? ARE WE TO BE INCLUDED IN YOUR PURGE?
OF COURSE. YOU EXPECT CHIVALRY FROM A YOUNGER GIRL?
I SEE...
IF SO, WOULD YOU MIND SPARING MY BELLY?
YOU SEE, I HAVE A BABY IN THERE.
MURMUR!
WHA-- HUH?!
Y-YOU LIAR! YOUR BELLY ISN'T SWOLLEN!
WHAT'S THIS? HAVEN'T LEARNED ABOUT THE BIRDS & THE BEES YET?
THIS IS WHAT EARLY PREG-NANCY'S LIKE, SWEETIE.
B-BUT YOU'RE STILL IN HIGH SCHOOL!
WELLLL, IT'S COMMON ONCE YOU'VE HIT HIGH-SCHOOL AGE, SEE?
THERE'RE TEN BABIES BORN TO TEEN PARENTS EVERY MONTH!
HA HA HA!
NOW FOR HER, IIN WOULD BELIEVE IT!
OH MY.
POINT
THIS KID'S SERI-OUSLY ASKING FOR IT--OH!

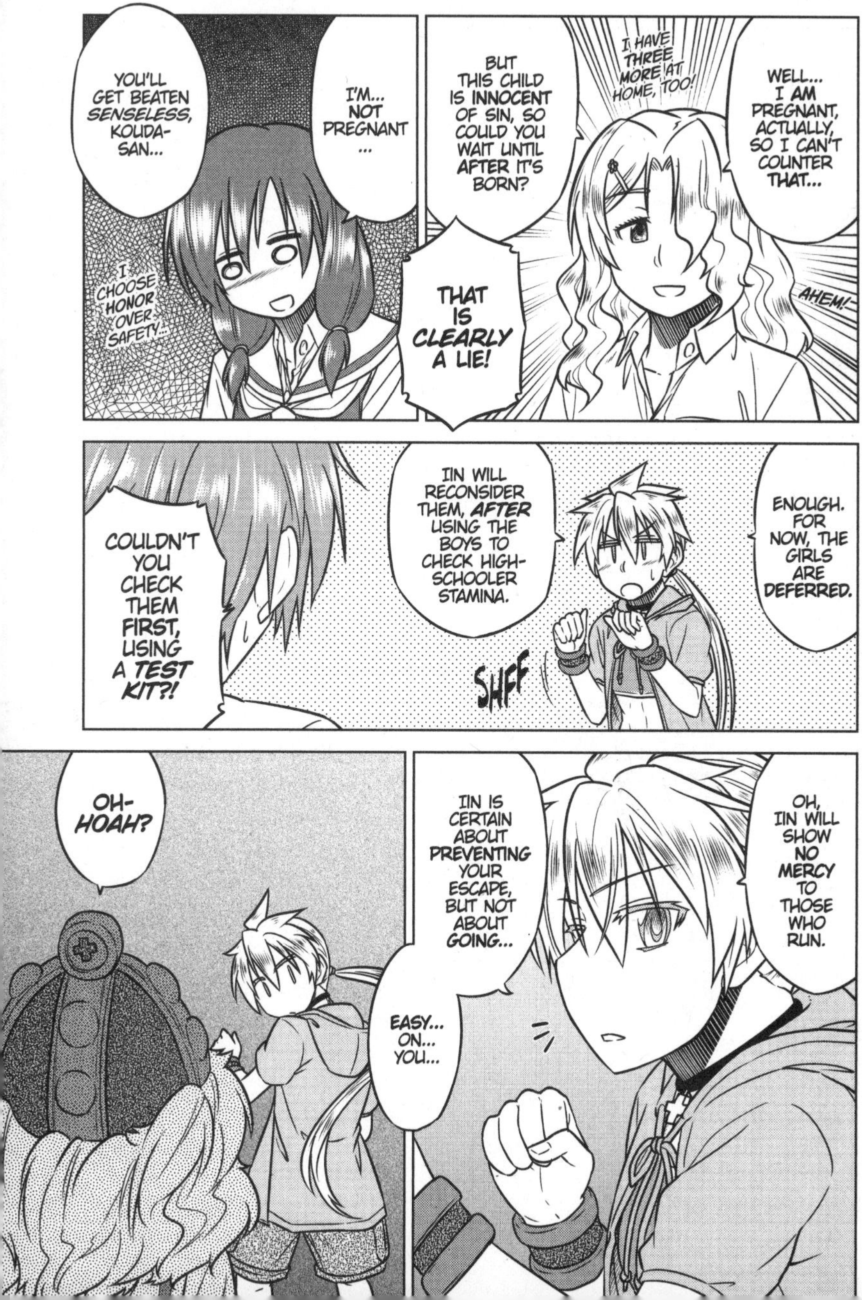
WELL... I AM PREGNANT, ACTUALLY, SO I CAN'T COUNTER THAT...
I HAVE THREE MORE AT HOME, TOO!
AHEM!
BUT THIS CHILD IS INNOCENT OF SIN, SO COULD YOU WAIT UNTIL AFTER IT'S BORN?
THAT IS CLEARLY A LIE!
I'M... NOT PREGNANT...
YOU'LL GET BEATEN SENSELESS, KOUDA-SAN...
I CHOOSE HONOR OVER SAFETY...
ENOUGH. FOR NOW, THE GIRLS ARE DEFERRED.
IIN WILL RECONSIDER THEM, AFTER USING THE BOYS TO CHECK HIGH-SCHOOLER STAMINA.
SHFF
COULDN'T YOU CHECK THEM FIRST, USING A TEST KIT?!
OH, IIN WILL SHOW NO MERCY TO THOSE WHO RUN.
IIN IS CERTAIN ABOUT PREVENTING YOUR ESCAPE, BUT NOT ABOUT GOING...
EASY... ON... YOU...
OH-HOAH?

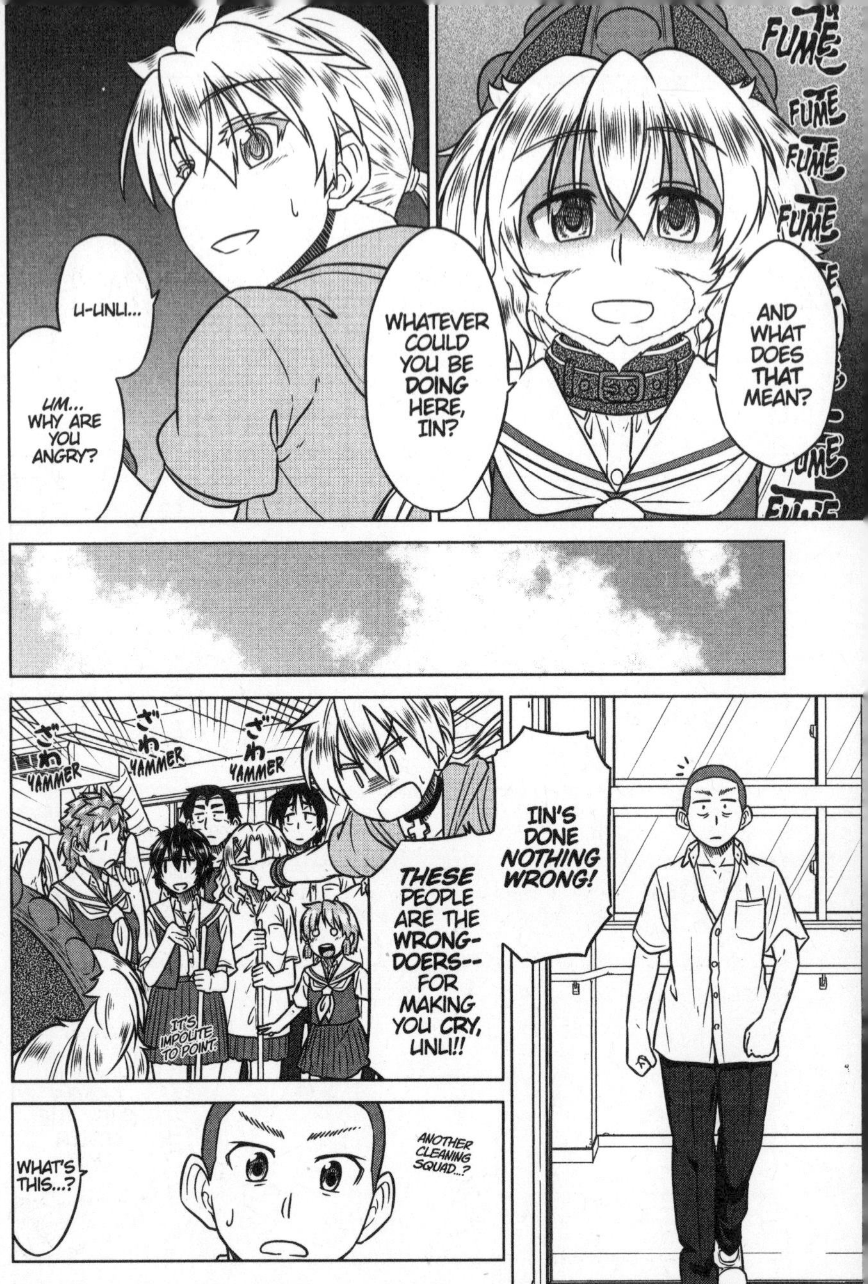

FUME FUME FUME FUME FUME FUME
AND WHAT DOES THAT MEAN?
WHATEVER COULD YOU BE DOING HERE, IIN?
U-UNLI...
UM... WHY ARE YOU ANGRY?
IIN'S DONE NOTHING WRONG!
THESE PEOPLE ARE THE WRONG-DOERS-- FOR MAKING YOU CRY, UNLI!!
ざわ YAMMER
ざわ YAMMER
ざわ YAMMER
IT'S IMPOLITE TO POINT.
ANOTHER CLEANING SQUAD...?
WHAT'S THIS...?

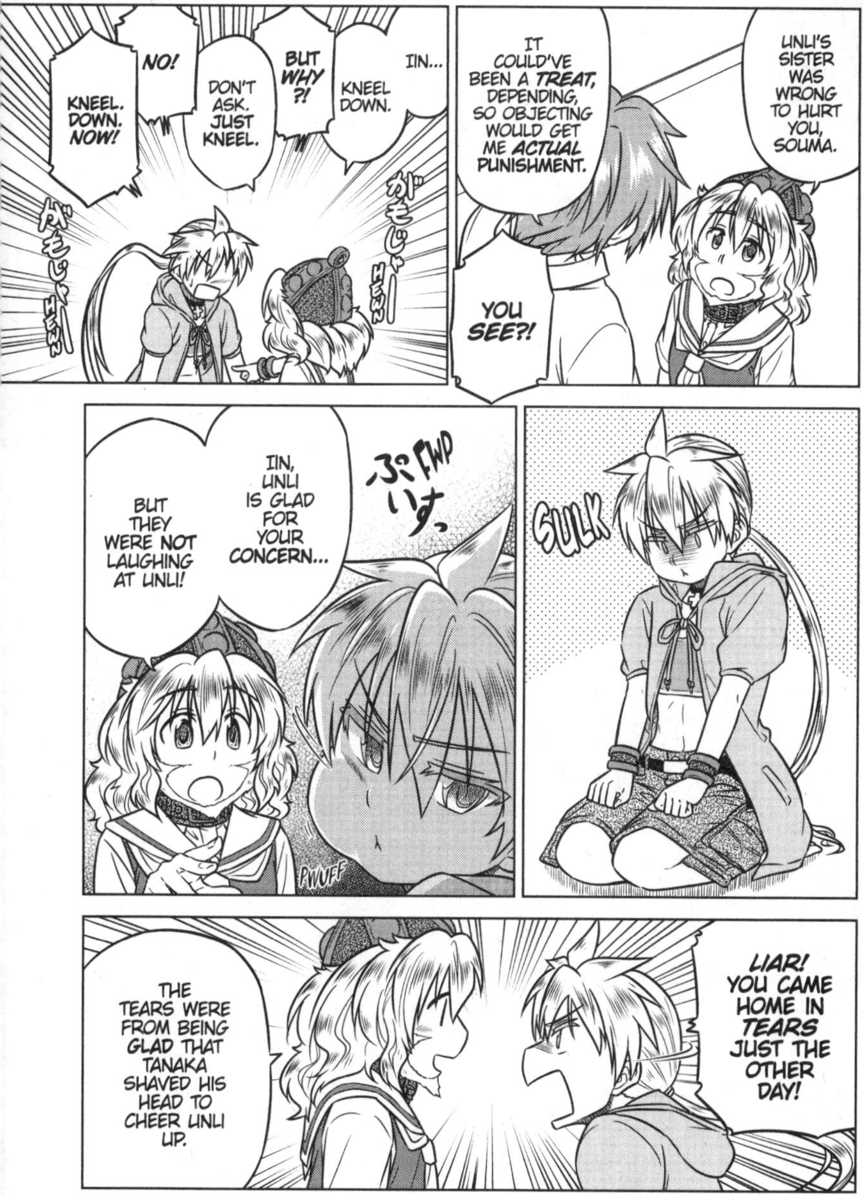
UNLI'S SISTER WAS WRONG TO HURT YOU, SOUMA.
IT COULD'VE BEEN A TREAT, DEPENDING, SO OBJECTING WOULD GET ME ACTUAL PUNISHMENT.
YOU SEE?!
IIN...
KNEEL DOWN.
BUT WHY?!
DON'T ASK. JUST KNEEL.
NO!
KNEEL. DOWN. NOW!
がもじゃー HEWN
がもじゃー HEWN
SULK
ぷいすっ FWP
IIN, UNLI IS GLAD FOR YOUR CONCERN...
BUT THEY WERE NOT LAUGHING AT UNLI!
PWUFF
LIAR! YOU CAME HOME IN TEARS JUST THE OTHER DAY!
THE TEARS WERE FROM BEING GLAD THAT TANAKA SHAVED HIS HEAD TO CHEER UNLI UP.

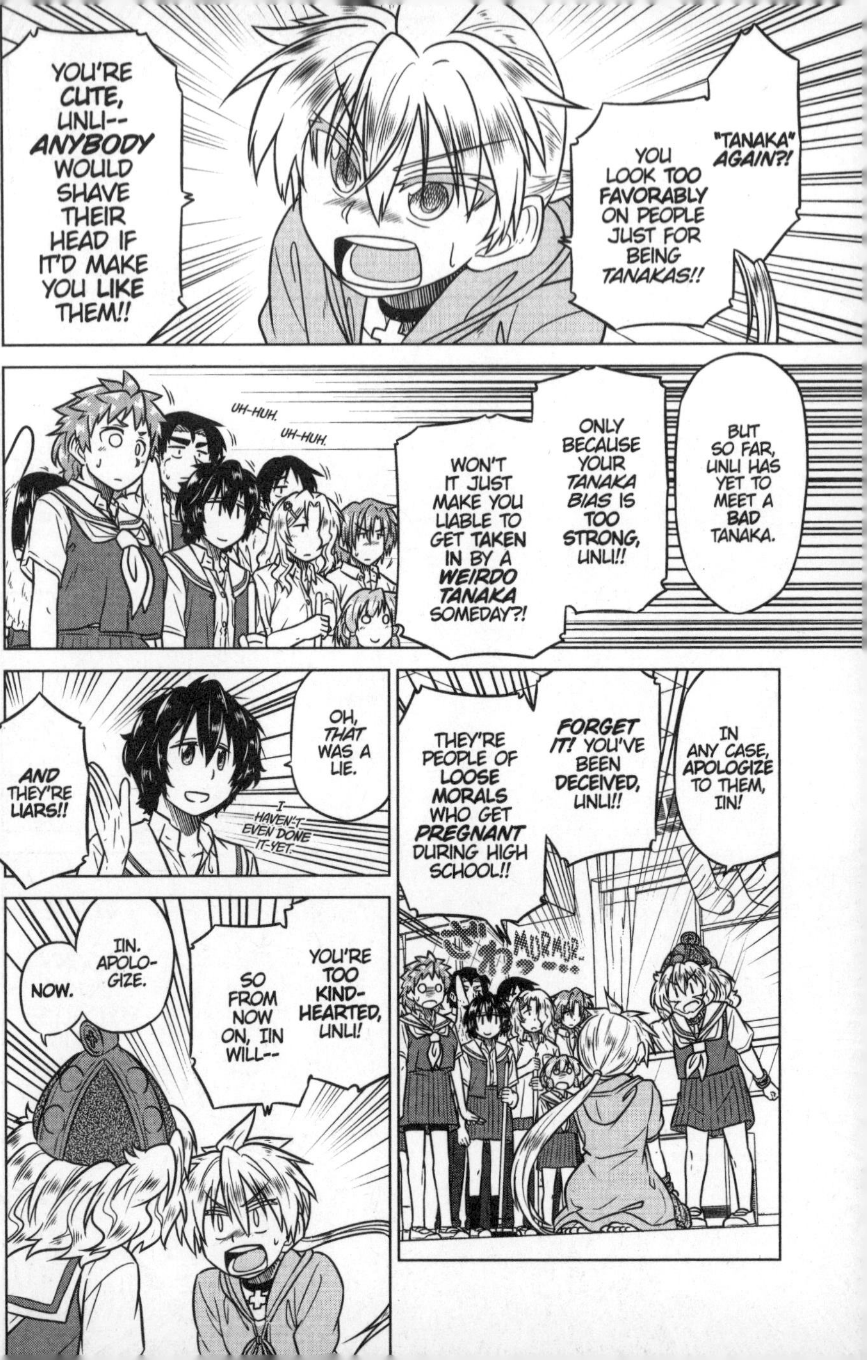

"TANAKA" AGAIN?!
YOU LOOK TOO FAVORABLY ON PEOPLE JUST FOR BEING TANAKAS!!
YOU'RE CUTE, UNLI-- ANYBODY WOULD SHAVE THEIR HEAD IF IT'D MAKE YOU LIKE THEM!!
BUT SO FAR, UNLI HAS YET TO MEET A BAD TANAKA.
ONLY BECAUSE YOUR TANAKA BIAS IS TOO STRONG, UNLI!!
WON'T IT JUST MAKE YOU LIABLE TO GET TAKEN IN BY A WEIRDO TANAKA SOMEDAY?!
UH-HUH.
UH-HUH.
IN ANY CASE, APOLOGIZE TO THEM, IIN!
FORGET IT! YOU'VE BEEN DECEIVED, UNLI!!
THEY'RE PEOPLE OF LOOSE MORALS WHO GET PREGNANT DURING HIGH SCHOOL!!
MURMUR
OH, THAT WAS A LIE.
I HAVEN'T EVEN DONE IT YET.
AND THEY'RE LIARS!!
YOU'RE TOO KIND-HEARTED, UNLI!
SO FROM NOW ON, IIN WILL--
IIN. APOLOGIZE.
NOW.

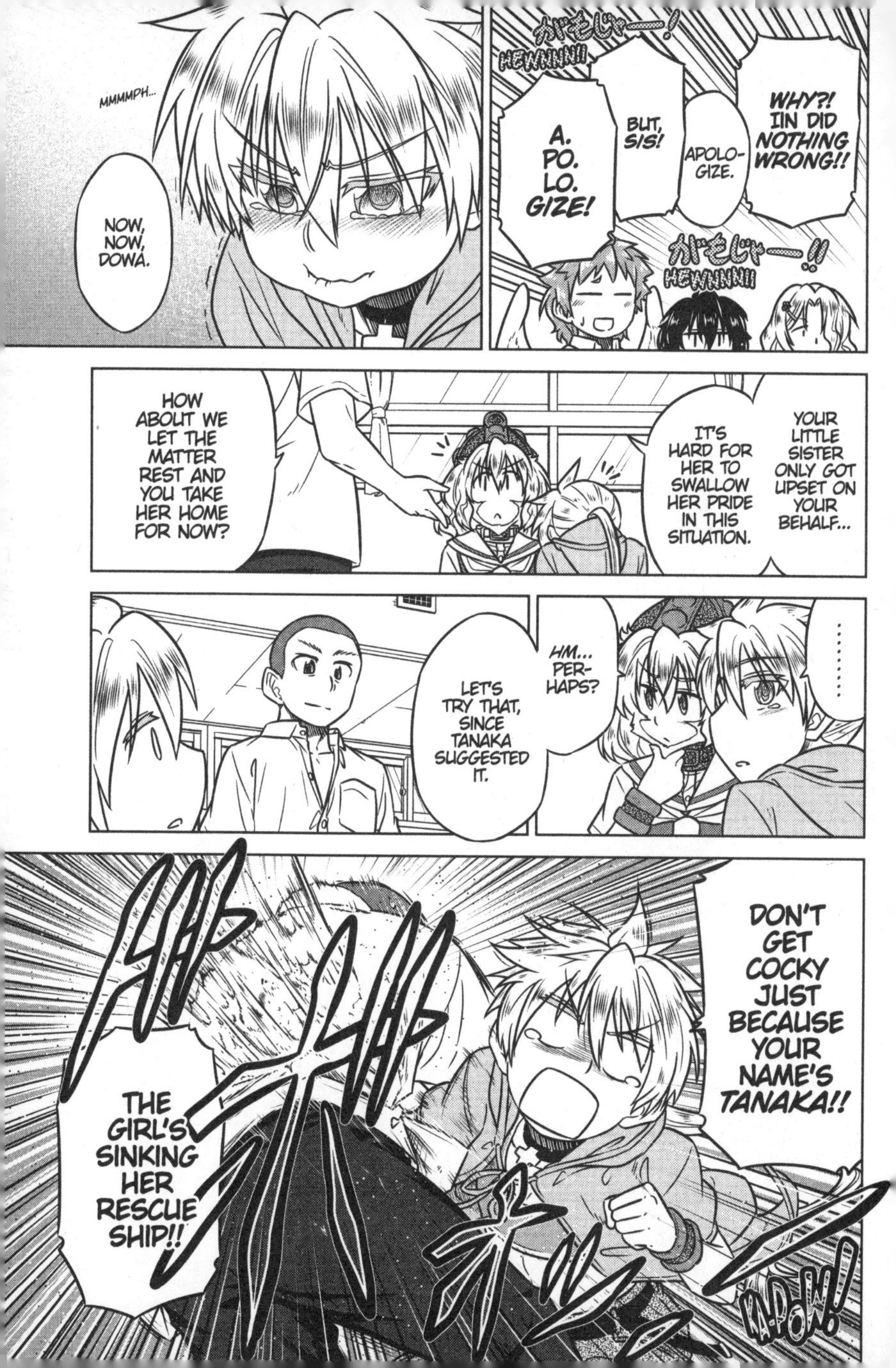
がもじゃー!
HEWNNNII
WHY?! IIN DID NOTHING WRONG!!
APOLO-GIZE.
BUT, SIS!
A. PO. LO. GIZE!
がもじゃー!!
HEWNNNII
MMMMPH...
NOW, NOW, DOWA.
YOUR LITTLE SISTER ONLY GOT UPSET ON YOUR BEHALF...
IT'S HARD FOR HER TO SWALLOW HER PRIDE IN THIS SITUATION.
HOW ABOUT WE LET THE MATTER REST AND YOU TAKE HER HOME FOR NOW?
......
HM... PER-HAPS?
LET'S TRY THAT, SINCE TANAKA SUGGESTED IT.
DON'T GET COCKY JUST BECAUSE YOUR NAME'S TANAKA!!
THE GIRL'S SINKING HER RESCUE SHIP!!
KA-POW!!

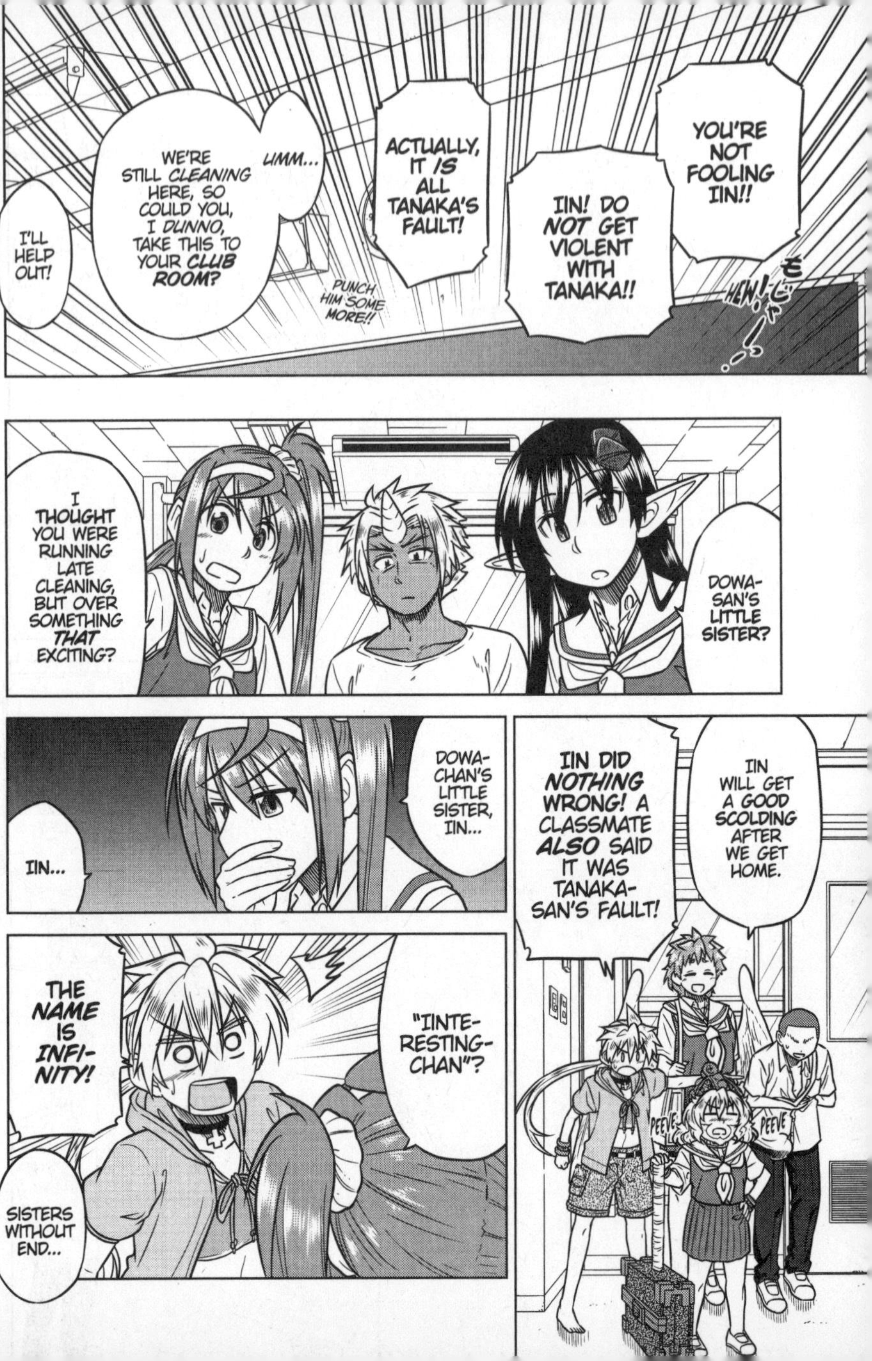
YOU'RE NOT FOOLING IIN!!
HEW!
IIN! DO *NOT* GET VIOLENT WITH TANAKA!!
ACTUALLY, IT *IS* ALL TANAKA'S FAULT!
UMM...
PUNCH HIM SOME MORE!!
WE'RE STILL *CLEANING* HERE, SO COULD YOU, I *DUNNO*, TAKE THIS TO YOUR **CLUB ROOM?**
I'LL HELP OUT!
DOWA-SAN'S LITTLE SISTER?
I THOUGHT YOU WERE RUNNING LATE CLEANING, BUT OVER SOMETHING ***THAT*** EXCITING?
IIN WILL GET A *GOOD* SCOLDING AFTER WE GET HOME.
IIN DID ***NOTHING*** WRONG! A CLASSMATE ***ALSO*** SAID IT WAS TANAKA-SAN'S FAULT!
PEEVE
PEEVE
DOWA-CHAN'S LITTLE SISTER, IIN...
IIN...
"IINTE-RESTING-CHAN"?
THE ***NAME*** IS ***INFINITY!***
SISTERS WITHOUT END...

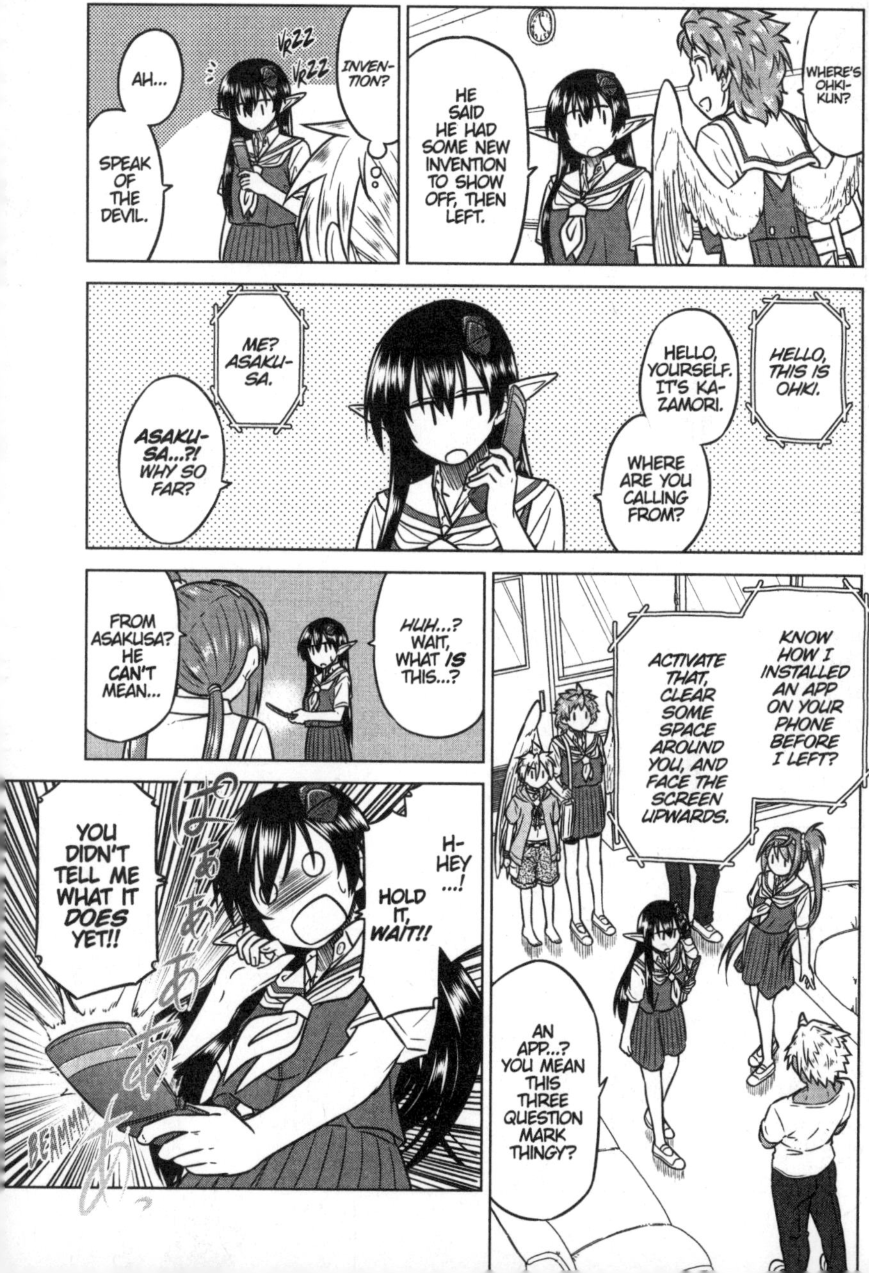
WHERE'S OHKI-KUN?
HE SAID HE HAD SOME NEW INVENTION TO SHOW OFF, THEN LEFT.
INVENTION?
VRZZ
VRZZ
AH...
SPEAK OF THE DEVIL.
HELLO, THIS IS OHKI.
HELLO, YOURSELF. IT'S KA-ZAMORI.
WHERE ARE YOU CALLING FROM?
ME? ASAKU-SA.
ASAKU-SA...?! WHY SO FAR?
KNOW HOW I INSTALLED AN APP ON YOUR PHONE BEFORE I LEFT?
ACTIVATE THAT, CLEAR SOME SPACE AROUND YOU, AND FACE THE SCREEN UPWARDS.
AN APP...? YOU MEAN THIS THREE QUESTION MARK THINGY?
HUH...? WAIT, WHAT IS THIS...?
FROM ASAKUSA? HE CAN'T MEAN...
H-HEY...!
HOLD IT, WAIT!!
YOU DIDN'T TELL ME WHAT IT DOES YET!!
BEAMMM

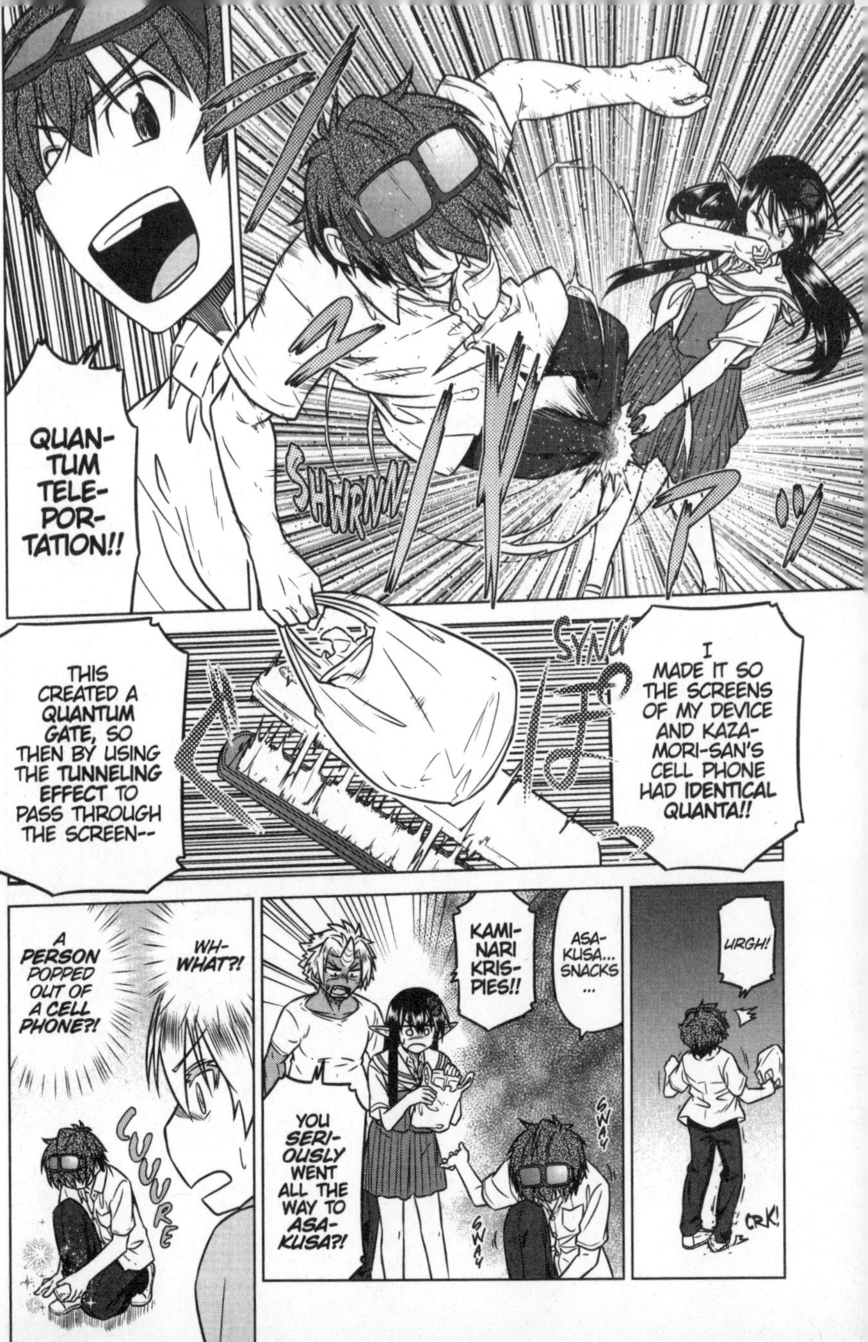
QUANTUM TELEPORTATION!!
SHWRNN
I MADE IT SO THE SCREENS OF MY DEVICE AND KAZAMORI-SAN'S CELL PHONE HAD IDENTICAL QUANTA!!
SYNC
THIS CREATED A QUANTUM GATE, SO THEN BY USING THE TUNNELING EFFECT TO PASS THROUGH THE SCREEN--
URGH!
CRK!
ASAKUSA... SNACKS ...
KAMINARI KRISPIES!!
YOU SERIOUSLY WENT ALL THE WAY TO ASAKUSA?!
SWAY
SWAY
WH-WHAT?!
A PERSON POPPED OUT OF A CELL PHONE?!
LUUURE

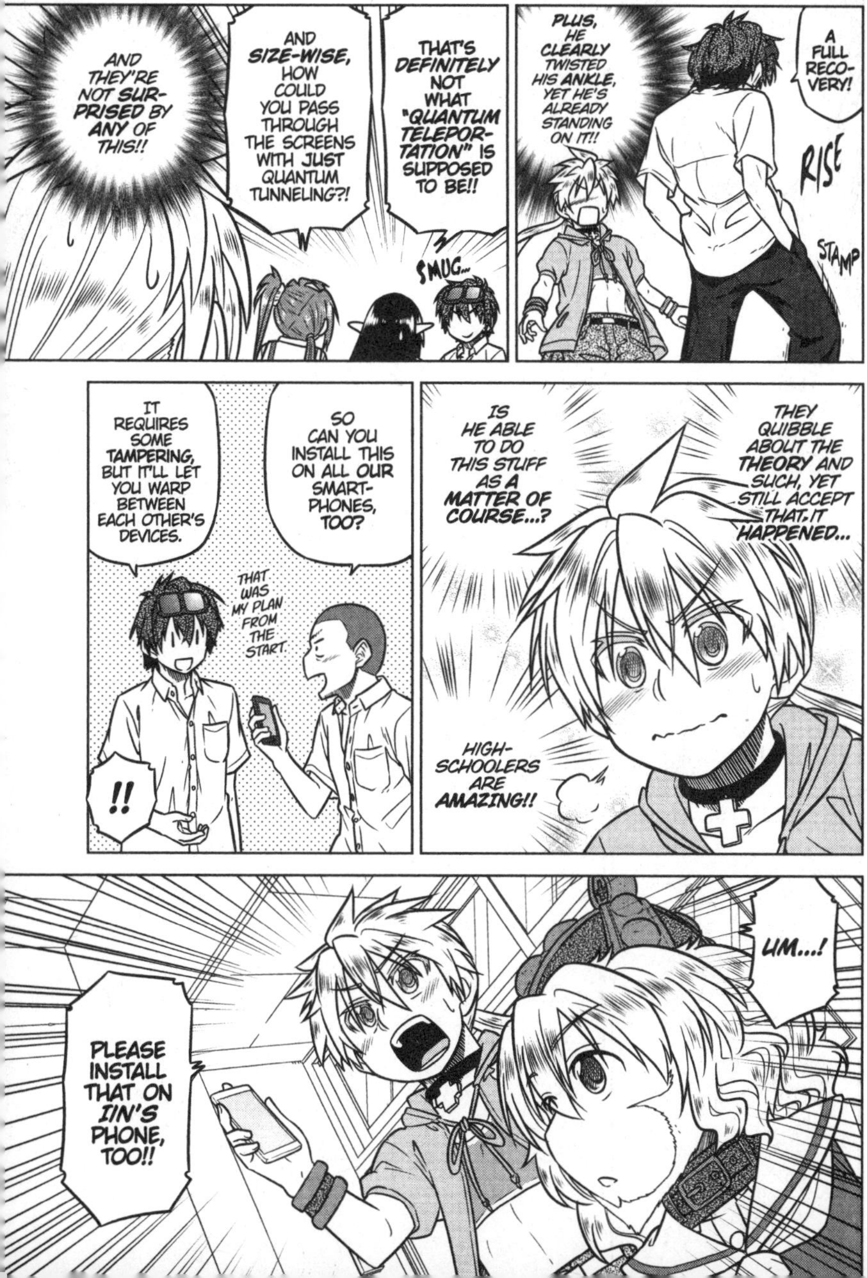

A FULL RECOVERY!
PLUS, HE CLEARLY TWISTED HIS ANKLE, YET HE'S ALREADY STANDING ON IT!!
RISE
STAMP
THAT'S DEFINITELY NOT WHAT "QUANTUM TELEPORTATION" IS SUPPOSED TO BE!!
AND SIZE-WISE, HOW COULD YOU PASS THROUGH THE SCREENS WITH JUST QUANTUM TUNNELING?!
AND THEY'RE NOT SURPRISED BY ANY OF THIS!!
SMUG...
THEY QUIBBLE ABOUT THE THEORY AND SUCH, YET STILL ACCEPT THAT IT HAPPENED...
IS HE ABLE TO DO THIS STUFF AS A MATTER OF COURSE...?
HIGH-SCHOOLERS ARE AMAZING!!
SO CAN YOU INSTALL THIS ON ALL OUR SMARTPHONES, TOO?
IT REQUIRES SOME TAMPERING, BUT IT'LL LET YOU WARP BETWEEN EACH OTHER'S DEVICES.
THAT WAS MY PLAN FROM THE START.
!!
UM...!
PLEASE INSTALL THAT ON IIN'S PHONE, TOO!!

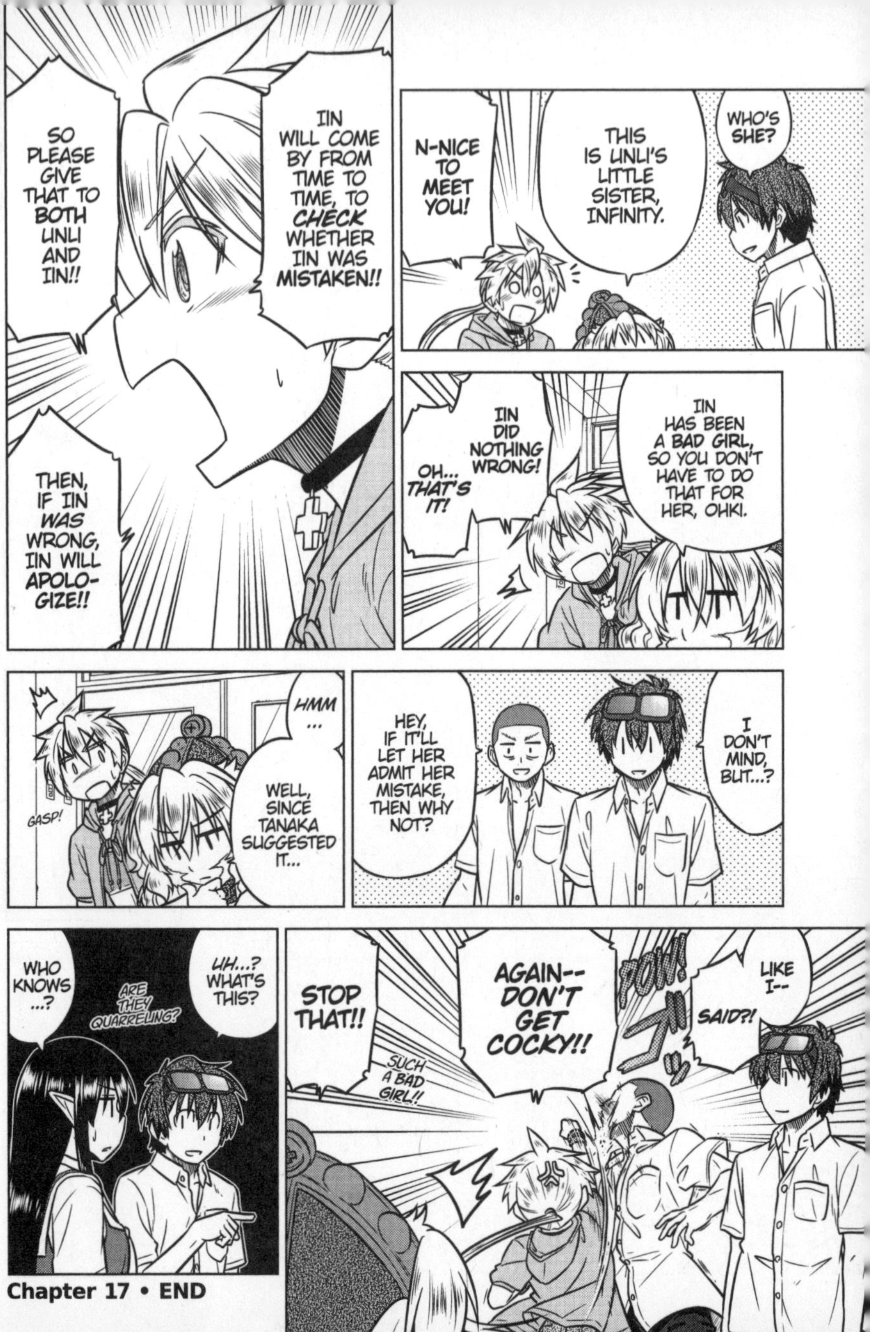
WHO'S SHE?
THIS IS UNLI'S LITTLE SISTER, INFINITY.
N-NICE TO MEET YOU!
IIN HAS BEEN A BAD GIRL, SO YOU DON'T HAVE TO DO THAT FOR HER, OHKI.
IIN DID NOTHING WRONG!
OH... THAT'S IT!
IIN WILL COME BY FROM TIME TO TIME, TO CHECK WHETHER IIN WAS MISTAKEN!!
SO PLEASE GIVE THAT TO BOTH UNLI AND IIN!!
THEN, IF IIN WAS WRONG, IIN WILL APOLOGIZE!!
I DON'T MIND, BUT...?
HEY, IF IT'LL LET HER ADMIT HER MISTAKE, THEN WHY NOT?
HMM...
WELL, SINCE TANAKA SUGGESTED IT...
GASP!
LIKE I--
SAID?!
POW!
AGAIN-- DON'T GET COCKY!!
STOP THAT!!
SUCH A BAD GIRL!!
UH...? WHAT'S THIS?
ARE THEY QUARRELING?
WHO KNOWS...?

Chapter 17 • END

Chapter 18: Kazamori-san Turns Sappy

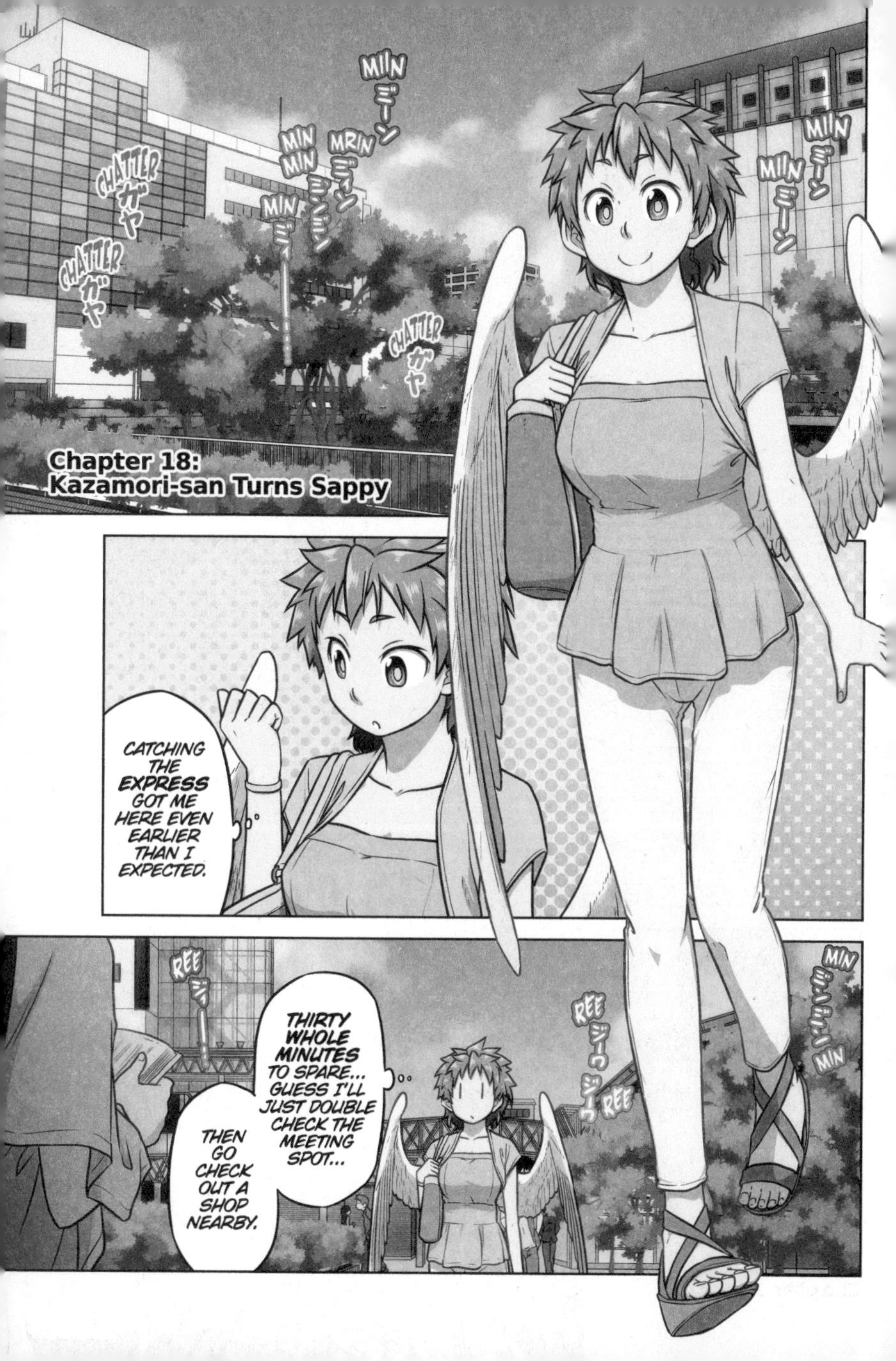
MIIN ミーン
MIIN ミーン
MIIN ミーン
MRIN ミィーン
MIN MIN
MIN ミィ
CHATTER ガヤ
CHATTER ガヤ
CHATTER ガヤ
CATCHING THE EXPRESS GOT ME HERE EVEN EARLIER THAN I EXPECTED.
MIN MIN
REE ジーワ ジーワ REE
THIRTY WHOLE MINUTES TO SPARE... GUESS I'LL JUST DOUBLE CHECK THE MEETING SPOT...
THEN GO CHECK OUT A SHOP NEARBY.
REE

Chapter 18: Kazamori-san Turns Sappy

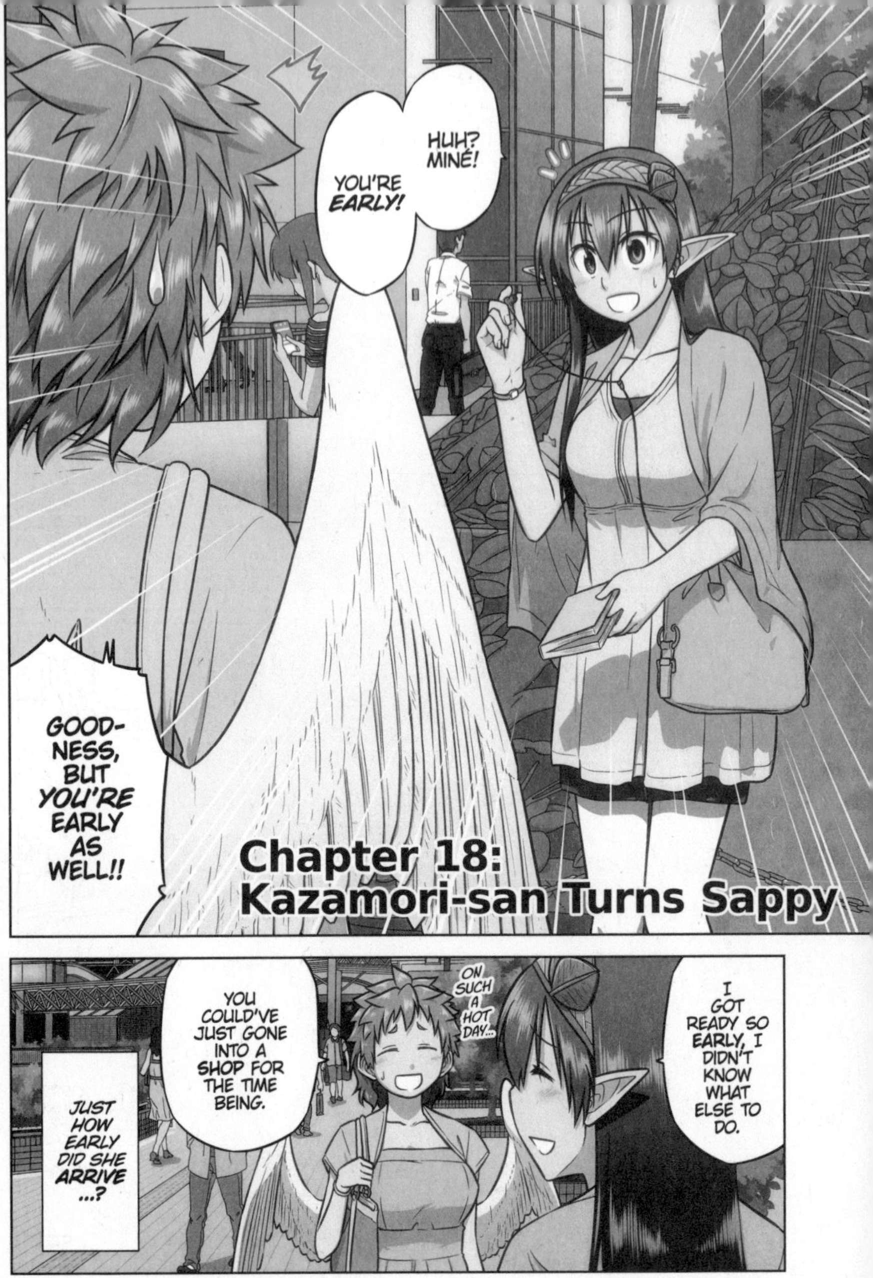
HUH? MINÉ! YOU'RE EARLY!
GOODNESS, BUT YOU'RE EARLY AS WELL!!
I GOT READY SO EARLY, I DIDN'T KNOW WHAT ELSE TO DO.
ON SUCH A HOT DAY...
YOU COULD'VE JUST GONE INTO A SHOP FOR THE TIME BEING.
JUST HOW EARLY DID SHE ARRIVE ...?

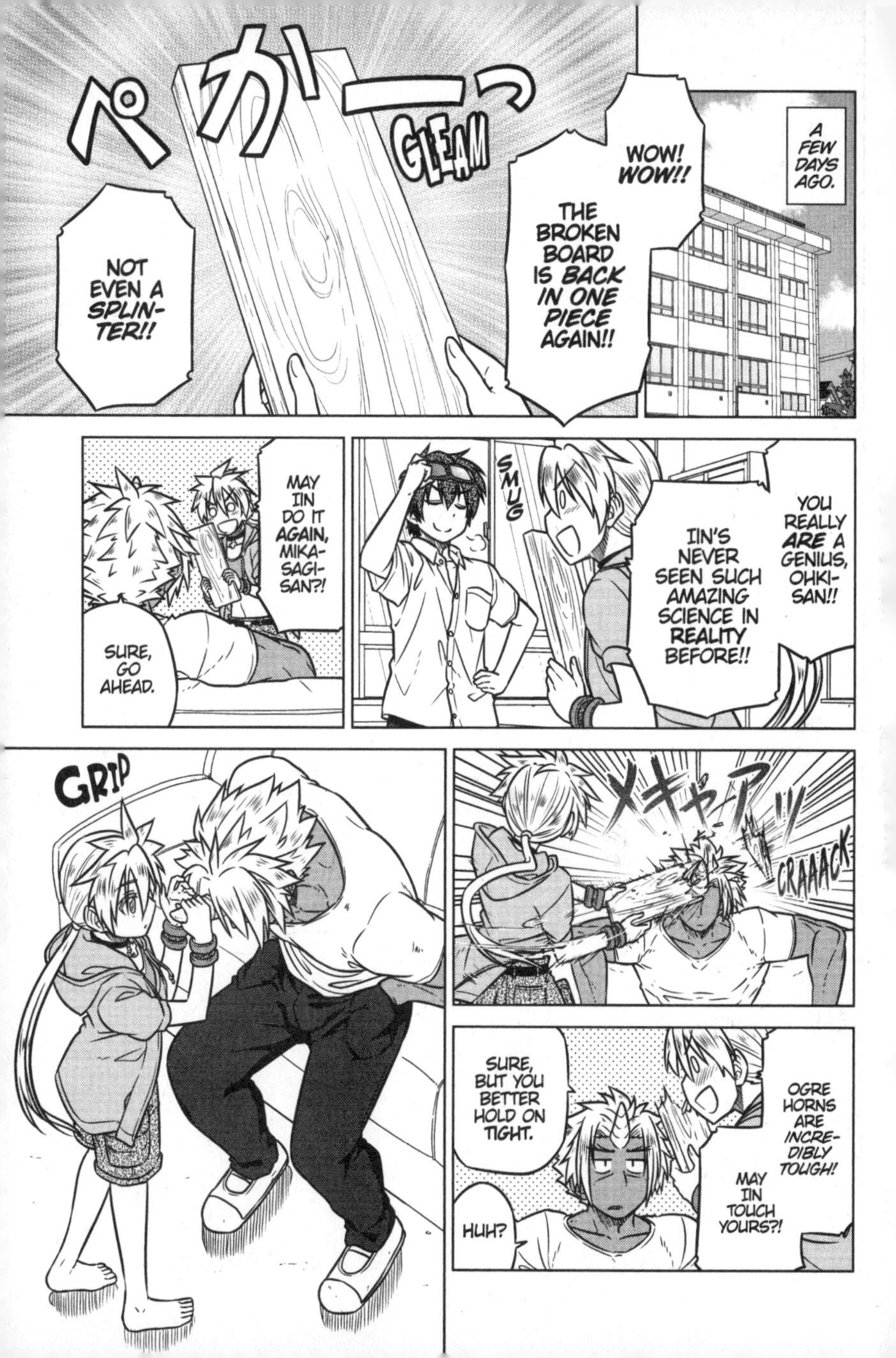
A FEW DAYS AGO.
WOW! WOW!!
THE BROKEN BOARD IS BACK IN ONE PIECE AGAIN!!
ぺかーっ
GLEAM
NOT EVEN A SPLINTER!!
YOU REALLY ARE A GENIUS, OHKI-SAN!!
IIN'S NEVER SEEN SUCH AMAZING SCIENCE IN REALITY BEFORE!!
SMUG
MAY IIN DO IT AGAIN, MIKASAGI-SAN?!
SURE, GO AHEAD.
メキャア!!
CRAAACK
OGRE HORNS ARE INCREDIBLY TOUGH!
MAY IIN TOUCH YOURS?!
SURE, BUT YOU BETTER HOLD ON TIGHT.
HUH?
GRIP

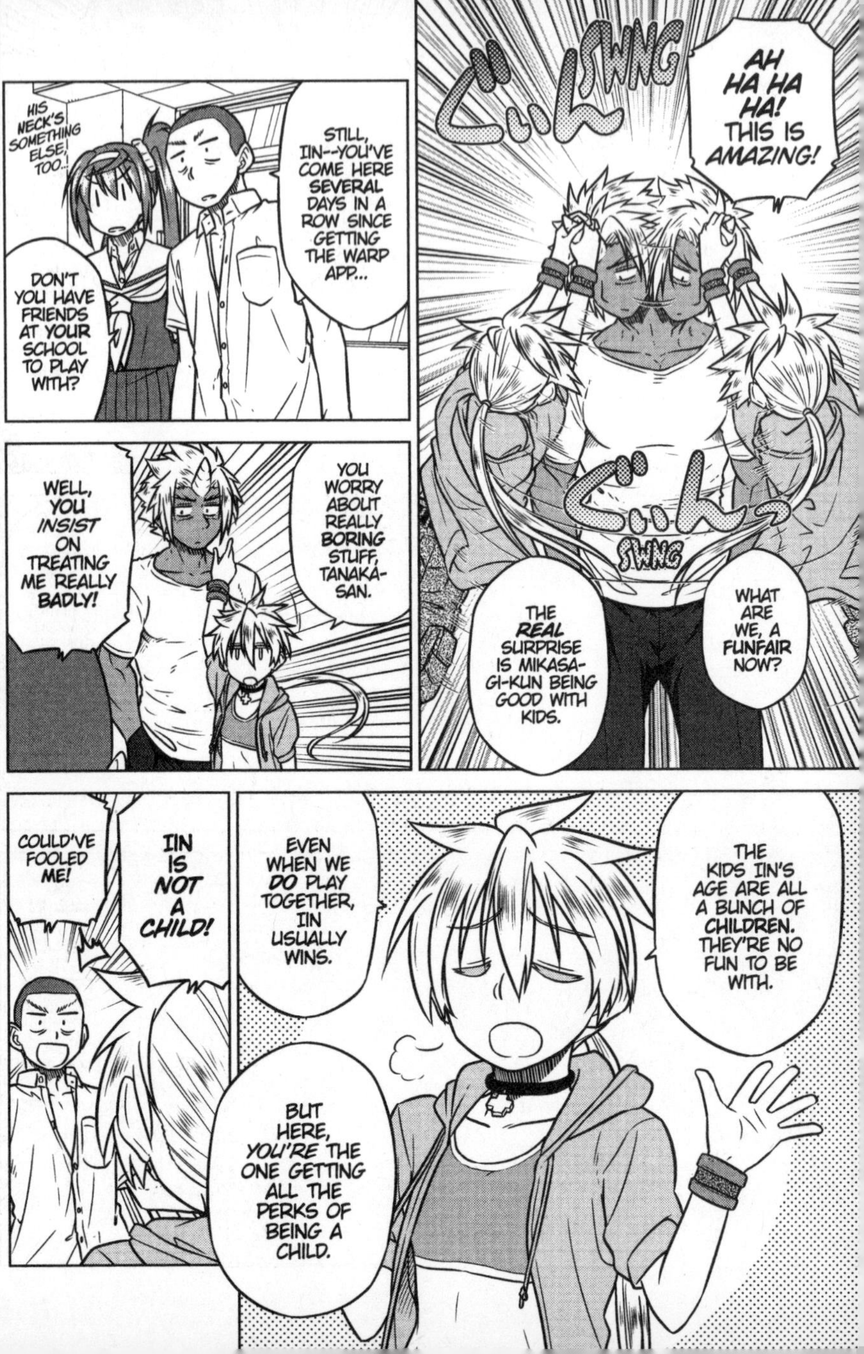
SWNG
AH HA HA HA! THIS IS AMAZING!
SWNG
WHAT ARE WE, A FUNFAIR NOW?
THE REAL SURPRISE IS MIKASAGI-KUN BEING GOOD WITH KIDS.
STILL, IIN--YOU'VE COME HERE SEVERAL DAYS IN A ROW SINCE GETTING THE WARP APP...
HIS NECK'S SOMETHING ELSE, TOO...
DON'T YOU HAVE FRIENDS AT YOUR SCHOOL TO PLAY WITH?
YOU WORRY ABOUT REALLY BORING STUFF, TANAKA-SAN.
WELL, YOU INSIST ON TREATING ME REALLY BADLY!
THE KIDS IIN'S AGE ARE ALL A BUNCH OF CHILDREN. THEY'RE NO FUN TO BE WITH.
EVEN WHEN WE DO PLAY TOGETHER, IIN USUALLY WINS.
BUT HERE, YOU'RE THE ONE GETTING ALL THE PERKS OF BEING A CHILD.
IIN IS NOT A CHILD!
COULD'VE FOOLED ME!

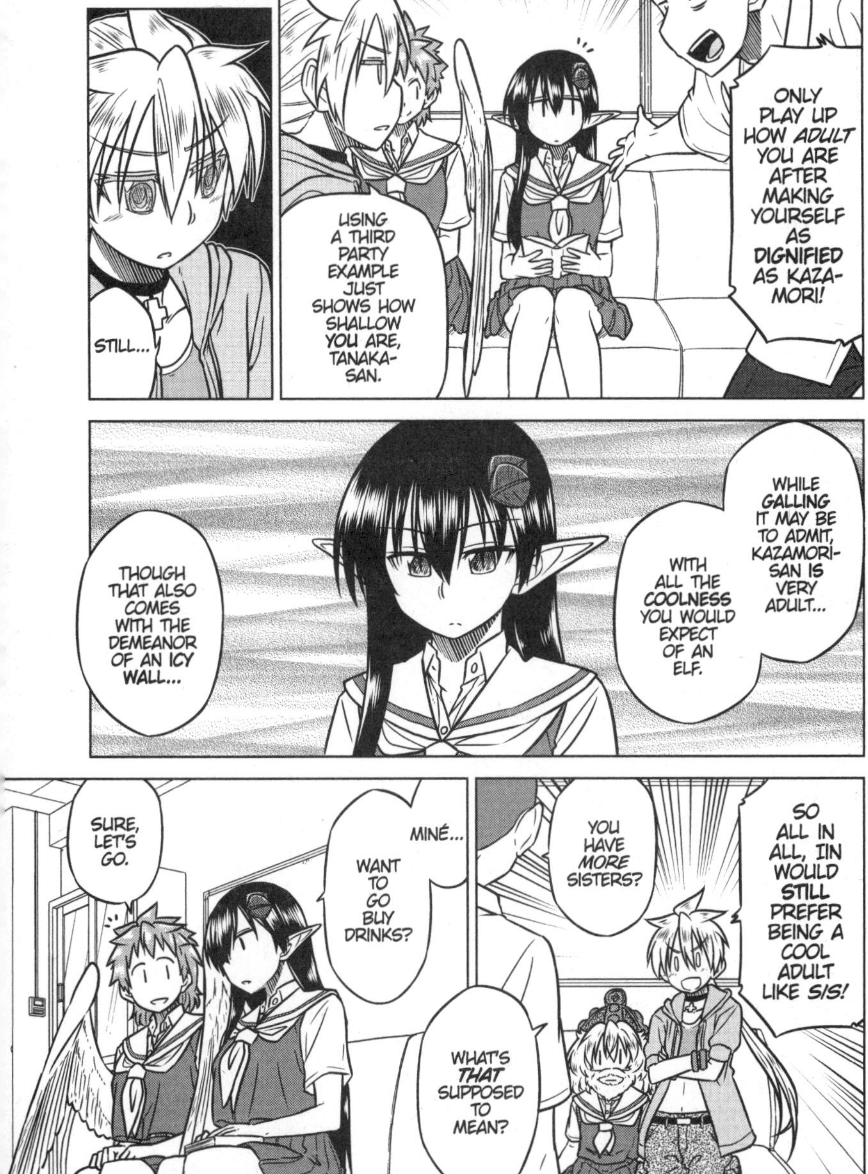
ONLY PLAY UP HOW ADULT YOU ARE AFTER MAKING YOURSELF AS DIGNIFIED AS KAZAMORI!
USING A THIRD PARTY EXAMPLE JUST SHOWS HOW SHALLOW YOU ARE, TANAKA-SAN.
STILL...
WHILE GALLING IT MAY BE TO ADMIT, KAZAMORI-SAN IS VERY ADULT...
WITH ALL THE COOLNESS YOU WOULD EXPECT OF AN ELF.
THOUGH THAT ALSO COMES WITH THE DEMEANOR OF AN ICY WALL...
SO ALL IN ALL, IIN WOULD STILL PREFER BEING A COOL ADULT LIKE SIS!
YOU HAVE MORE SISTERS?
WHAT'S THAT SUPPOSED TO MEAN?
MINÉ...
WANT TO GO BUY DRINKS?
SURE, LET'S GO.

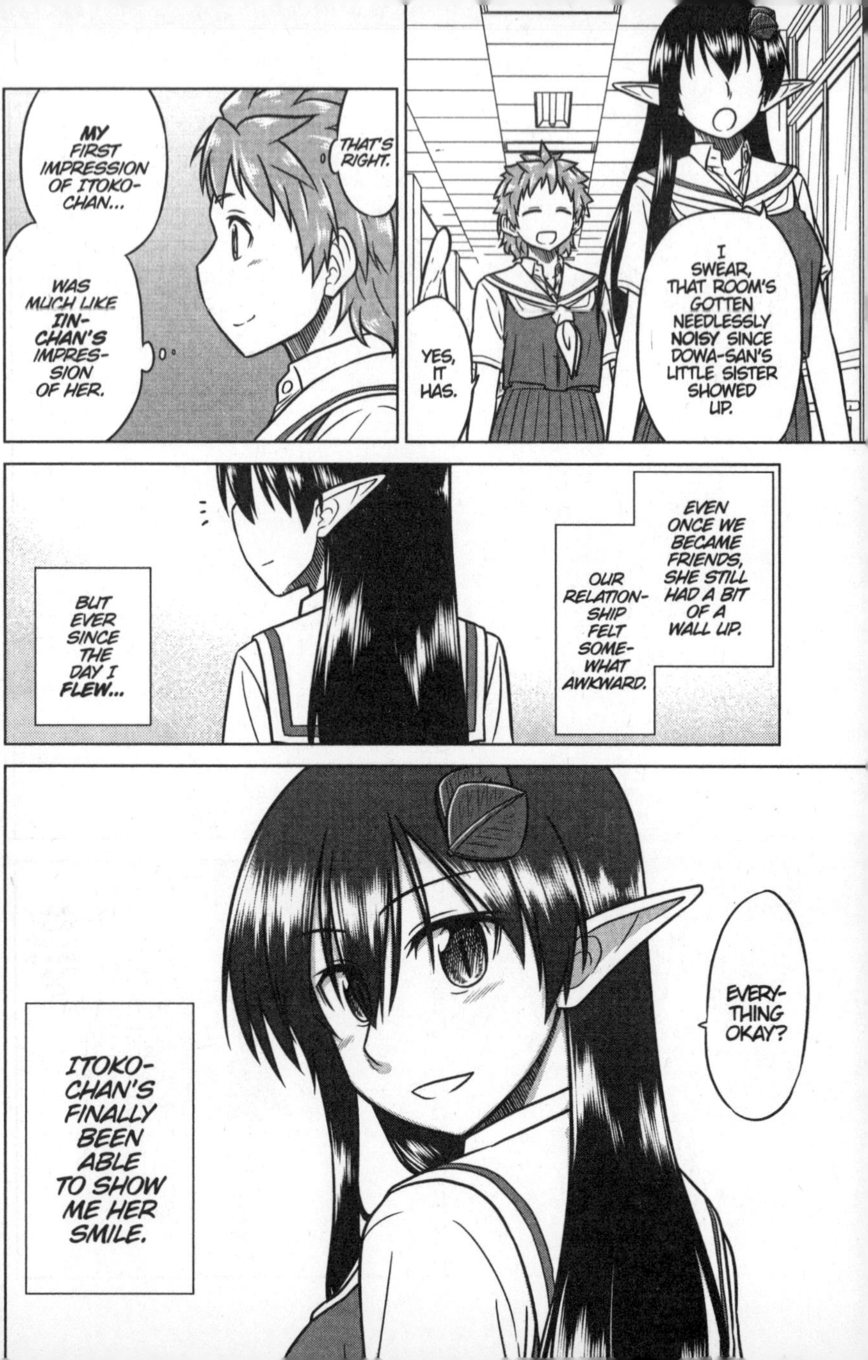
I SWEAR, THAT ROOM'S GOTTEN NEEDLESSLY NOISY SINCE DOWA-SAN'S LITTLE SISTER SHOWED UP.
YES, IT HAS.
THAT'S RIGHT.
MY FIRST IMPRESSION OF ITOKO-CHAN...
WAS MUCH LIKE IIN-CHAN'S IMPRESSION OF HER.
EVEN ONCE WE BECAME FRIENDS, SHE STILL HAD A BIT OF A WALL UP.
OUR RELATIONSHIP FELT SOMEWHAT AWKWARD.
BUT EVER SINCE THE DAY I FLEW...
EVERYTHING OKAY?
ITOKO-CHAN'S FINALLY BEEN ABLE TO SHOW ME HER SMILE.

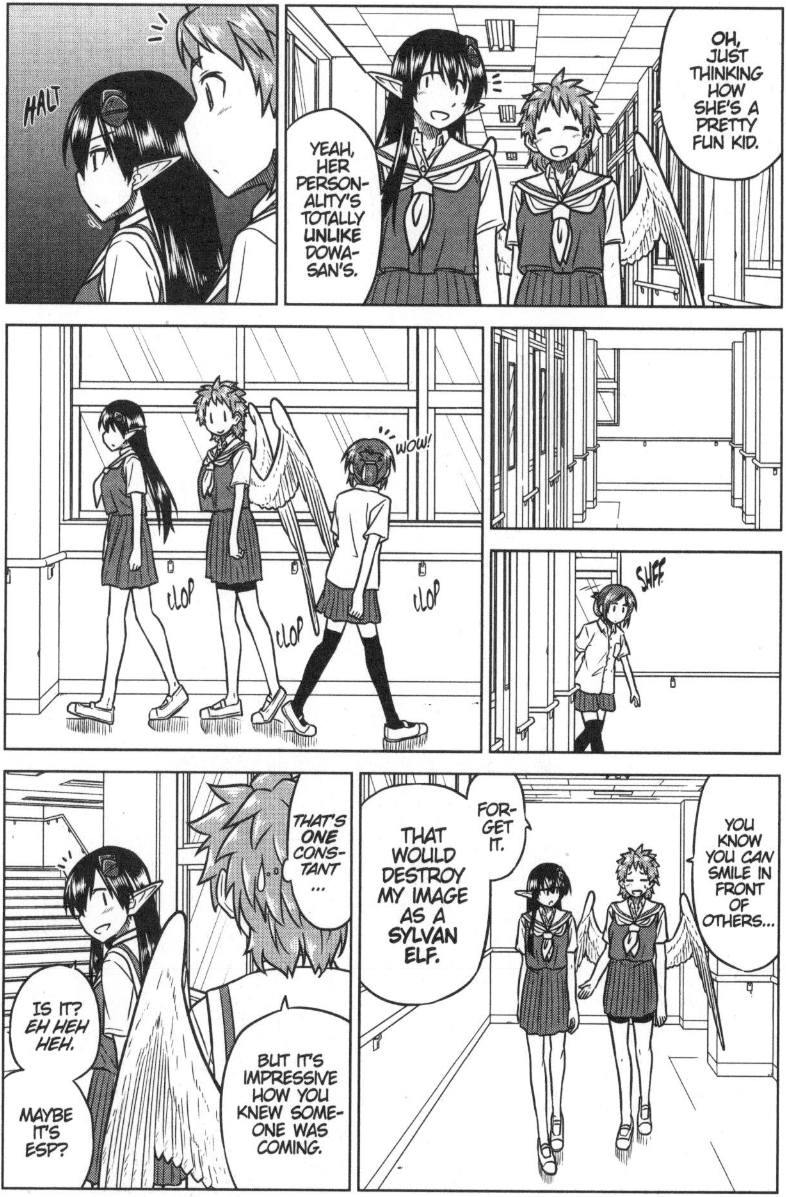
OH, JUST THINKING HOW SHE'S A PRETTY FUN KID.
YEAH, HER PERSONALITY'S TOTALLY UNLIKE DOWA-SAN'S.
HALT
SHFF
WOW!
CLOP
CLOP
CLOP
YOU KNOW YOU CAN SMILE IN FRONT OF OTHERS...
FOR-GET IT.
THAT WOULD DESTROY MY IMAGE AS A SYLVAN ELF.
THAT'S ONE CONSTANT...
BUT IT'S IMPRESSIVE HOW YOU KNEW SOME-ONE WAS COMING.
IS IT? EH HEH HEH.
MAYBE IT'S ESP?

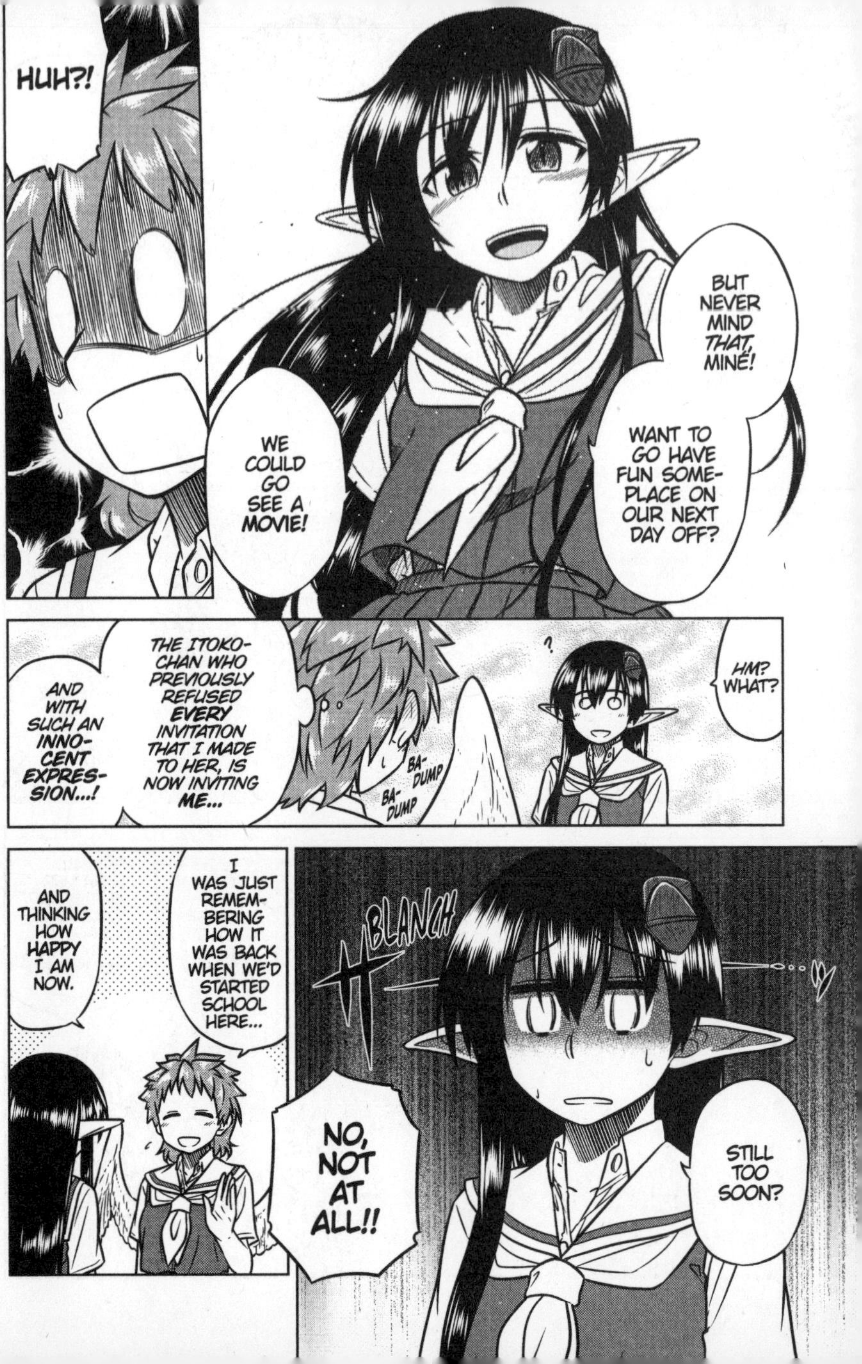
BUT NEVER MIND THAT, MINÉ!
WANT TO GO HAVE FUN SOME-PLACE ON OUR NEXT DAY OFF?
WE COULD GO SEE A MOVIE!
HUH?!
HM? WHAT?
?
BA-DUMP
BA-DUMP
THE ITOKO-CHAN WHO PREVIOUSLY REFUSED EVERY INVITATION THAT I MADE TO HER, IS NOW INVITING ME...
AND WITH SUCH AN INNO-CENT EXPRES-SION...!
BLANCH
STILL TOO SOON?
NO, NOT AT ALL!!
I WAS JUST REMEM-BERING HOW IT WAS BACK WHEN WE'D STARTED SCHOOL HERE...
AND THINKING HOW HAPPY I AM NOW.

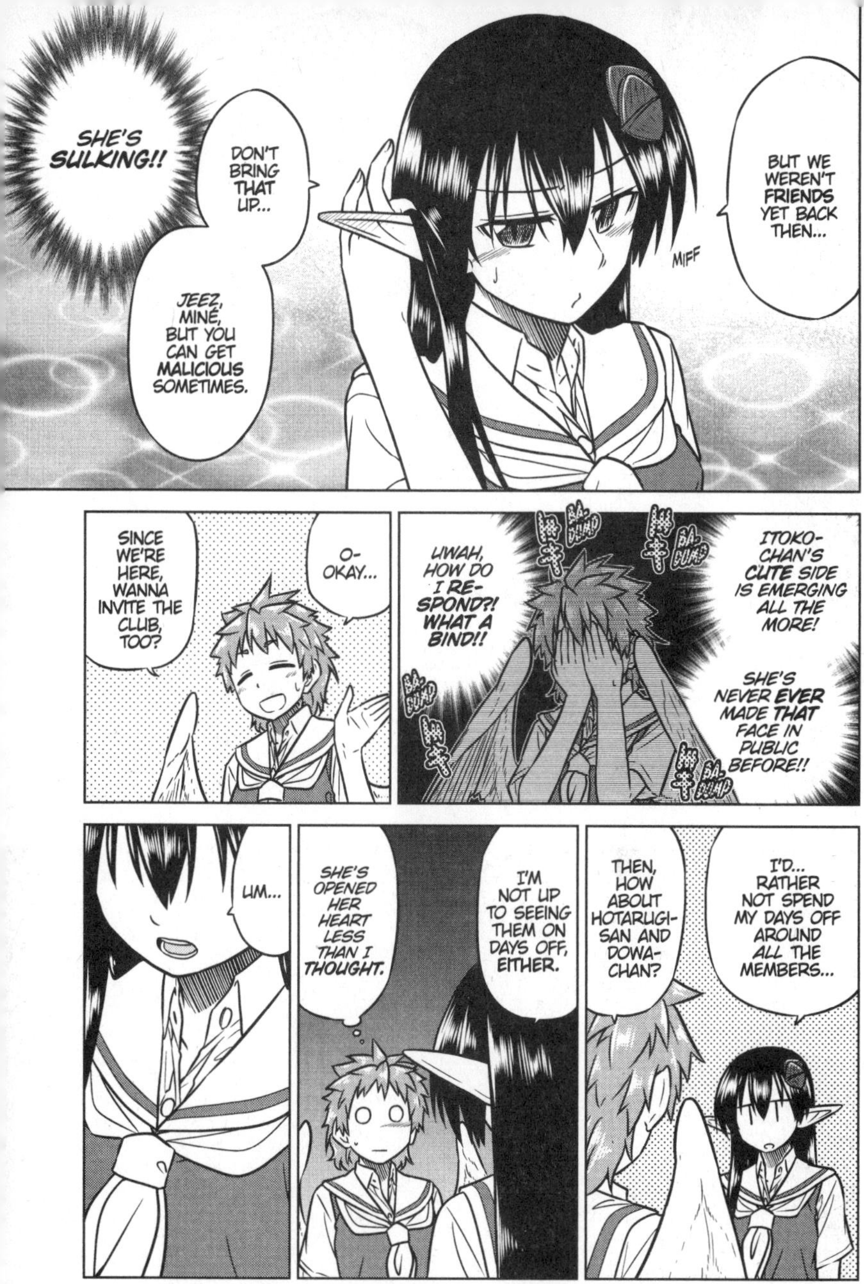
BUT WE WEREN'T FRIENDS YET BACK THEN...
MIFF
DON'T BRING THAT UP...
JEEZ, MINÉ, BUT YOU CAN GET MALICIOUS SOMETIMES.
SHE'S SULKING!!
ITOKO-CHAN'S CUTE SIDE IS EMERGING ALL THE MORE!
SHE'S NEVER EVER MADE THAT FACE IN PUBLIC BEFORE!!
UWAH, HOW DO I RE-SPOND?! WHAT A BIND!!
BA-DUMP
BA-DUMP
BA-DUMP
BA-DUMP
O-OKAY...
SINCE WE'RE HERE, WANNA INVITE THE CLUB, TOO?
I'D... RATHER NOT SPEND MY DAYS OFF AROUND ALL THE MEMBERS...
THEN, HOW ABOUT HOTARUGI-SAN AND DOWA-CHAN?
I'M NOT UP TO SEEING THEM ON DAYS OFF, EITHER.
SHE'S OPENED HER HEART LESS THAN I THOUGHT.
UM...

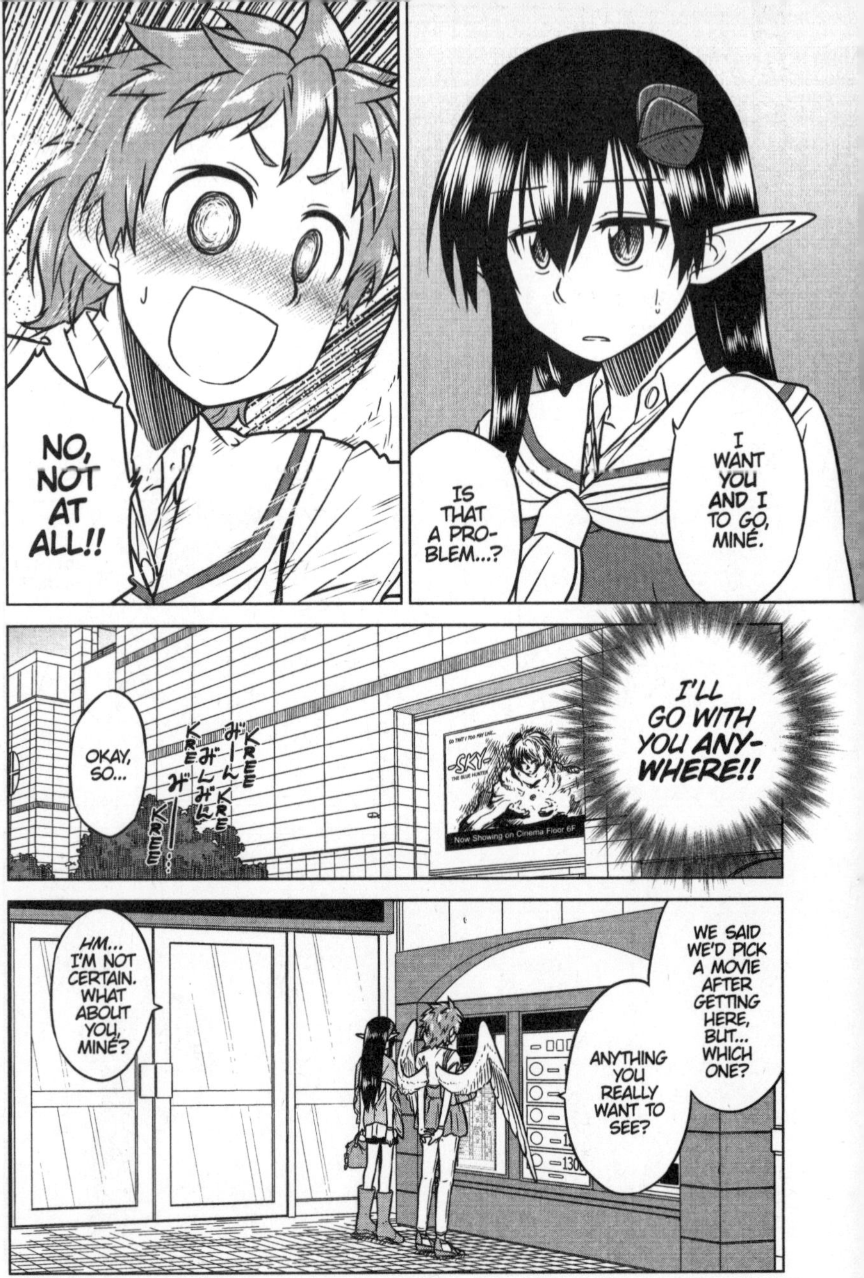
I WANT YOU AND I TO GO, MINÉ.
IS THAT A PROBLEM...?
NO, NOT AT ALL!!
I'LL GO WITH YOU ANYWHERE!!
SO THAT I TOO MAY LIVE...
-SKY-
THE BLUE HUNTER
Now Showing on Cinema Floor 6F
KREE KREE
KREE
KREE...
OKAY, SO...
WE SAID WE'D PICK A MOVIE AFTER GETTING HERE, BUT... WHICH ONE?
ANYTHING YOU REALLY WANT TO SEE?
HM... I'M NOT CERTAIN. WHAT ABOUT YOU, MINÉ?

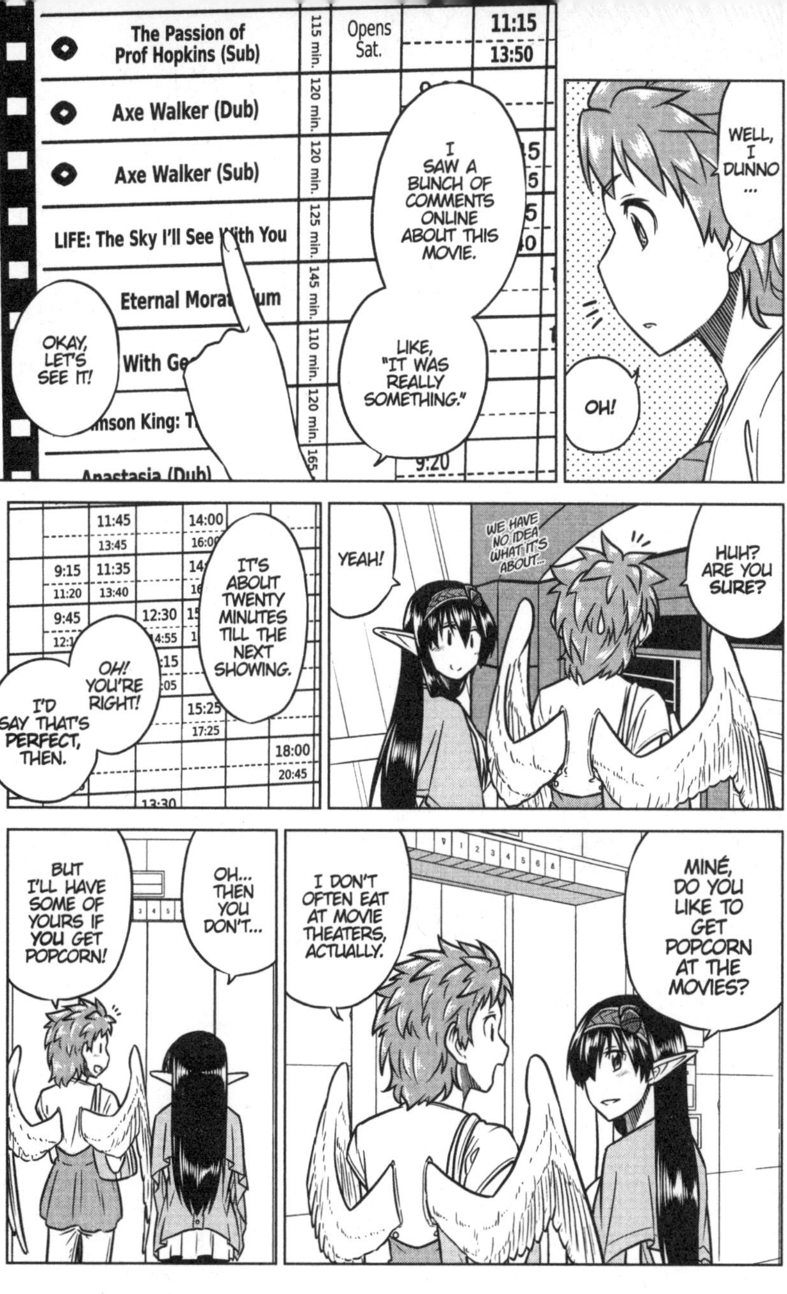
WELL, I DUNNO ...
OH!
The Passion of Prof Hopkins (Sub)
115 min.
Opens Sat.
11:15
13:50
Axe Walker (Dub)
120 min.
Axe Walker (Sub)
120 min.
125 min.
145 min.
110 min.
120 min.
9:20
I SAW A BUNCH OF COMMENTS ONLINE ABOUT THIS MOVIE.
LIKE, "IT WAS REALLY SOMETHING."
OKAY, LET'S SEE IT!
HUH? ARE YOU SURE?
WE HAVE NO IDEA WHAT IT'S ABOUT...
YEAH!
11:45
13:45
14:00
9:15
11:35
11:20
13:40
9:45
12:30
15:25
17:25
18:00
20:45
IT'S ABOUT TWENTY MINUTES TILL THE NEXT SHOWING.
OH! YOU'RE RIGHT!
I'D SAY THAT'S PERFECT, THEN.
MINÉ, DO YOU LIKE TO GET POPCORN AT THE MOVIES?
I DON'T OFTEN EAT AT MOVIE THEATERS, ACTUALLY.
OH... THEN YOU DON'T...
BUT I'LL HAVE SOME OF YOURS IF YOU GET POPCORN!

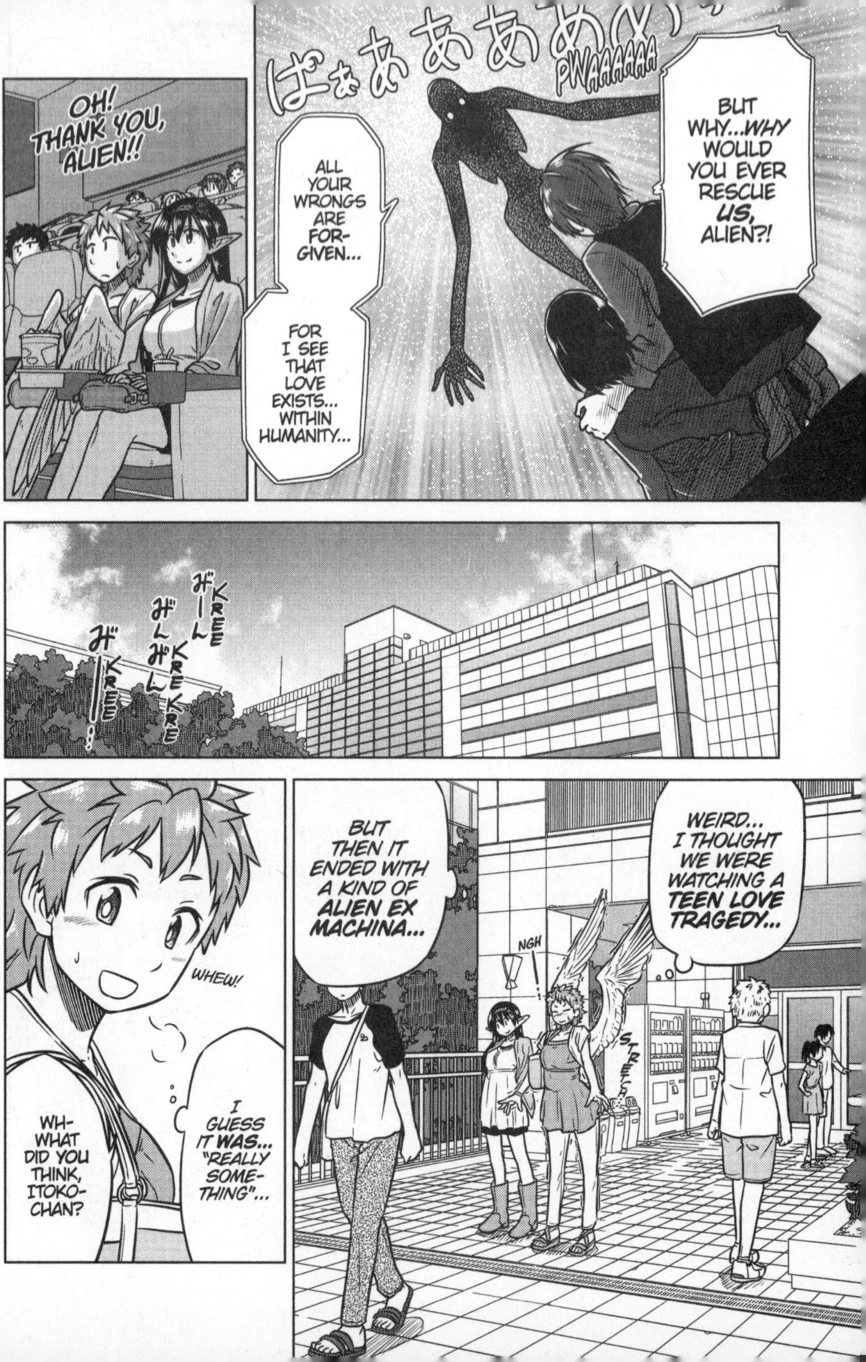
PWAAAAAA
BUT WHY...WHY WOULD YOU EVER RESCUE US, ALIEN?!
ALL YOUR WRONGS ARE FOR-GIVEN...
FOR I SEE THAT LOVE EXISTS... WITHIN HUMANITY...
OH! THANK YOU, ALIEN!!
みーん KREE
みんみん KREKRE
み… KREE...
WEIRD... I THOUGHT WE WERE WATCHING A TEEN LOVE TRAGEDY...
BUT THEN IT ENDED WITH A KIND OF ALIEN EX MACHINA...
STRETCH
NGH
WHEW!
I GUESS IT WAS... "REALLY SOMETHING"...
WH-WHAT DID YOU THINK, ITOKO-CHAN?

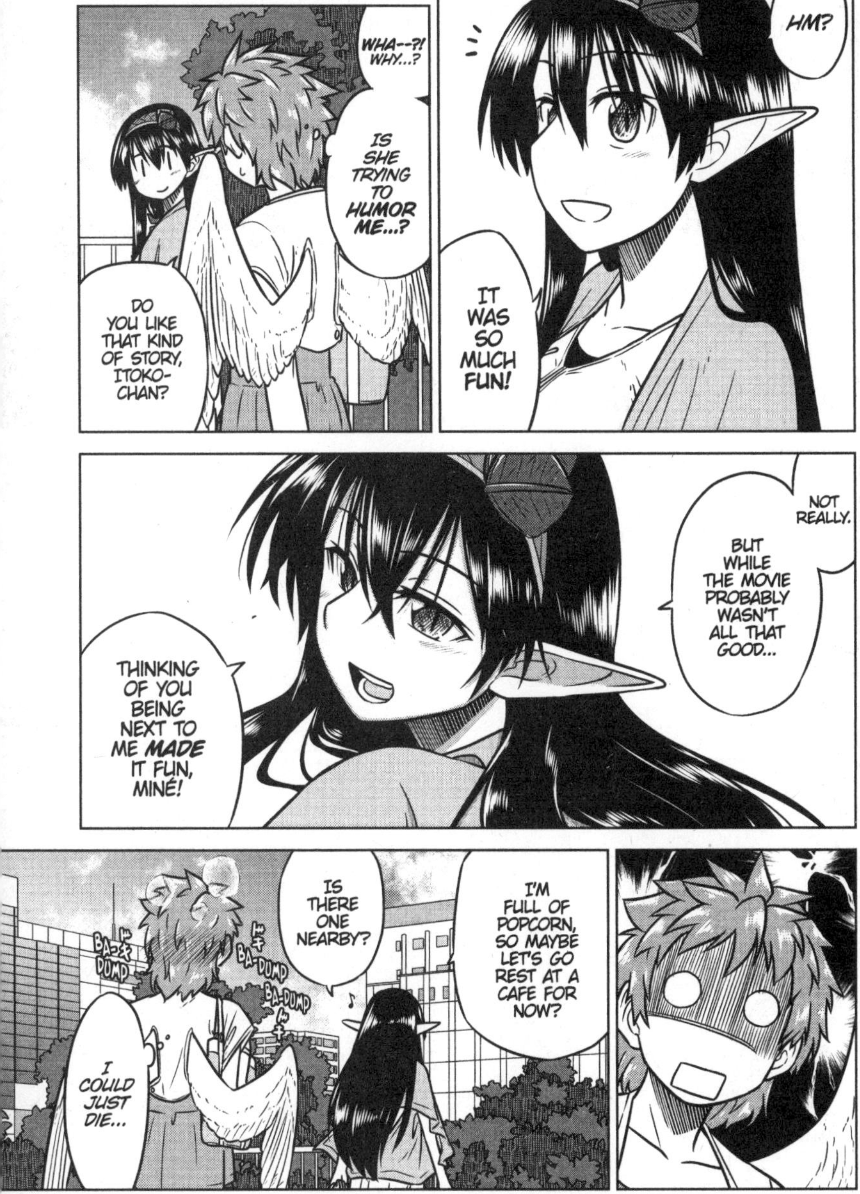
HM?
IT WAS SO MUCH FUN!
WHA--?! WHY...?
IS SHE TRYING TO HUMOR ME...?
DO YOU LIKE THAT KIND OF STORY, ITOKO-CHAN?
NOT REALLY.
BUT WHILE THE MOVIE PROBABLY WASN'T ALL THAT GOOD...
THINKING OF YOU BEING NEXT TO ME MADE IT FUN, MINÉ!
I'M FULL OF POPCORN, SO MAYBE LET'S GO REST AT A CAFE FOR NOW?
IS THERE ONE NEARBY?
ドキ BA-DUMP
ドキ BA-DUMP
ドキ BA-DUMP
I COULD JUST DIE...

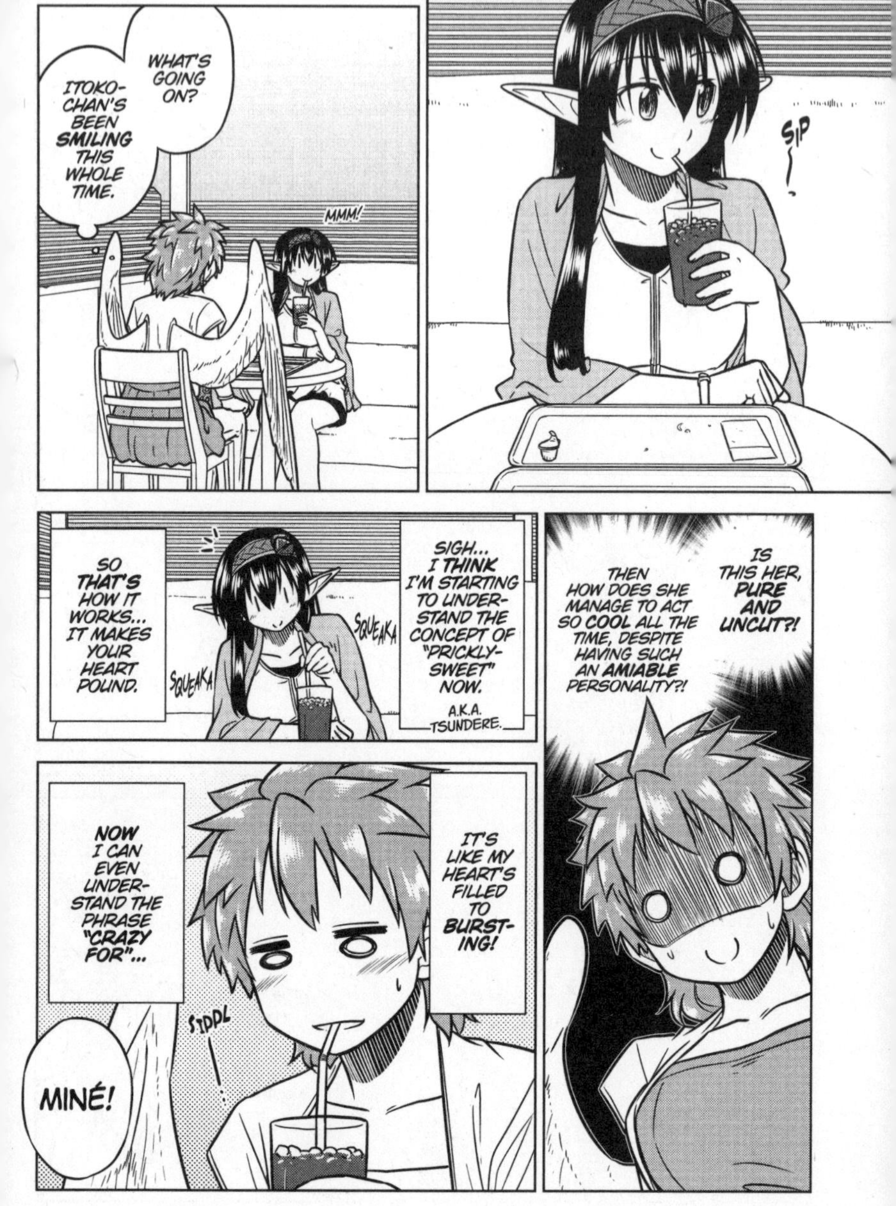
SIP
WHAT'S GOING ON?
ITOKO-CHAN'S BEEN SMILING THIS WHOLE TIME.
MMM!
IS THIS HER, PURE AND UNCUT?!
THEN HOW DOES SHE MANAGE TO ACT SO COOL ALL THE TIME, DESPITE HAVING SUCH AN AMIABLE PERSONALITY?!
SIGH... I THINK I'M STARTING TO UNDER-STAND THE CONCEPT OF "PRICKLY-SWEET" NOW.
A.K.A. TSUNDERE.
SQUEAKA
SO THAT'S HOW IT WORKS... IT MAKES YOUR HEART POUND.
SQUEAKA
IT'S LIKE MY HEART'S FILLED TO BURST-ING!
NOW I CAN EVEN UNDER-STAND THE PHRASE "CRAZY FOR"...
SIPPL
MINÉ!

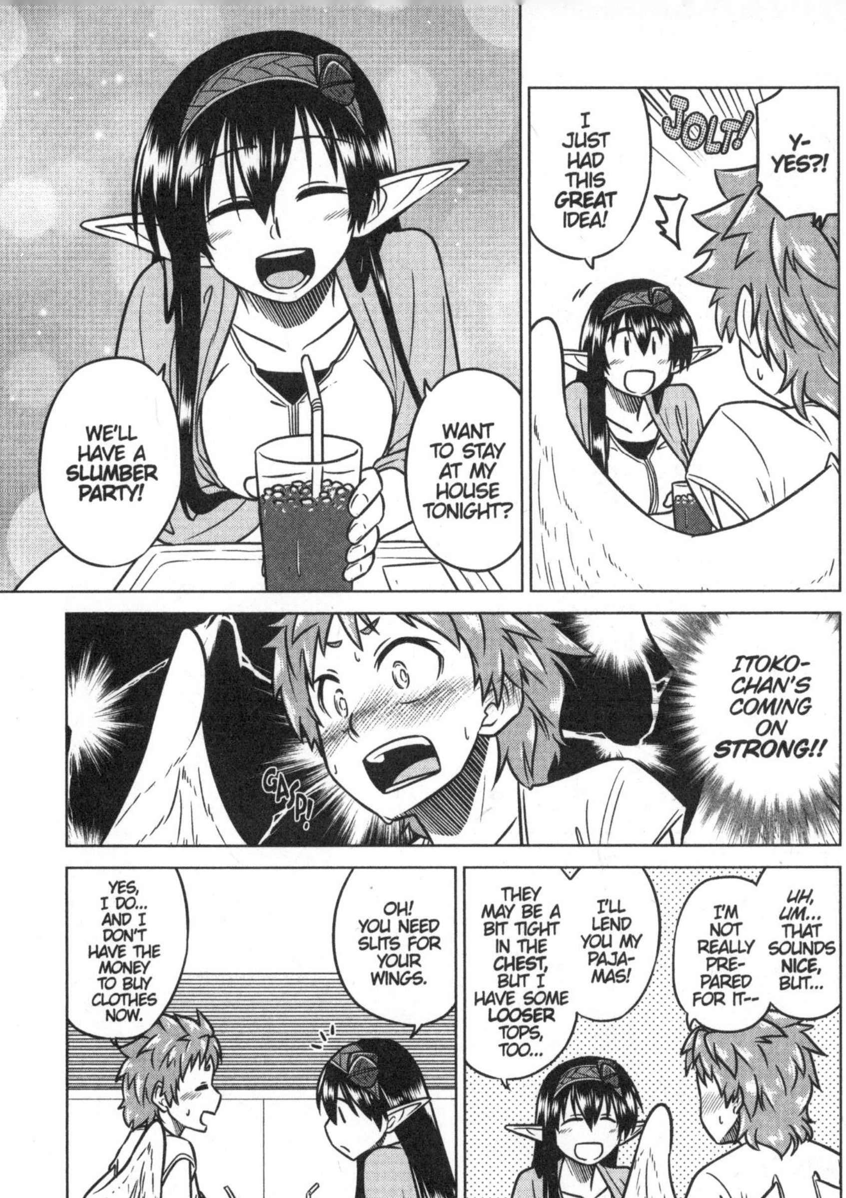
JOLT!
Y- YES?!
I JUST HAD THIS GREAT IDEA!
WANT TO STAY AT MY HOUSE TONIGHT?
WE'LL HAVE A SLUMBER PARTY!
ITOKO-CHAN'S COMING ON STRONG!!
GASP!
UH, UM... THAT SOUNDS NICE, BUT...
I'M NOT REALLY PRE-PARED FOR IT--
I'LL LEND YOU MY PAJA-MAS!
THEY MAY BE A BIT TIGHT IN THE CHEST, BUT I HAVE SOME LOOSER TOPS, TOO...
OH! YOU NEED SLITS FOR YOUR WINGS.
YES, I DO... AND I DON'T HAVE THE MONEY TO BUY CLOTHES NOW.

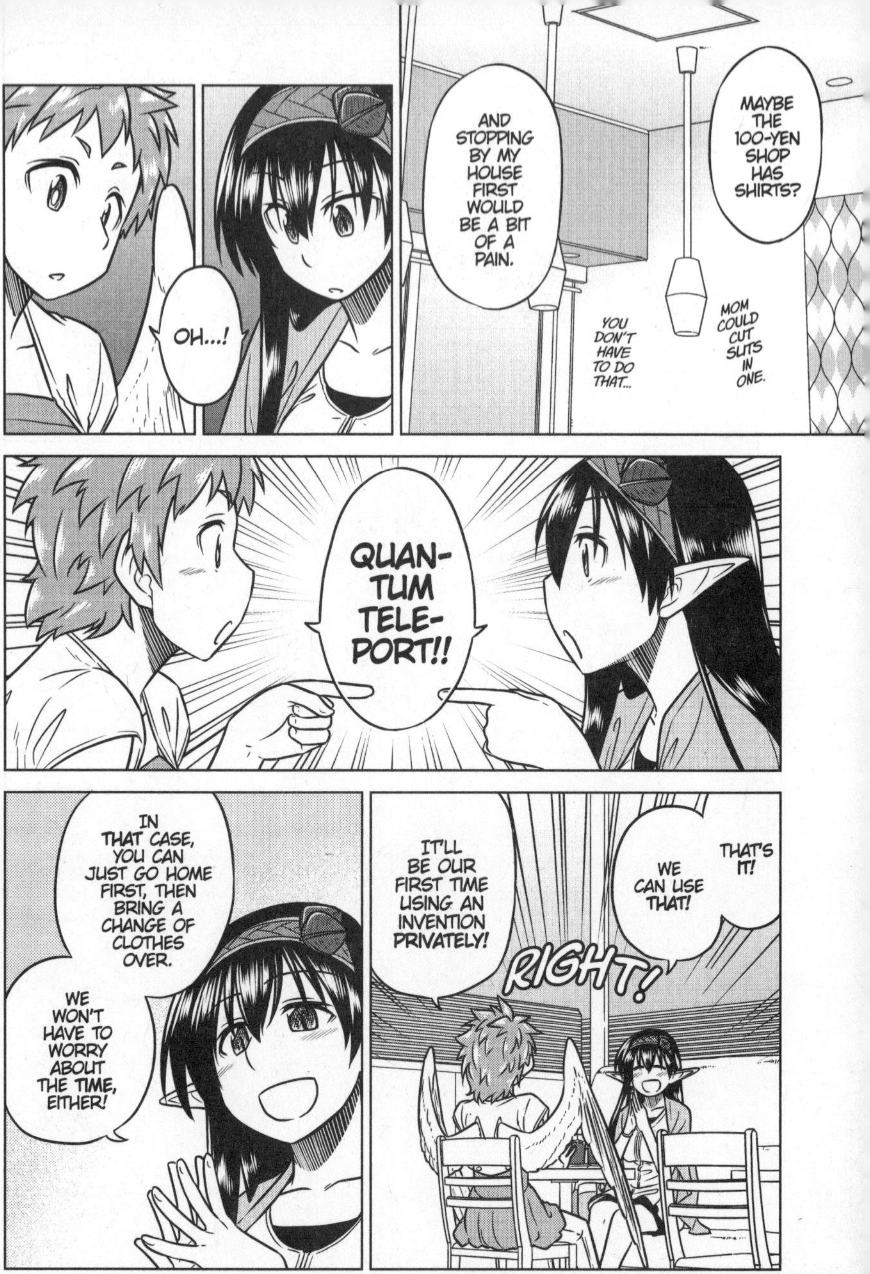
MAYBE THE 100-YEN SHOP HAS SHIRTS?
MOM COULD CUT SLITS IN ONE.
YOU DON'T HAVE TO DO THAT...
AND STOPPING BY MY HOUSE FIRST WOULD BE A BIT OF A PAIN.
OH...!
QUANTUM TELEPORT!!
THAT'S IT!
WE CAN USE THAT!
IT'LL BE OUR FIRST TIME USING AN INVENTION PRIVATELY!
RIGHT!
IN THAT CASE, YOU CAN JUST GO HOME FIRST, THEN BRING A CHANGE OF CLOTHES OVER.
WE WON'T HAVE TO WORRY ABOUT THE TIME, EITHER!

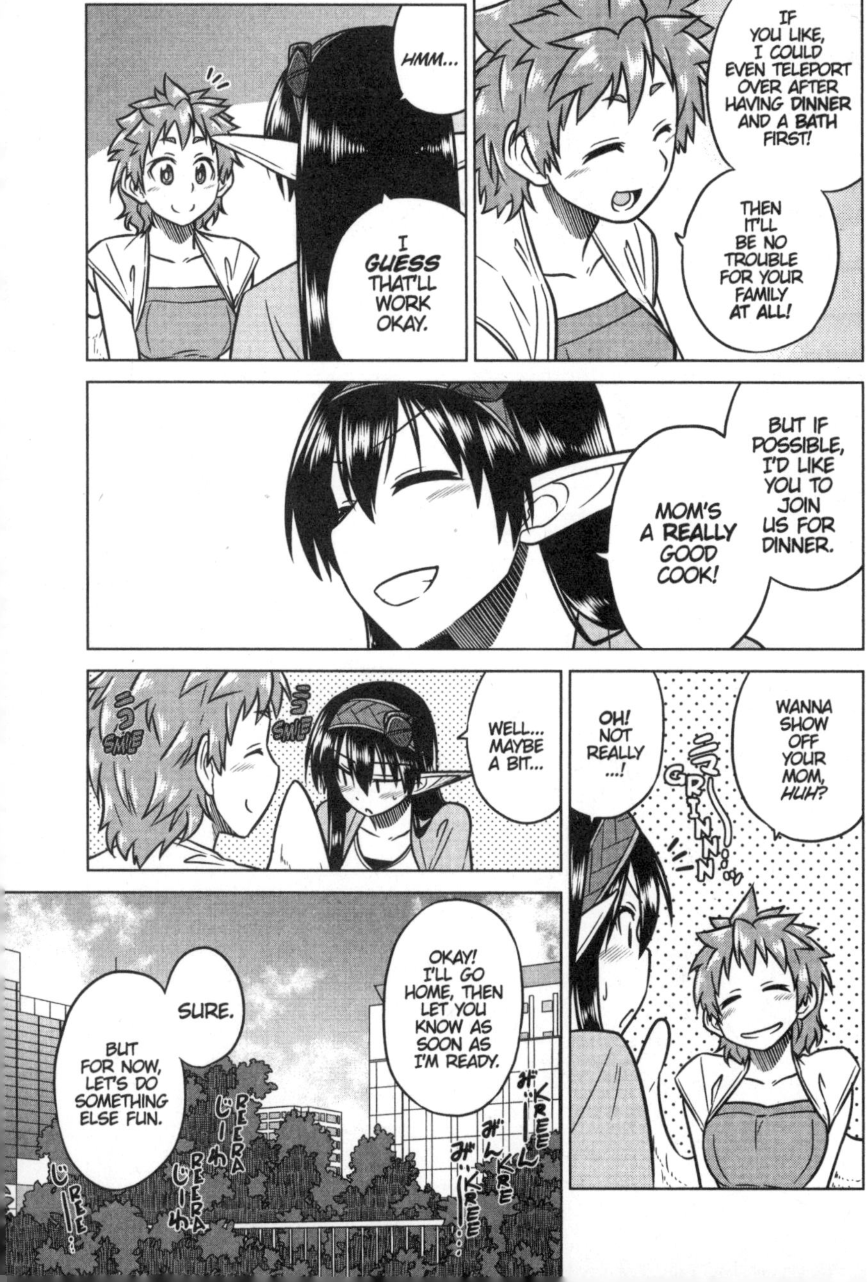
IF YOU LIKE, I COULD EVEN TELEPORT OVER AFTER HAVING DINNER AND A BATH FIRST!
THEN IT'LL BE NO TROUBLE FOR YOUR FAMILY AT ALL!
HMM...
I GUESS THAT'LL WORK OKAY.
BUT IF POSSIBLE, I'D LIKE YOU TO JOIN US FOR DINNER.
MOM'S A REALLY GOOD COOK!
WANNA SHOW OFF YOUR MOM, HUH?
GRINNN
OH! NOT REALLY ...!
WELL... MAYBE A BIT...
SMILE
SMILE
OKAY! I'LL GO HOME, THEN LET YOU KNOW AS SOON AS I'M READY.
SURE.
BUT FOR NOW, LET'S DO SOMETHING ELSE FUN.
KREE
KRE
KREE...
REERA
REERA
REE...

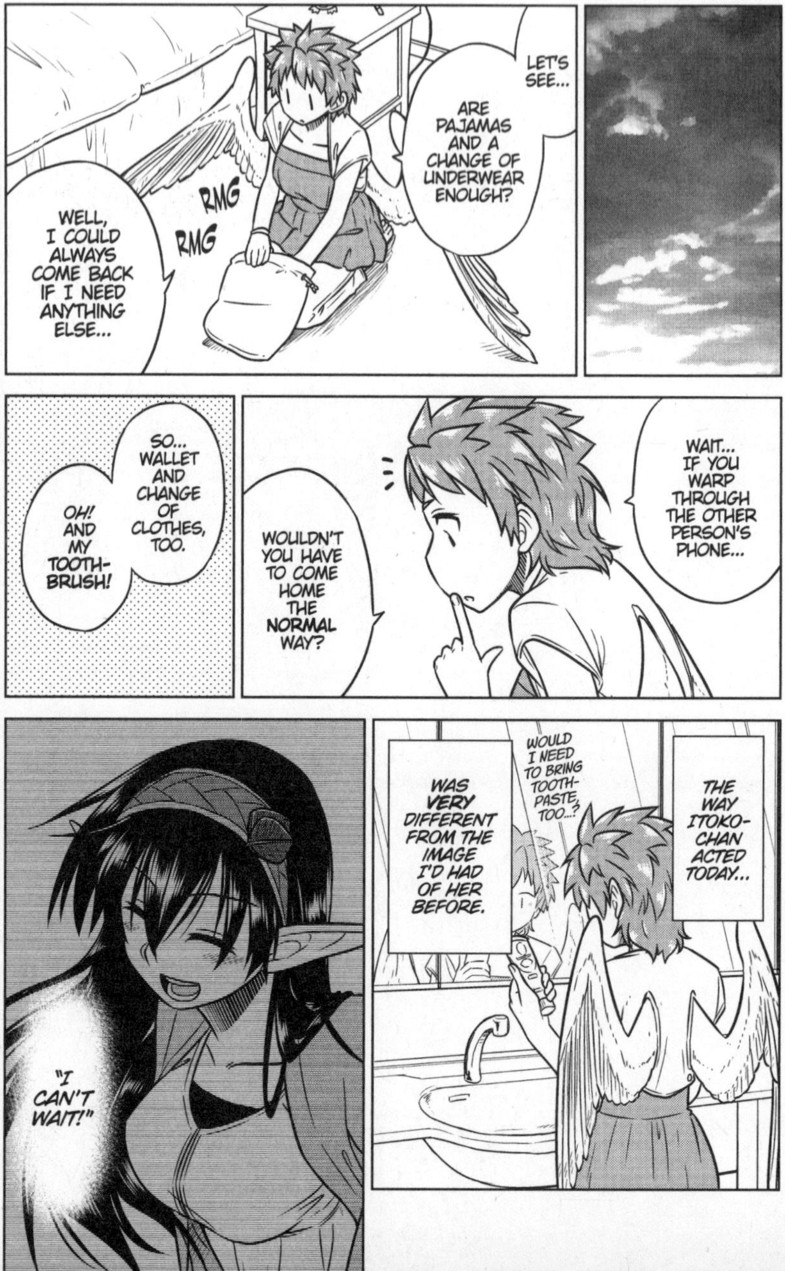
LET'S SEE...
ARE PAJAMAS AND A CHANGE OF UNDERWEAR ENOUGH?
RMG
RMG
WELL, I COULD ALWAYS COME BACK IF I NEED ANYTHING ELSE...
WAIT... IF YOU WARP THROUGH THE OTHER PERSON'S PHONE...
WOULDN'T YOU HAVE TO COME HOME THE NORMAL WAY?
SO... WALLET AND CHANGE OF CLOTHES, TOO.
OH! AND MY TOOTH-BRUSH!
THE WAY ITOKO-CHAN ACTED TODAY...
WOULD I NEED TO BRING TOOTH-PASTE, TOO...?
WAS VERY DIFFERENT FROM THE IMAGE I'D HAD OF HER BEFORE.
"I CAN'T WAIT!"

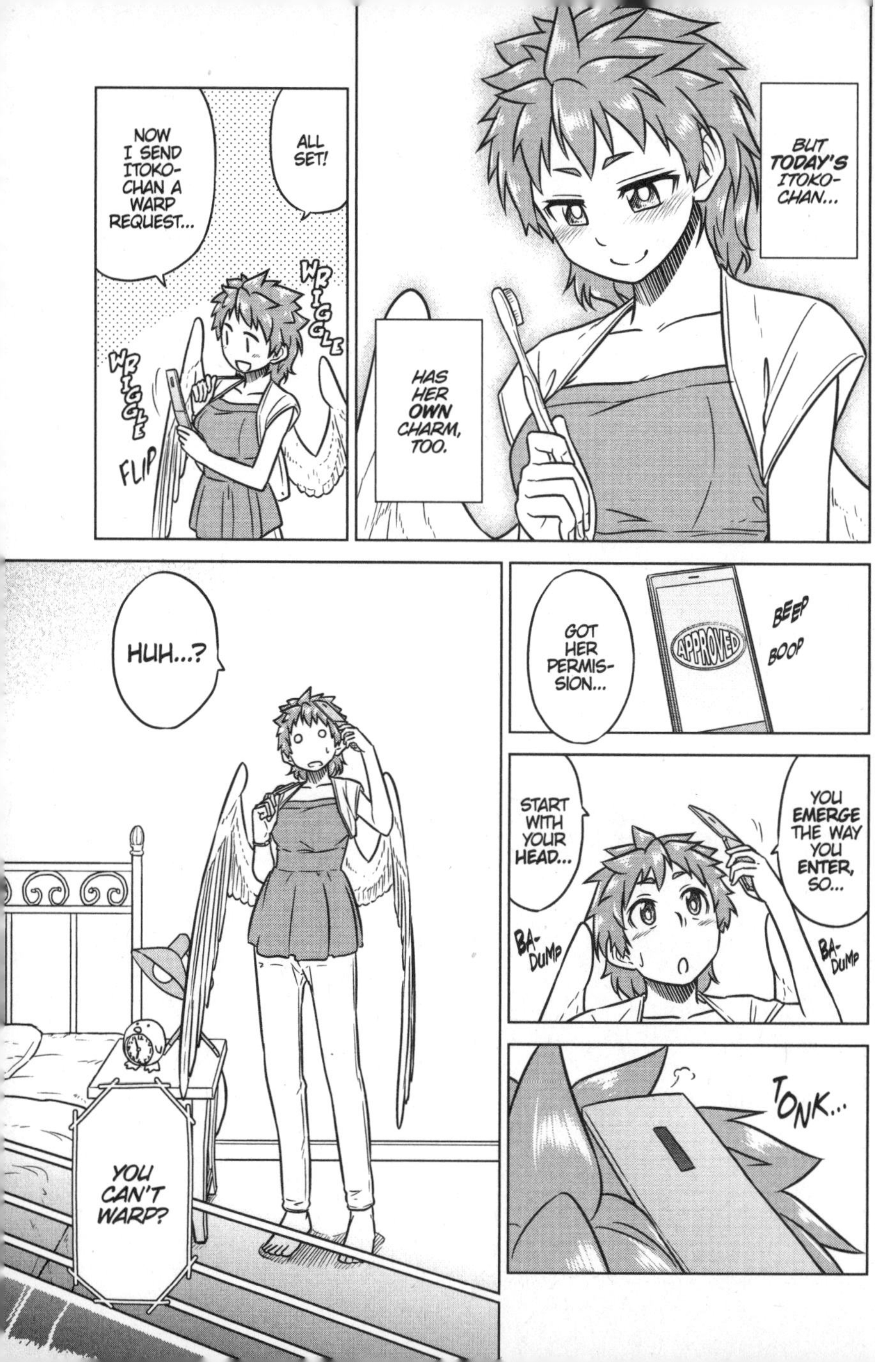
BUT TODAY'S ITOKO-CHAN...
HAS HER OWN CHARM, TOO.
ALL SET!
NOW I SEND ITOKO-CHAN A WARP REQUEST...
WRIGGLE
WRIGGLE
FLIP
GOT HER PERMISSION...
APPROVED
BEEP
BOOP
YOU EMERGE THE WAY YOU ENTER, SO...
START WITH YOUR HEAD...
BA-DUMP
BA-DUMP
TONK...
HUH...?
YOU CAN'T WARP?

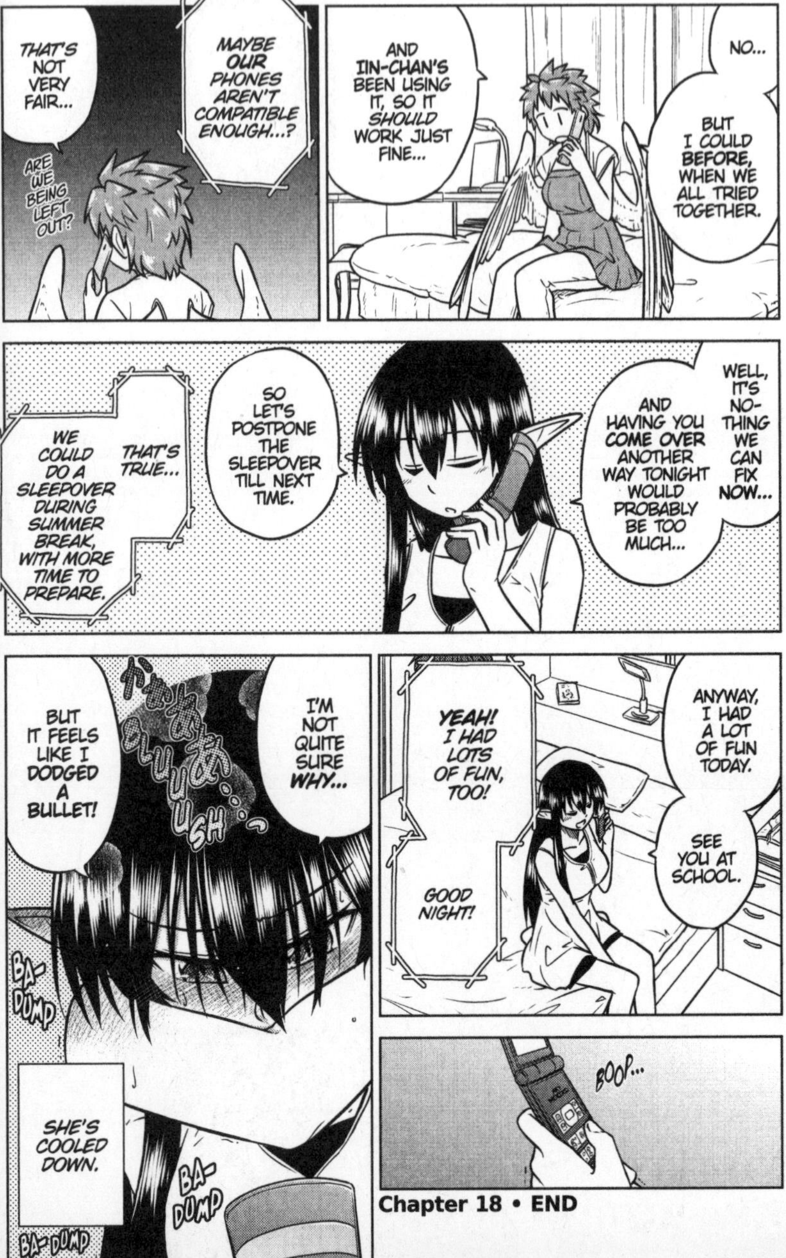
NO...
BUT I COULD BEFORE, WHEN WE ALL TRIED TOGETHER.
AND IIN-CHAN'S BEEN USING IT, SO IT SHOULD WORK JUST FINE...
MAYBE OUR PHONES AREN'T COMPATIBLE ENOUGH...?
THAT'S NOT VERY FAIR...
ARE WE BEING LEFT OUT?
WELL, IT'S NOTHING WE CAN FIX NOW...
AND HAVING YOU COME OVER ANOTHER WAY TONIGHT WOULD PROBABLY BE TOO MUCH...
SO LET'S POSTPONE THE SLEEPOVER TILL NEXT TIME.
THAT'S TRUE...
WE COULD DO A SLEEPOVER DURING SUMMER BREAK, WITH MORE TIME TO PREPARE.
ANYWAY, I HAD A LOT OF FUN TODAY.
SEE YOU AT SCHOOL.
YEAH! I HAD LOTS OF FUN, TOO!
GOOD NIGHT!
BOOP...
I'M NOT QUITE SURE WHY...
BUT IT FEELS LIKE I DODGED A BULLET!
BLUUUSH
BA-DUMP
SHE'S COOLED DOWN.
BA-DUMP
BA-DUMP

Chapter 18 • END

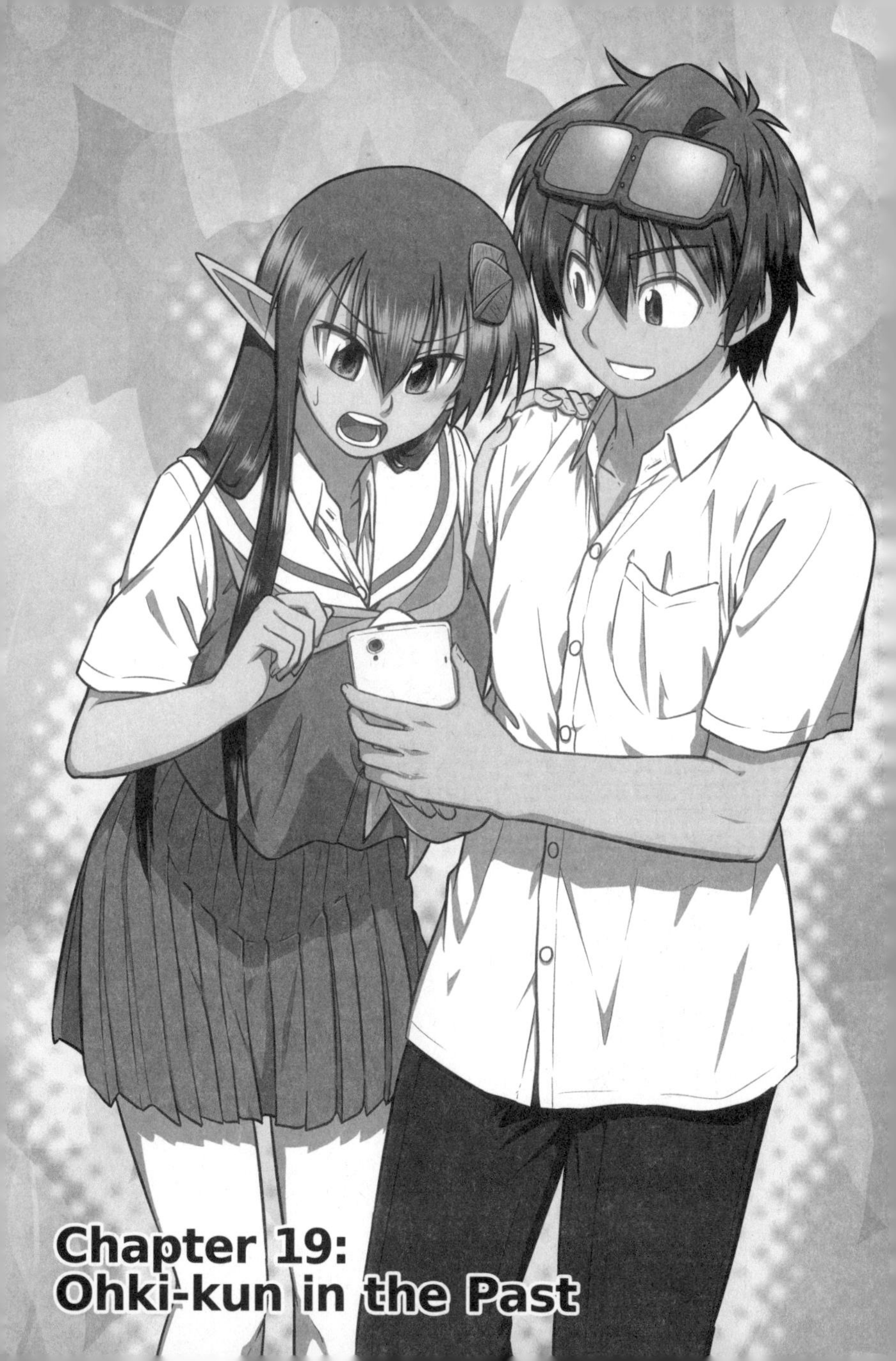

Chapter 19: Ohki-kun in the Past

WAS I INTOXICATED? I DID SOME HORRIBLY EMBARRASSING THINGS...
IF I HADN'T GOTTEN THAT COOL-DOWN TIME, WHO KNOWS WHAT MIGHT'VE HAPPENED...
MINÉ! ♪ LET'S BATHE TOGETHER!
EEEP...
MINÉ! ♪ LET'S SLEEP TOGETHER!
EEEP...
AGGGGGHHHHH!!
OH, NO! THAT WOULD'VE DEFINITELY BEEN ALL WRONG!!
NONE OF THAT FALLS UNDER THE CATEGORY OF FRIENDSHIP!!

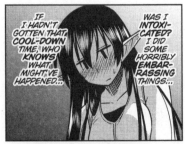

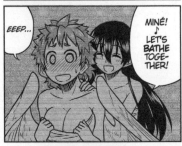

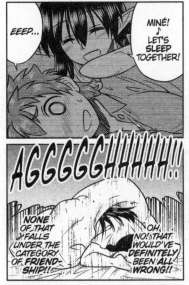

She had a relapse.

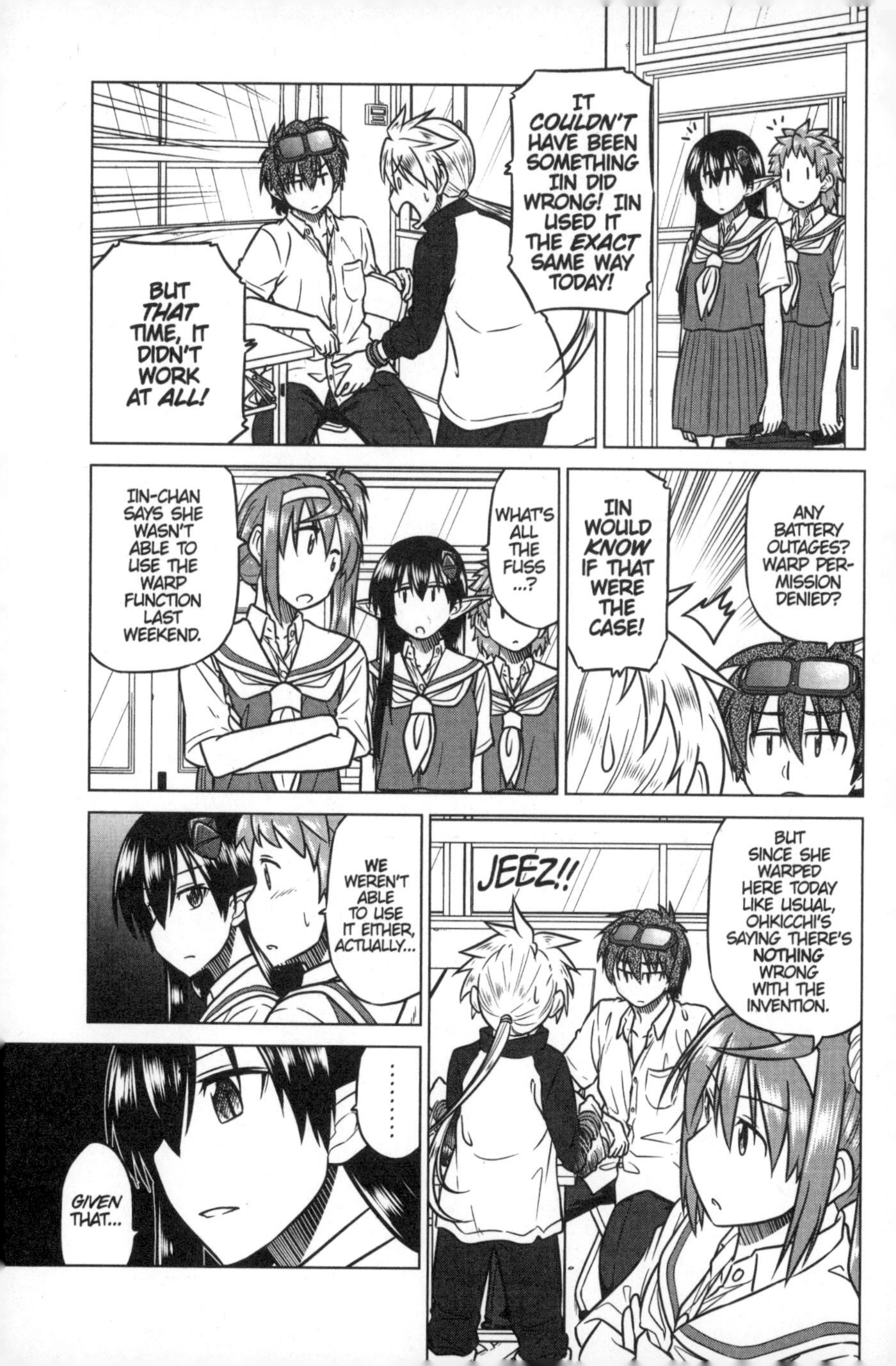
IT COULDN'T HAVE BEEN SOMETHING IIN DID WRONG! IIN USED IT THE EXACT SAME WAY TODAY!
BUT THAT TIME, IT DIDN'T WORK AT ALL!
ANY BATTERY OUTAGES? WARP PER-MISSION DENIED?
IIN WOULD KNOW IF THAT WERE THE CASE!
WHAT'S ALL THE FUSS ...?
IIN-CHAN SAYS SHE WASN'T ABLE TO USE THE WARP FUNCTION LAST WEEKEND.
JEEZ!!
BUT SINCE SHE WARPED HERE TODAY LIKE USUAL, OHKICCHI'S SAYING THERE'S NOTHING WRONG WITH THE INVENTION.
WE WEREN'T ABLE TO USE IT EITHER, ACTUALLY...
......
GIVEN THAT...

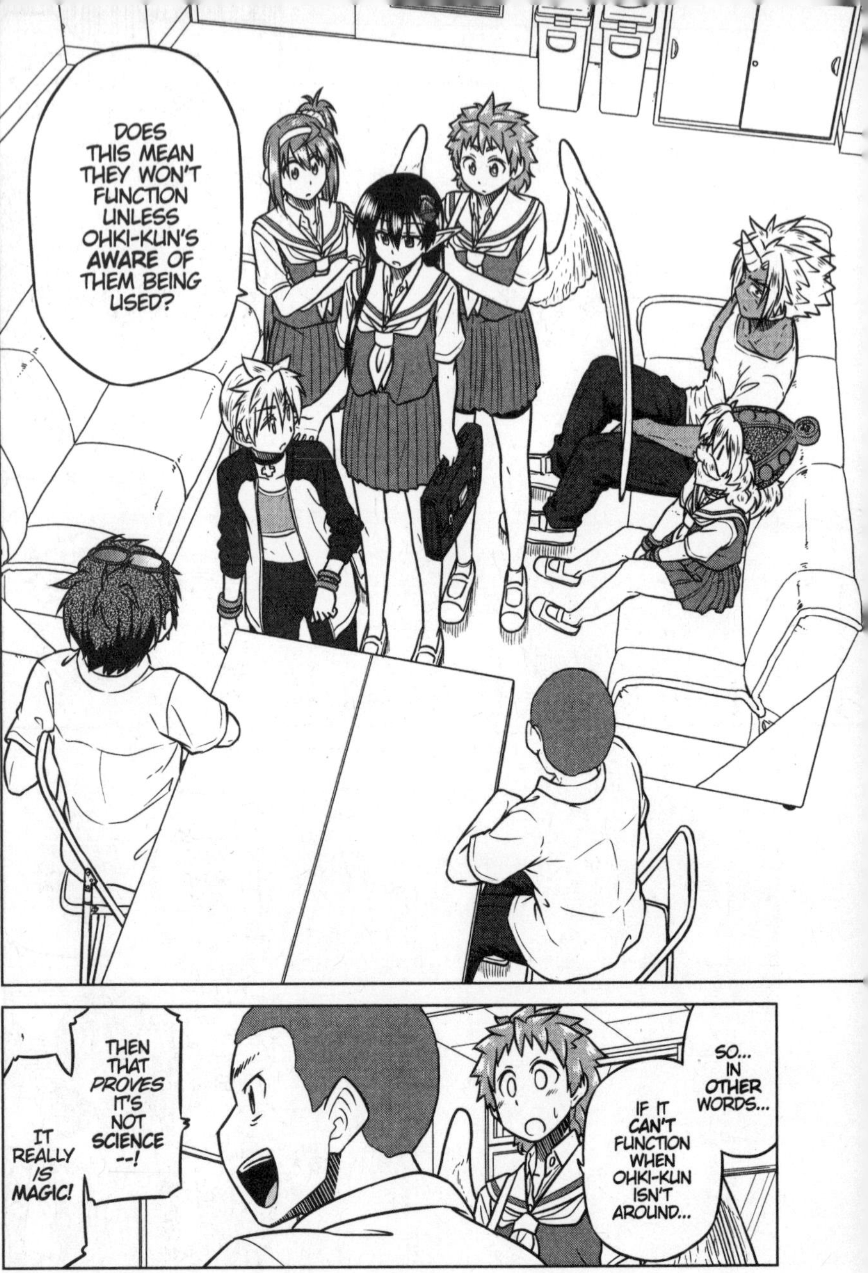
DOES THIS MEAN THEY WON'T FUNCTION UNLESS OHKI-KUN'S AWARE OF THEM BEING USED?
SO... IN OTHER WORDS...
IF IT CAN'T FUNCTION WHEN OHKI-KUN ISN'T AROUND...
THEN THAT *PROVES* IT'S NOT SCIENCE --!
IT REALLY *IS* MAGIC!

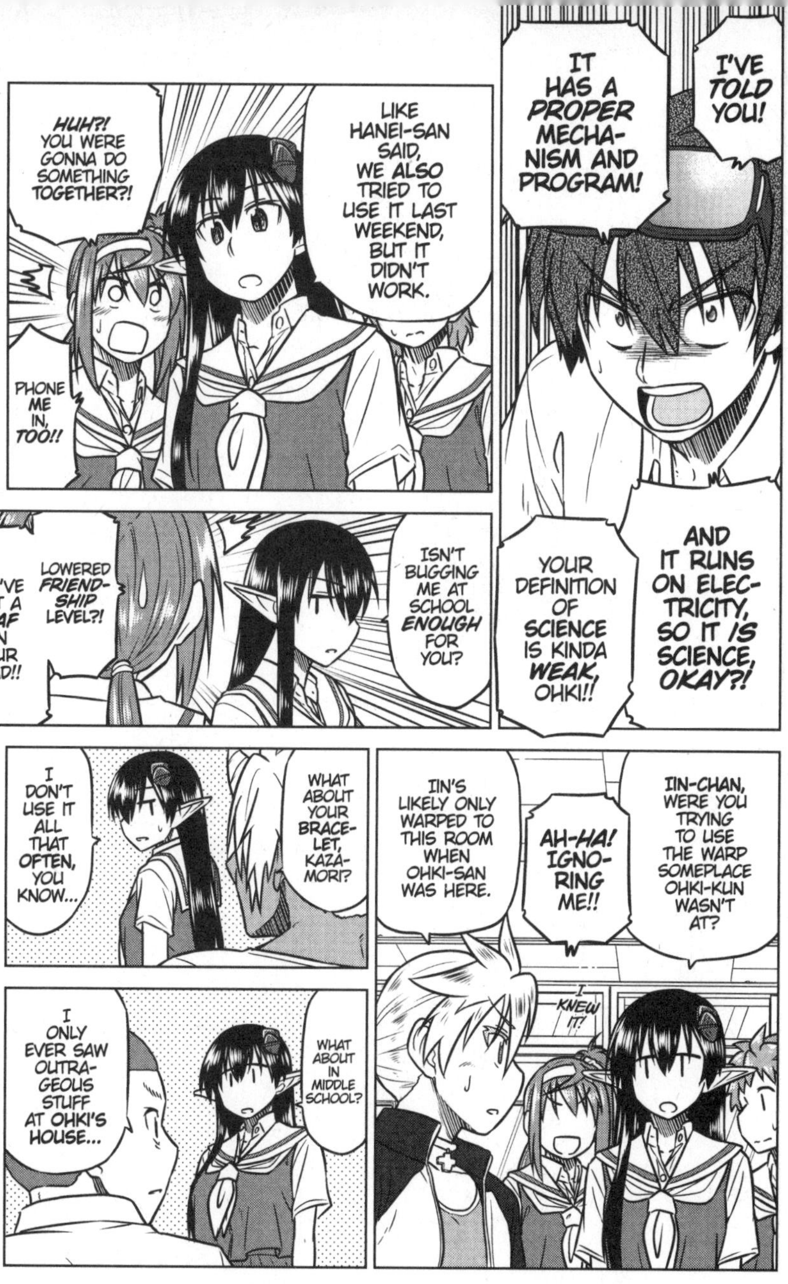
I'VE TOLD YOU!
IT HAS A PROPER MECHANISM AND PROGRAM!
AND IT RUNS ON ELECTRICITY, SO IT IS SCIENCE, OKAY?!
YOUR DEFINITION OF SCIENCE IS KINDA WEAK, OHKI!!
LIKE HANEI-SAN SAID, WE ALSO TRIED TO USE IT LAST WEEKEND, BUT IT DIDN'T WORK.
HUH?! YOU WERE GONNA DO SOMETHING TOGETHER?!
PHONE ME IN, TOO!!
ISN'T BUGGING ME AT SCHOOL ENOUGH FOR YOU?
LOWERED FRIENDSHIP LEVEL?!
YOU'VE GOT A LEAF ON YOUR HEAD!!
IIN-CHAN, WERE YOU TRYING TO USE THE WARP SOMEPLACE OHKI-KUN WASN'T AT?
AH-HA! IGNORING ME!!
IIN'S LIKELY ONLY WARPED TO THIS ROOM WHEN OHKI-SAN WAS HERE.
I KNEW IT!
WHAT ABOUT YOUR BRACELET, KAZAMORI?
I DON'T USE IT ALL THAT OFTEN, YOU KNOW...
WHAT ABOUT IN MIDDLE SCHOOL?
I ONLY EVER SAW OUTRAGEOUS STUFF AT OHKI'S HOUSE...

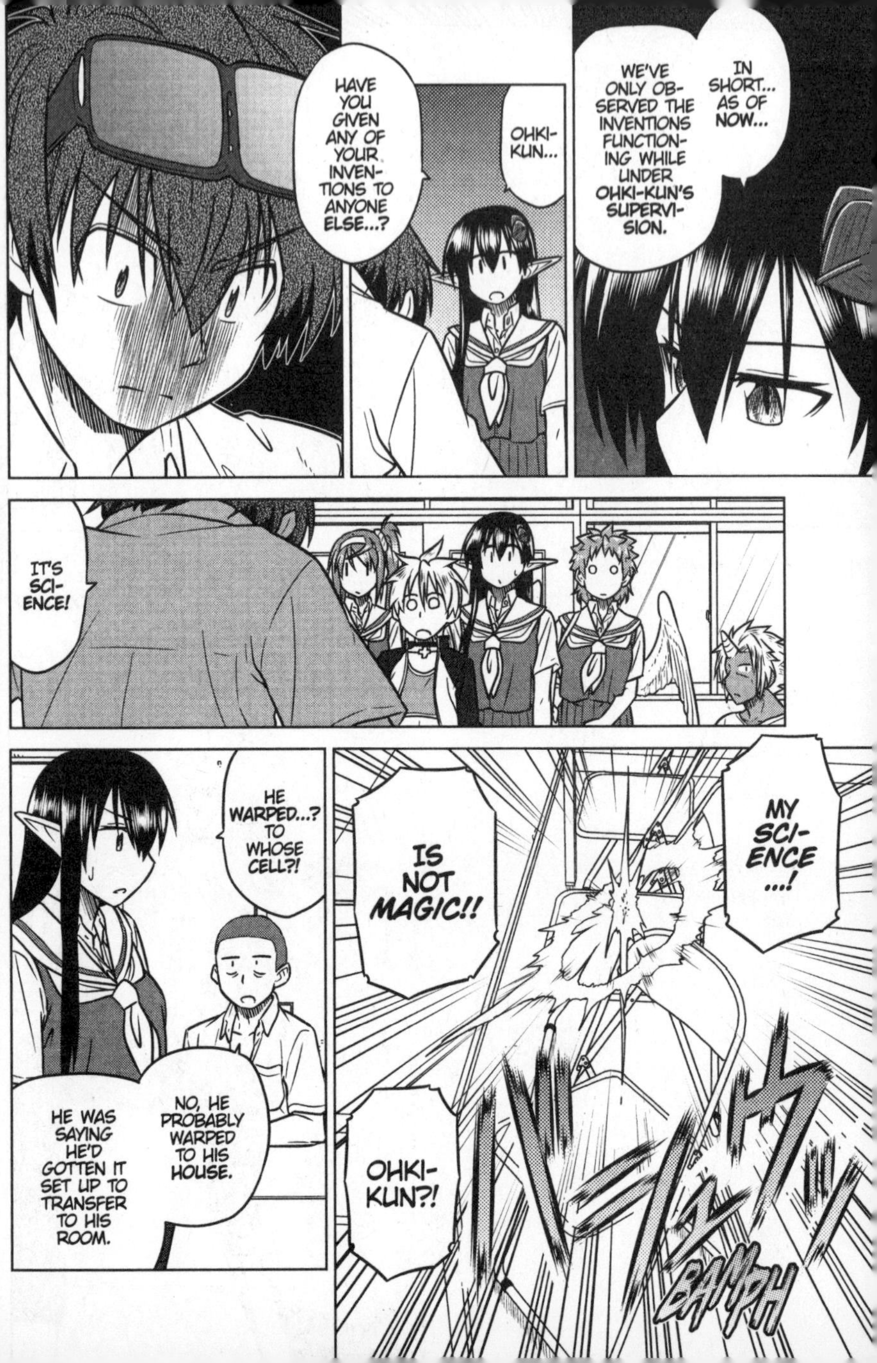
IN SHORT... AS OF NOW...
WE'VE ONLY OBSERVED THE INVENTIONS FUNCTIONING WHILE UNDER OHKI-KUN'S SUPERVISION.
OHKI-KUN...
HAVE YOU GIVEN ANY OF YOUR INVENTIONS TO ANYONE ELSE...?
IT'S SCIENCE!
MY SCIENCE...!
IS NOT MAGIC!!
BAMPH
OHKI-KUN?!
HE WARPED...? TO WHOSE CELL?!
NO, HE PROBABLY WARPED TO HIS HOUSE.
HE WAS SAYING HE'D GOTTEN IT SET UP TO TRANSFER TO HIS ROOM.

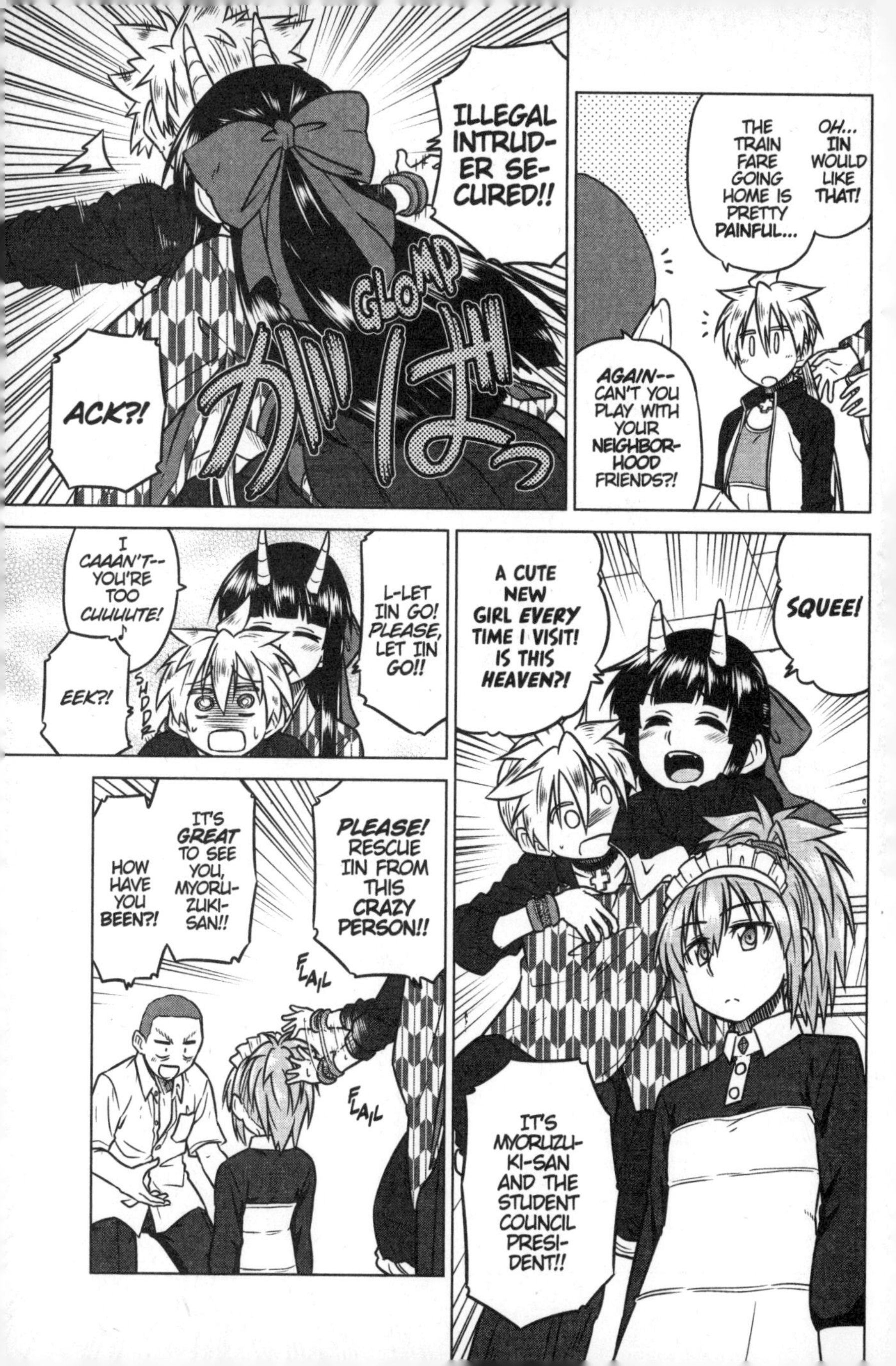
OH... IIN WOULD LIKE THAT!
THE TRAIN FARE GOING HOME IS PRETTY PAINFUL...
AGAIN-- CAN'T YOU PLAY WITH YOUR NEIGHBOR-HOOD FRIENDS?!
ILLEGAL INTRUD-ER SE-CURED!!
GLOMP
ACK?!
SQUEE!
A CUTE NEW GIRL EVERY TIME I VISIT! IS THIS HEAVEN?!
IT'S MYORUZU-KI-SAN AND THE STUDENT COUNCIL PRESI-DENT!!
L-LET IIN GO! PLEASE, LET IIN GO!!
I CAAAN'T-- YOU'RE TOO CUUUUTE! ♪
EEK?!
SHDDR
PLEASE! RESCUE IIN FROM THIS CRAZY PERSON!!
IT'S GREAT TO SEE YOU, MYORU-ZUKI-SAN!!
HOW HAVE YOU BEEN?!
FLAIL
FLAIL

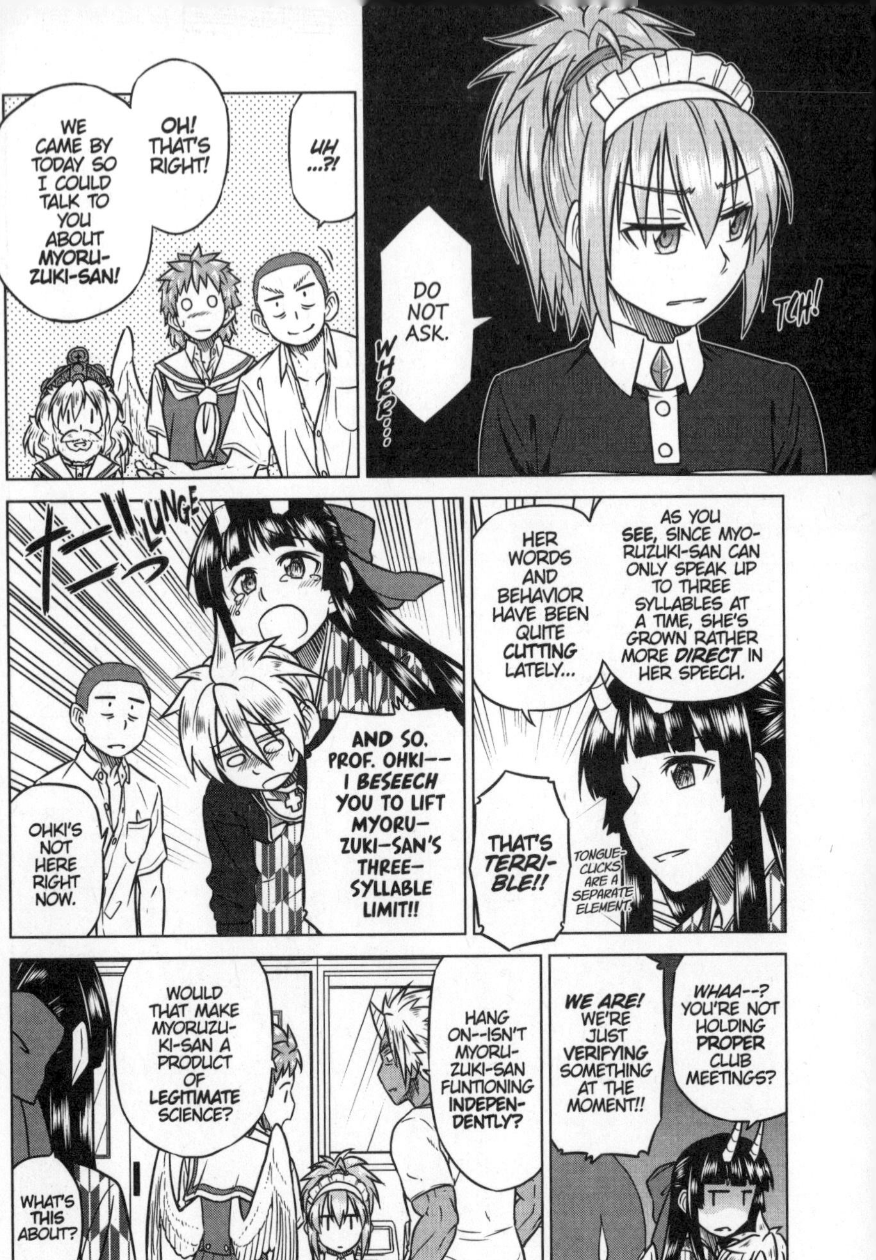
DO NOT ASK.
WHRRR...
TCH!
UH ...?!
OH! THAT'S RIGHT!
WE CAME BY TODAY SO I COULD TALK TO YOU ABOUT MYORUZUKI-SAN!
AS YOU SEE, SINCE MYORUZUKI-SAN CAN ONLY SPEAK UP TO THREE SYLLABLES AT A TIME, SHE'S GROWN RATHER MORE DIRECT IN HER SPEECH.
HER WORDS AND BEHAVIOR HAVE BEEN QUITE CUTTING LATELY...
THAT'S TERRIBLE!!
TONGUE-CLICKS ARE A SEPARATE ELEMENT.
LUNGE
AND SO. PROF. OHKI-- I BESEECH YOU TO LIFT MYORUZUKI-SAN'S THREE-SYLLABLE LIMIT!!
OHKI'S NOT HERE RIGHT NOW.
WHAA--? YOU'RE NOT HOLDING PROPER CLUB MEETINGS?
WE ARE! WE'RE JUST VERIFYING SOMETHING AT THE MOMENT!!
HANG ON--ISN'T MYORUZUKI-SAN FUNTIONING INDEPENDENTLY?
WOULD THAT MAKE MYORUZUKI-SAN A PRODUCT OF LEGITIMATE SCIENCE?
WHAT'S THIS ABOUT?

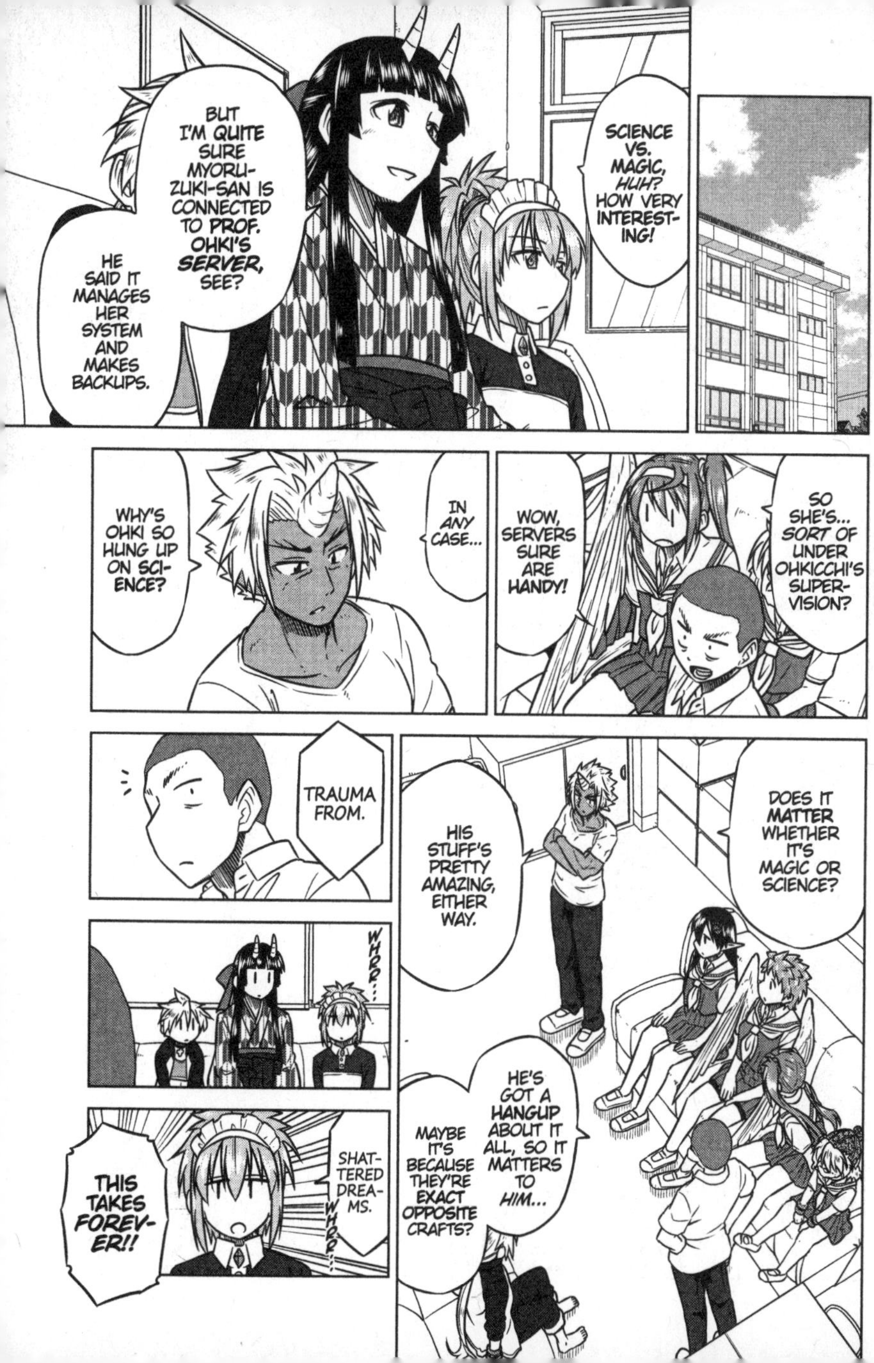
SCIENCE VS. MAGIC, HUH? HOW VERY INTERESTING!
BUT I'M QUITE SURE MYORUZUKI-SAN IS CONNECTED TO PROF. OHKI'S SERVER, SEE?
HE SAID IT MANAGES HER SYSTEM AND MAKES BACKUPS.
SO SHE'S... SORT OF UNDER OHKICCHI'S SUPERVISION?
WOW, SERVERS SURE ARE HANDY!
IN ANY CASE...
WHY'S OHKI SO HUNG UP ON SCIENCE?
DOES IT MATTER WHETHER IT'S MAGIC OR SCIENCE?
HIS STUFF'S PRETTY AMAZING, EITHER WAY.
HE'S GOT A HANGUP ABOUT IT ALL, SO IT MATTERS TO HIM...
MAYBE IT'S BECAUSE THEY'RE EXACT OPPOSITE CRAFTS?
TRAUMA FROM.
WHRR...
SHATTERED DREAMS.
WHRR...
THIS TAKES FOREVER!!

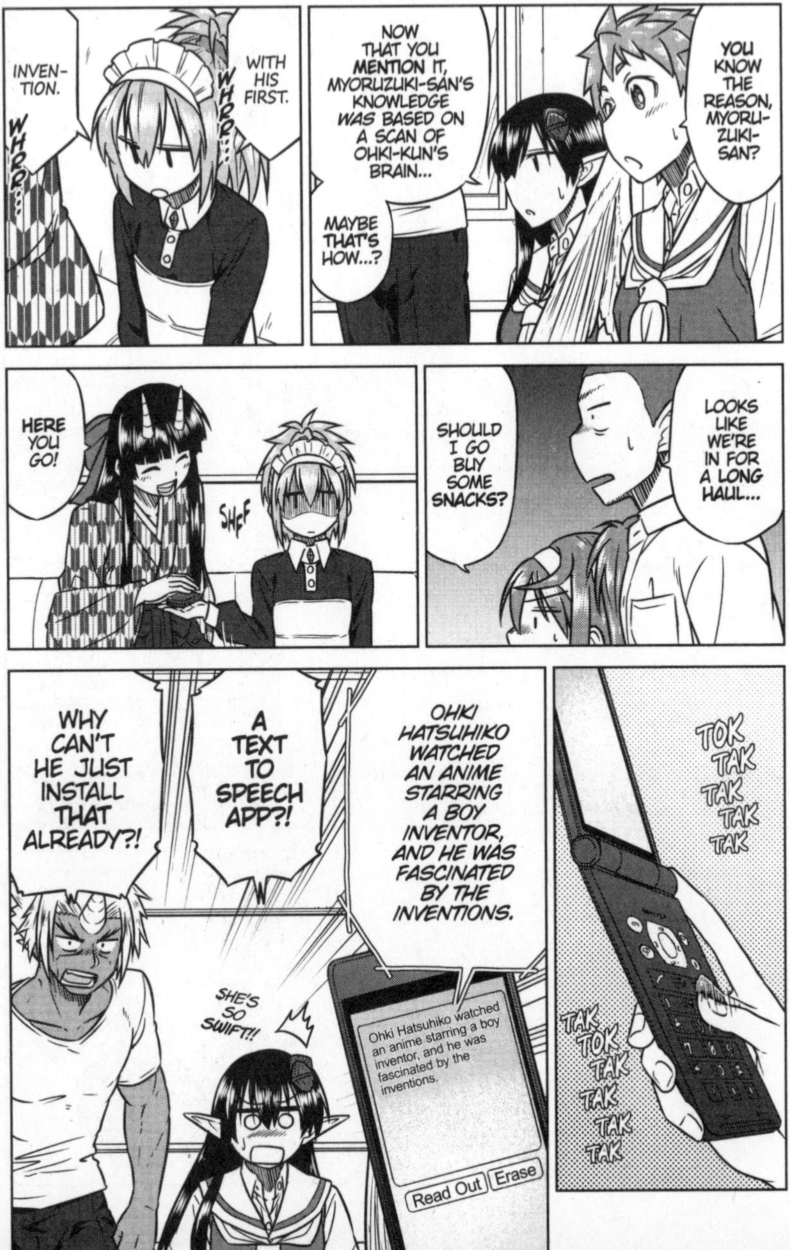
YOU KNOW THE REASON, MYORUZUKI-SAN?
NOW THAT YOU MENTION IT, MYORUZUKI-SAN'S KNOWLEDGE WAS BASED ON A SCAN OF OHKI-KUN'S BRAIN...
MAYBE THAT'S HOW...?
WHRR...
WITH HIS FIRST.
INVENTION.
WHRR...
LOOKS LIKE WE'RE IN FOR A LONG HAUL...
SHOULD I GO BUY SOME SNACKS?
SHFF
HERE YOU GO!
TOK TAK TAK TAK TAK
TAK TOK TAK TAK TAK TAK
OHKI HATSUHIKO WATCHED AN ANIME STARRING A BOY INVENTOR, AND HE WAS FASCINATED BY THE INVENTIONS.
A TEXT TO SPEECH APP?!
WHY CAN'T HE JUST INSTALL THAT ALREADY?!
Ohki Hatsuhiko watched an anime starring a boy inventor, and he was fascinated by the inventions.
Erase
Read Out
SHE'S SO SWIFT!!

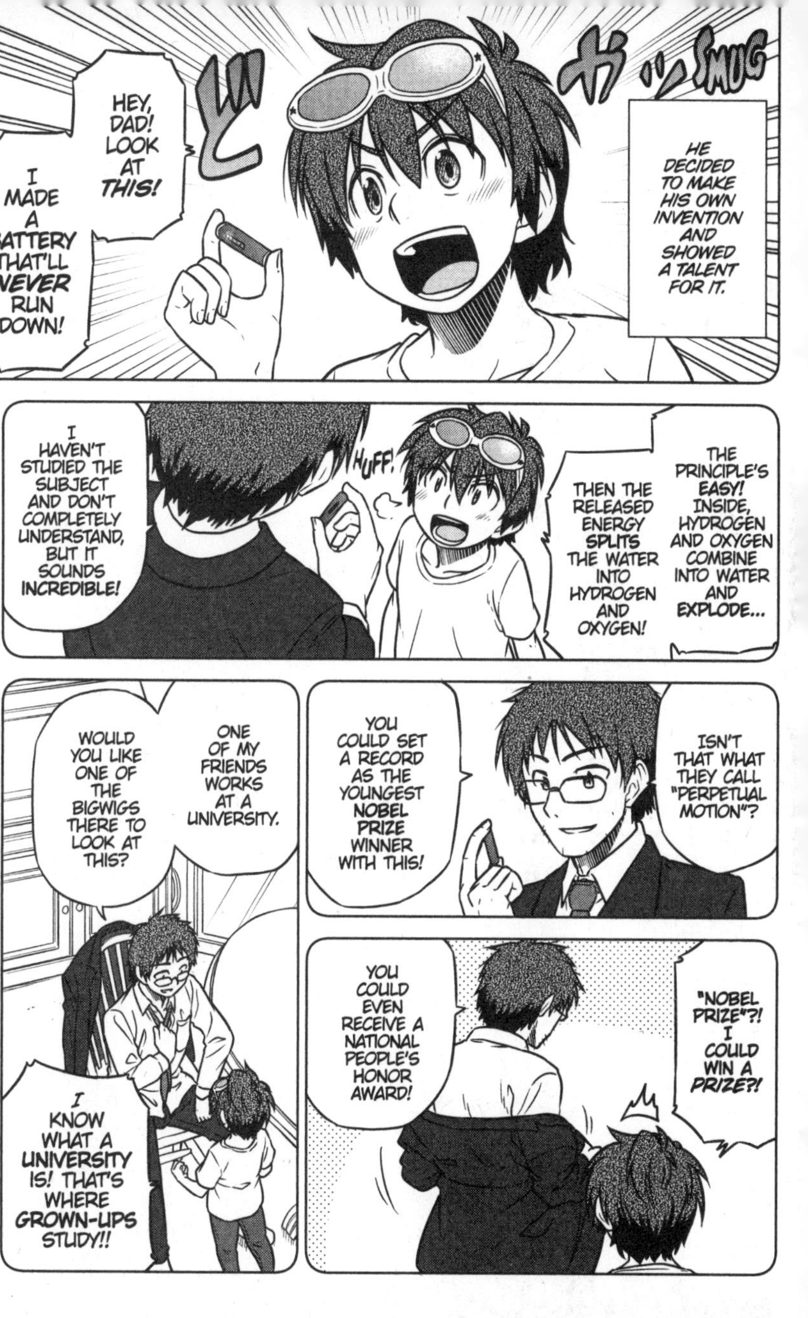
HE DECIDED TO MAKE HIS OWN INVENTION AND SHOWED A TALENT FOR IT.
SMUG
HEY, DAD! LOOK AT *THIS!*
I MADE A BATTERY THAT'LL ***NEVER*** RUN DOWN!
THE PRINCIPLE'S **EASY!** INSIDE, HYDROGEN AND OXYGEN COMBINE INTO WATER AND **EXPLODE...**
THEN THE RELEASED ENERGY **SPLITS** THE WATER INTO HYDROGEN AND OXYGEN!
HUFF!
I HAVEN'T STUDIED THE SUBJECT AND DON'T COMPLETELY UNDERSTAND, BUT IT SOUNDS **INCREDIBLE!**
ISN'T THAT WHAT THEY CALL "PERPETUAL MOTION"?
YOU COULD SET A RECORD AS THE YOUNGEST **NOBEL PRIZE** WINNER WITH THIS!
"NOBEL PRIZE"?! I COULD WIN A ***PRIZE?!***
YOU COULD EVEN RECEIVE A NATIONAL PEOPLE'S HONOR AWARD!
ONE OF MY FRIENDS WORKS AT A UNIVERSITY.
WOULD YOU LIKE ONE OF THE BIGWIGS THERE TO LOOK AT THIS?
I KNOW WHAT A **UNIVERSITY** IS! THAT'S WHERE **GROWN-UPS** STUDY!!

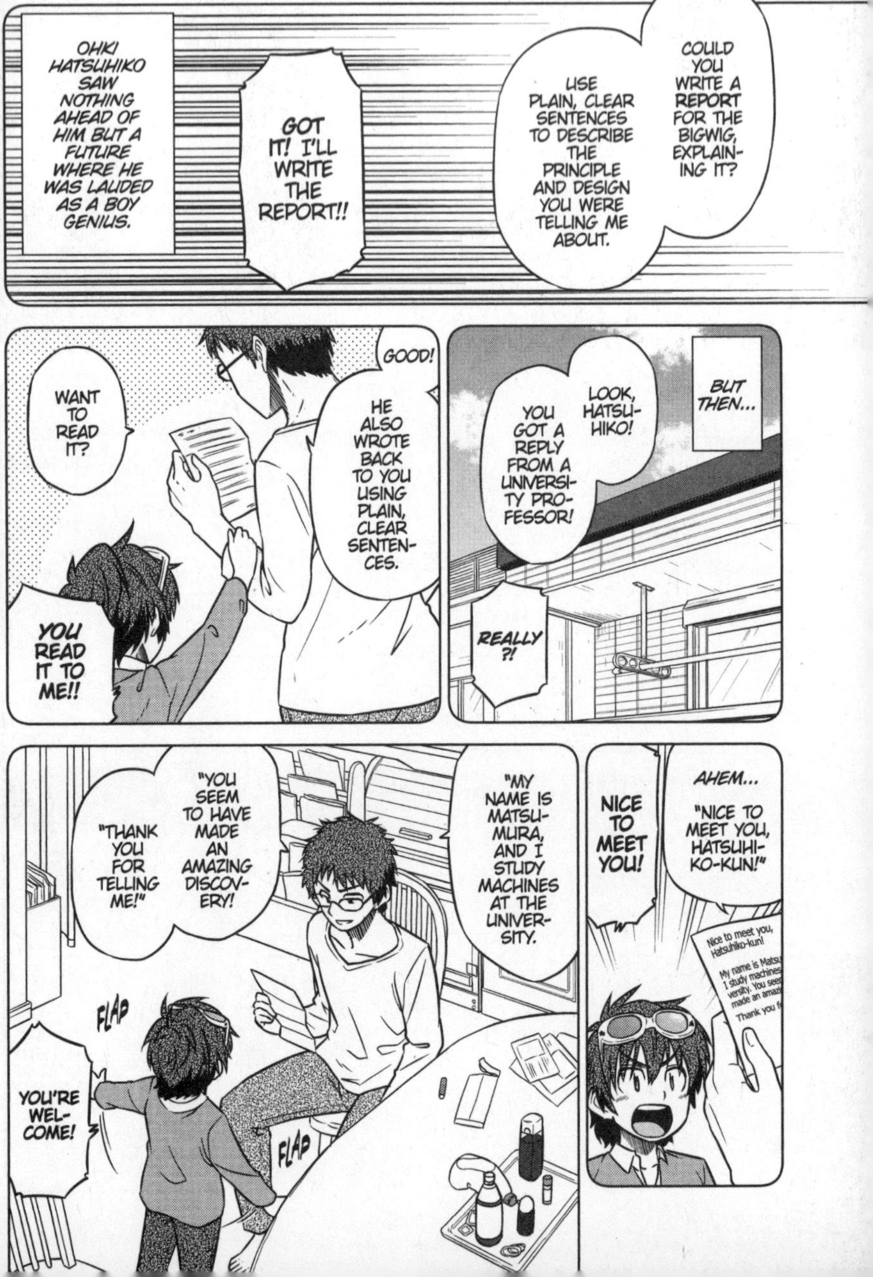
COULD YOU WRITE A REPORT FOR THE BIGWIG, EXPLAINING IT?
USE PLAIN, CLEAR SENTENCES TO DESCRIBE THE PRINCIPLE AND DESIGN YOU WERE TELLING ME ABOUT.
GOT IT! I'LL WRITE THE REPORT!!
OHKI HATSUHIKO SAW NOTHING AHEAD OF HIM BUT A FUTURE WHERE HE WAS LAUDED AS A BOY GENIUS.
BUT THEN...
LOOK, HATSUHIKO!
YOU GOT A REPLY FROM A UNIVERSITY PROFESSOR!
REALLY?!
GOOD!
HE ALSO WROTE BACK TO YOU USING PLAIN, CLEAR SENTENCES.
WANT TO READ IT?
YOU READ IT TO ME!!
AHEM... "NICE TO MEET YOU, HATSUHIKO-KUN!"
NICE TO MEET YOU!
Nice to meet you, Hatsuhiko-kun!
"MY NAME IS MATSUMURA, AND I STUDY MACHINES AT THE UNIVERSITY.
"YOU SEEM TO HAVE MADE AN AMAZING DISCOVERY!
"THANK YOU FOR TELLING ME!"
FLAP
FLAP
YOU'RE WELCOME!

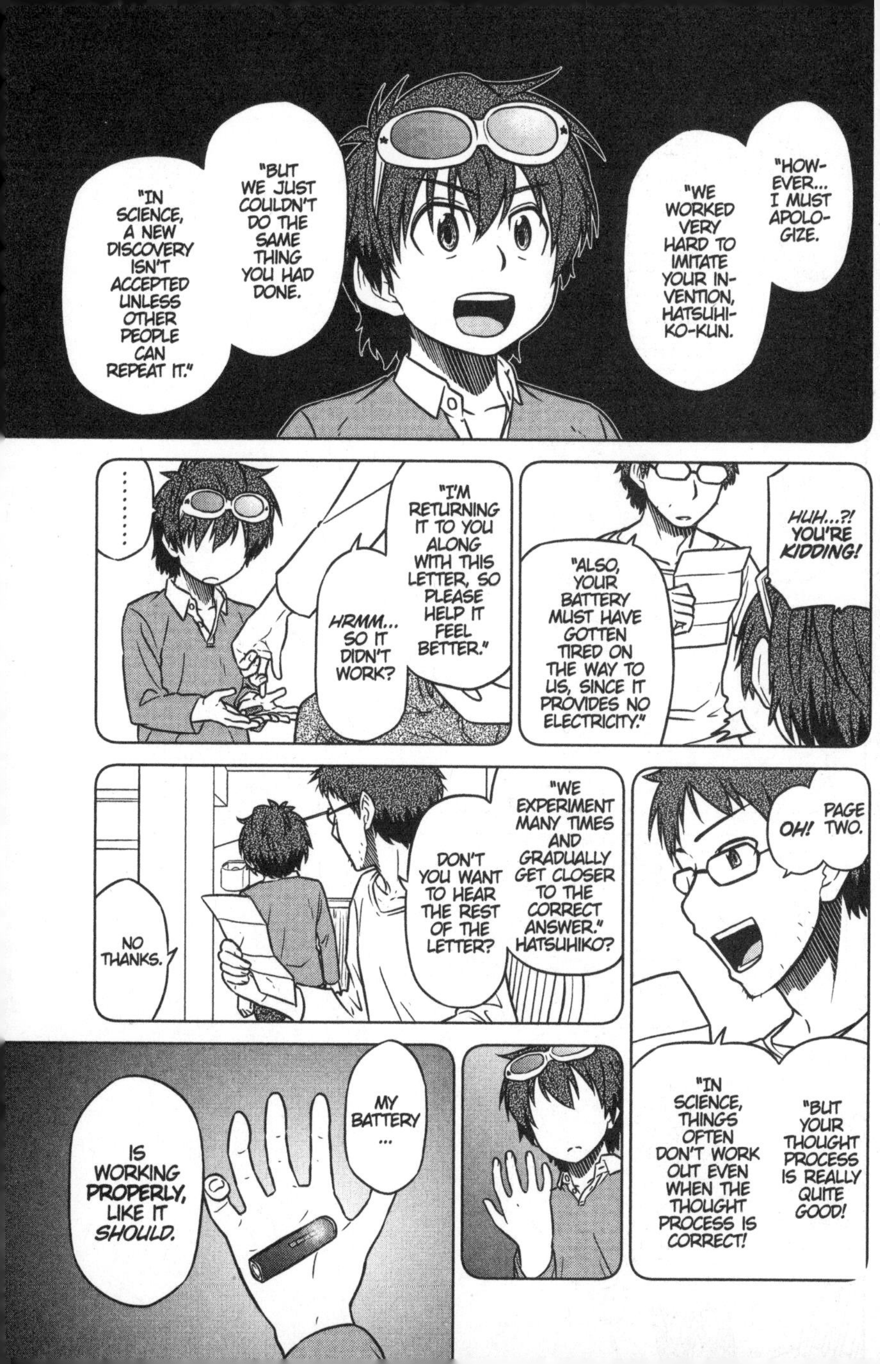
"HOW-EVER... I MUST APOLO-GIZE.
"WE WORKED VERY HARD TO IMITATE YOUR IN-VENTION, HATSUHI-KO-KUN.
"BUT WE JUST COULDN'T DO THE SAME THING YOU HAD DONE.
"IN SCIENCE, A NEW DISCOVERY ISN'T ACCEPTED UNLESS OTHER PEOPLE CAN REPEAT IT."
HUH...?! YOU'RE *KIDDING!*
"ALSO, YOUR BATTERY MUST HAVE GOTTEN TIRED ON THE WAY TO US, SINCE IT PROVIDES NO ELECTRICITY."
"I'M RETURNING IT TO YOU ALONG WITH THIS LETTER, SO PLEASE HELP IT FEEL BETTER."
HRMM... SO IT DIDN'T WORK?
......
PAGE TWO.
OH!
"BUT YOUR THOUGHT PROCESS IS REALLY QUITE GOOD!
"IN SCIENCE, THINGS OFTEN DON'T WORK OUT EVEN WHEN THE THOUGHT PROCESS IS CORRECT!
"WE EXPERIMENT MANY TIMES AND GRADUALLY GET CLOSER TO THE CORRECT ANSWER." HATSUHIKO?
DON'T YOU WANT TO HEAR THE REST OF THE LETTER?
NO THANKS.
MY BATTERY ...
IS WORKING **PROPERLY,** LIKE IT *SHOULD.*

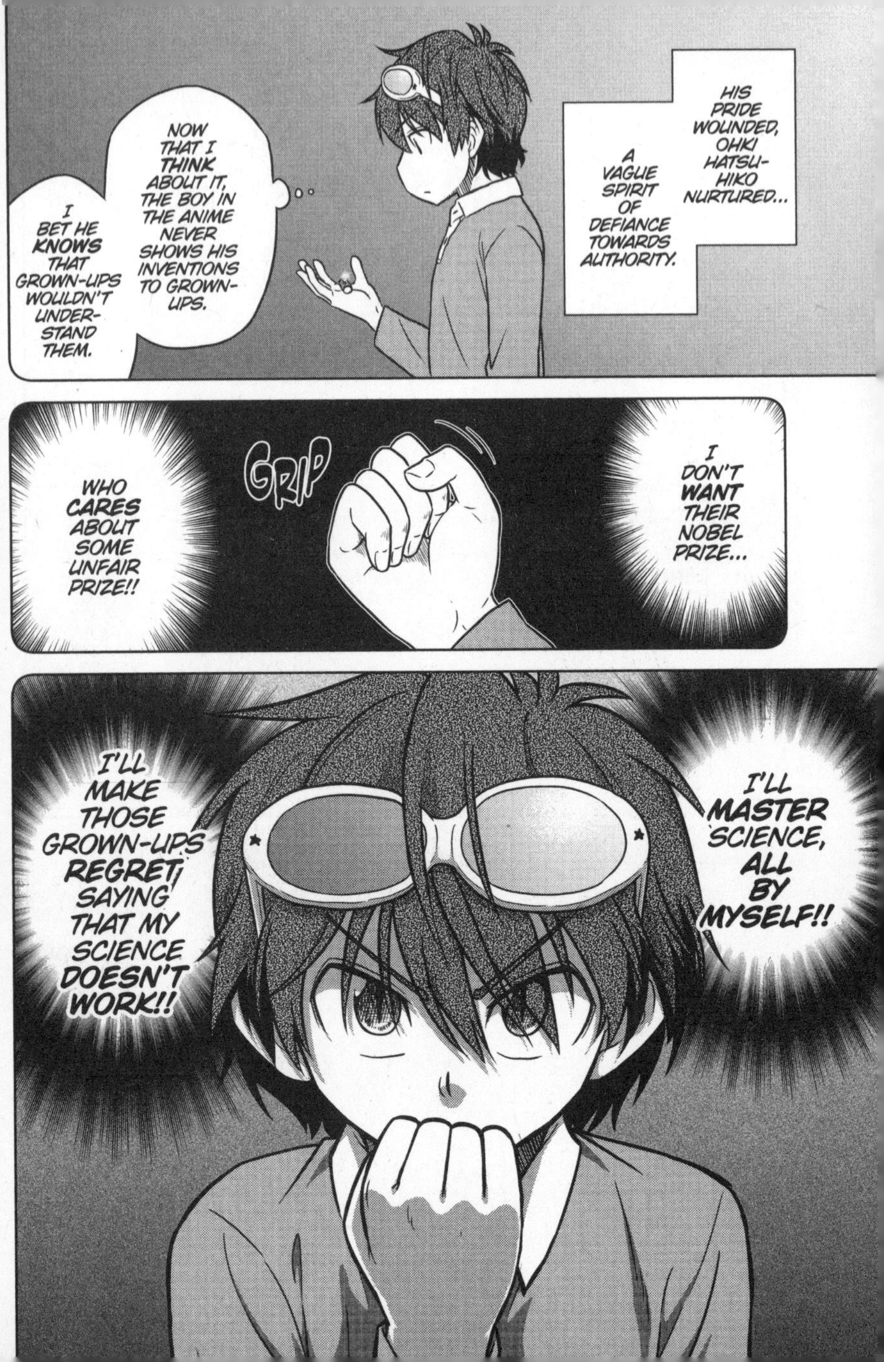
HIS PRIDE WOUNDED, OHKI HATSUHIKO NURTURED...
A VAGUE SPIRIT OF DEFIANCE TOWARDS AUTHORITY.
NOW THAT I THINK ABOUT IT, THE BOY IN THE ANIME NEVER SHOWS HIS INVENTIONS TO GROWN-UPS.
I BET HE KNOWS THAT GROWN-UPS WOULDN'T UNDERSTAND THEM.
I DON'T WANT THEIR NOBEL PRIZE...
GRIP
WHO CARES ABOUT SOME UNFAIR PRIZE!!
I'LL MASTER SCIENCE, ALL BY MYSELF!!
I'LL MAKE THOSE GROWN-UPS REGRET SAYING THAT MY SCIENCE DOESN'T WORK!!

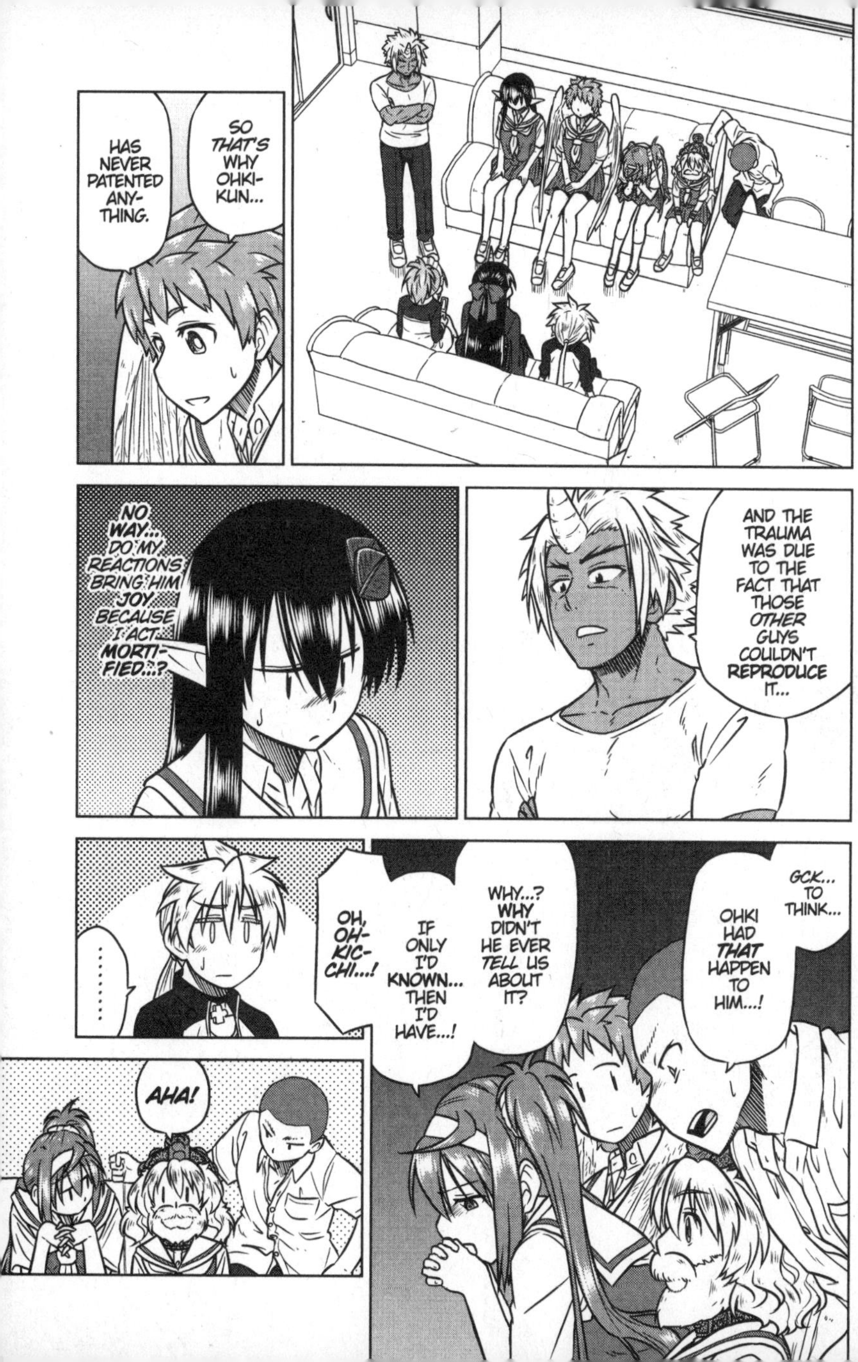
SO THAT'S WHY OHKI-KUN...
HAS NEVER PATENTED ANYTHING.
AND THE TRAUMA WAS DUE TO THE FACT THAT THOSE OTHER GUYS COULDN'T REPRODUCE IT...
NO WAY... DO MY REACTIONS BRING HIM JOY BECAUSE I ACT MORTIFIED...?
GCK... TO THINK...
OHKI HAD THAT HAPPEN TO HIM...!
WHY...? WHY DIDN'T HE EVER TELL US ABOUT IT?
IF ONLY I'D KNOWN... THEN I'D HAVE...!
OH, OH-KICCHI...!
......
AHA!

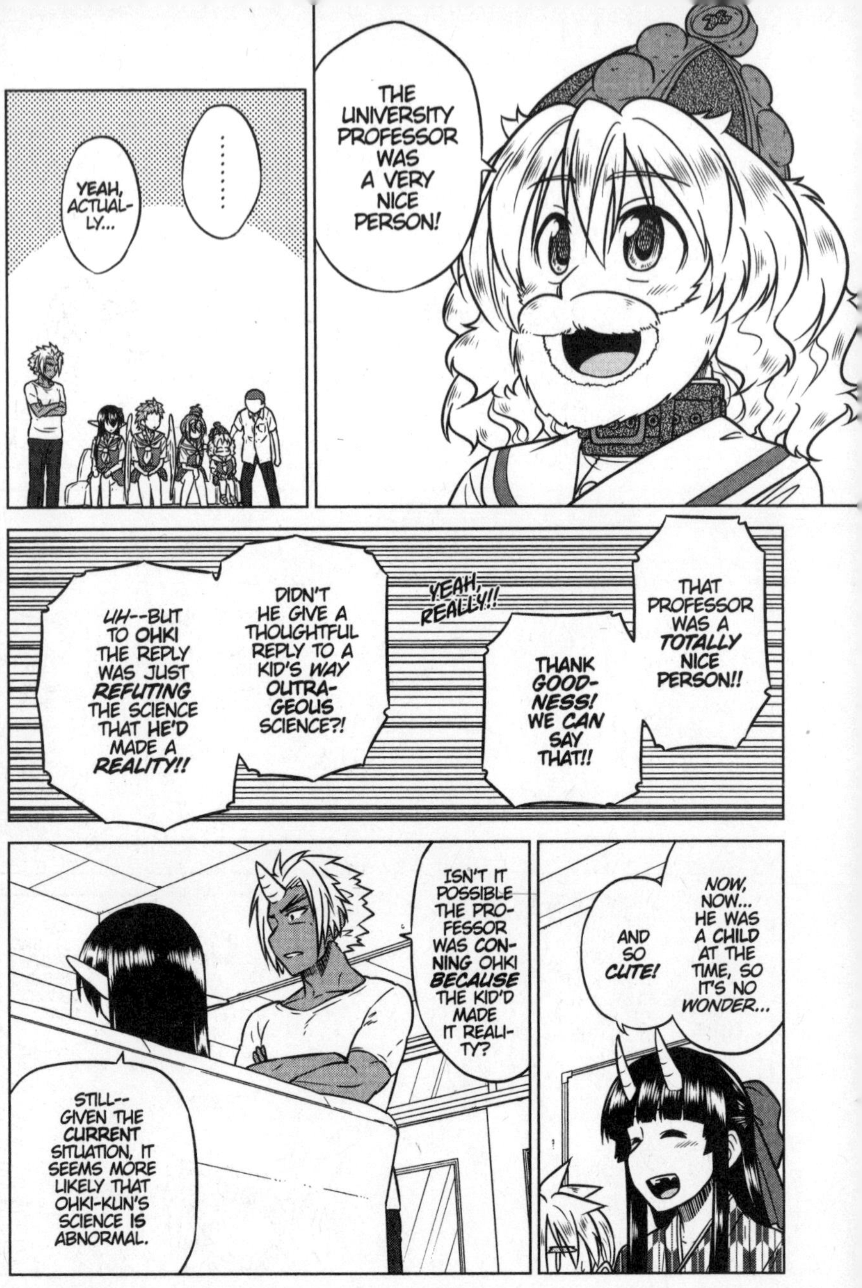
THE UNIVERSITY PROFESSOR WAS A VERY NICE PERSON!
......
YEAH, ACTUALLY...
THAT PROFESSOR WAS A TOTALLY NICE PERSON!!
THANK GOODNESS! WE CAN SAY THAT!!
YEAH, REALLY!!
DIDN'T HE GIVE A THOUGHTFUL REPLY TO A KID'S WAY OUTRAGEOUS SCIENCE?!
UH--BUT TO OHKI THE REPLY WAS JUST REFUTING THE SCIENCE THAT HE'D MADE A REALITY!!
NOW, NOW... HE WAS A CHILD AT THE TIME, SO IT'S NO WONDER...
AND SO CUTE!
ISN'T IT POSSIBLE THE PROFESSOR WAS CONNING OHKI BECAUSE THE KID'D MADE IT REALITY?
STILL-- GIVEN THE CURRENT SITUATION, IT SEEMS MORE LIKELY THAT OHKI-KUN'S SCIENCE IS ABNORMAL.

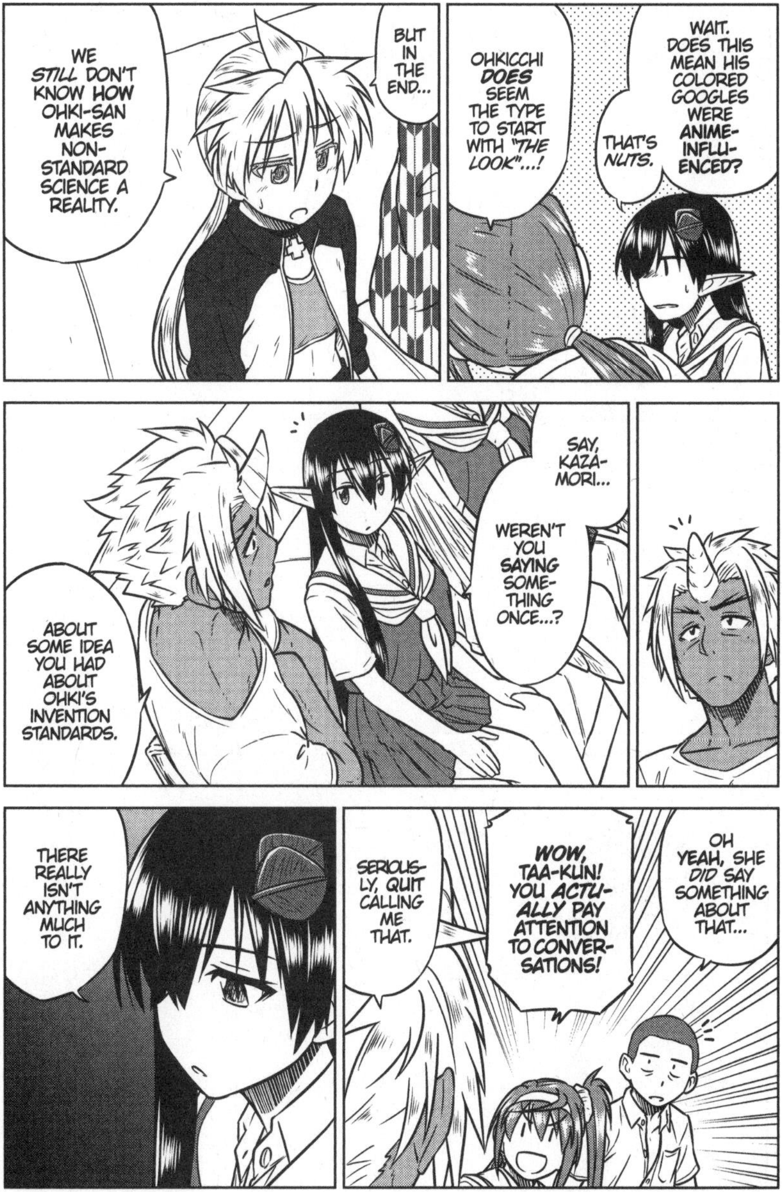
WAIT. DOES THIS MEAN HIS COLORED GOOGLES WERE ANIME-INFLUENCED?
THAT'S NUTS.
OHKICCHI DOES SEEM THE TYPE TO START WITH "THE LOOK"...!
BUT IN THE END...
WE STILL DON'T KNOW HOW OHKI-SAN MAKES NON-STANDARD SCIENCE A REALITY.
SAY, KAZAMORI...
WEREN'T YOU SAYING SOMETHING ONCE...?
ABOUT SOME IDEA YOU HAD ABOUT OHKI'S INVENTION STANDARDS.
OH YEAH, SHE DID SAY SOMETHING ABOUT THAT...
WOW, TAA-KUN! YOU ACTUALLY PAY ATTENTION TO CONVERSATIONS!
SERIOUSLY, QUIT CALLING ME THAT.
THERE REALLY ISN'T ANYTHING MUCH TO IT.

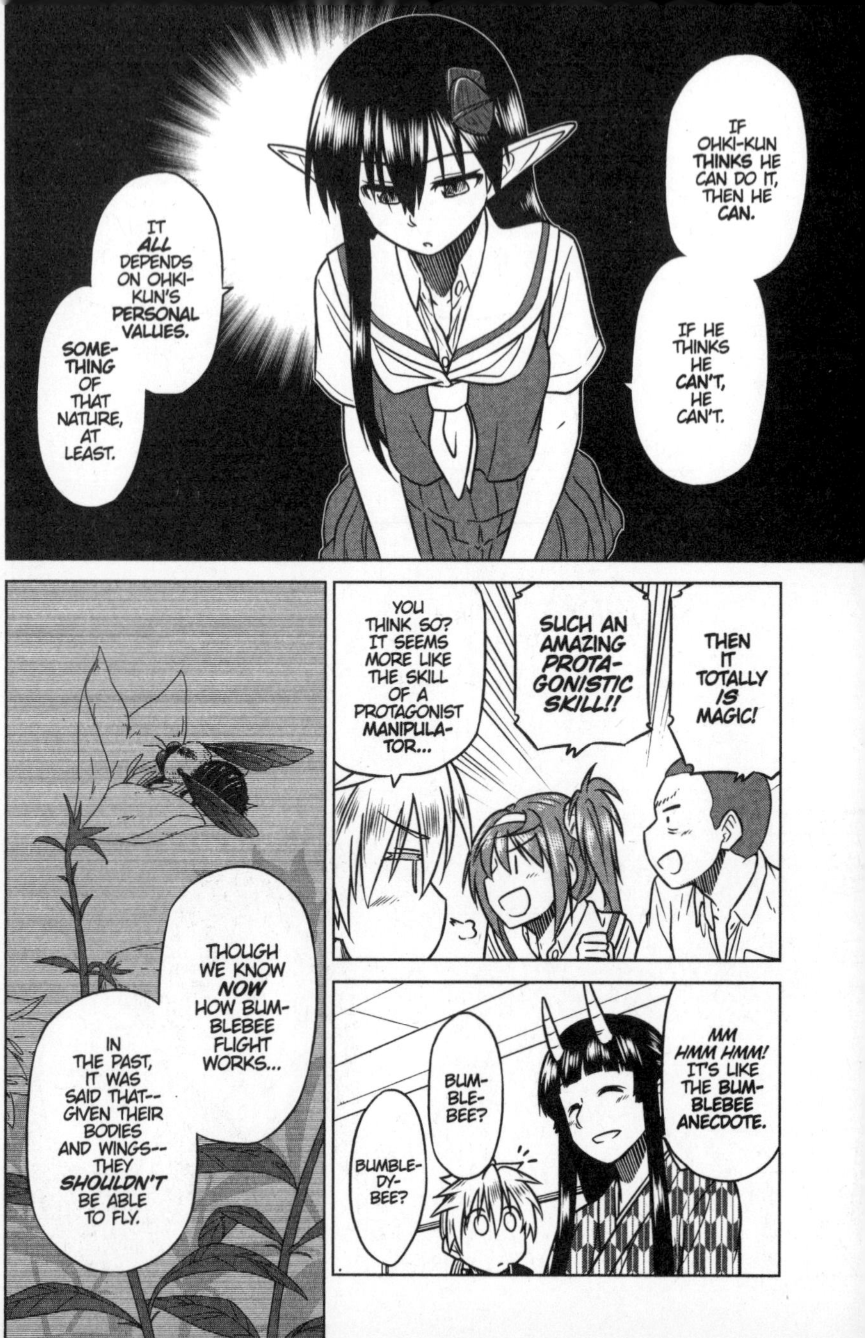
IF OHKI-KUN THINKS HE CAN DO IT, THEN HE CAN.
IF HE THINKS HE CAN'T, HE CAN'T.
IT *ALL* DEPENDS ON OHKI-KUN'S PERSONAL VALUES.
SOME-THING OF THAT NATURE, AT LEAST.
THEN IT TOTALLY *IS* MAGIC!
SUCH AN AMAZING *PROTA-GONISTIC* SKILL!!
YOU THINK SO? IT SEEMS MORE LIKE THE SKILL OF A PROTAGONIST MANIPULA-TOR...
MM HMM HMM! IT'S LIKE THE BUM-BLEBEE ANECDOTE.
BUM-BLE-BEE?
BUMBLE-DY-BEE?
THOUGH WE KNOW *NOW* HOW BUM-BLEBEE FLIGHT WORKS...
IN THE PAST, IT WAS SAID THAT-- GIVEN THEIR BODIES AND WINGS-- THEY *SHOULDN'T* BE ABLE TO FLY.

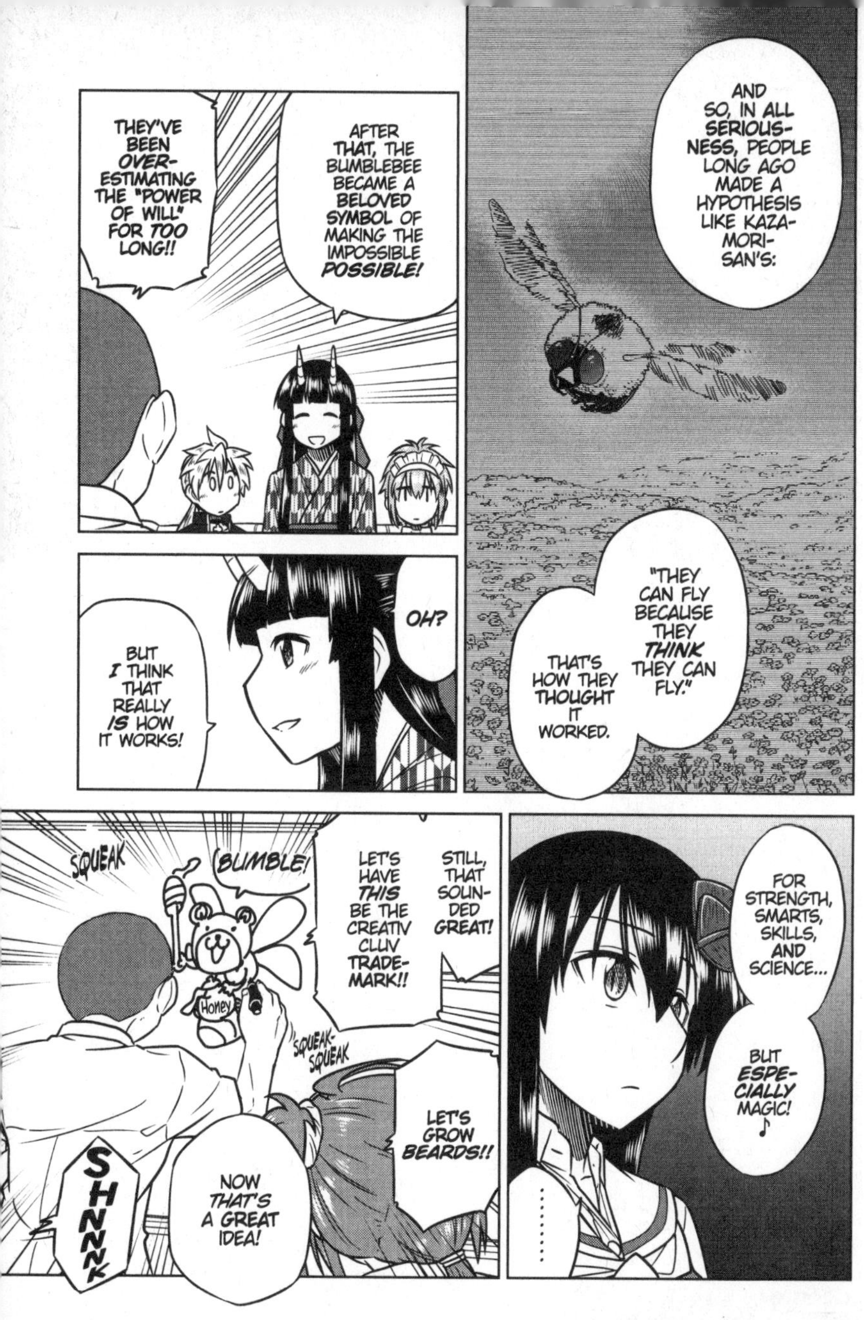
AND SO, IN ALL SERIOUSNESS, PEOPLE LONG AGO MADE A HYPOTHESIS LIKE KAZAMORI-SAN'S:
"THEY CAN FLY BECAUSE THEY THINK THEY CAN FLY."
THAT'S HOW THEY THOUGHT IT WORKED.
AFTER THAT, THE BUMBLEBEE BECAME A BELOVED SYMBOL OF MAKING THE IMPOSSIBLE POSSIBLE!
THEY'VE BEEN OVER-ESTIMATING THE "POWER OF WILL" FOR TOO LONG!!
OH?
BUT I THINK THAT REALLY IS HOW IT WORKS!
FOR STRENGTH, SMARTS, SKILLS, AND SCIENCE...
BUT ESPECIALLY MAGIC! ♪
......
STILL, THAT SOUNDED GREAT!
LET'S HAVE THIS BE THE CREATIV CLUV TRADEMARK!!
BUMBLE!
SQUEAK
Honey
SQUEAK-SQUEAK
LET'S GROW BEARDS!!
NOW THAT'S A GREAT IDEA!
SHNNNK

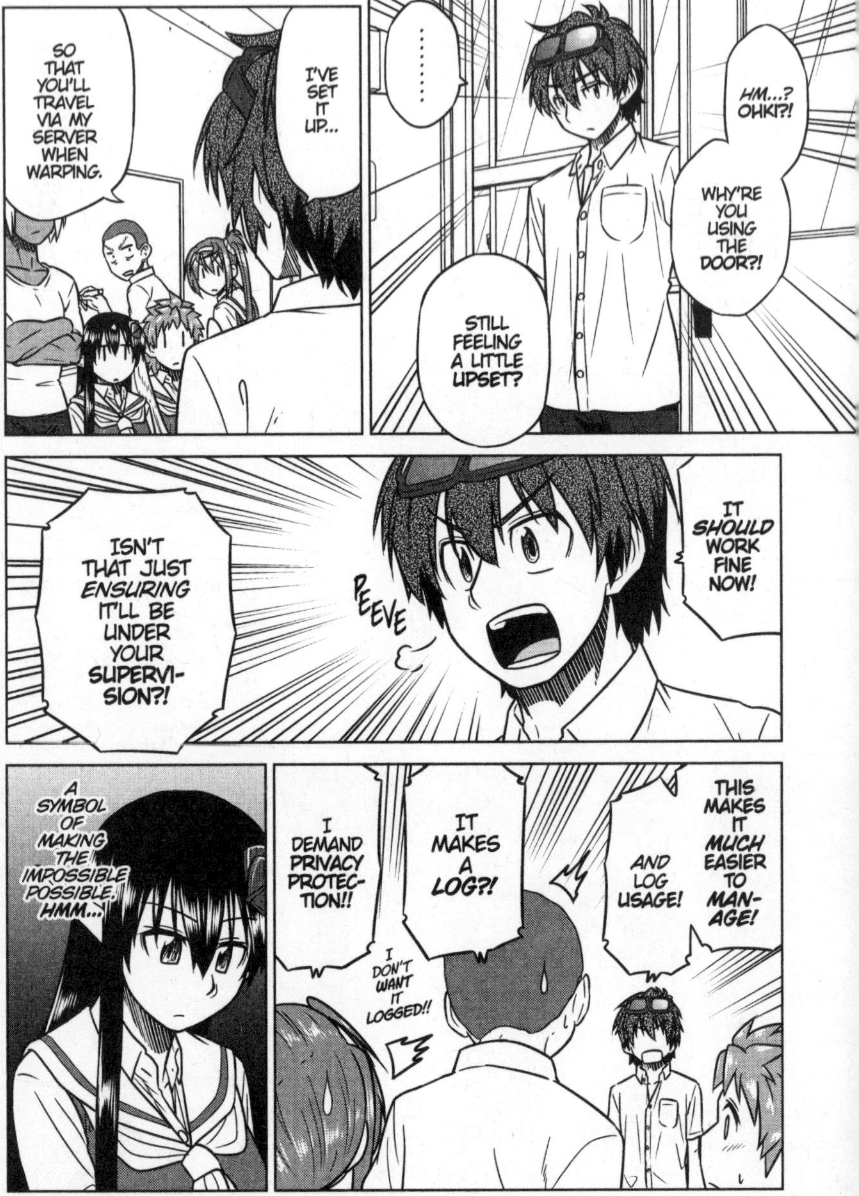
HM...? OHKI?!
WHY'RE YOU USING THE DOOR?!
......
STILL FEELING A LITTLE UPSET?
I'VE SET IT UP...
SO THAT YOU'LL TRAVEL VIA MY SERVER WHEN WARPING.
IT SHOULD WORK FINE NOW!
PEEVE
ISN'T THAT JUST ENSURING IT'LL BE UNDER YOUR SUPERVISION?!
THIS MAKES IT MUCH EASIER TO MANAGE!
AND LOG USAGE!
IT MAKES A LOG?!
I DEMAND PRIVACY PROTECTION!!
I DON'T WANT IT LOGGED!!
A SYMBOL OF MAKING THE IMPOSSIBLE POSSIBLE. HMM...

Chapter 19 • END

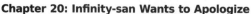

Chapter 20: Infinity-san Wants to Apologize

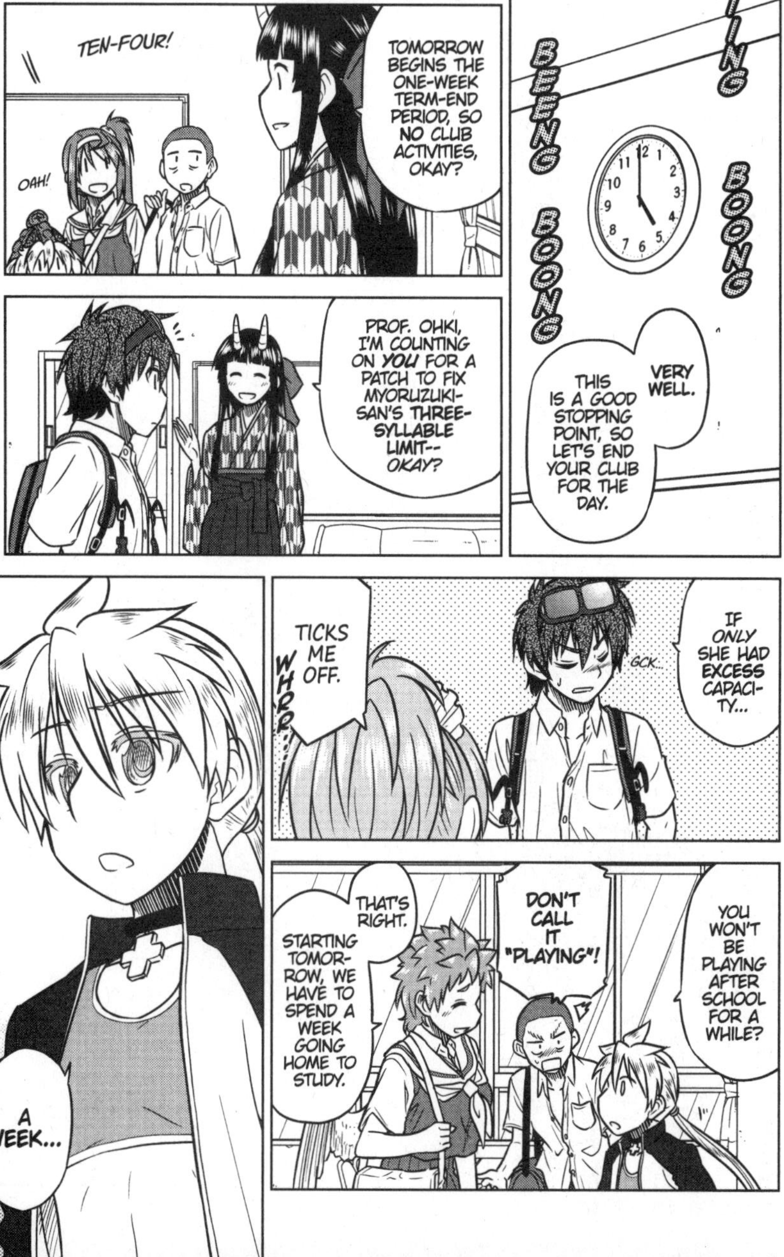
BIING
BOONG
BEENG
BOONG
VERY WELL.
THIS IS A GOOD STOPPING POINT, SO LET'S END YOUR CLUB FOR THE DAY.
TOMORROW BEGINS THE ONE-WEEK TERM-END PERIOD, SO NO CLUB ACTIVITIES, OKAY?
TEN-FOUR!
OAH!
PROF. OHKI, I'M COUNTING ON YOU FOR A PATCH TO FIX MYORUZUKI-SAN'S THREE-SYLLABLE LIMIT-- OKAY?
IF ONLY SHE HAD EXCESS CAPACITY...
GCK...
TICKS ME OFF.
WHRR...
YOU WON'T BE PLAYING AFTER SCHOOL FOR A WHILE?
DON'T CALL IT "PLAYING"!
THAT'S RIGHT.
STARTING TOMORROW, WE HAVE TO SPEND A WEEK GOING HOME TO STUDY.
A WEEK...

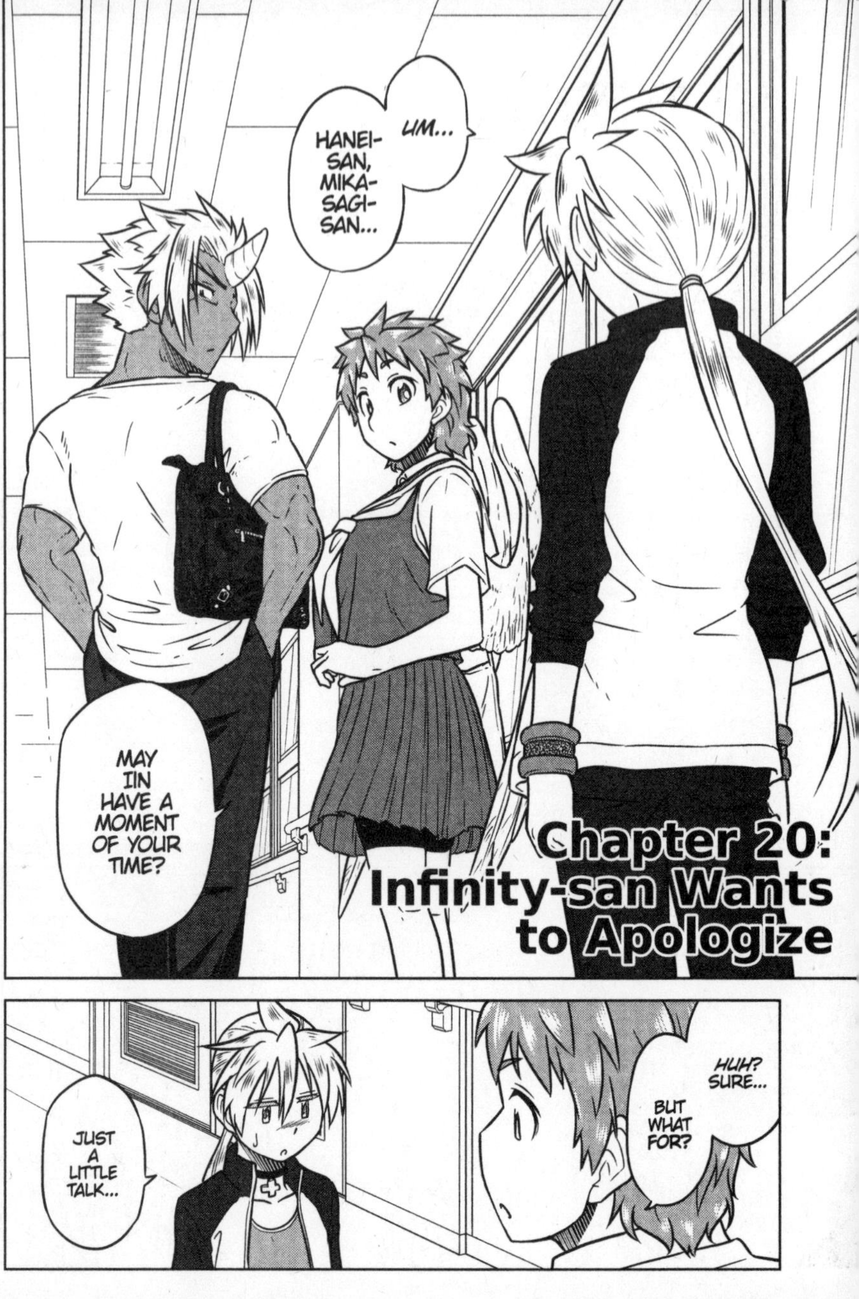
UM...
HANEI-SAN, MIKA-SAGI-SAN...
MAY IIN HAVE A MOMENT OF YOUR TIME?
Chapter 20: Infinity-san Wants to Apologize
HUH? SURE...
BUT WHAT FOR?
JUST A LITTLE TALK...

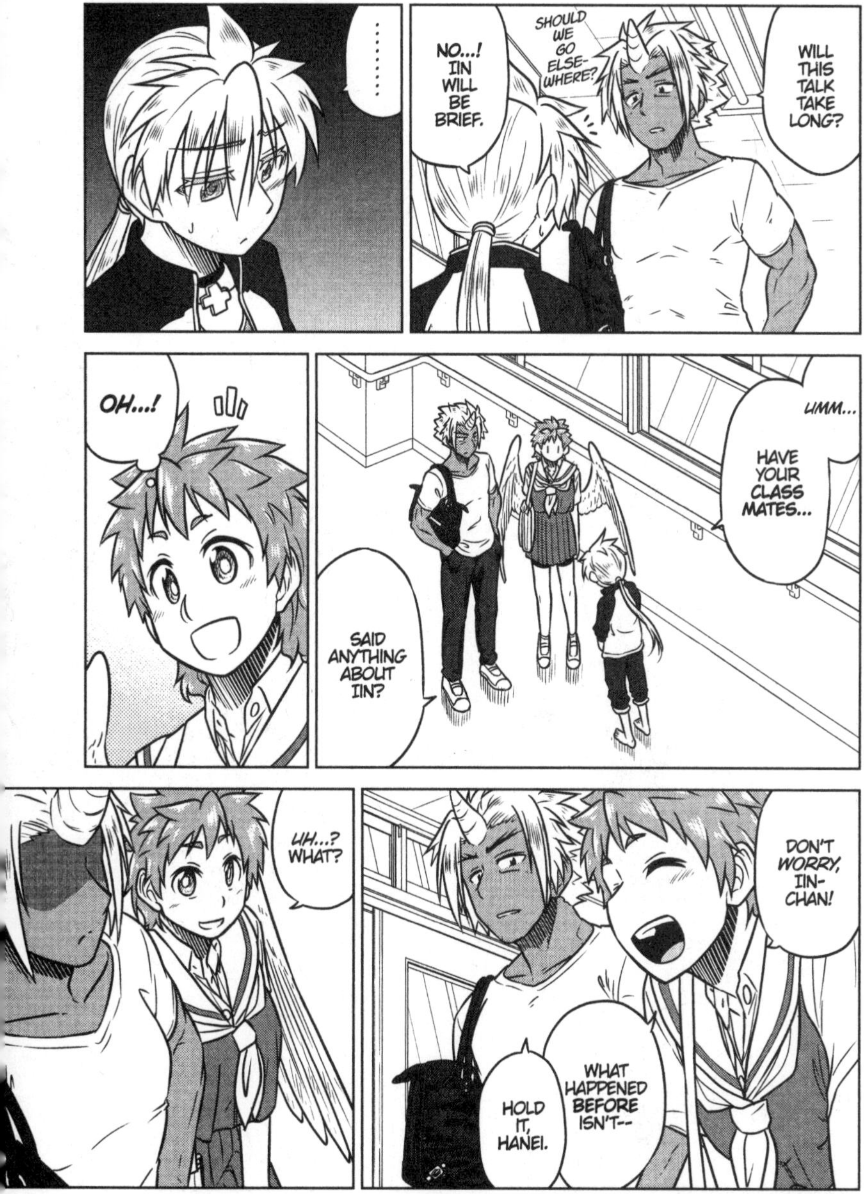
WILL THIS TALK TAKE LONG?
SHOULD WE GO ELSEWHERE?
NO...! IIN WILL BE BRIEF.
......
UMM...
HAVE YOUR CLASS MATES...
SAID ANYTHING ABOUT IIN?
OH...!
DON'T *WORRY*, IIN-CHAN!
WHAT HAPPENED BEFORE ISN'T--
HOLD IT, HANEI.
UH...? WHAT?

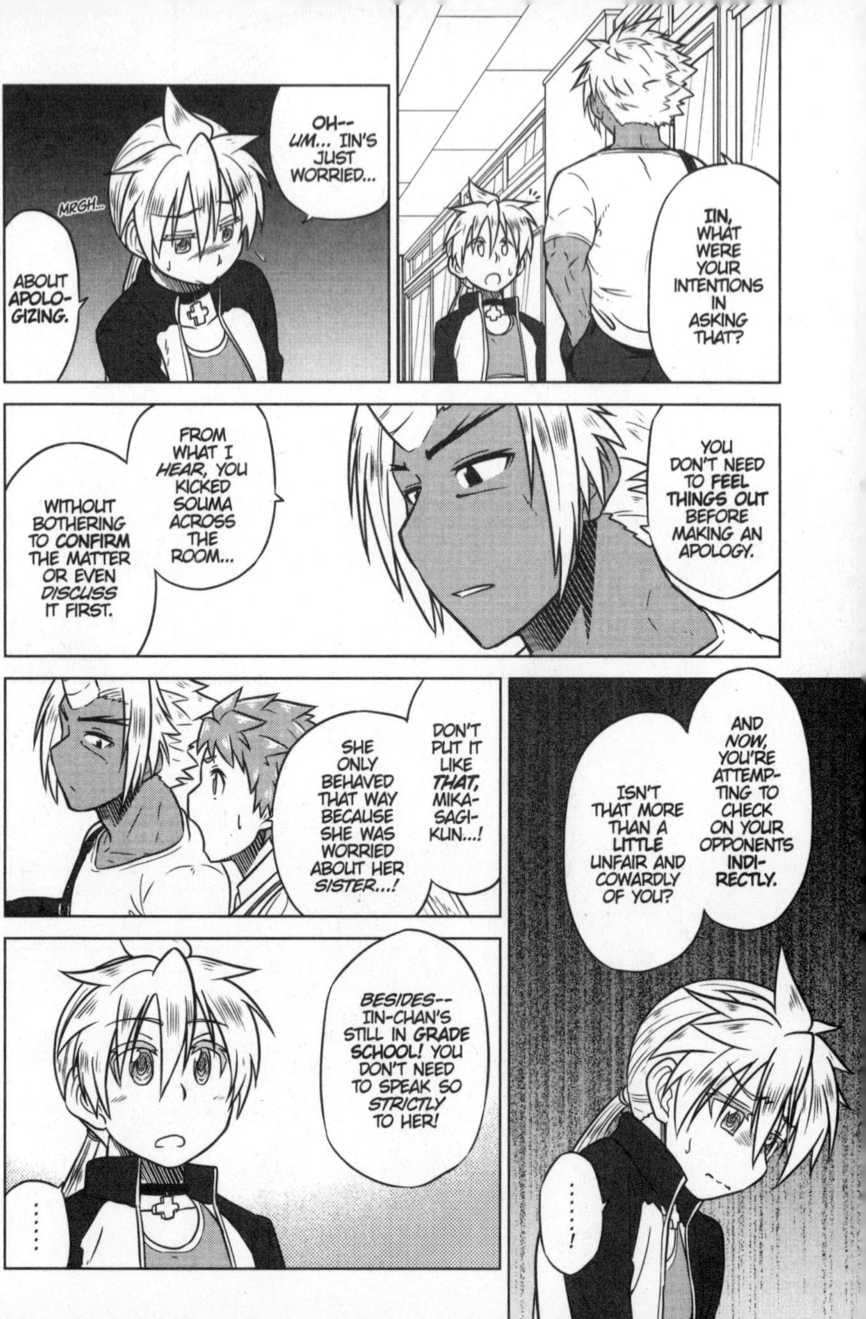
IIN, WHAT WERE YOUR INTENTIONS IN ASKING THAT?
OH-- UM... IIN'S JUST WORRIED...
MRGH...
ABOUT APOLOGIZING.
YOU DON'T NEED TO FEEL THINGS OUT BEFORE MAKING AN APOLOGY.
FROM WHAT I HEAR, YOU KICKED SOUMA ACROSS THE ROOM...
WITHOUT BOTHERING TO CONFIRM THE MATTER OR EVEN DISCUSS IT FIRST.
AND NOW, YOU'RE ATTEMPTING TO CHECK ON YOUR OPPONENTS INDIRECTLY.
ISN'T THAT MORE THAN A LITTLE UNFAIR AND COWARDLY OF YOU?
......!
DON'T PUT IT LIKE THAT, MIKASAGI-KUN...!
SHE ONLY BEHAVED THAT WAY BECAUSE SHE WAS WORRIED ABOUT HER SISTER...!
BESIDES-- IIN-CHAN'S STILL IN GRADE SCHOOL! YOU DON'T NEED TO SPEAK SO STRICTLY TO HER!
......

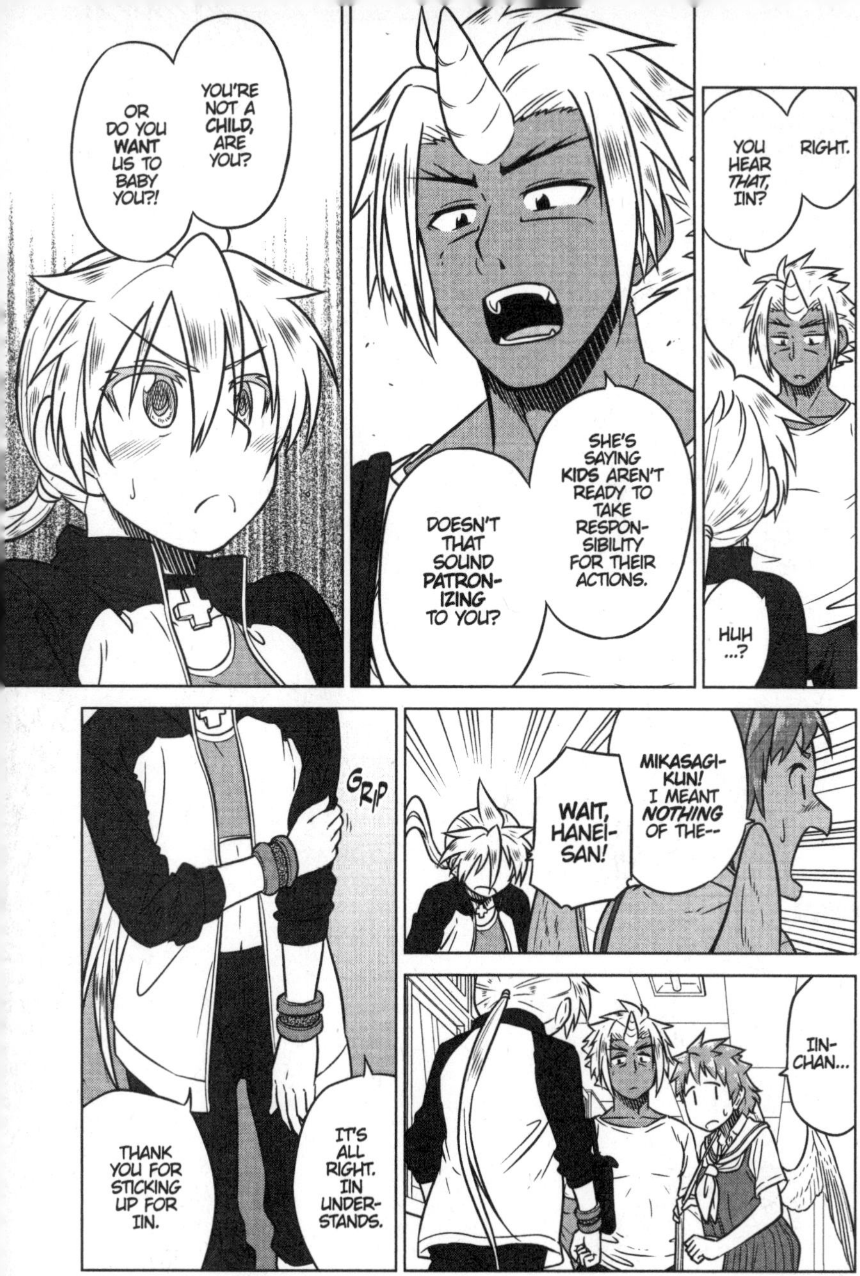
RIGHT.
YOU HEAR *THAT*, IIN?
HUH ...?
SHE'S SAYING KIDS AREN'T READY TO TAKE RESPONSIBILITY FOR THEIR ACTIONS.
DOESN'T THAT SOUND **PATRONIZING** TO YOU?
YOU'RE NOT A CHILD, ARE YOU?
OR DO YOU **WANT** US TO BABY YOU?!
MIKASAGI-KUN! I MEANT ***NOTHING*** OF THE--
WAIT, HANEI-SAN!
IIN-CHAN...
GRIP
IT'S ALL RIGHT. IIN UNDERSTANDS.
THANK YOU FOR STICKING UP FOR IIN.

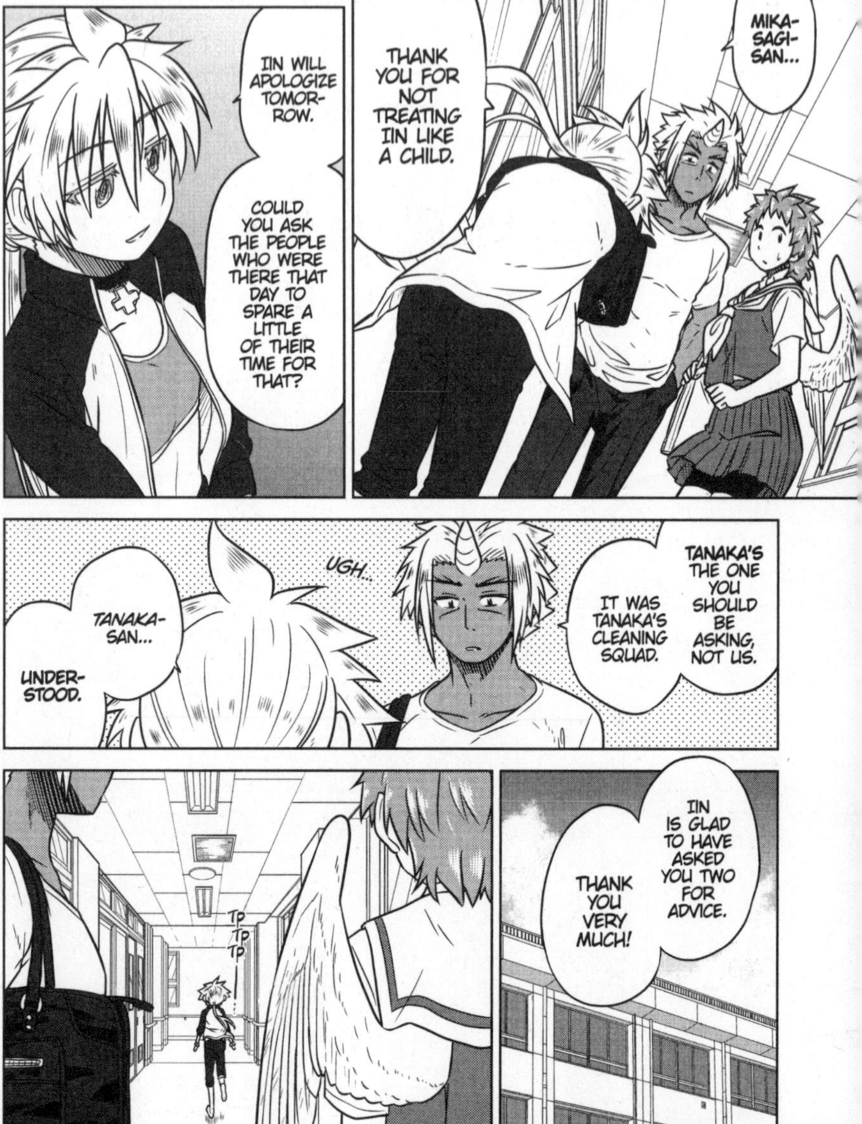
MIKA-SAGI-SAN...
THANK YOU FOR NOT TREATING IIN LIKE A CHILD.
IIN WILL APOLOGIZE TOMOR-ROW.
COULD YOU ASK THE PEOPLE WHO WERE THERE THAT DAY TO SPARE A LITTLE OF THEIR TIME FOR THAT?
TANAKA'S THE ONE YOU SHOULD BE ASKING, NOT US.
IT WAS TANAKA'S CLEANING SQUAD.
UGH...
TANAKA-SAN...
UNDER-STOOD.
IIN IS GLAD TO HAVE ASKED YOU TWO FOR ADVICE.
THANK YOU VERY MUCH!
TP TP TP

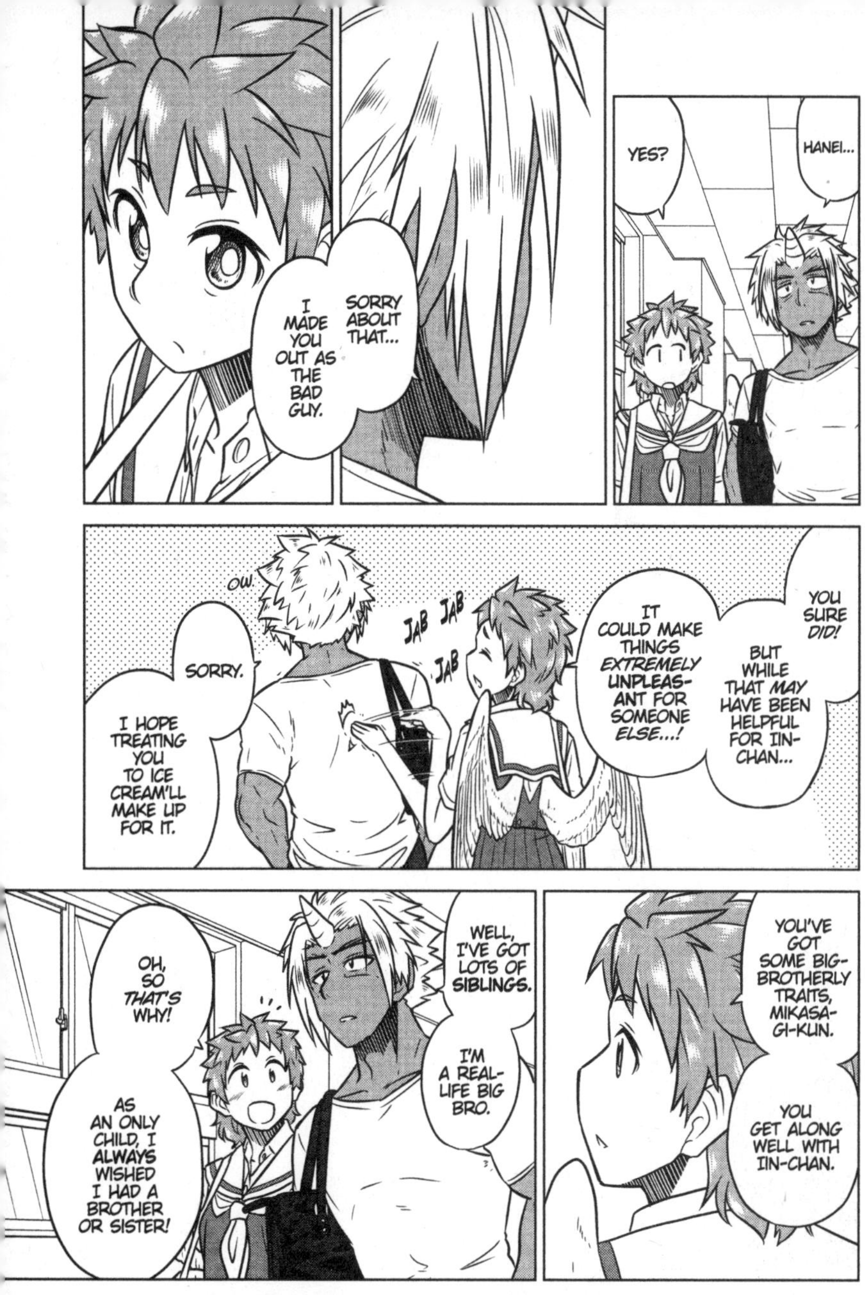
HANEI...
YES?
SORRY ABOUT THAT...
I MADE YOU OUT AS THE BAD GUY.
YOU SURE DID!
BUT WHILE THAT MAY HAVE BEEN HELPFUL FOR IIN-CHAN...
IT COULD MAKE THINGS EXTREMELY UNPLEASANT FOR SOMEONE ELSE...!
JAB JAB
JAB
OW.
SORRY.
I HOPE TREATING YOU TO ICE CREAM'LL MAKE UP FOR IT.
YOU'VE GOT SOME BIG-BROTHERLY TRAITS, MIKASAGI-KUN.
YOU GET ALONG WELL WITH IIN-CHAN.
WELL, I'VE GOT LOTS OF SIBLINGS.
I'M A REAL-LIFE BIG BRO.
OH, SO THAT'S WHY!
AS AN ONLY CHILD, I ALWAYS WISHED I HAD A BROTHER OR SISTER!

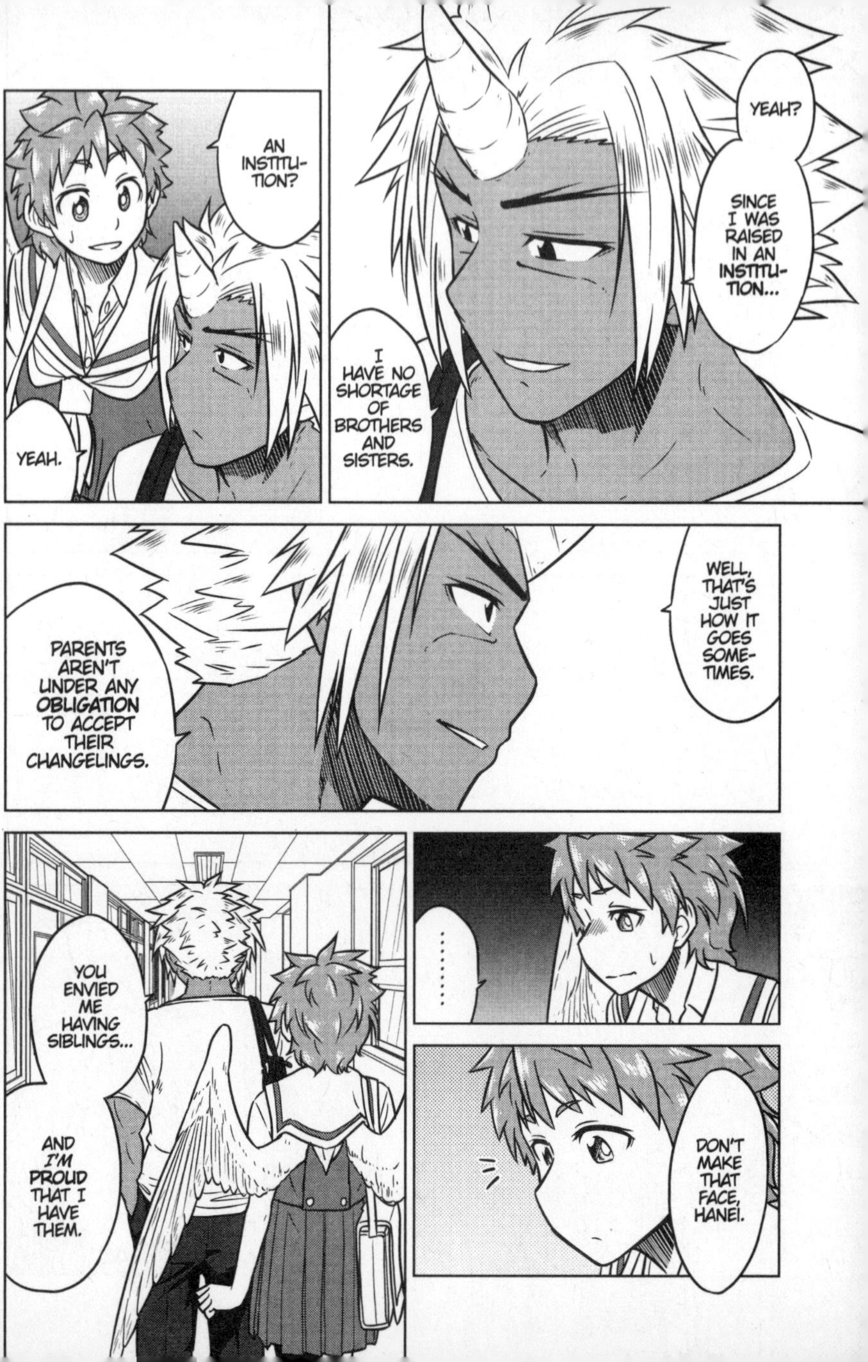
YEAH?
SINCE I WAS RAISED IN AN INSTITUTION...
I HAVE NO SHORTAGE OF BROTHERS AND SISTERS.
AN INSTITUTION?
YEAH.
WELL, THAT'S JUST HOW IT GOES SOMETIMES.
PARENTS AREN'T UNDER ANY OBLIGATION TO ACCEPT THEIR CHANGELINGS.
......
DON'T MAKE THAT FACE, HANEI.
YOU ENVIED ME HAVING SIBLINGS...
AND I'M PROUD THAT I HAVE THEM.

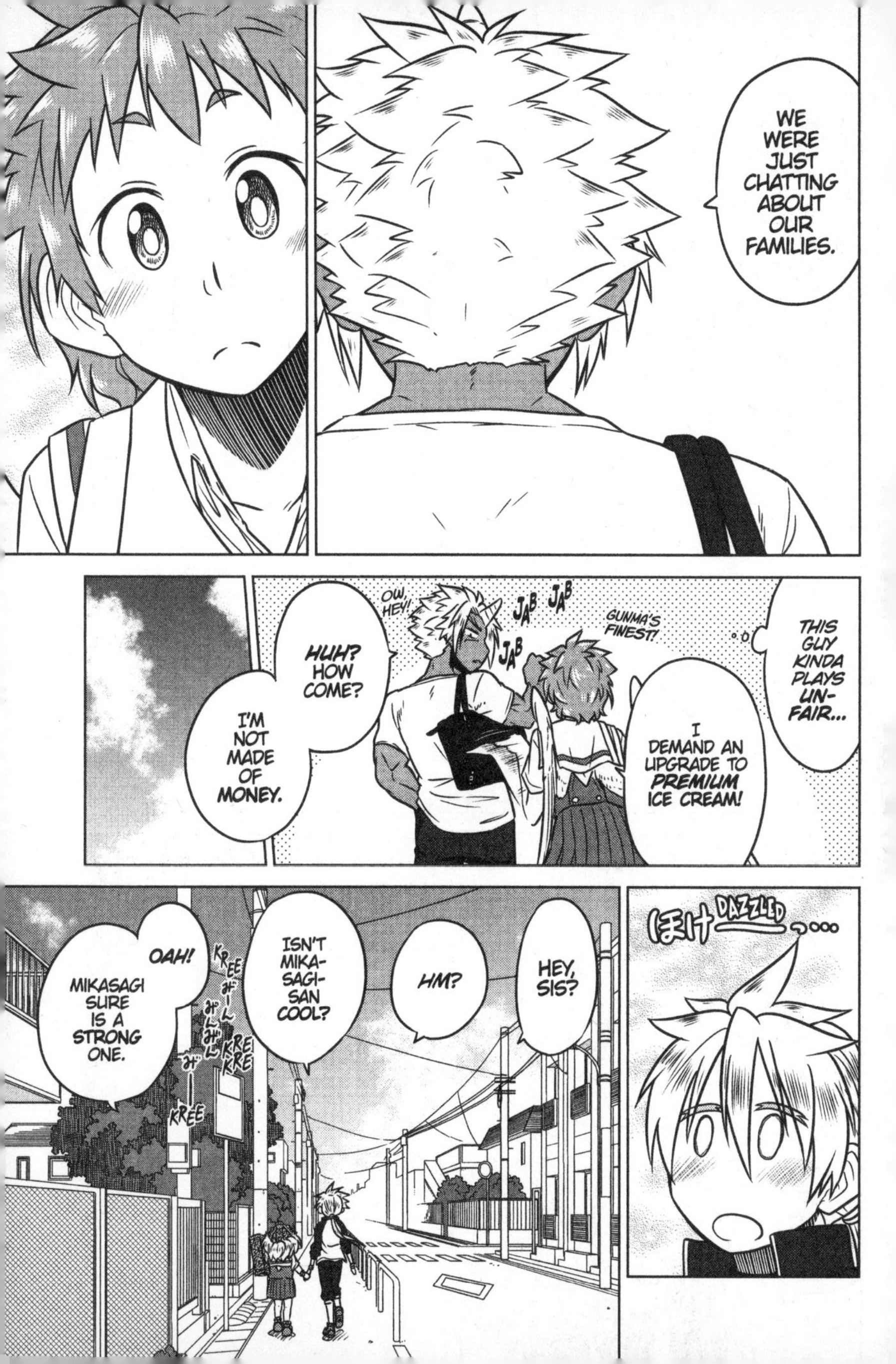

WE WERE JUST CHATTING ABOUT OUR FAMILIES.
THIS GUY KINDA PLAYS UN-FAIR...
GUNMA'S FINEST!
I DEMAND AN UPGRADE TO PREMIUM ICE CREAM!
JAB JAB JAB
OW, HEY!
HUH? HOW COME?
I'M NOT MADE OF MONEY.
ほけ DAZZLED っ...
HEY, SIS?
HM?
ISN'T MIKASAGI-SAN COOL?
KREE みーん
KREE KREE みんみん
KREE みー
OAH! MIKASAGI SURE IS A STRONG ONE.

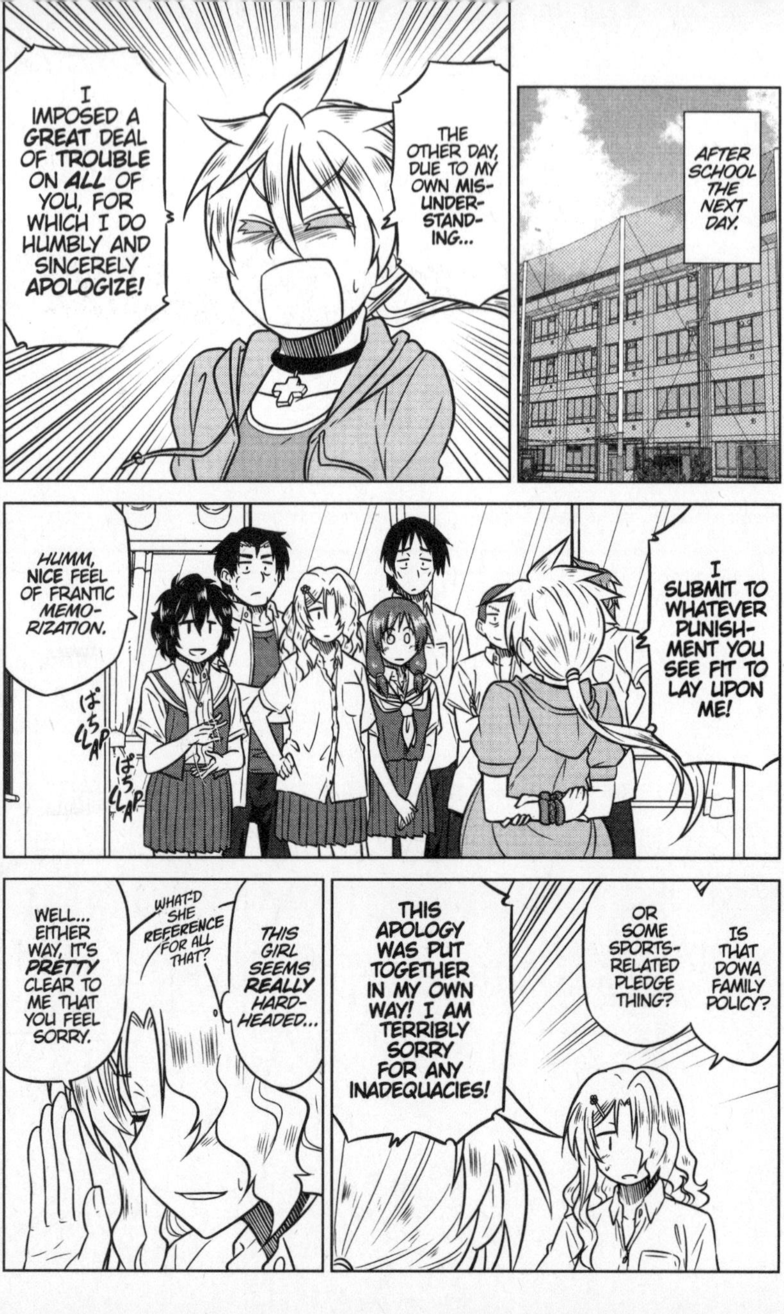
AFTER SCHOOL THE NEXT DAY.
THE OTHER DAY, DUE TO MY OWN MISUNDERSTANDING...
I IMPOSED A GREAT DEAL OF TROUBLE ON ALL OF YOU, FOR WHICH I DO HUMBLY AND SINCERELY APOLOGIZE!
I SUBMIT TO WHATEVER PUNISHMENT YOU SEE FIT TO LAY UPON ME!
HUMM, NICE FEEL OF FRANTIC MEMORIZATION.
ぱち CLAP
ぱち CLAP
IS THAT DOWA FAMILY POLICY?
OR SOME SPORTS-RELATED PLEDGE THING?
THIS APOLOGY WAS PUT TOGETHER IN MY OWN WAY! I AM TERRIBLY SORRY FOR ANY INADEQUACIES!
THIS GIRL SEEMS REALLY HARD-HEADED...
WHAT'D SHE REFERENCE FOR ALL THAT?
WELL... EITHER WAY, IT'S PRETTY CLEAR TO ME THAT YOU FEEL SORRY.

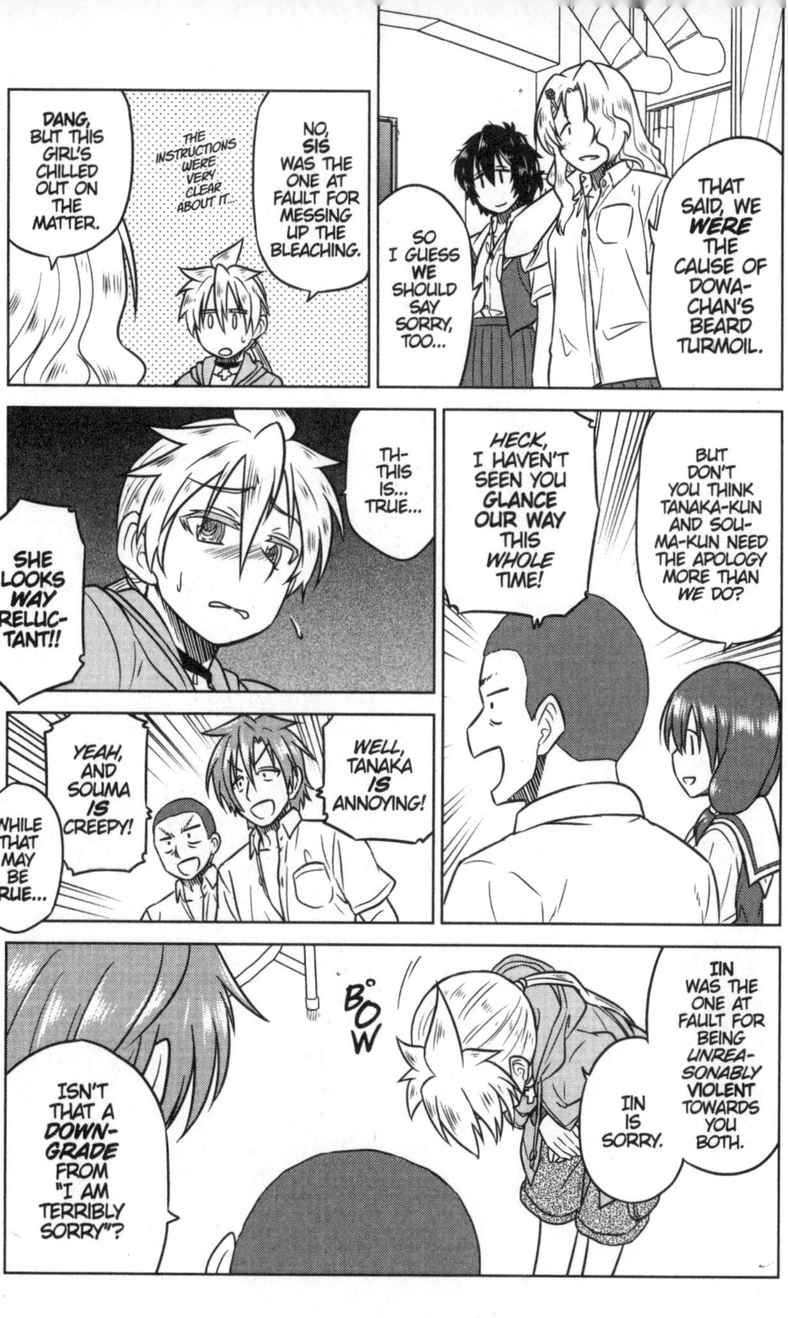
THAT SAID, WE WERE THE CAUSE OF DOWA-CHAN'S BEARD TURMOIL.
SO I GUESS WE SHOULD SAY SORRY, TOO...
NO, SIS WAS THE ONE AT FAULT FOR MESSING UP THE BLEACHING.
THE INSTRUCTIONS WERE VERY CLEAR ABOUT IT...
DANG, BUT THIS GIRL'S CHILLED OUT ON THE MATTER.
BUT DON'T YOU THINK TANAKA-KUN AND SOUMA-KUN NEED THE APOLOGY MORE THAN WE DO?
HECK, I HAVEN'T SEEN YOU GLANCE OUR WAY THIS WHOLE TIME!
TH- THIS IS... TRUE...
SHE LOOKS WAY RELUCTANT!!
WELL, TANAKA IS ANNOYING!
YEAH, AND SOUMA IS CREEPY!
WHILE THAT MAY BE TRUE...
IIN WAS THE ONE AT FAULT FOR BEING UNREASONABLY VIOLENT TOWARDS YOU BOTH.
IIN IS SORRY.
BOW
ISN'T THAT A DOWNGRADE FROM "I AM TERRIBLY SORRY"?

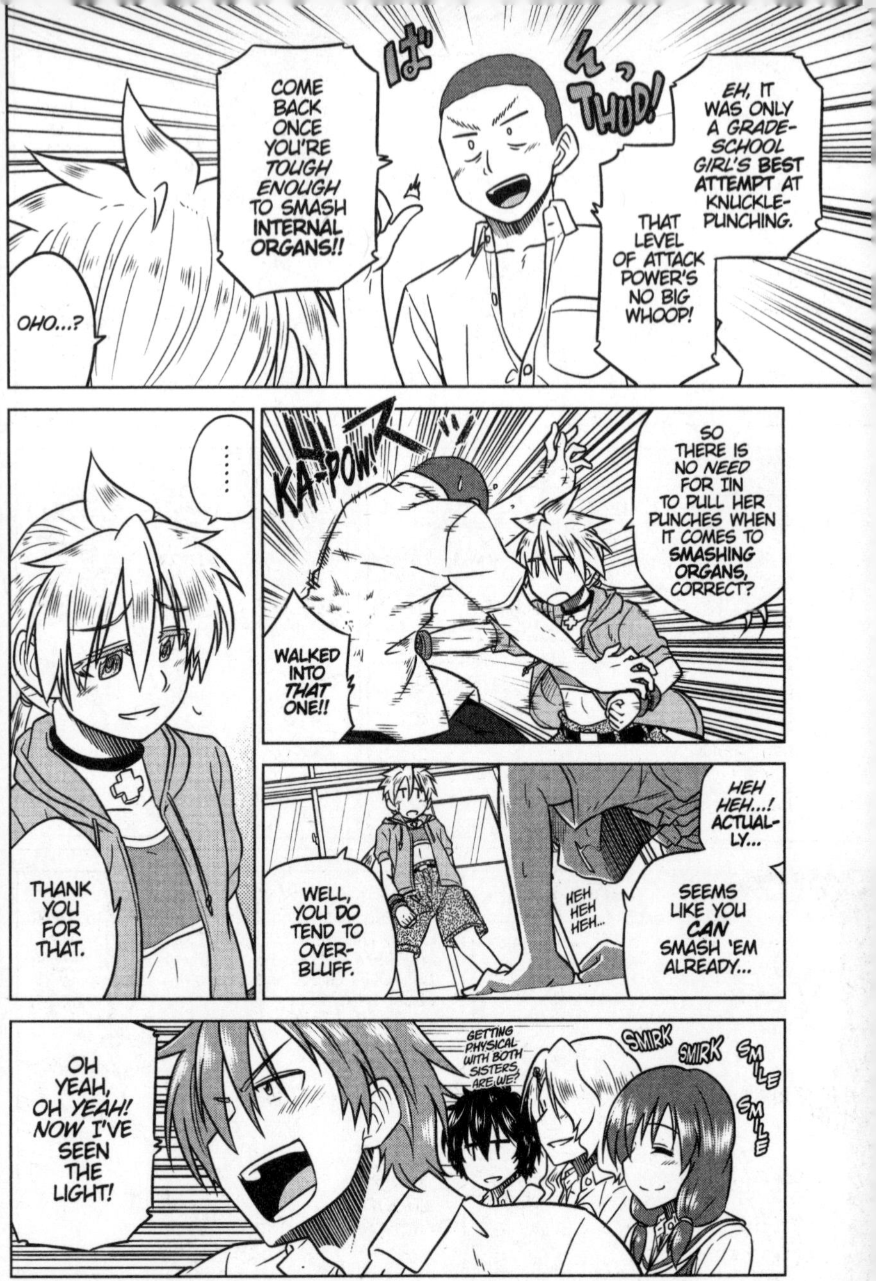
ばんっ
THUD!
EH, IT WAS ONLY A GRADE-SCHOOL GIRL'S BEST ATTEMPT AT KNUCKLE-PUNCHING.
THAT LEVEL OF ATTACK POWER'S NO BIG WHOOP!
COME BACK ONCE YOU'RE TOUGH ENOUGH TO SMASH INTERNAL ORGANS!!
OHO...?
SO THERE IS NO NEED FOR IIN TO PULL HER PUNCHES WHEN IT COMES TO SMASHING ORGANS, CORRECT?
KA-POW!
WALKED INTO THAT ONE!!
HEH HEH...! ACTUALLY...
SEEMS LIKE YOU CAN SMASH 'EM ALREADY...
HEH HEH HEH...
WELL, YOU DO TEND TO OVER-BLUFF.
......
THANK YOU FOR THAT.
SMIRK
SMIRK
SMILE
SMILE
GETTING PHYSICAL WITH BOTH SISTERS, ARE WE?
OH YEAH, OH YEAH! NOW I'VE SEEN THE LIGHT!

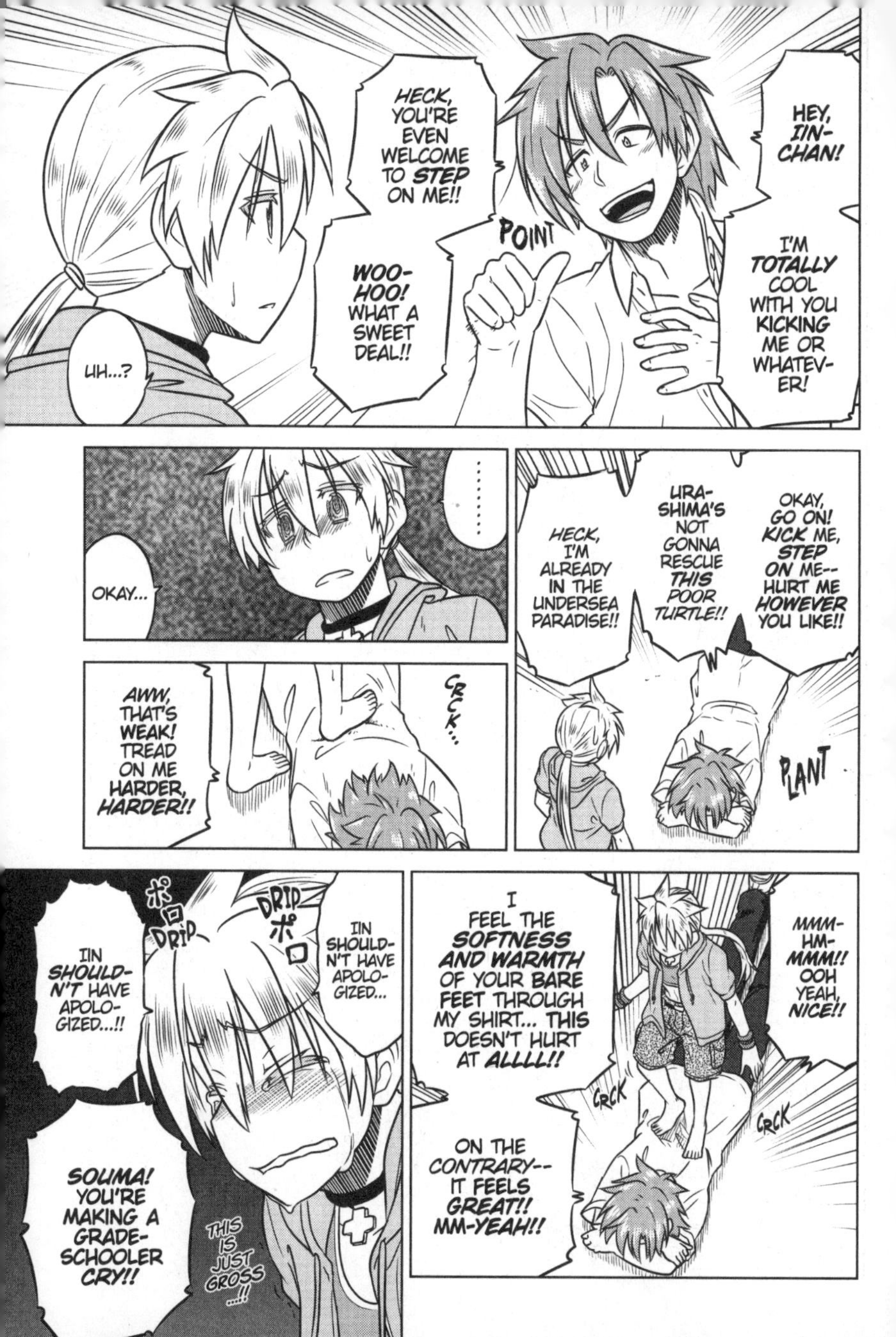

HEY, IIN-CHAN!
I'M TOTALLY COOL WITH YOU KICKING ME OR WHATEVER!
POINT
HECK, YOU'RE EVEN WELCOME TO STEP ON ME!!
WOO-HOO! WHAT A SWEET DEAL!!
UH...?
OKAY, GO ON! KICK ME, STEP ON ME-- HURT ME HOWEVER YOU LIKE!!
URA-SHIMA'S NOT GONNA RESCUE THIS POOR TURTLE!!
HECK, I'M ALREADY IN THE UNDERSEA PARADISE!!
PLANT
......
OKAY...
CRCK...
AWW, THAT'S WEAK! TREAD ON ME HARDER, HARDER!!
MMM-HM-MMM!! OOH YEAH, NICE!!
I FEEL THE SOFTNESS AND WARMTH OF YOUR BARE FEET THROUGH MY SHIRT... THIS DOESN'T HURT AT ALLLL!!
CRCK
CRCK
ON THE CONTRARY-- IT FEELS GREAT!! MM-YEAH!!
ポロ DRIP
IIN SHOULDN'T HAVE APOLOGIZED...
ポロ DRIP
IIN SHOULDN'T HAVE APOLOGIZED...!!
SOUMA! YOU'RE MAKING A GRADE-SCHOOLER CRY!!
THIS IS JUST GROSS...!!

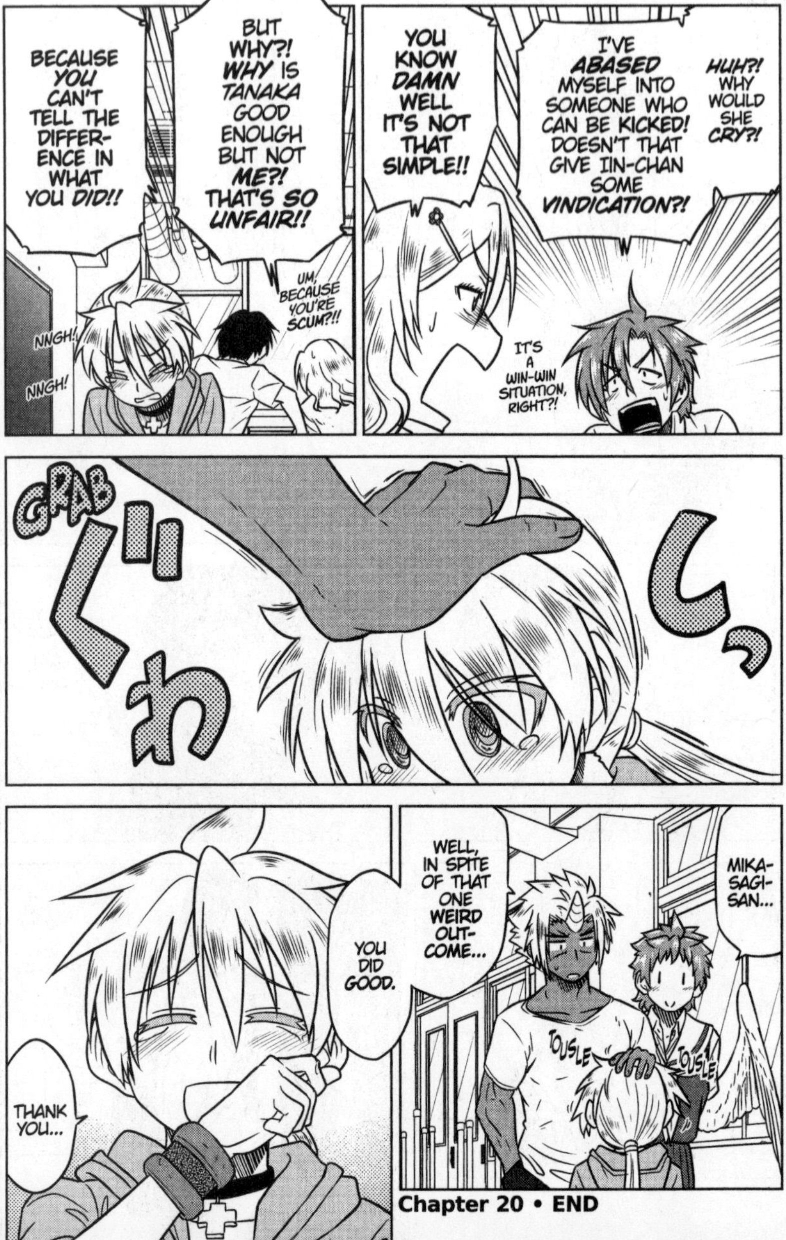
HUH?! WHY WOULD SHE CRY?!
I'VE ABASED MYSELF INTO SOMEONE WHO CAN BE KICKED! DOESN'T THAT GIVE IIN-CHAN SOME VINDICATION?!
IT'S A WIN-WIN SITUATION, RIGHT?!
YOU KNOW DAMN WELL IT'S NOT THAT SIMPLE!!
BUT WHY?! WHY IS TANAKA GOOD ENOUGH BUT NOT ME?! THAT'S SO UNFAIR!!
UM, BECAUSE YOU'RE SCUM?!!
BECAUSE YOU CAN'T TELL THE DIFFERENCE IN WHAT YOU DID!!
NNGH!
NNGH!
GRAB
MIKA-SAGI-SAN...
WELL, IN SPITE OF THAT ONE WEIRD OUT-COME...
TOUSLE
TOUSLE
YOU DID GOOD.
THANK YOU...

Chapter 20 • END

Chapter 21: Hanei-san Wants to Know

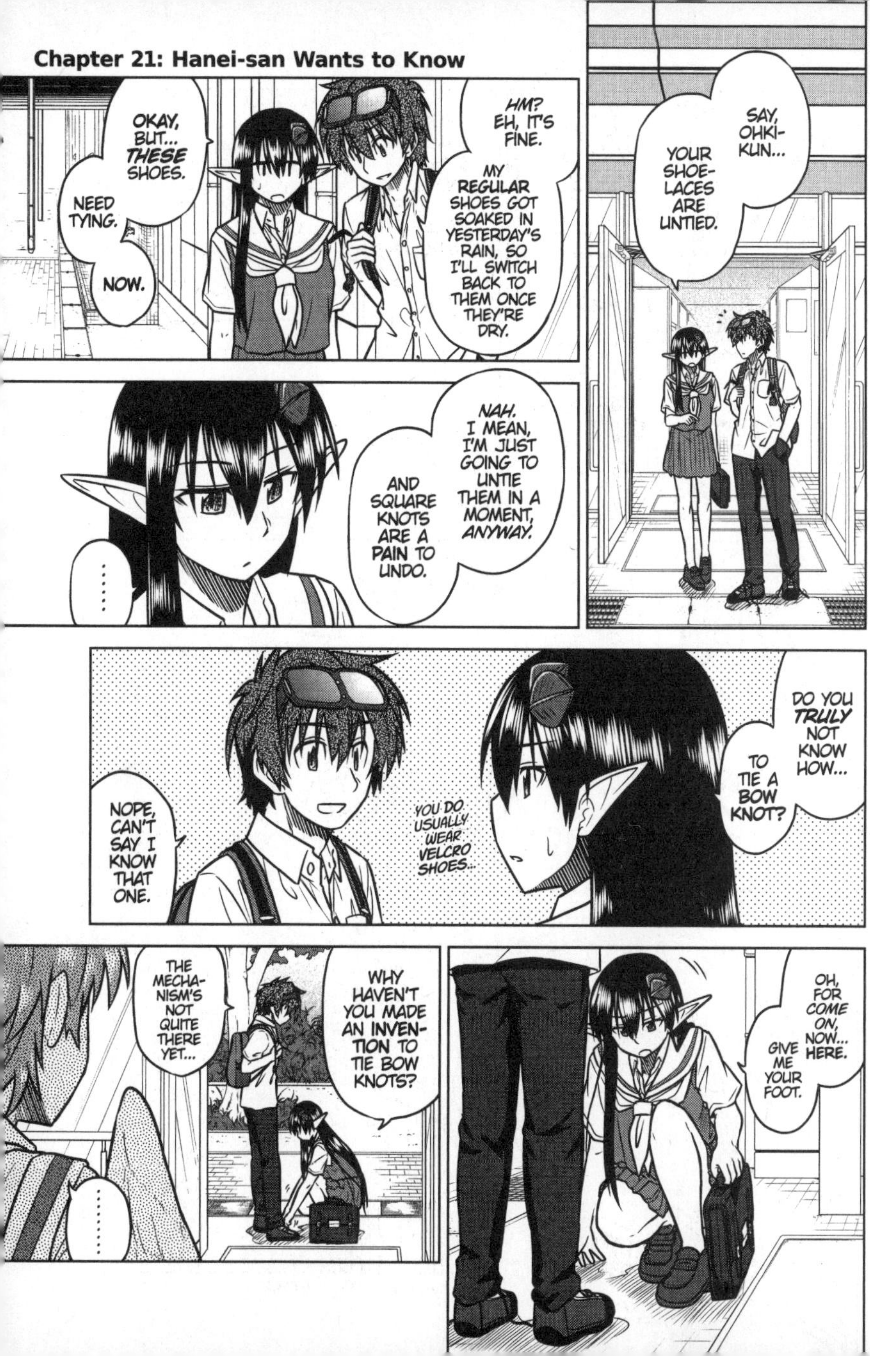
SAY, OHKI-KUN...
YOUR SHOELACES ARE UNTIED.
HM? EH, IT'S FINE.
MY REGULAR SHOES GOT SOAKED IN YESTERDAY'S RAIN, SO I'LL SWITCH BACK TO THEM ONCE THEY'RE DRY.
OKAY, BUT... THESE SHOES.
NEED TYING.
NOW.
NAH. I MEAN, I'M JUST GOING TO UNTIE THEM IN A MOMENT, ANYWAY.
AND SQUARE KNOTS ARE A PAIN TO UNDO.
......
DO YOU TRULY NOT KNOW HOW...
TO TIE A BOW KNOT?
YOU DO USUALLY WEAR VELCRO SHOES...
NOPE, CAN'T SAY I KNOW THAT ONE.
OH, FOR COME ON, NOW... HERE.
GIVE ME YOUR FOOT.
WHY HAVEN'T YOU MADE AN INVENTION TO TIE BOW KNOTS?
THE MECHANISM'S NOT QUITE THERE YET...
......

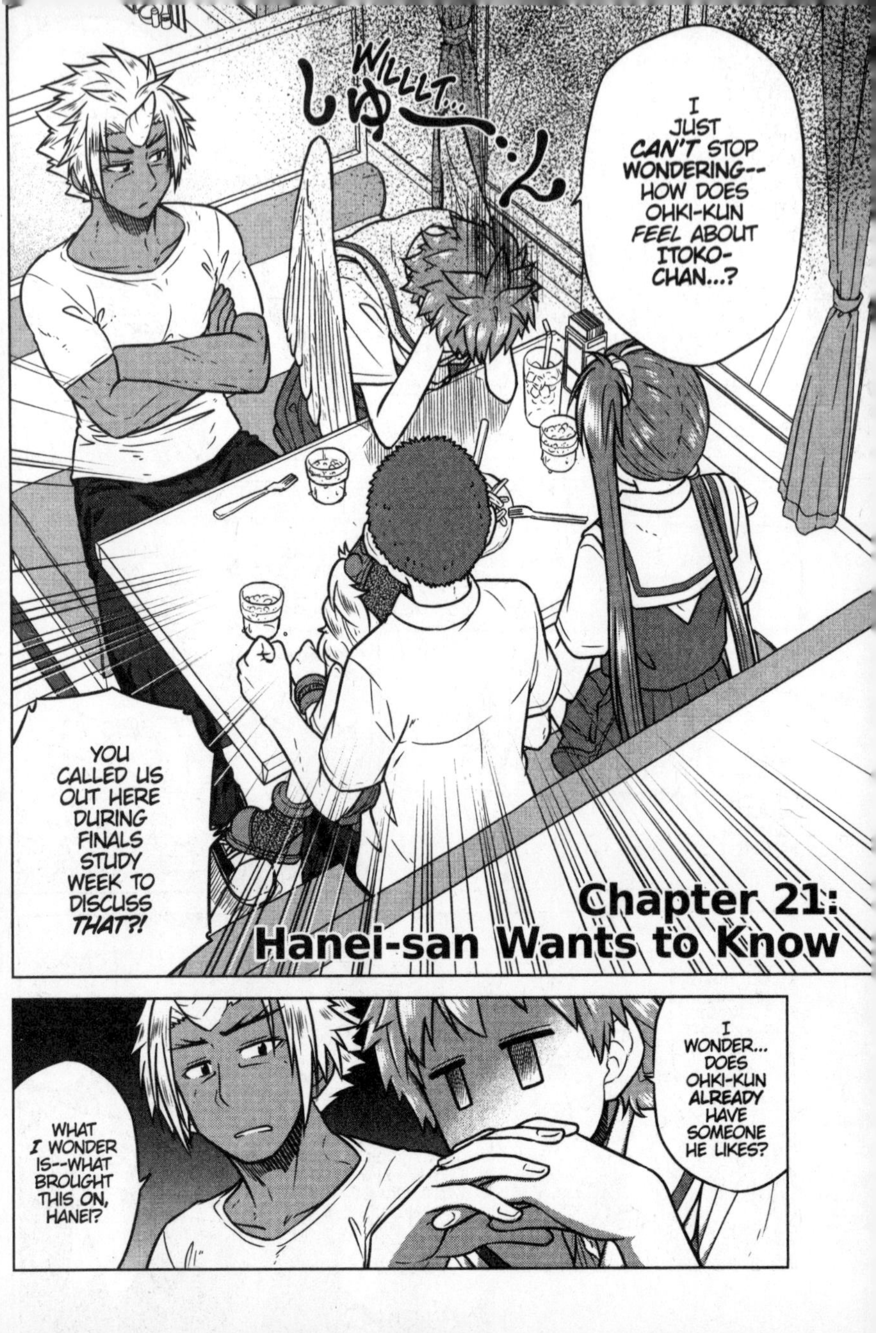
I JUST *CAN'T* STOP WONDERING-- HOW DOES OHKI-KUN *FEEL* ABOUT ITOKO-CHAN...?
WILLLT...
しゅーん
YOU CALLED US OUT HERE DURING FINALS STUDY WEEK TO DISCUSS *THAT?!*
Chapter 21: Hanei-san Wants to Know
I WONDER... DOES OHKI-KUN ALREADY HAVE SOMEONE HE LIKES?
WHAT *I* WONDER IS--WHAT BROUGHT THIS ON, HANEI?

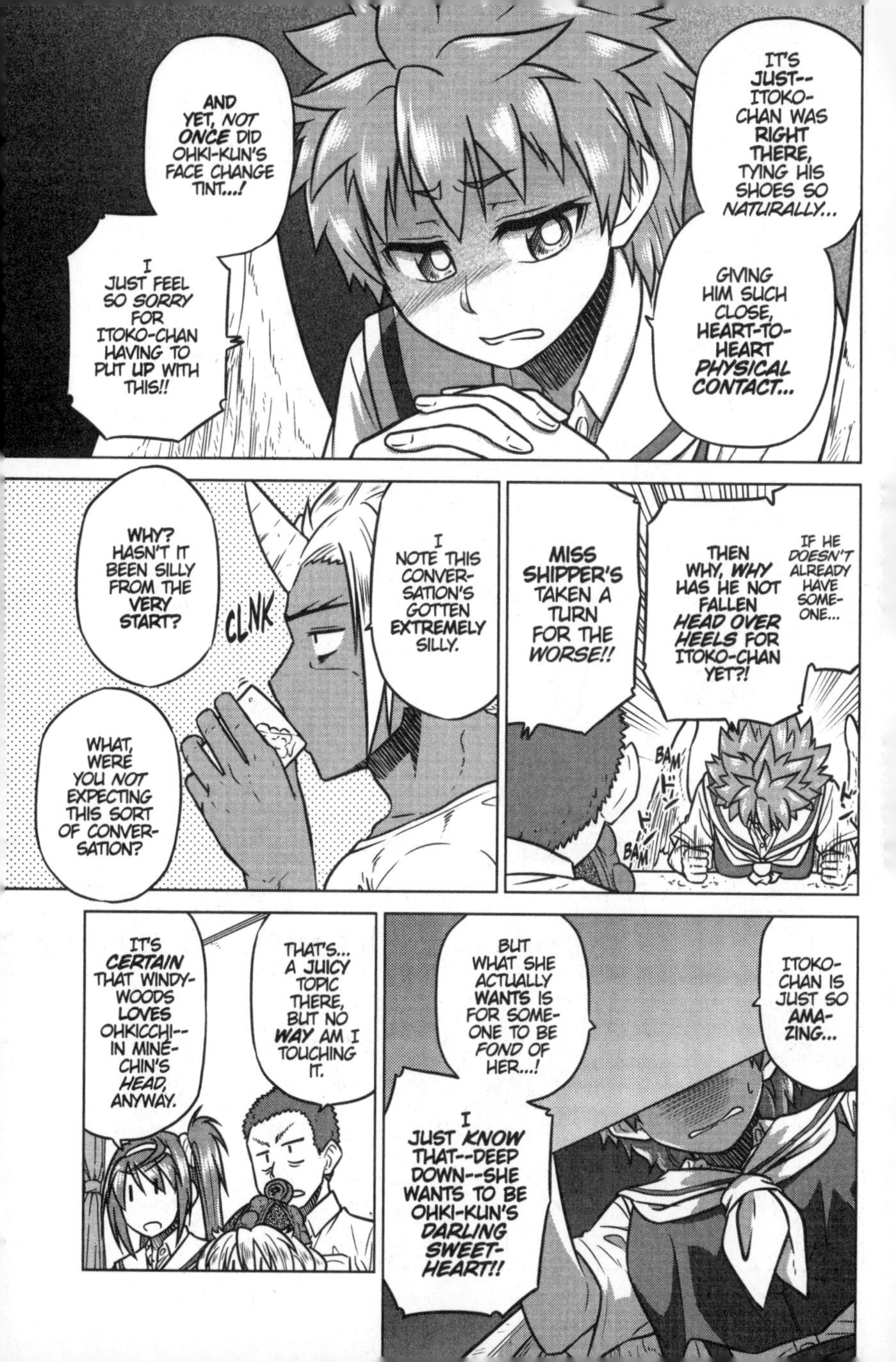
IT'S JUST-- ITOKO-CHAN WAS RIGHT THERE, TYING HIS SHOES SO NATURALLY...
GIVING HIM SUCH CLOSE, HEART-TO-HEART PHYSICAL CONTACT...
AND YET, NOT ONCE DID OHKI-KUN'S FACE CHANGE TINT...!
I JUST FEEL SO SORRY FOR ITOKO-CHAN HAVING TO PUT UP WITH THIS!!
IF HE DOESN'T ALREADY HAVE SOMEONE...
THEN WHY, WHY HAS HE NOT FALLEN HEAD OVER HEELS FOR ITOKO-CHAN YET?!
BAM
BAM
MISS SHIPPER'S TAKEN A TURN FOR THE WORSE!!
I NOTE THIS CONVERSATION'S GOTTEN EXTREMELY SILLY.
CLNK
WHY? HASN'T IT BEEN SILLY FROM THE VERY START?
WHAT, WERE YOU NOT EXPECTING THIS SORT OF CONVERSATION?
ITOKO-CHAN IS JUST SO AMAZING...
BUT WHAT SHE ACTUALLY WANTS IS FOR SOMEONE TO BE FOND OF HER...!
I JUST KNOW THAT--DEEP DOWN--SHE WANTS TO BE OHKI-KUN'S DARLING SWEETHEART!!
THAT'S... A JUICY TOPIC THERE, BUT NO WAY AM I TOUCHING IT.
IT'S CERTAIN THAT WINDYWOODS LOVES OHKICCHI-- IN MINECHIN'S HEAD, ANYWAY.

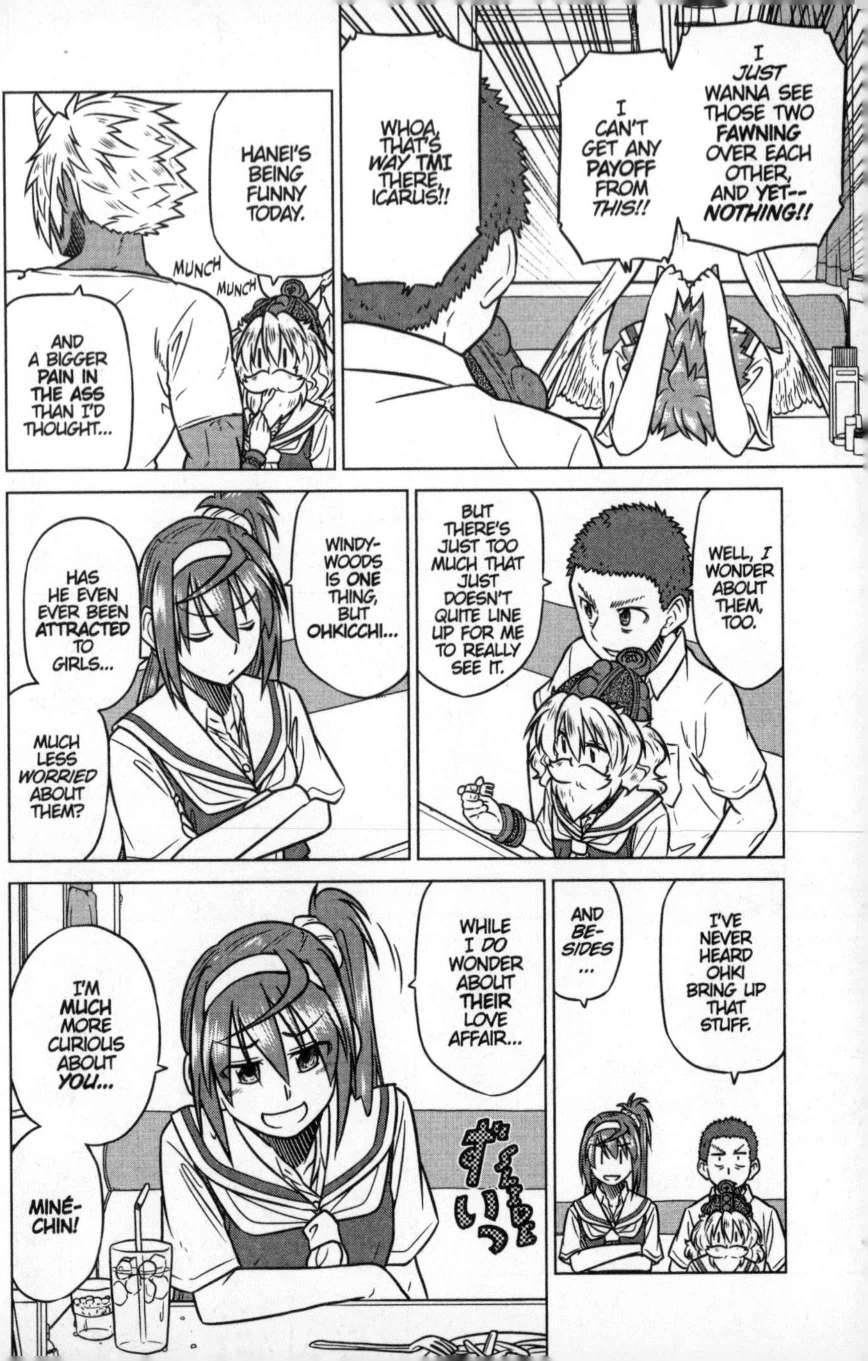
I JUST WANNA SEE THOSE TWO FAWNING OVER EACH OTHER, AND YET-- NOTHING!!
I CAN'T GET ANY PAYOFF FROM THIS!!
WHOA, THAT'S WAY TMI THERE, ICARUS!!
HANEI'S BEING FUNNY TODAY.
MUNCH
MUNCH
AND A BIGGER PAIN IN THE ASS THAN I'D THOUGHT...
WELL, I WONDER ABOUT THEM, TOO.
BUT THERE'S JUST TOO MUCH THAT JUST DOESN'T QUITE LINE UP FOR ME TO REALLY SEE IT.
WINDY-WOODS IS ONE THING, BUT OHKICCHI...
HAS HE EVEN EVER BEEN ATTRACTED TO GIRLS...
MUCH LESS WORRIED ABOUT THEM?
I'VE NEVER HEARD OHKI BRING UP THAT STUFF.
AND BE-SIDES...
WHILE I DO WONDER ABOUT THEIR LOVE AFFAIR...
I'M MUCH MORE CURIOUS ABOUT YOU...
MINÉ-CHIN!

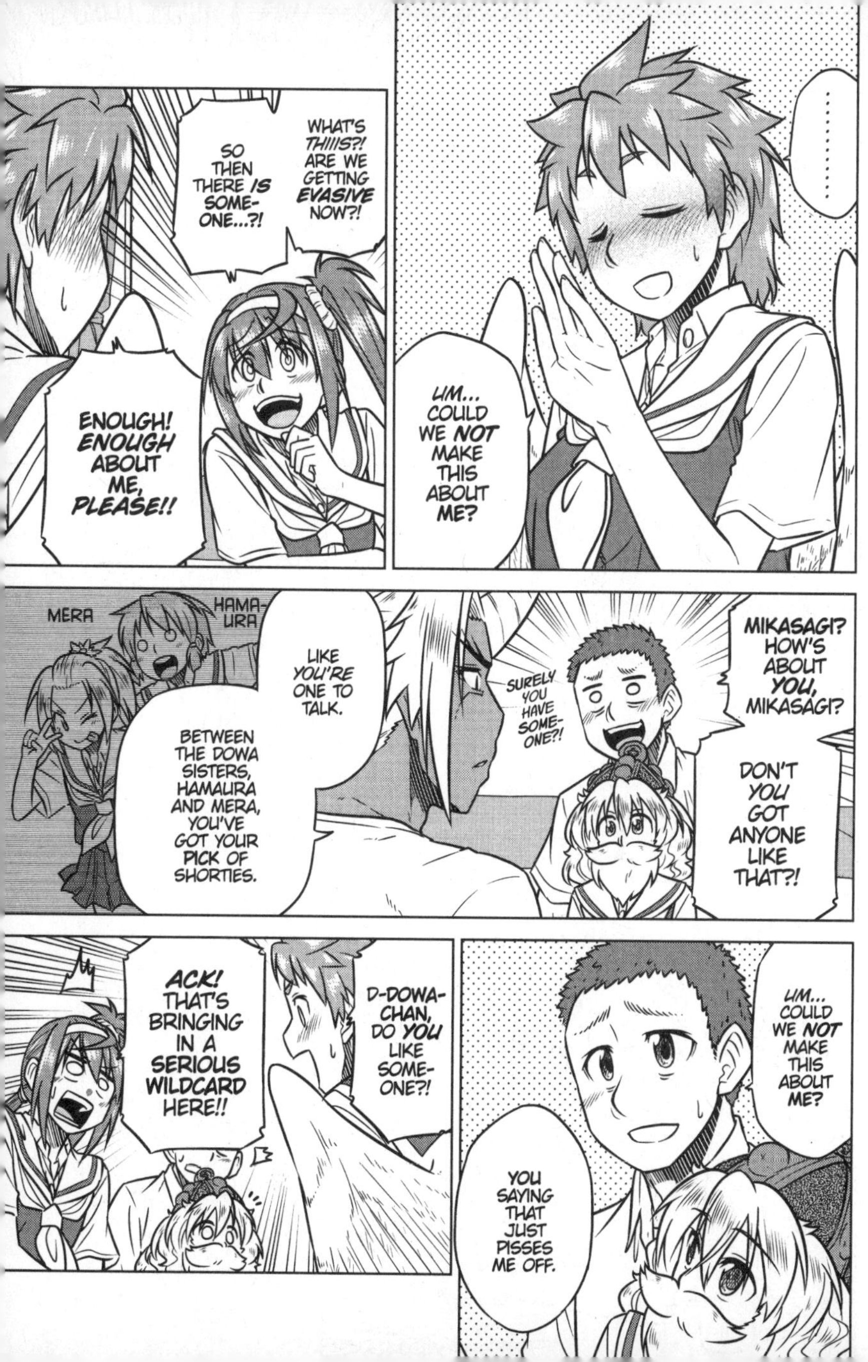
……
UM... COULD WE NOT MAKE THIS ABOUT ME?
WHAT'S THIIIS?! ARE WE GETTING EVASIVE NOW?!
SO THEN THERE IS SOME-ONE...?!
ENOUGH! ENOUGH ABOUT ME, PLEASE!!
MIKASAGI? HOW'S ABOUT YOU, MIKASAGI?
DON'T YOU GOT ANYONE LIKE THAT?!
SURELY YOU HAVE SOME-ONE?!
LIKE YOU'RE ONE TO TALK.
BETWEEN THE DOWA SISTERS, HAMAURA AND MERA, YOU'VE GOT YOUR PICK OF SHORTIES.
HAMA-URA
MERA
UM... COULD WE NOT MAKE THIS ABOUT ME?
YOU SAYING THAT JUST PISSES ME OFF.
D-DOWA-CHAN, DO YOU LIKE SOME-ONE?!
ACK! THAT'S BRINGING IN A SERIOUS WILDCARD HERE!!

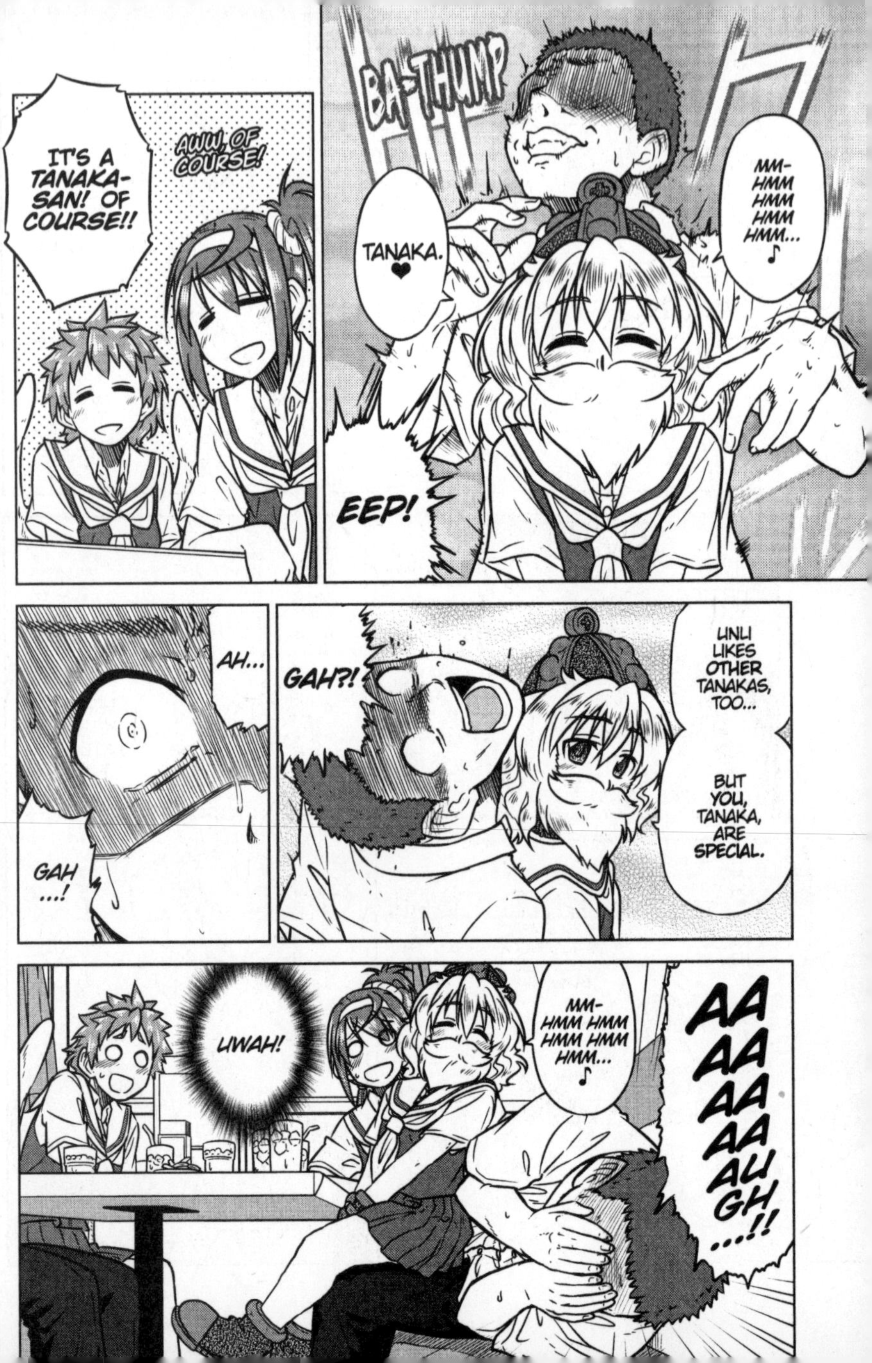
BA-THUMP
MM-HMM HMM HMM HMM... ♪
TANAKA. ❤
EEP!
AWW, OF COURSE!
IT'S A TANAKA-SAN! OF COURSE!!
UNLI LIKES OTHER TANAKAS, TOO...
BUT YOU, TANAKA, ARE SPECIAL.
GAH?!
AH...
GAH ...!
AAAAAAAAAAAUGH...!!
MM-HMM HMM HMM HMM HMM... ♪
UWAH!

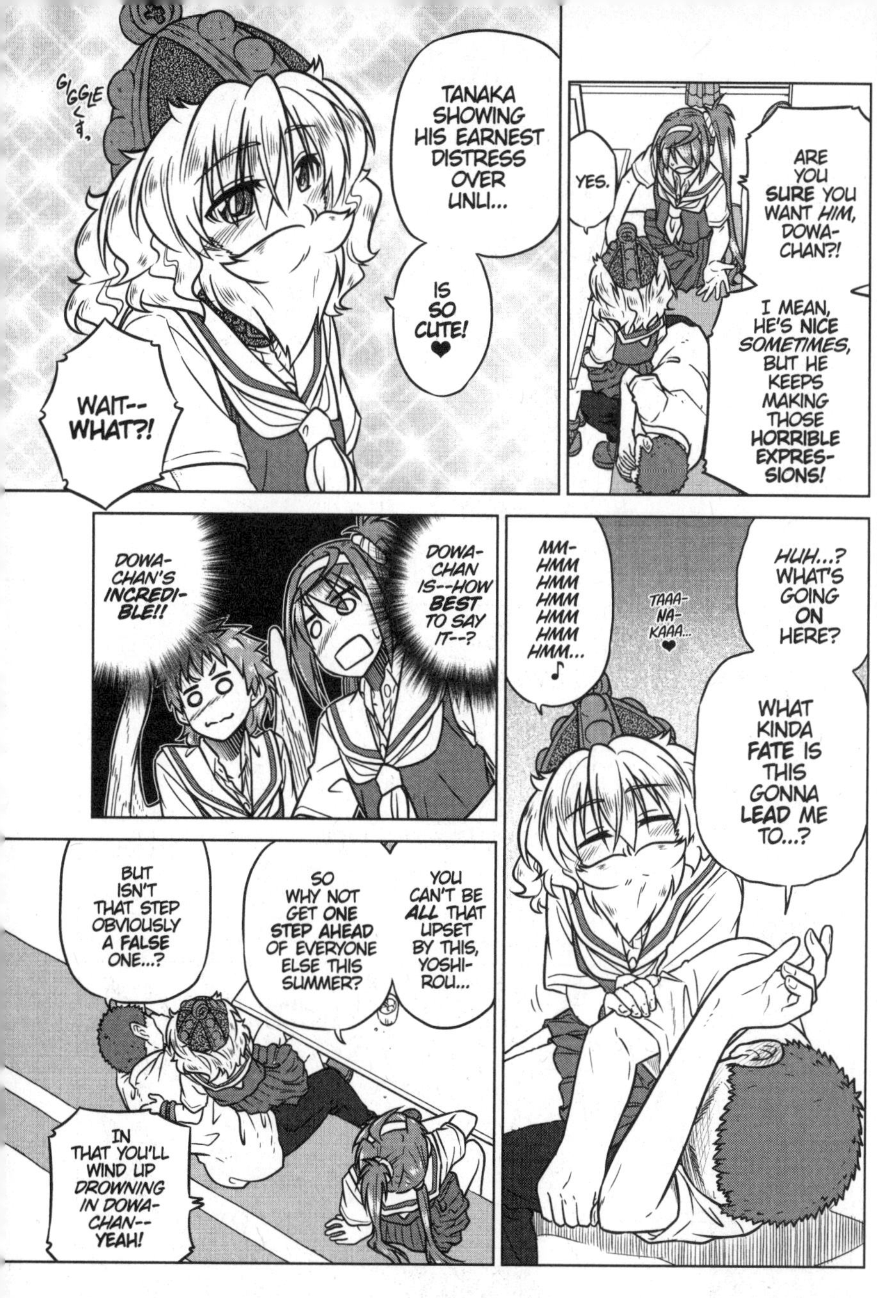
ARE YOU SURE YOU WANT HIM, DOWA-CHAN?!
YES.
I MEAN, HE'S NICE SOMETIMES, BUT HE KEEPS MAKING THOSE HORRIBLE EXPRES-SIONS!
TANAKA SHOWING HIS EARNEST DISTRESS OVER UNLI...
GIGGLE くす
IS SO CUTE! ❤
WAIT--WHAT?!
HUH...? WHAT'S GOING ON HERE?
WHAT KINDA FATE IS THIS GONNA LEAD ME TO...?
TAAA-NA-KAAA... ❤
MM-HMM HMM HMM HMM HMM HMM... ♪
DOWA-CHAN IS--HOW BEST TO SAY IT--?
DOWA-CHAN'S INCREDI-BLE!!
YOU CAN'T BE ALL THAT UPSET BY THIS, YOSHI-ROU...
SO WHY NOT GET ONE STEP AHEAD OF EVERYONE ELSE THIS SUMMER?
BUT ISN'T THAT STEP OBVIOUSLY A FALSE ONE...?
IN THAT YOU'LL WIND UP DROWNING IN DOWA-CHAN--YEAH!

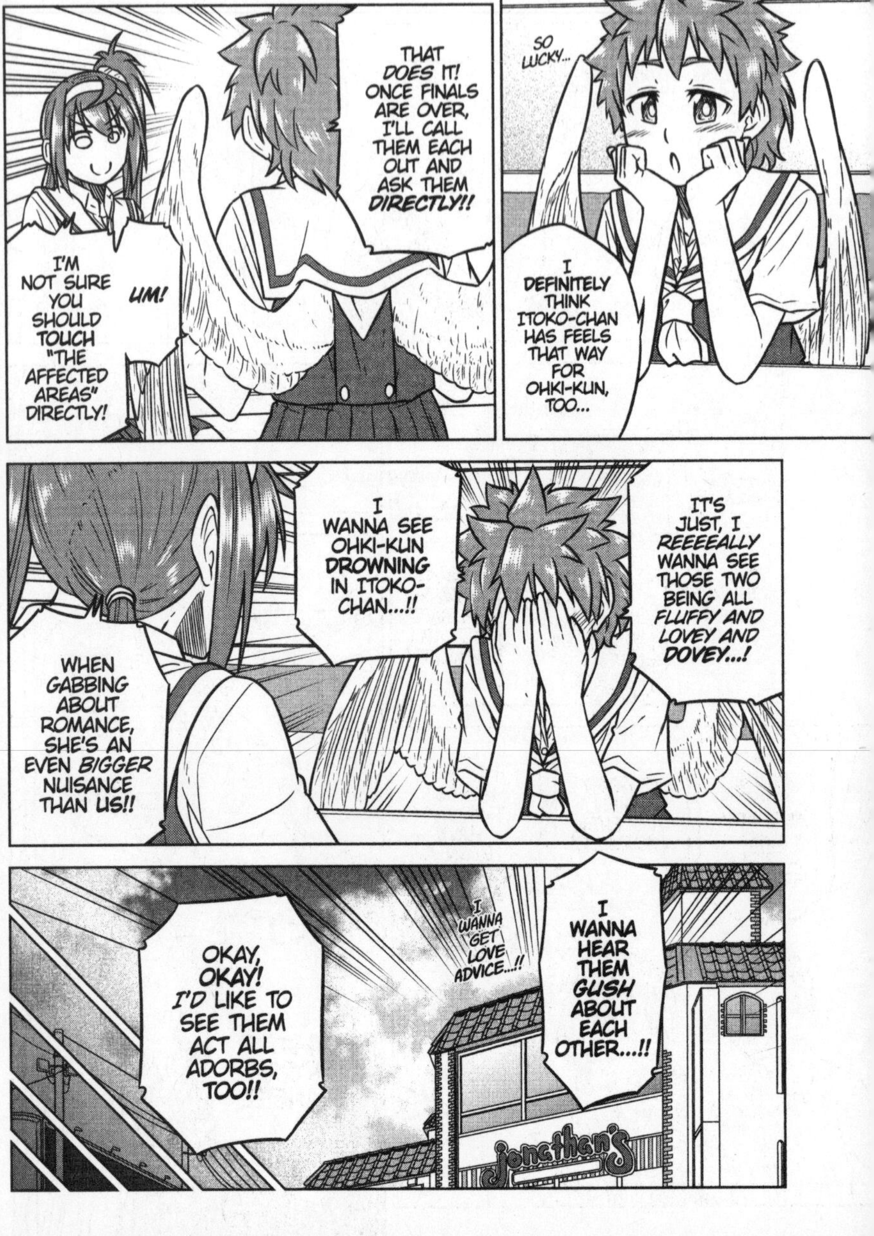
SO LUCKY...
I DEFINITELY THINK ITOKO-CHAN HAS FEELS THAT WAY FOR OHKI-KUN, TOO...
THAT DOES IT! ONCE FINALS ARE OVER, I'LL CALL THEM EACH OUT AND ASK THEM DIRECTLY!!
UM!
I'M NOT SURE YOU SHOULD TOUCH "THE AFFECTED AREAS" DIRECTLY!
IT'S JUST, I REEEEALLY WANNA SEE THOSE TWO BEING ALL FLUFFY AND LOVEY AND DOVEY...!
I WANNA SEE OHKI-KUN DROWNING IN ITOKO-CHAN...!!
WHEN GABBING ABOUT ROMANCE, SHE'S AN EVEN BIGGER NUISANCE THAN US!!
I WANNA HEAR THEM GUSH ABOUT EACH OTHER...!!
I WANNA GET LOVE ADVICE...!!
OKAY, OKAY! I'D LIKE TO SEE THEM ACT ALL ADORBS, TOO!!
jonathan's

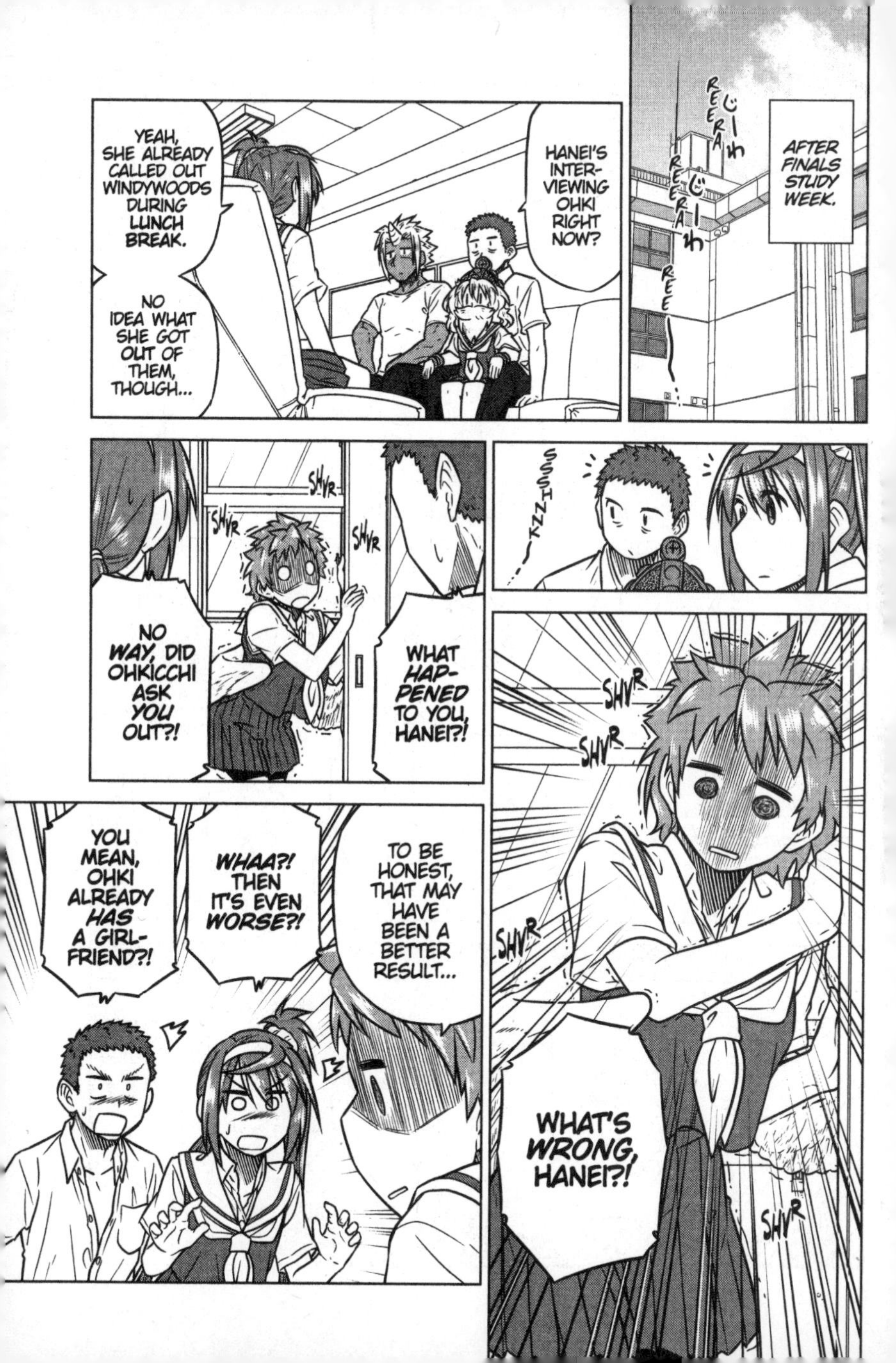

AFTER FINALS STUDY WEEK.
REERA
REERA
REE
HANEI'S INTER-VIEWING OHKI RIGHT NOW?
YEAH, SHE ALREADY CALLED OUT WINDYWOODS DURING LUNCH BREAK.
NO IDEA WHAT SHE GOT OUT OF THEM, THOUGH...
SSSHNNK
SHVR
SHVR
SHVR
WHAT HAP-PENED TO YOU, HANEI?!
NO WAY, DID OHKICCHI ASK YOU OUT?!
SHVR
SHVR
SHVR
SHVR
WHAT'S WRONG, HANEI?!
TO BE HONEST, THAT MAY HAVE BEEN A BETTER RESULT...
WHAA?! THEN IT'S EVEN WORSE?!
YOU MEAN, OHKI ALREADY HAS A GIRL-FRIEND?!

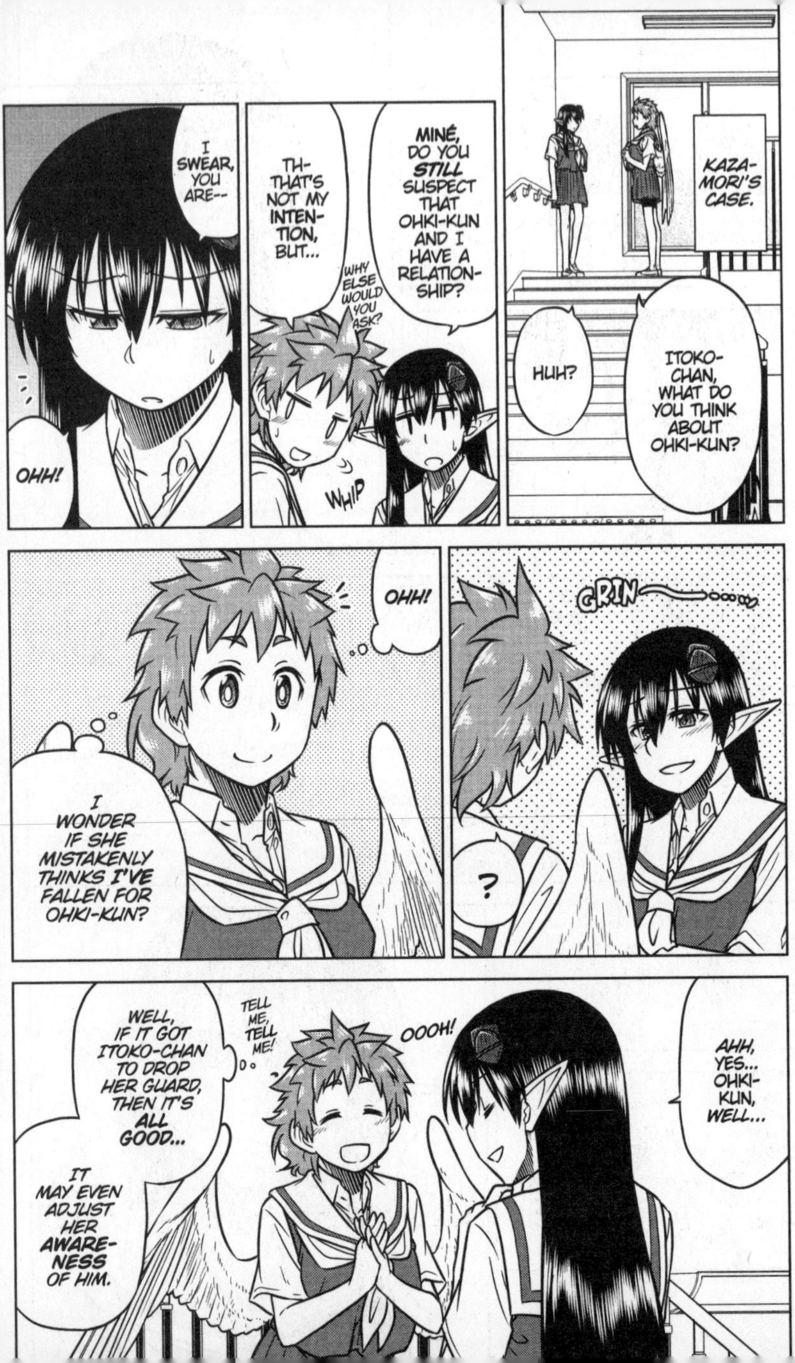
KAZAMORI'S CASE.
ITOKO-CHAN, WHAT DO YOU THINK ABOUT OHKI-KUN?
HUH?
MINÉ, DO YOU STILL SUSPECT THAT OHKI-KUN AND I HAVE A RELATIONSHIP?
WHY ELSE WOULD YOU ASK?
TH-THAT'S NOT MY INTENTION, BUT...
WHIP
I SWEAR, YOU ARE--
OHH!
GRIN
?
OHH!
I WONDER IF SHE MISTAKENLY THINKS I'VE FALLEN FOR OHKI-KUN?
AHH, YES... OHKI-KUN, WELL...
OOOH!
TELL ME, TELL ME!
WELL, IF IT GOT ITOKO-CHAN TO DROP HER GUARD, THEN IT'S ALL GOOD...
IT MAY EVEN ADJUST HER AWARENESS OF HIM.

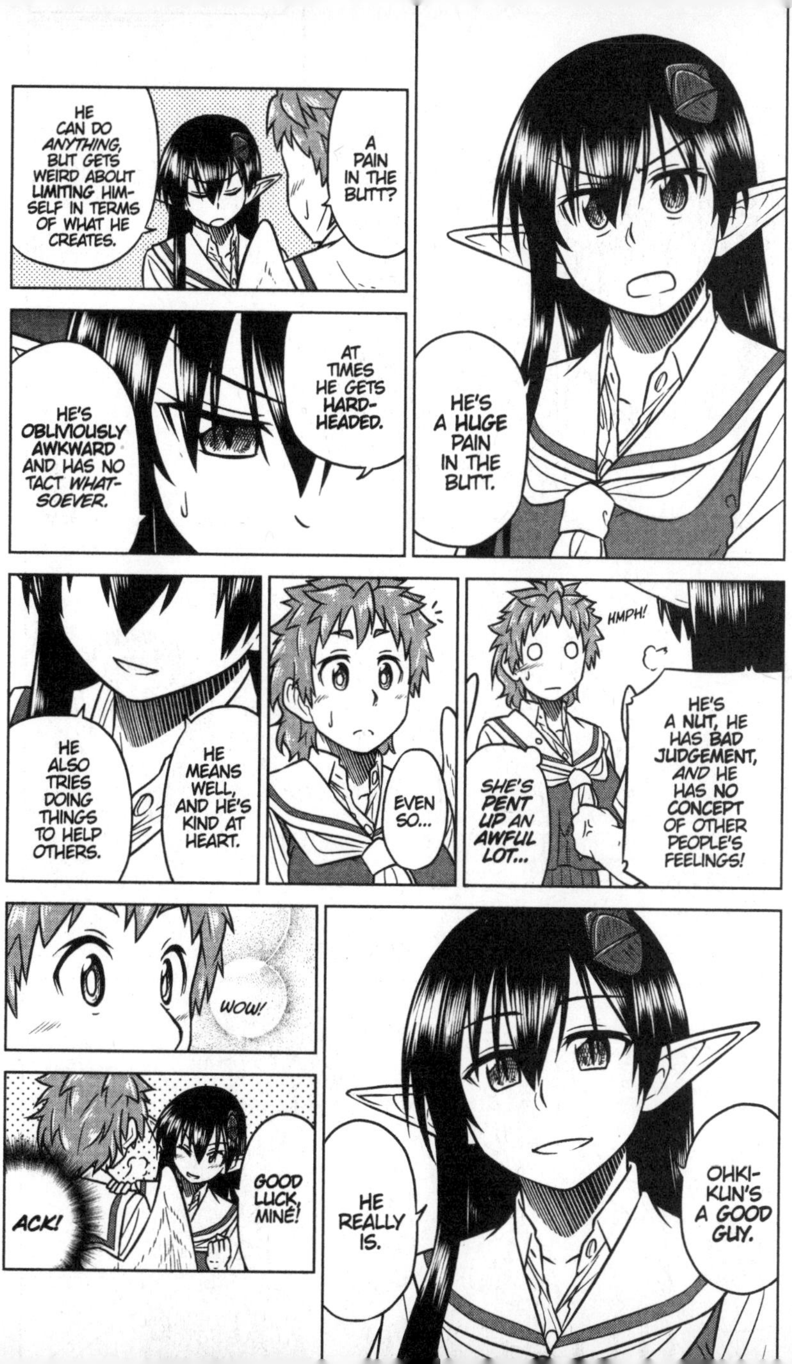
HE'S A HUGE PAIN IN THE BUTT.
A PAIN IN THE BUTT?
HE CAN DO *ANYTHING*, BUT GETS WEIRD ABOUT LIMITING HIM-SELF IN TERMS OF WHAT HE CREATES.
AT TIMES HE GETS HARD-HEADED.
HE'S OBLIVIOUSLY AWKWARD AND HAS NO TACT *WHAT-SOEVER*.
HMPH!
HE'S A NUT, HE HAS BAD JUDGEMENT, *AND* HE HAS NO CONCEPT OF OTHER PEOPLE'S FEELINGS!
SHE'S PENT UP AN AWFUL LOT...
EVEN SO...
HE MEANS WELL, AND HE'S KIND AT HEART.
HE ALSO TRIES DOING THINGS TO HELP OTHERS.
OHKI-KUN'S A GOOD GUY.
HE REALLY IS.
WOW!
GOOD LUCK, MINÉ!
ACK!

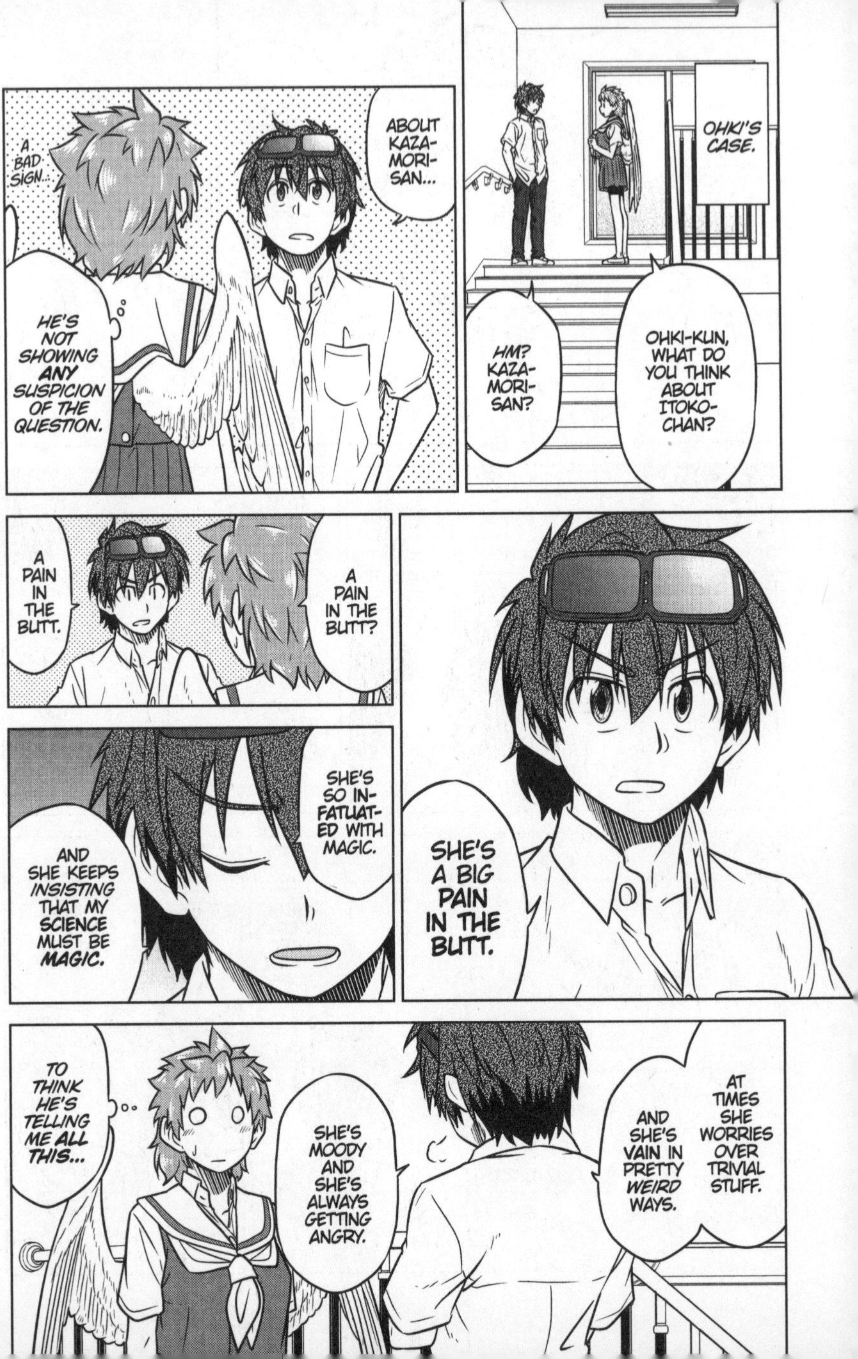
OHKI'S CASE.
OHKI-KUN, WHAT DO YOU THINK ABOUT ITOKO-CHAN?
HM? KAZAMORI-SAN?
ABOUT KAZAMORI-SAN...
A BAD SIGN...
HE'S NOT SHOWING ANY SUSPICION OF THE QUESTION.
SHE'S A BIG PAIN IN THE BUTT.
A PAIN IN THE BUTT?
A PAIN IN THE BUTT.
SHE'S SO INFATUATED WITH MAGIC.
AND SHE KEEPS INSISTING THAT MY SCIENCE MUST BE MAGIC.
AT TIMES SHE WORRIES OVER TRIVIAL STUFF.
AND SHE'S VAIN IN PRETTY WEIRD WAYS.
SHE'S MOODY AND SHE'S ALWAYS GETTING ANGRY.
TO THINK HE'S TELLING ME ALL THIS...

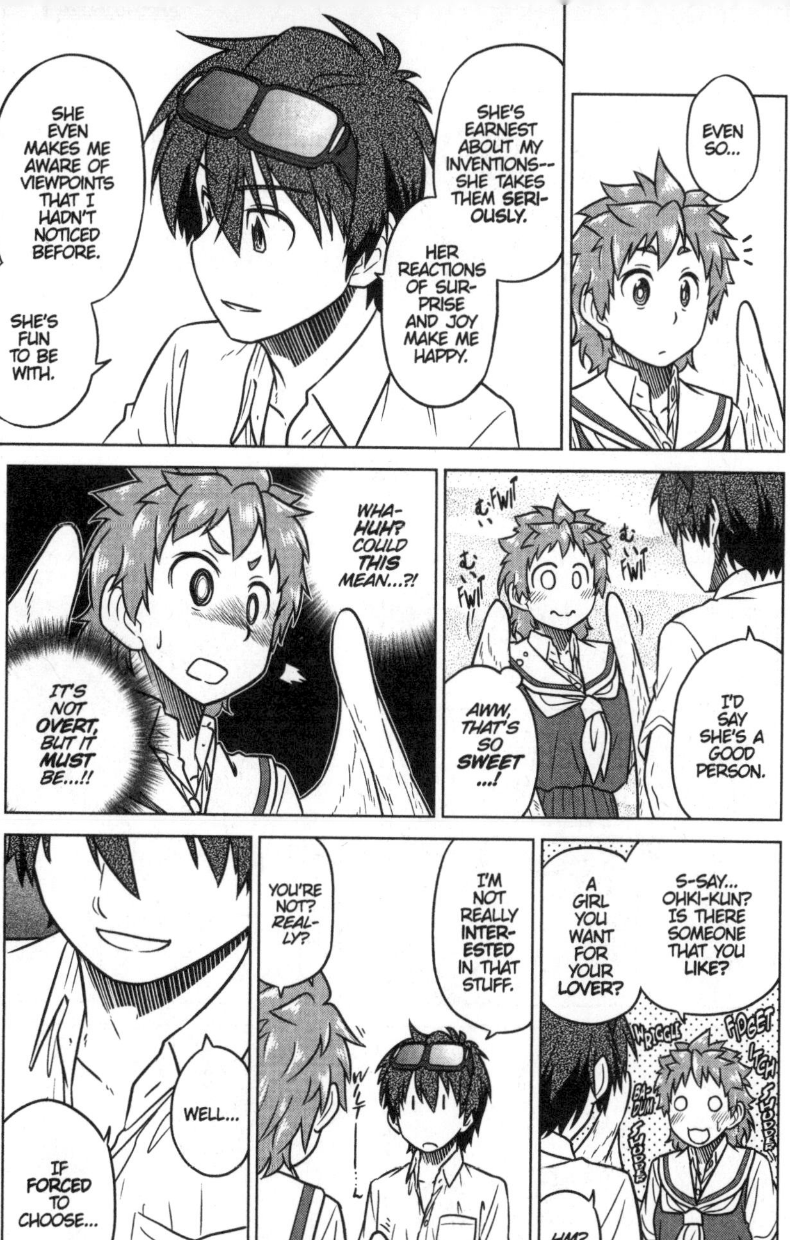
EVEN SO...
SHE'S EARNEST ABOUT MY INVENTIONS--SHE TAKES THEM SERIOUSLY.
HER REACTIONS OF SURPRISE AND JOY MAKE ME HAPPY.
SHE EVEN MAKES ME AWARE OF VIEWPOINTS THAT I HADN'T NOTICED BEFORE.
SHE'S FUN TO BE WITH.
I'D SAY SHE'S A GOOD PERSON.
FWIT
FWIT
FWIT
AWW, THAT'S SO SWEET...!
WHA-HUH? COULD THIS MEAN...?!
IT'S NOT OVERT, BUT IT MUST BE...!!
S-SAY... OHKI-KUN? IS THERE SOMEONE THAT YOU LIKE?
A GIRL YOU WANT FOR YOUR LOVER?
FIDGET
HM?
I'M NOT REALLY INTERESTED IN THAT STUFF.
YOU'RE NOT? REALLY?
WILT
WELL...
IF FORCED TO CHOOSE...

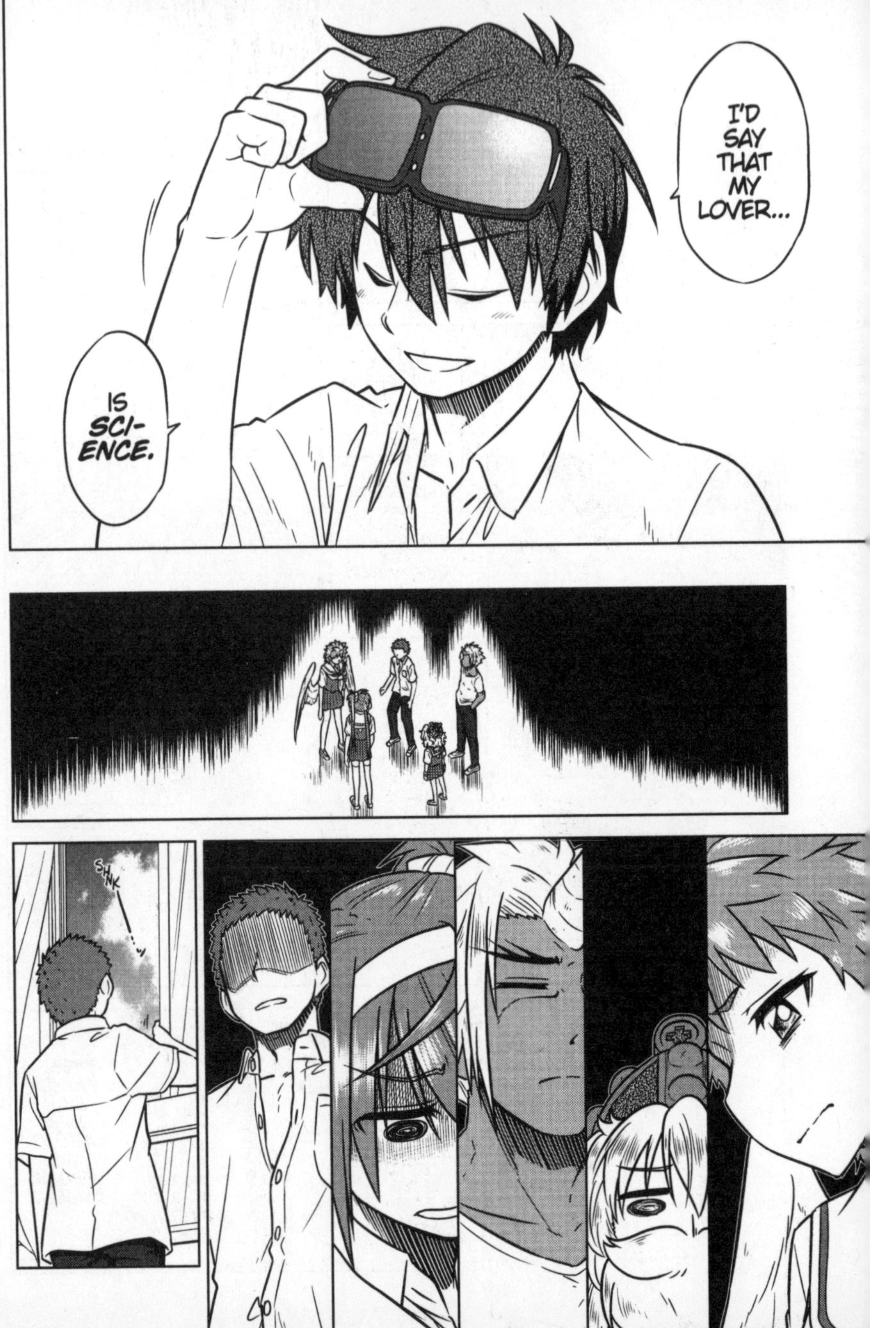
I'D SAY THAT MY LOVER...
IS SCI-ENCE.
SHNK

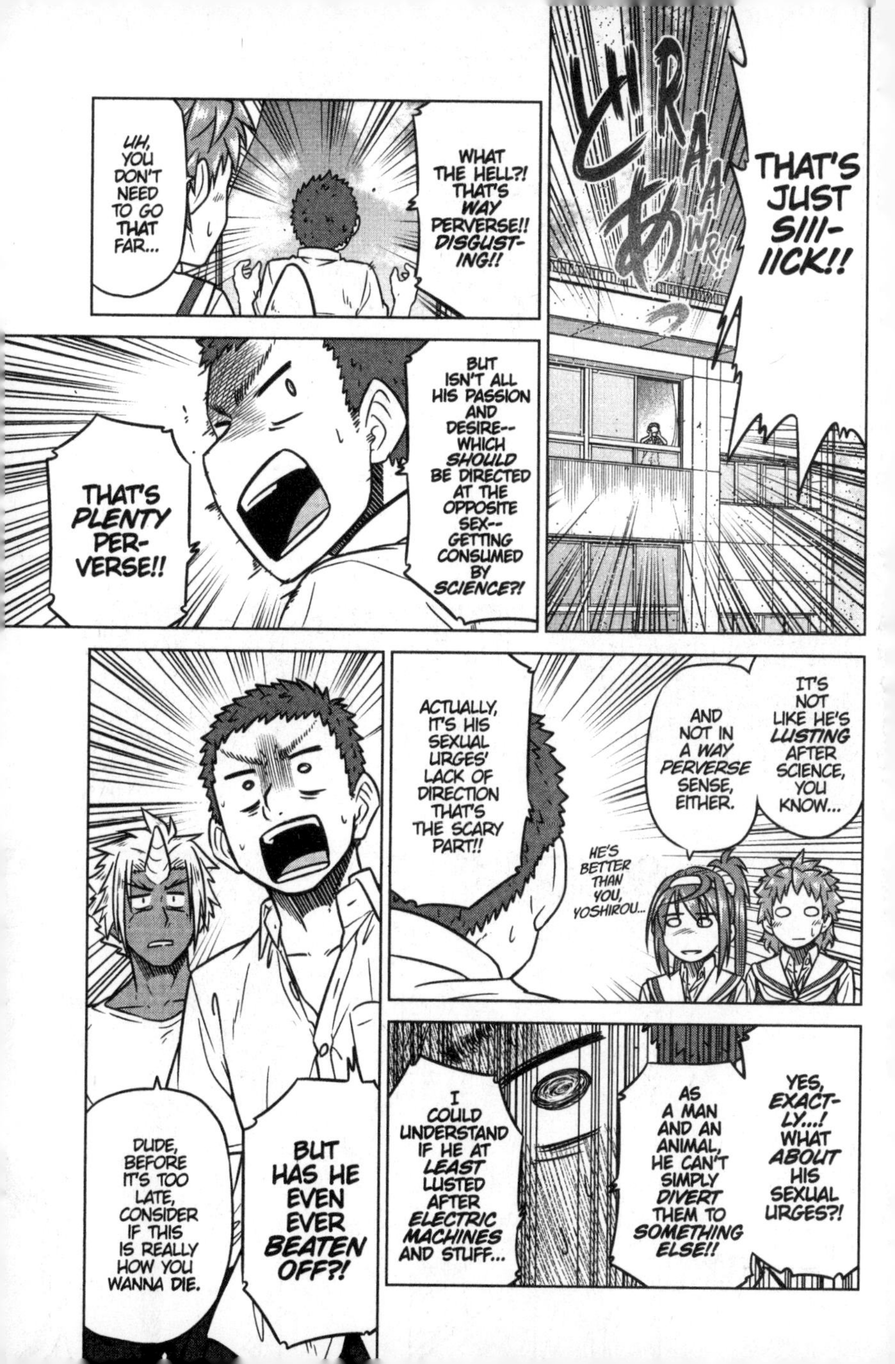

どあ
RAAAWR!!
THAT'S JUST SIII-IICK!!
WHAT THE HELL?! THAT'S WAY PERVERSE!! DISGUSTING!!
UH, YOU DON'T NEED TO GO THAT FAR...
BUT ISN'T ALL HIS PASSION AND DESIRE-- WHICH SHOULD BE DIRECTED AT THE OPPOSITE SEX-- GETTING CONSUMED BY SCIENCE?!
THAT'S PLENTY PERVERSE!!
IT'S NOT LIKE HE'S LUSTING AFTER SCIENCE, YOU KNOW...
AND NOT IN A WAY PERVERSE SENSE, EITHER.
HE'S BETTER THAN YOU, YOSHIROU...
ACTUALLY, IT'S HIS SEXUAL URGES' LACK OF DIRECTION THAT'S THE SCARY PART!!
YES, EXACTLY...! WHAT ABOUT HIS SEXUAL URGES?!
AS A MAN AND AN ANIMAL, HE CAN'T SIMPLY DIVERT THEM TO SOMETHING ELSE!!
I COULD UNDERSTAND IF HE AT LEAST LUSTED AFTER ELECTRIC MACHINES AND STUFF...
BUT HAS HE EVEN EVER BEATEN OFF?!
DUDE, BEFORE IT'S TOO LATE, CONSIDER IF THIS IS REALLY HOW YOU WANNA DIE.

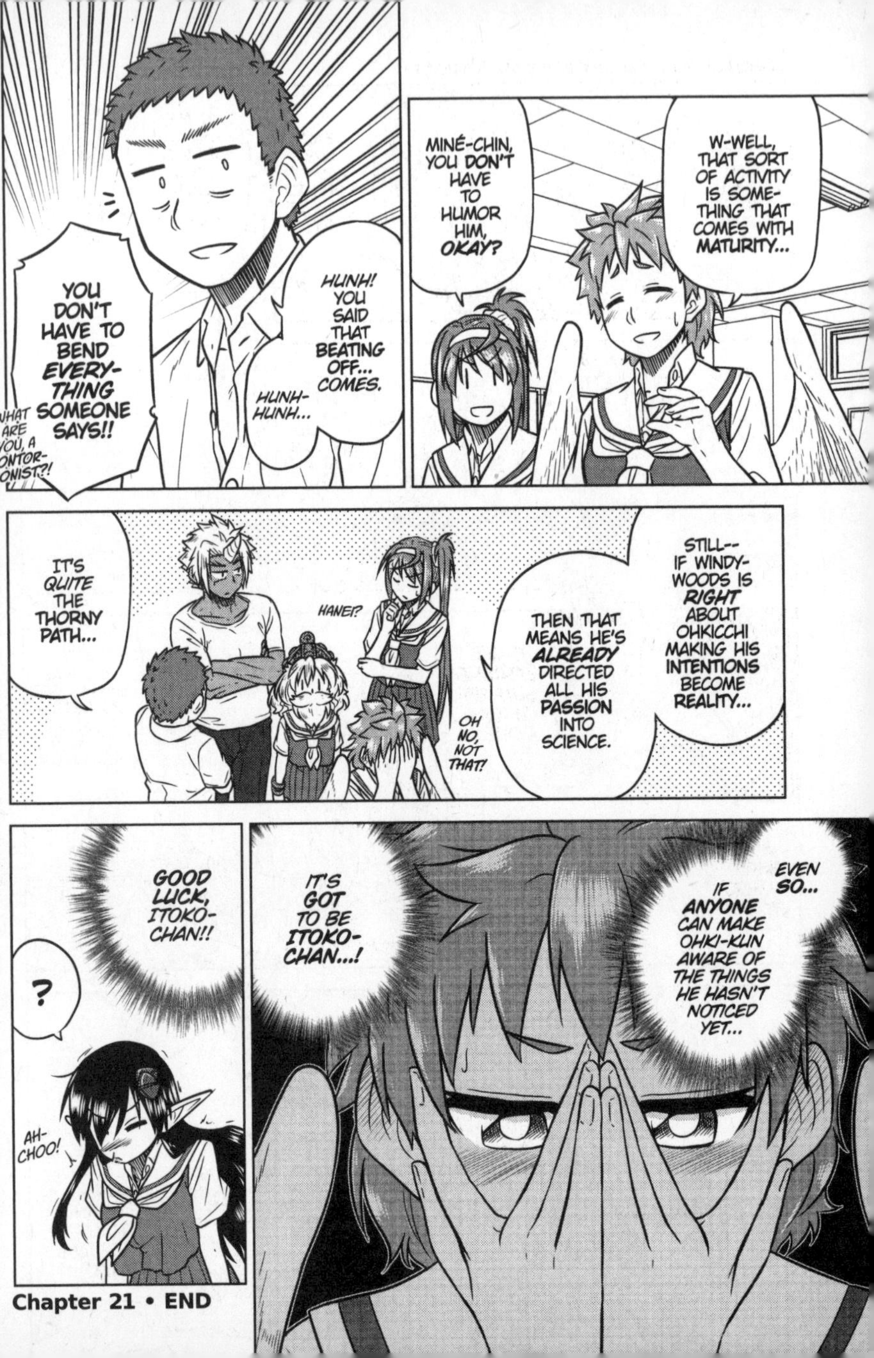
W-WELL, THAT SORT OF ACTIVITY IS SOME-THING THAT COMES WITH MATURITY...
MINÉ-CHIN, YOU DON'T HAVE TO HUMOR HIM, OKAY?
HUNH! YOU SAID THAT BEATING OFF... COMES.
HUNH-HUNH...
YOU DON'T HAVE TO BEND EVERY-THING SOMEONE SAYS!!
WHAT ARE YOU, A CONTOR-TIONIST?!
STILL-- IF WINDY-WOODS IS RIGHT ABOUT OHKICCHI MAKING HIS INTENTIONS BECOME REALITY...
THEN THAT MEANS HE'S ALREADY DIRECTED ALL HIS PASSION INTO SCIENCE.
OH NO, NOT THAT!
HANE!?
IT'S QUITE THE THORNY PATH...
EVEN SO... IF ANYONE CAN MAKE OHKI-KUN AWARE OF THE THINGS HE HASN'T NOTICED YET...
IT'S GOT TO BE ITOKO-CHAN...!
GOOD LUCK, ITOKO-CHAN!!
?
AH-CHOO!

Chapter 21 • END

Chapter 22: Kazamori-san Shoots

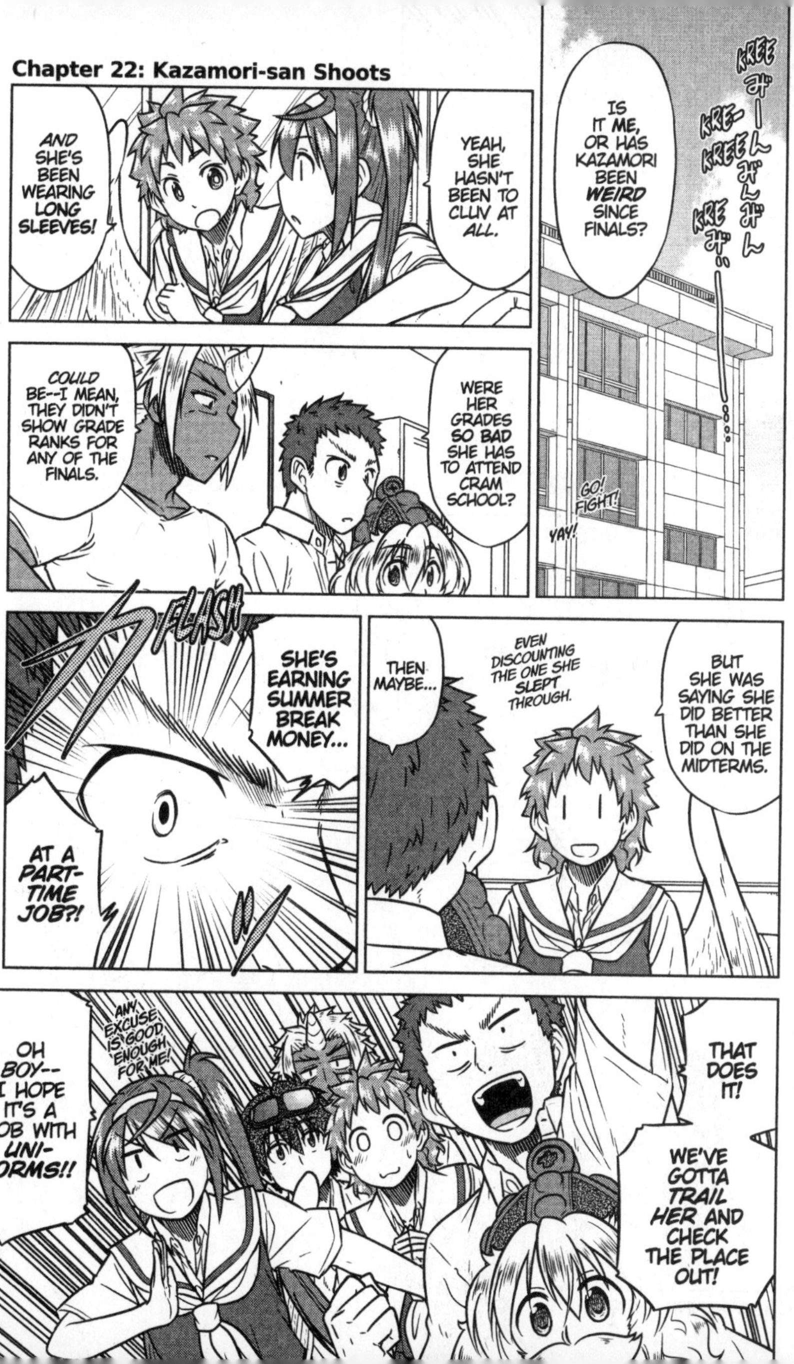
KREE
KRE-
KREE
KRE
IS IT ME, OR HAS KAZAMORI BEEN WEIRD SINCE FINALS?
GO! FIGHT!
YAY!
YEAH, SHE HASN'T BEEN TO CLUV AT ALL.
AND SHE'S BEEN WEARING LONG SLEEVES!
WERE HER GRADES SO BAD SHE HAS TO ATTEND CRAM SCHOOL?
COULD BE--I MEAN, THEY DIDN'T SHOW GRADE RANKS FOR ANY OF THE FINALS.
BUT SHE WAS SAYING SHE DID BETTER THAN SHE DID ON THE MIDTERMS.
EVEN DISCOUNTING THE ONE SHE SLEPT THROUGH.
THEN MAYBE...
SHE'S EARNING SUMMER BREAK MONEY...
FLASH
AT A PART-TIME JOB?!
THAT DOES IT!
WE'VE GOTTA TRAIL HER AND CHECK THE PLACE OUT!
ANY EXCUSE IS GOOD ENOUGH FOR ME!
OH BOY--I HOPE IT'S A JOB WITH UNI-FORMS!!

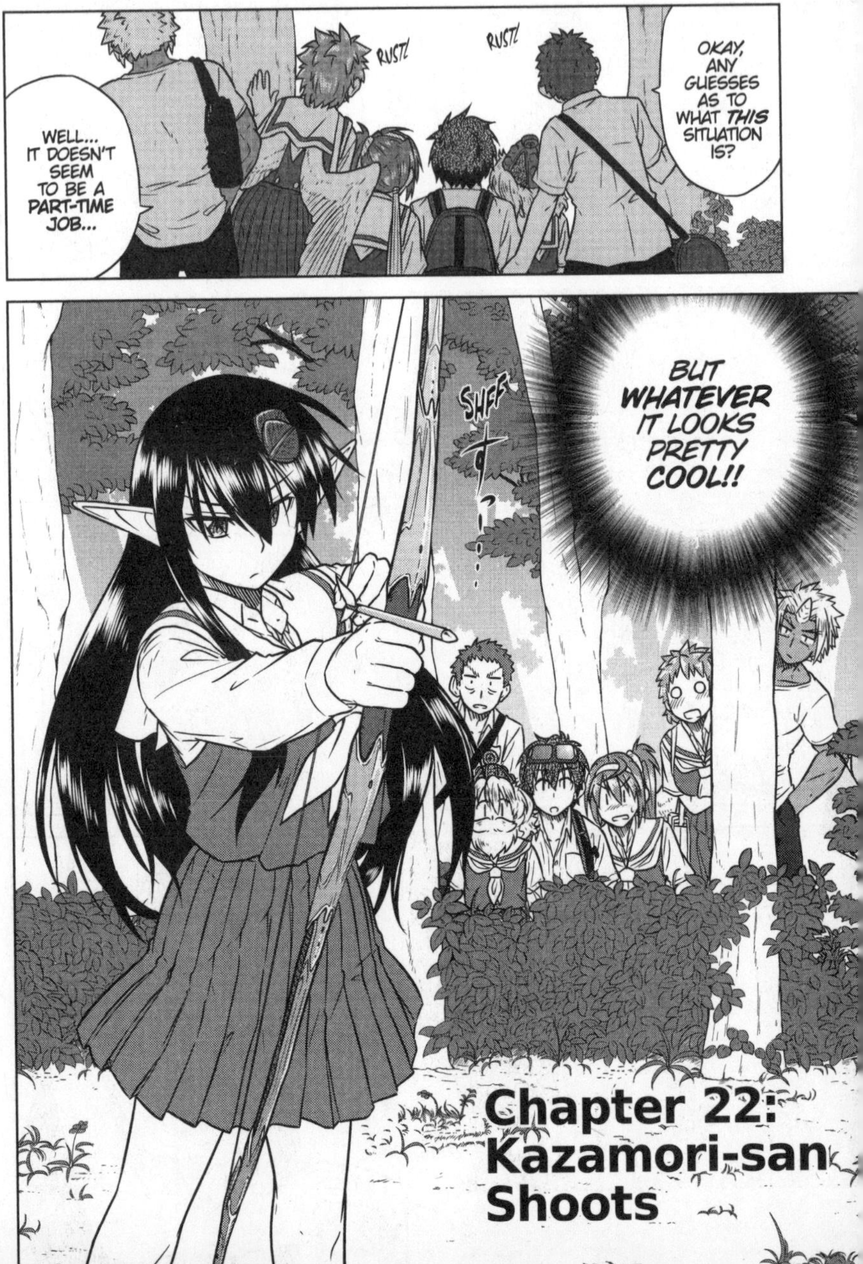
OKAY, ANY GUESSES AS TO WHAT *THIS* SITUATION IS?
RUSTL
RUSTL
WELL... IT DOESN'T SEEM TO BE A PART-TIME JOB...
BUT *WHATEVER* IT LOOKS PRETTY COOL!!
SHFF
Chapter 22: Kazamori-san Shoots

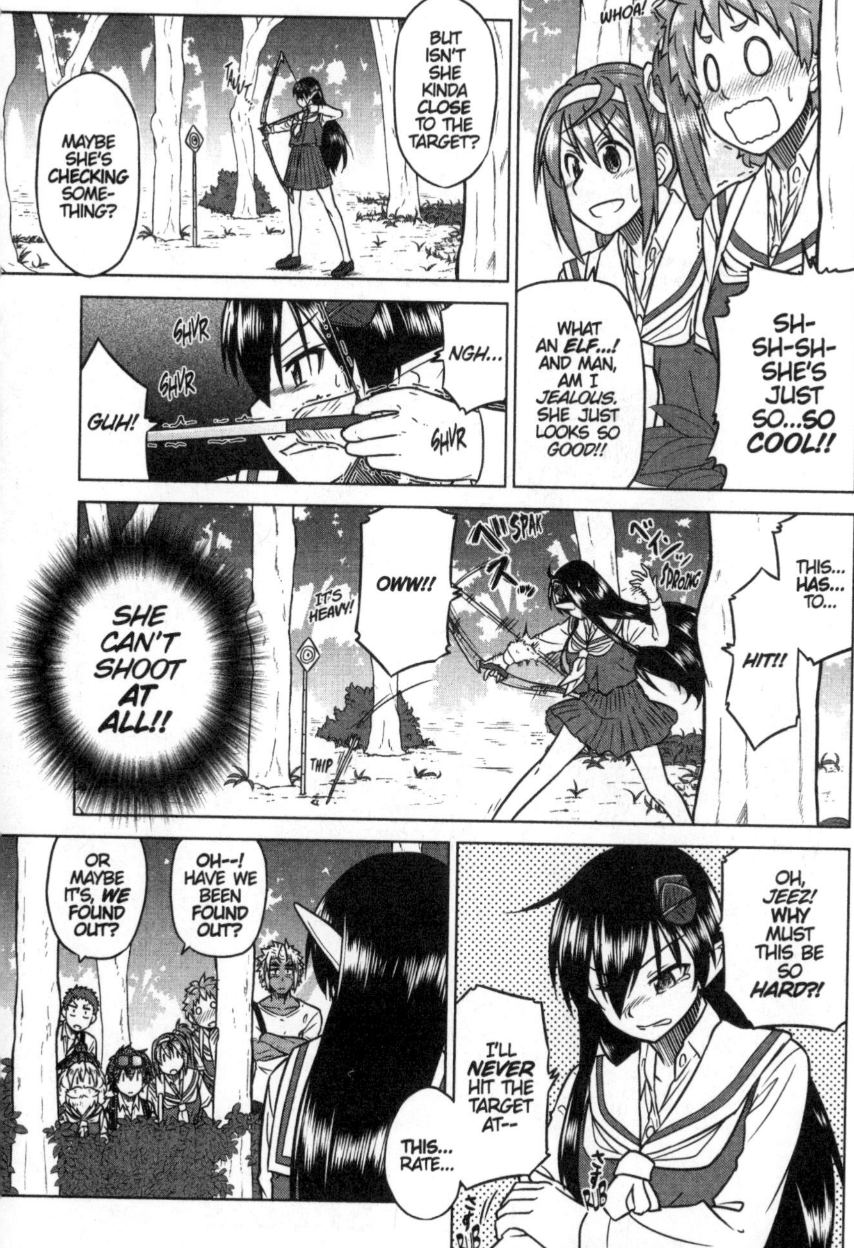
WHOA!
SH-SH-SH-SHE'S JUST SO...SO COOL!!
WHAT AN ELF...! AND MAN, AM I JEALOUS. SHE JUST LOOKS SO GOOD!!
BUT ISN'T SHE KINDA CLOSE TO THE TARGET?
TAUT...
MAYBE SHE'S CHECKING SOME-THING?
NGH...
SHVR
SHVR
SHVR
GUH!
THIS... HAS... TO...
HIT!!
SPROING
SPAK
OWW!!
IT'S HEAVY!
THIP
SHE CAN'T SHOOT AT ALL!!
OH, JEEZ! WHY MUST THIS BE SO HARD?!
I'LL NEVER HIT THE TARGET AT--
THIS... RATE...
RUB
RUB
OH--! HAVE WE BEEN FOUND OUT?
OR MAYBE IT'S, WE FOUND OUT?

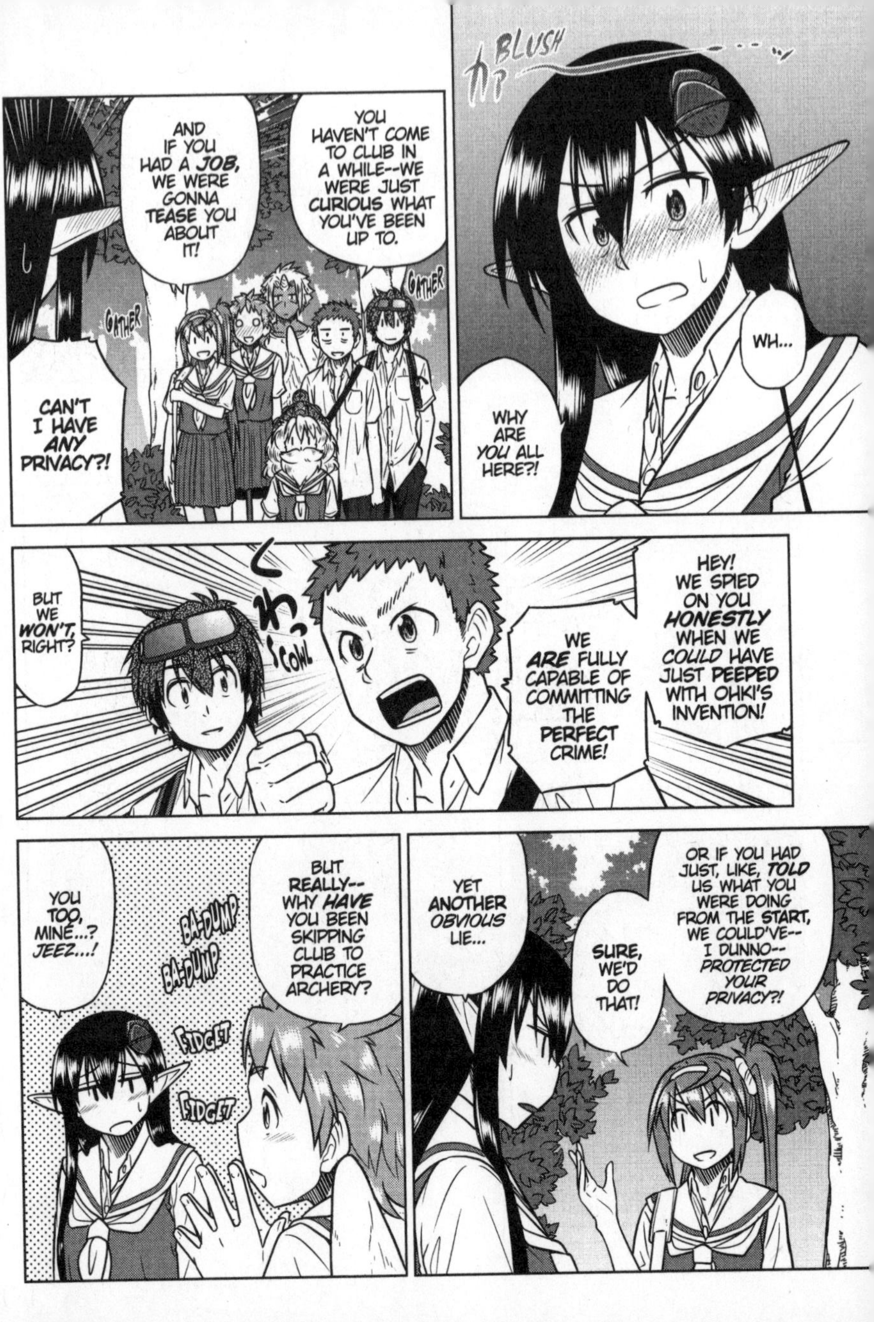
BLUSH
WH...
WHY ARE YOU ALL HERE?!
YOU HAVEN'T COME TO CLUB IN A WHILE--WE WERE JUST CURIOUS WHAT YOU'VE BEEN UP TO.
AND IF YOU HAD A JOB, WE WERE GONNA TEASE YOU ABOUT IT!
GATHER
GATHER
CAN'T I HAVE ANY PRIVACY?!
HEY! WE SPIED ON YOU HONESTLY WHEN WE COULD HAVE JUST PEEPED WITH OHKI'S INVENTION!
WE ARE FULLY CAPABLE OF COMMITTING THE PERFECT CRIME!
SCOWL
BUT WE WON'T, RIGHT?
OR IF YOU HAD JUST, LIKE, TOLD US WHAT YOU WERE DOING FROM THE START, WE COULD'VE-- I DUNNO-- PROTECTED YOUR PRIVACY?!
SURE, WE'D DO THAT!
YET ANOTHER OBVIOUS LIE...
BUT REALLY-- WHY HAVE YOU BEEN SKIPPING CLUB TO PRACTICE ARCHERY?
BA-DUMP
BA-DUMP
YOU TOO, MINE...? JEEZ...!
FIDGET
FIDGET

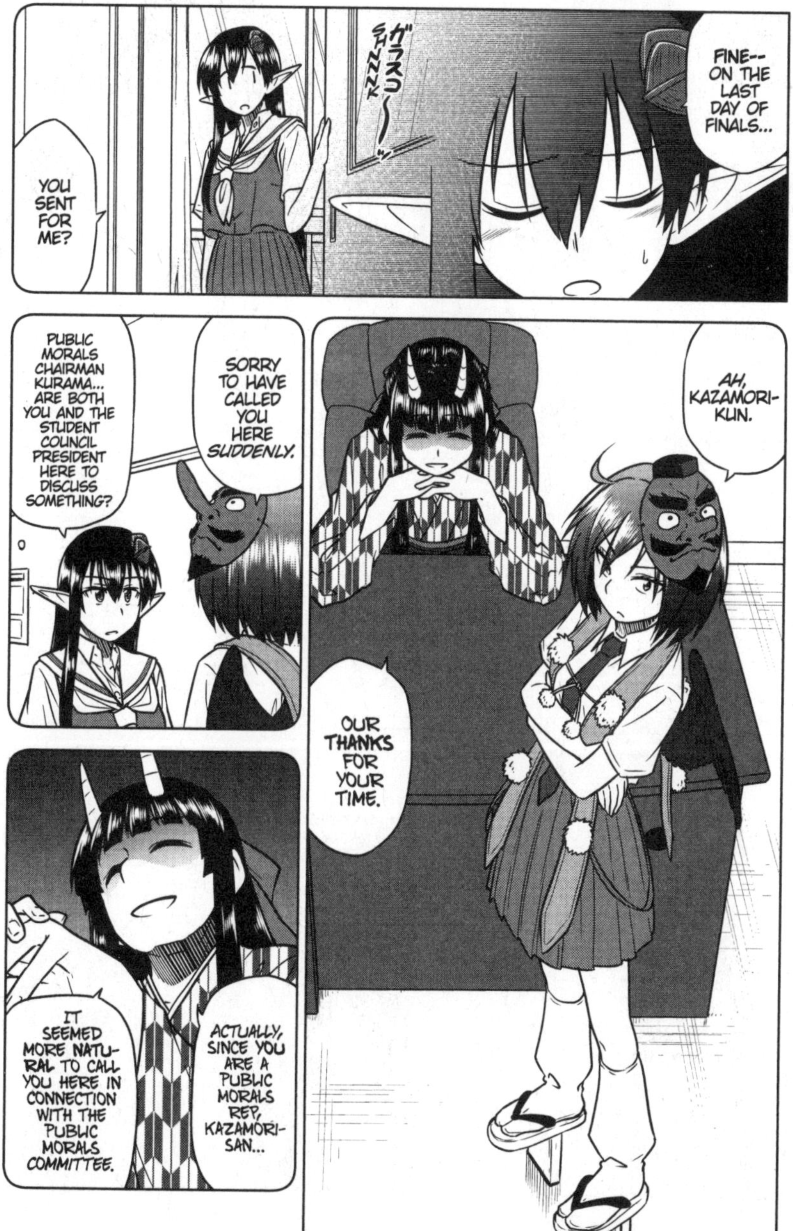
FINE-- ON THE LAST DAY OF FINALS...
SHNNNK
YOU SENT FOR ME?
AH, KAZAMORI-KUN.
OUR THANKS FOR YOUR TIME.
SORRY TO HAVE CALLED YOU HERE *SUDDENLY.*
PUBLIC MORALS CHAIRMAN KURAMA... ARE BOTH YOU AND THE STUDENT COUNCIL PRESIDENT HERE TO DISCUSS SOMETHING?
ACTUALLY, SINCE YOU ARE A PUBLIC MORALS REP, KAZAMORI-SAN...
IT SEEMED MORE NATURAL TO CALL YOU HERE IN CONNECTION WITH THE PUBLIC MORALS COMMITTEE.

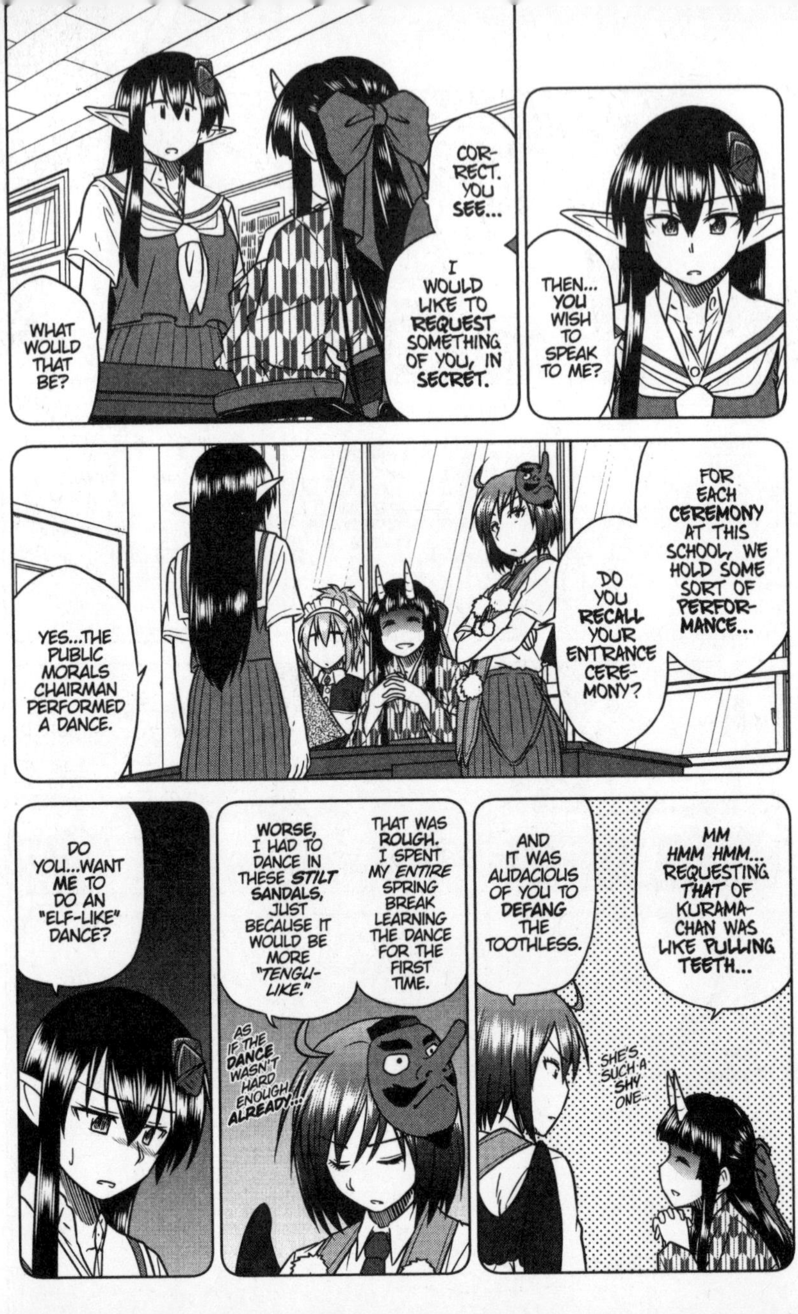
THEN... YOU WISH TO SPEAK TO ME?
COR-RECT. YOU SEE...
I WOULD LIKE TO REQUEST SOMETHING OF YOU, IN SECRET.
WHAT WOULD THAT BE?
FOR EACH CEREMONY AT THIS SCHOOL, WE HOLD SOME SORT OF PERFORMANCE...
DO YOU RECALL YOUR ENTRANCE CEREMONY?
YES...THE PUBLIC MORALS CHAIRMAN PERFORMED A DANCE.
MM HMM HMM... REQUESTING THAT OF KURAMA-CHAN WAS LIKE PULLING TEETH...
AND IT WAS AUDACIOUS OF YOU TO DEFANG THE TOOTHLESS.
SHE'S SUCH A SHY ONE...
THAT WAS ROUGH. I SPENT MY ENTIRE SPRING BREAK LEARNING THE DANCE FOR THE FIRST TIME.
WORSE, I HAD TO DANCE IN THESE STILT SANDALS, JUST BECAUSE IT WOULD BE MORE "TENGU-LIKE."
AS IF THE DANCE WASN'T HARD ENOUGH ALREADY...
DO YOU...WANT ME TO DO AN "ELF-LIKE" DANCE?

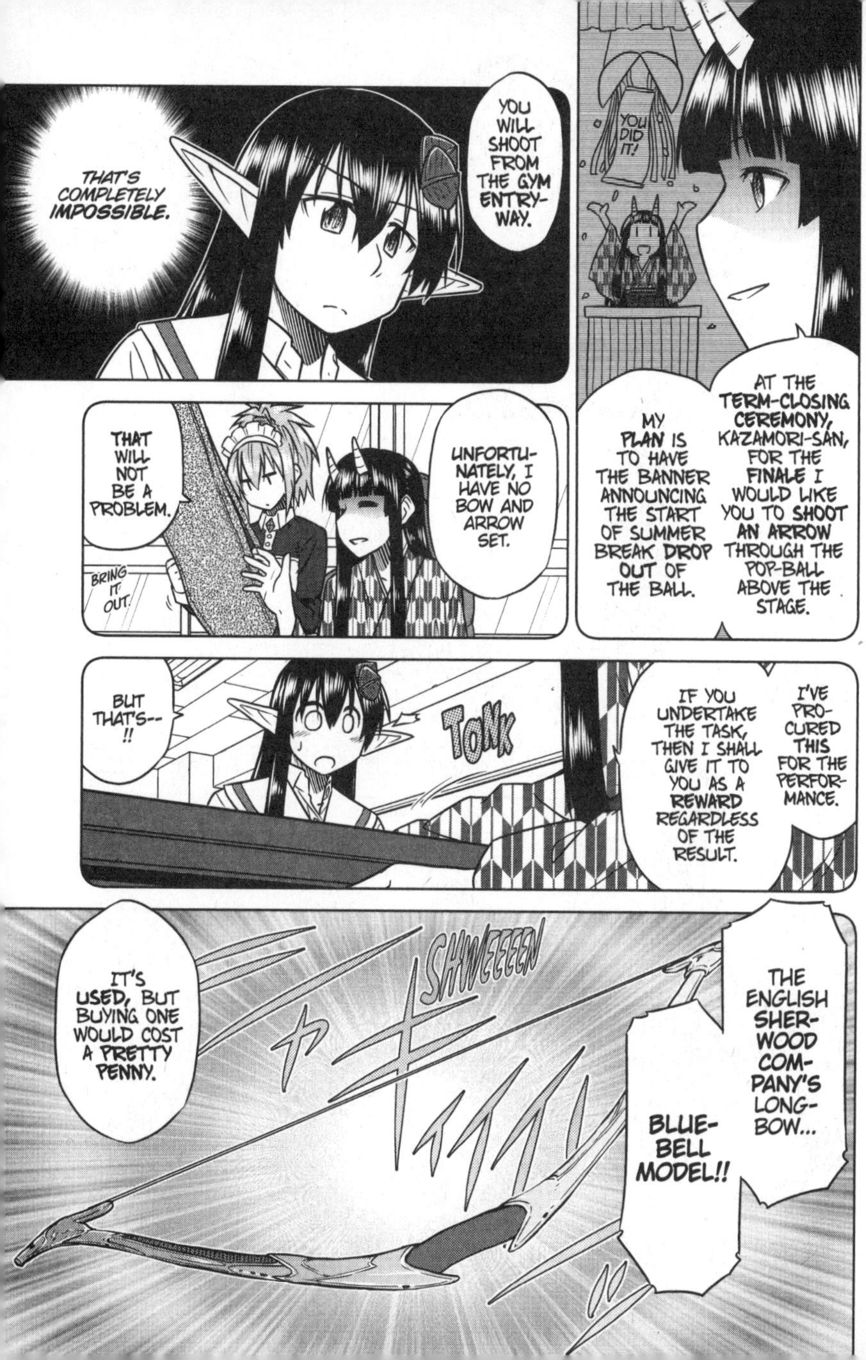

YOU DID IT!
AT THE TERM-CLOSING CEREMONY, KAZAMORI-SAN, FOR THE FINALE I WOULD LIKE YOU TO SHOOT AN ARROW THROUGH THE POP-BALL ABOVE THE STAGE.
MY PLAN IS TO HAVE THE BANNER ANNOUNCING THE START OF SUMMER BREAK DROP OUT OF THE BALL.
YOU WILL SHOOT FROM THE GYM ENTRY-WAY.
THAT'S COMPLETELY IMPOSSIBLE.
UNFORTU-NATELY, I HAVE NO BOW AND ARROW SET.
THAT WILL NOT BE A PROBLEM.
BRING IT OUT.
I'VE PRO-CURED THIS FOR THE PERFOR-MANCE.
IF YOU UNDERTAKE THE TASK, THEN I SHALL GIVE IT TO YOU AS A REWARD REGARDLESS OF THE RESULT.
TONK
BUT THAT'S--!!
THE ENGLISH SHER-WOOD COM-PANY'S LONG-BOW...
BLUE-BELL MODEL!!
SHWEEEEN
IT'S USED, BUT BUYING ONE WOULD COST A PRETTY PENNY.

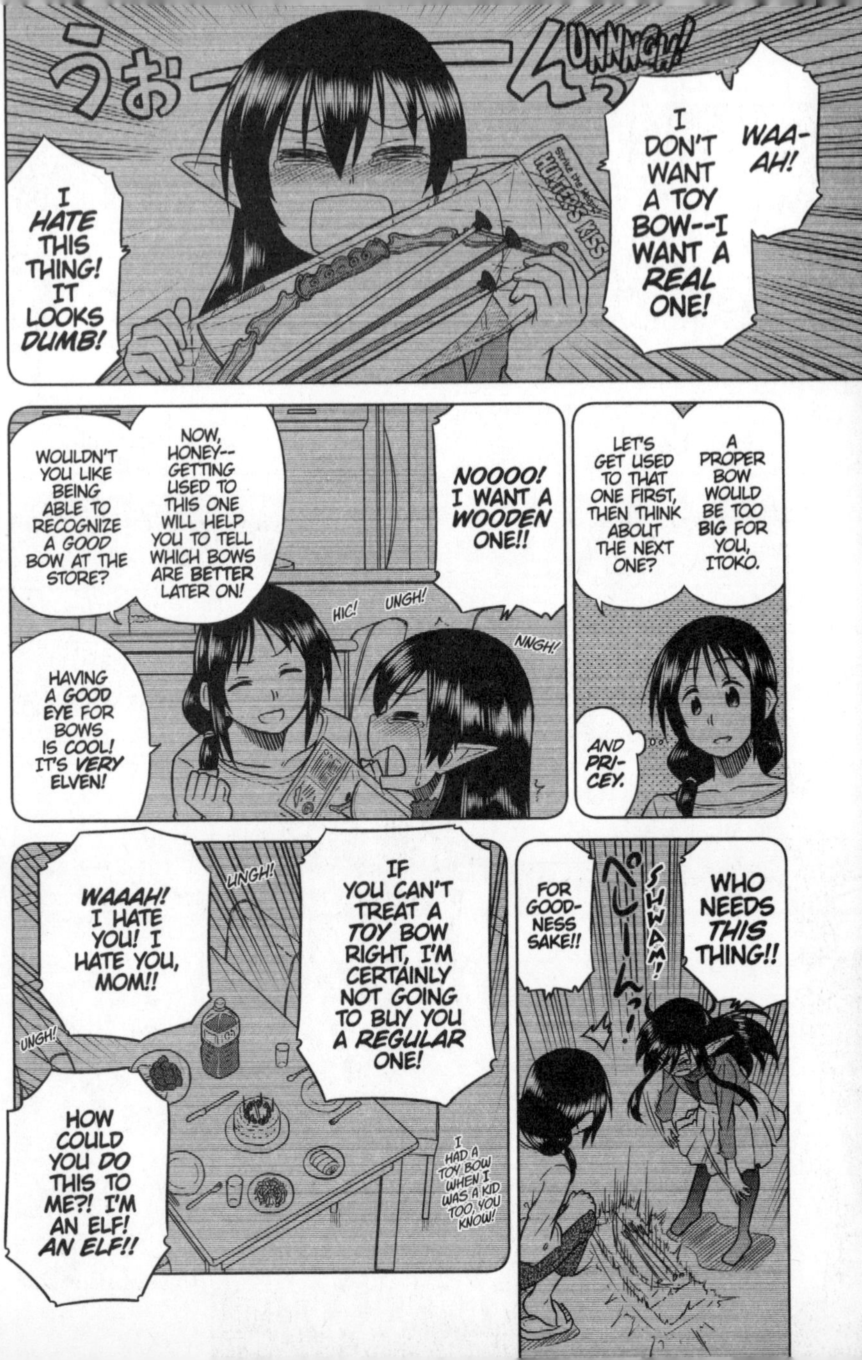
うおーーーんっ
UNNNGH!!
WAA-AH!
I DON'T WANT A TOY BOW--I WANT A REAL ONE!
HUNTER'S KISS
I HATE THIS THING! IT LOOKS DUMB!
A PROPER BOW WOULD BE TOO BIG FOR YOU, ITOKO.
LET'S GET USED TO THAT ONE FIRST, THEN THINK ABOUT THE NEXT ONE?
AND PRICEY.
NOOOO! I WANT A WOODEN ONE!!
NOW, HONEY-- GETTING USED TO THIS ONE WILL HELP YOU TO TELL WHICH BOWS ARE BETTER LATER ON!
WOULDN'T YOU LIKE BEING ABLE TO RECOGNIZE A GOOD BOW AT THE STORE?
UNGH!
HIC!
NNGH!
HAVING A GOOD EYE FOR BOWS IS COOL! IT'S VERY ELVEN!
WHO NEEDS THIS THING!!
SHWAM!
ぺしーんっ
FOR GOODNESS SAKE!!
IF YOU CAN'T TREAT A TOY BOW RIGHT, I'M CERTAINLY NOT GOING TO BUY YOU A REGULAR ONE!
UNGH!
WAAAH! I HATE YOU! I HATE YOU, MOM!!
UNGH!
I HAD A TOY BOW WHEN I WAS A KID TOO, YOU KNOW!
HOW COULD YOU DO THIS TO ME?! I'M AN ELF! AN ELF!!

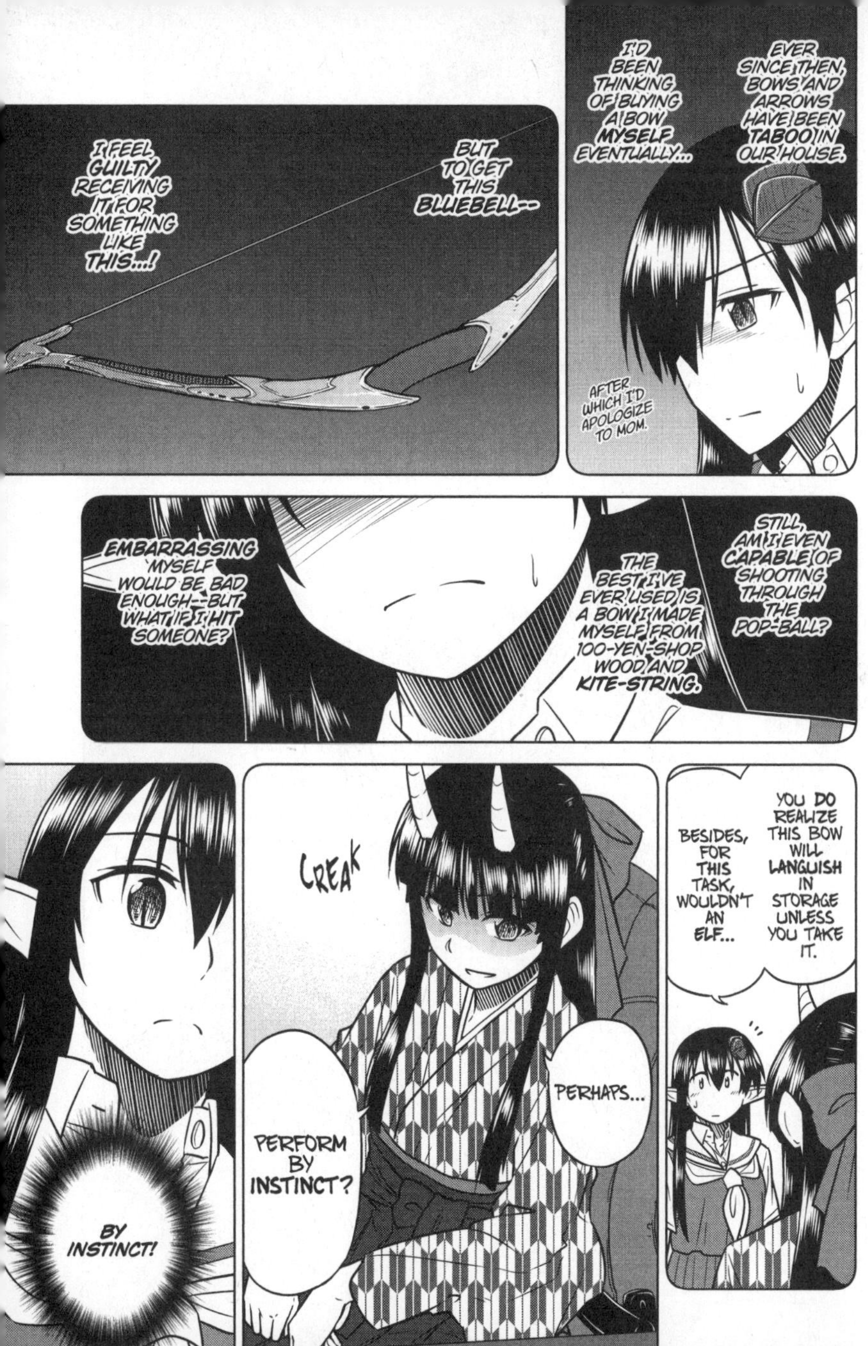
EVER SINCE THEN, BOWS AND ARROWS HAVE BEEN TABOO IN OUR HOUSE.
I'D BEEN THINKING OF BUYING A BOW MYSELF EVENTUALLY...
AFTER WHICH I'D APOLOGIZE TO MOM.
BUT TO GET THIS BLUEBELL--
I FEEL GUILTY RECEIVING IT FOR SOMETHING LIKE THIS...!
STILL, AM I EVEN CAPABLE OF SHOOTING THROUGH THE POP-BALL?
THE BEST I'VE EVER USED IS A BOW I MADE MYSELF FROM 100-YEN-SHOP WOOD AND KITE-STRING.
EMBARRASSING MYSELF WOULD BE BAD ENOUGH--BUT WHAT IF I HIT SOMEONE?
YOU DO REALIZE THIS BOW WILL LANGUISH IN STORAGE UNLESS YOU TAKE IT.
BESIDES, FOR THIS TASK, WOULDN'T AN ELF...
...
CREAK
PERHAPS...
PERFORM BY INSTINCT?
BY INSTINCT!

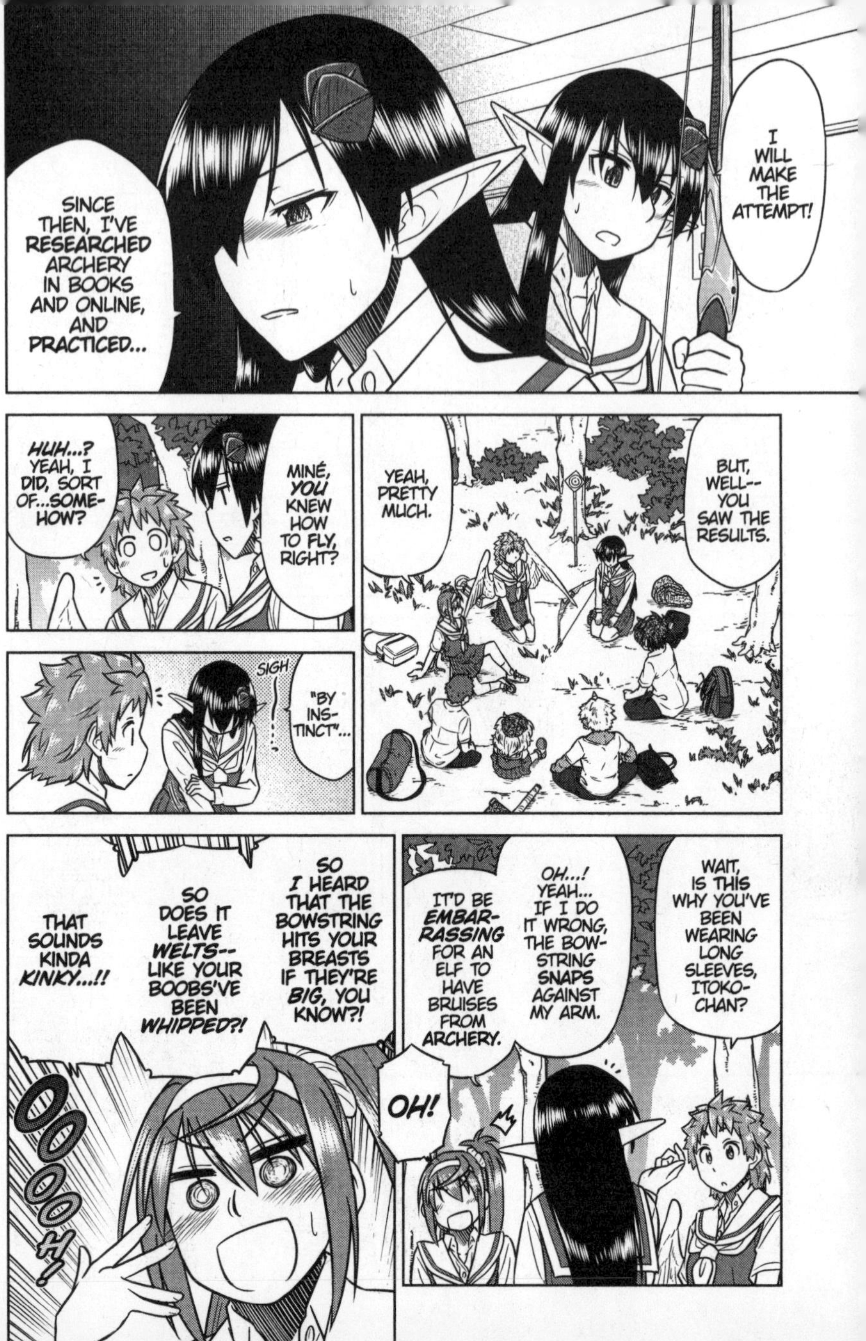
I WILL MAKE THE ATTEMPT!
SINCE THEN, I'VE RESEARCHED ARCHERY IN BOOKS AND ONLINE, AND PRACTICED...
BUT, WELL-- YOU SAW THE RESULTS.
YEAH, PRETTY MUCH.
MINÉ, *YOU* KNEW HOW TO FLY, RIGHT?
HUH...? YEAH, I DID, SORT OF...SOME-HOW?
SIGH
"BY INS-TINCT"...
WAIT, IS THIS WHY YOU'VE BEEN WEARING LONG SLEEVES, ITOKO-CHAN?
OH...! YEAH... IF I DO IT WRONG, THE BOW-STRING SNAPS AGAINST MY ARM.
IT'D BE *EMBAR-RASSING* FOR AN ELF TO HAVE BRUISES FROM ARCHERY.
OH!
SO *I* HEARD THAT THE BOWSTRING HITS YOUR BREASTS IF THEY'RE *BIG*, YOU KNOW?!
SO DOES IT LEAVE *WELTS*-- LIKE YOUR BOOBS'VE BEEN *WHIPPED?!*
THAT SOUNDS KINDA *KINKY...!!*
OOOOOH!

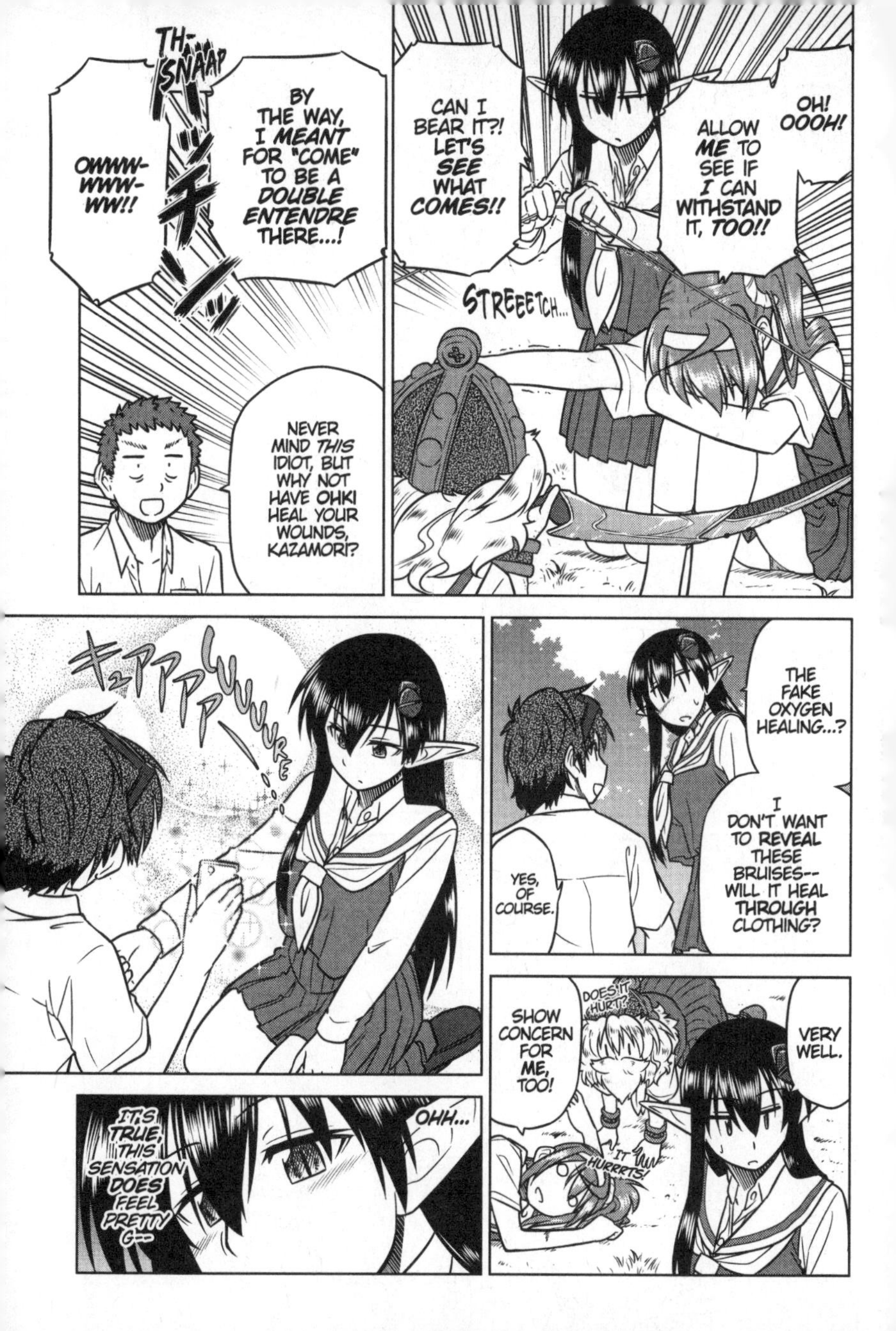
OH! OOOH!
ALLOW ME TO SEE IF I CAN WITHSTAND IT, TOO!!
CAN I BEAR IT?! LET'S SEE WHAT COMES!!
STREEETCH...
BY THE WAY, I MEANT FOR "COME" TO BE A DOUBLE ENTENDRE THERE...!
TH-SNAAP
OWWW-WWW-WW!!
NEVER MIND THIS IDIOT, BUT WHY NOT HAVE OHKI HEAL YOUR WOUNDS, KAZAMORI?
THE FAKE OXYGEN HEALING...?
I DON'T WANT TO REVEAL THESE BRUISES-- WILL IT HEAL THROUGH CLOTHING?
YES, OF COURSE.
VERY WELL.
DOES IT HURT?
SHOW CONCERN FOR ME, TOO!
IT HURRRTS!
キュアアアア
CUUUURE
OHH...
IT'S TRUE, THIS SENSATION DOES FEEL PRETTY G--

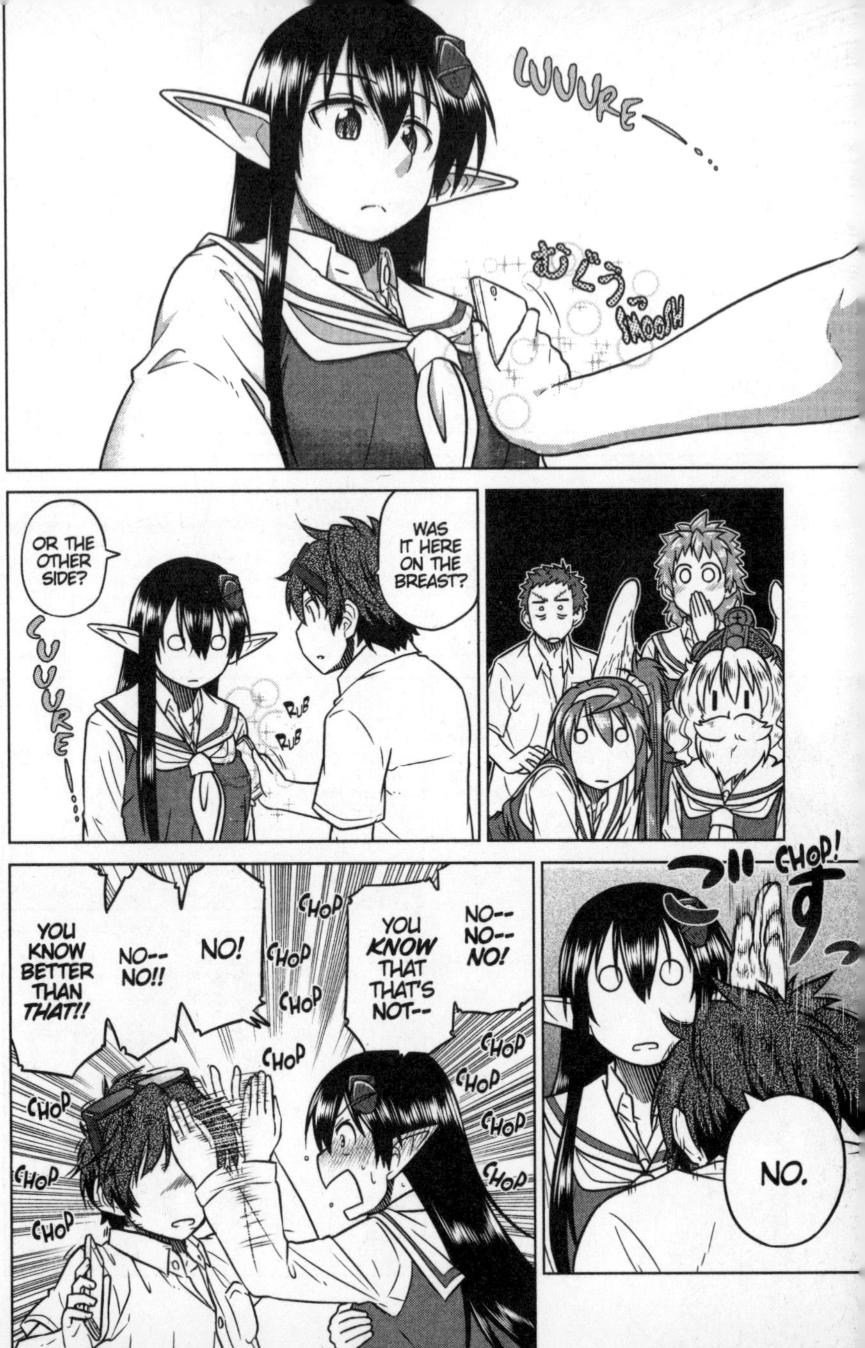
LUUURE—...
SMOOSH
WAS IT HERE ON THE BREAST?
OR THE OTHER SIDE?
RUB
RUB
LUUURE!...
CHOP!
NO.
NO-- NO-- NO!
YOU KNOW THAT THAT'S NOT--
NO!
NO-- NO!!
YOU KNOW BETTER THAN THAT!!
CHOP
CHOP
CHOP
CHOP
CHOP
CHOP
CHOP
CHOP
CHOP
CHOP

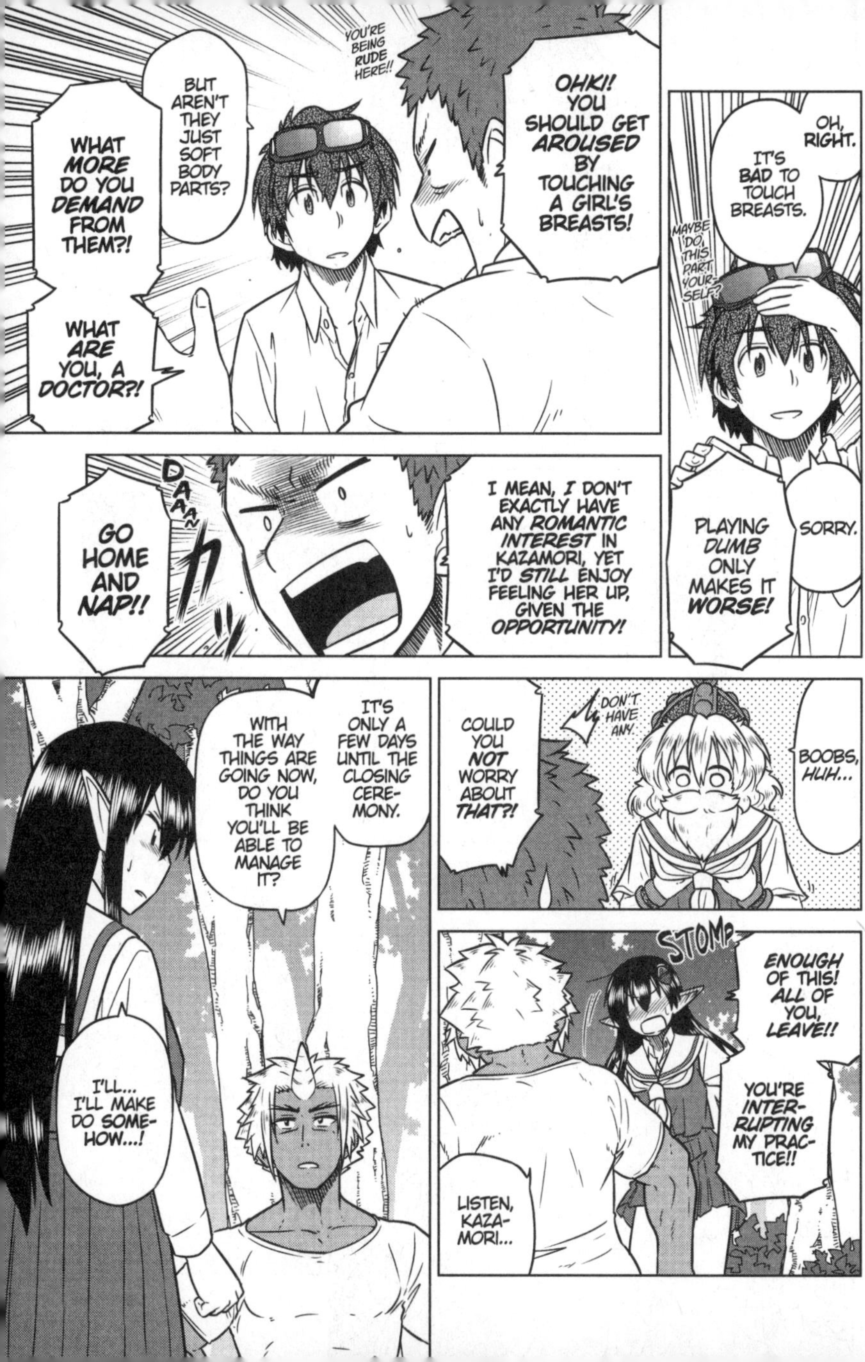
OHKI! YOU SHOULD GET AROUSED BY TOUCHING A GIRL'S BREASTS!
YOU'RE BEING RUDE HERE!!
BUT AREN'T THEY JUST SOFT BODY PARTS?
WHAT MORE DO YOU DEMAND FROM THEM?!
WHAT ARE YOU, A DOCTOR?!
OH, RIGHT.
IT'S BAD TO TOUCH BREASTS.
MAYBE DO THIS PART YOURSELF?
SORRY.
PLAYING DUMB ONLY MAKES IT WORSE!
I MEAN, I DON'T EXACTLY HAVE ANY ROMANTIC INTEREST IN KAZAMORI, YET I'D STILL ENJOY FEELING HER UP, GIVEN THE OPPORTUNITY!
DAAAN
GO HOME AND NAP!!
BOOBS, HUH...
COULD YOU NOT WORRY ABOUT THAT?!
DON'T HAVE ANY
STOMP
ENOUGH OF THIS! ALL OF YOU, LEAVE!!
YOU'RE INTER-RUPTING MY PRAC-TICE!!
LISTEN, KAZA-MORI...
IT'S ONLY A FEW DAYS UNTIL THE CLOSING CERE-MONY.
WITH THE WAY THINGS ARE GOING NOW, DO YOU THINK YOU'LL BE ABLE TO MANAGE IT?
I'LL... I'LL MAKE DO SOME-HOW...!

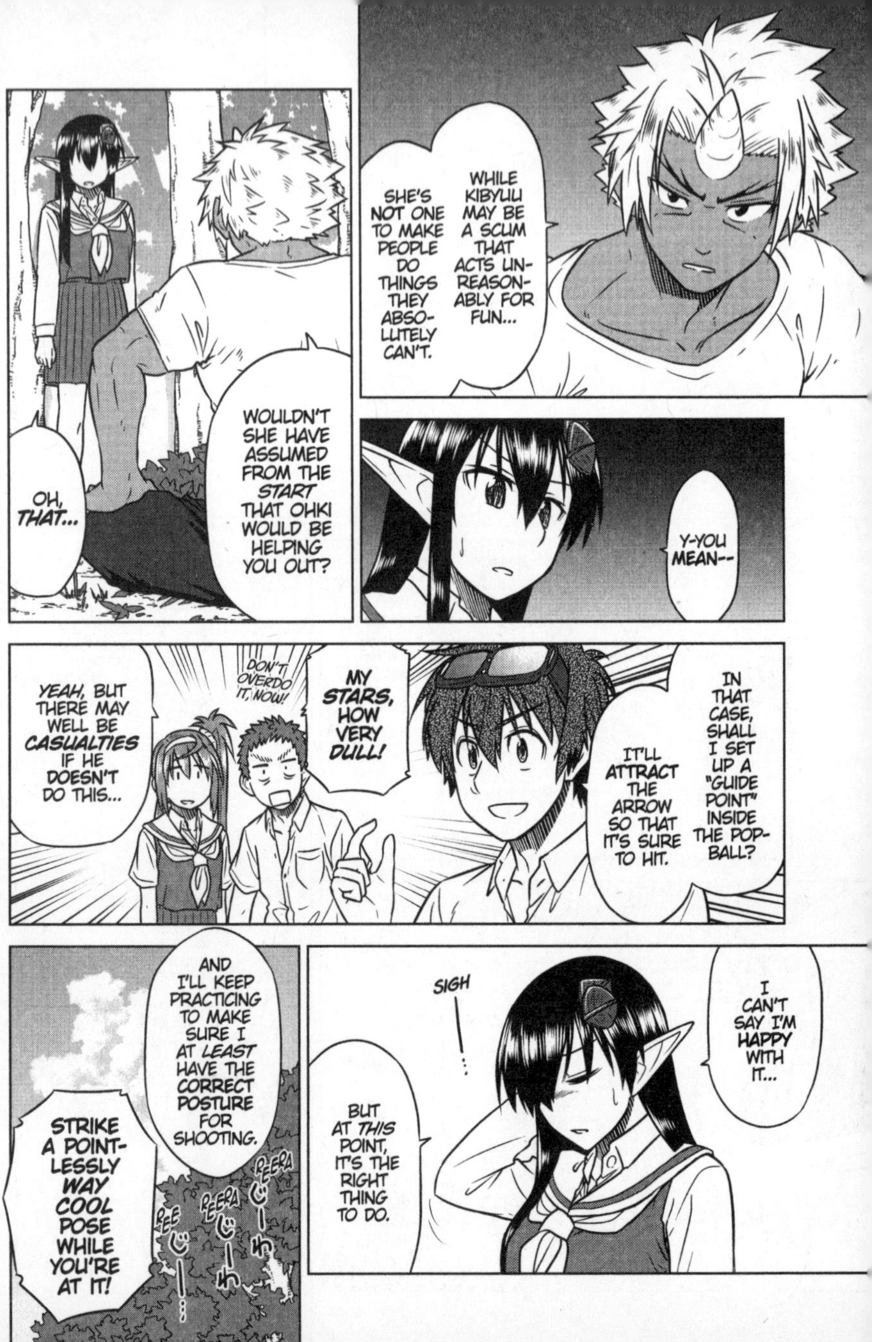
WHILE KIBYUU MAY BE A SCUM THAT ACTS UNREASONABLY FOR FUN...
SHE'S NOT ONE TO MAKE PEOPLE DO THINGS THEY ABSOLUTELY CAN'T.
Y-YOU MEAN--
WOULDN'T SHE HAVE ASSUMED FROM THE START THAT OHKI WOULD BE HELPING YOU OUT?
OH, THAT...
IN THAT CASE, SHALL I SET UP A "GUIDE POINT" INSIDE THE POP-BALL?
IT'LL ATTRACT THE ARROW SO THAT IT'S SURE TO HIT.
MY STARS, HOW VERY DULL!
DON'T OVERDO IT, NOW!
YEAH, BUT THERE MAY WELL BE CASUALTIES IF HE DOESN'T DO THIS...
I CAN'T SAY I'M HAPPY WITH IT...
SIGH
BUT AT THIS POINT, IT'S THE RIGHT THING TO DO.
AND I'LL KEEP PRACTICING TO MAKE SURE I AT LEAST HAVE THE CORRECT POSTURE FOR SHOOTING.
STRIKE A POINTLESSLY WAY COOL POSE WHILE YOU'RE AT IT!
REERA
REERA
REE

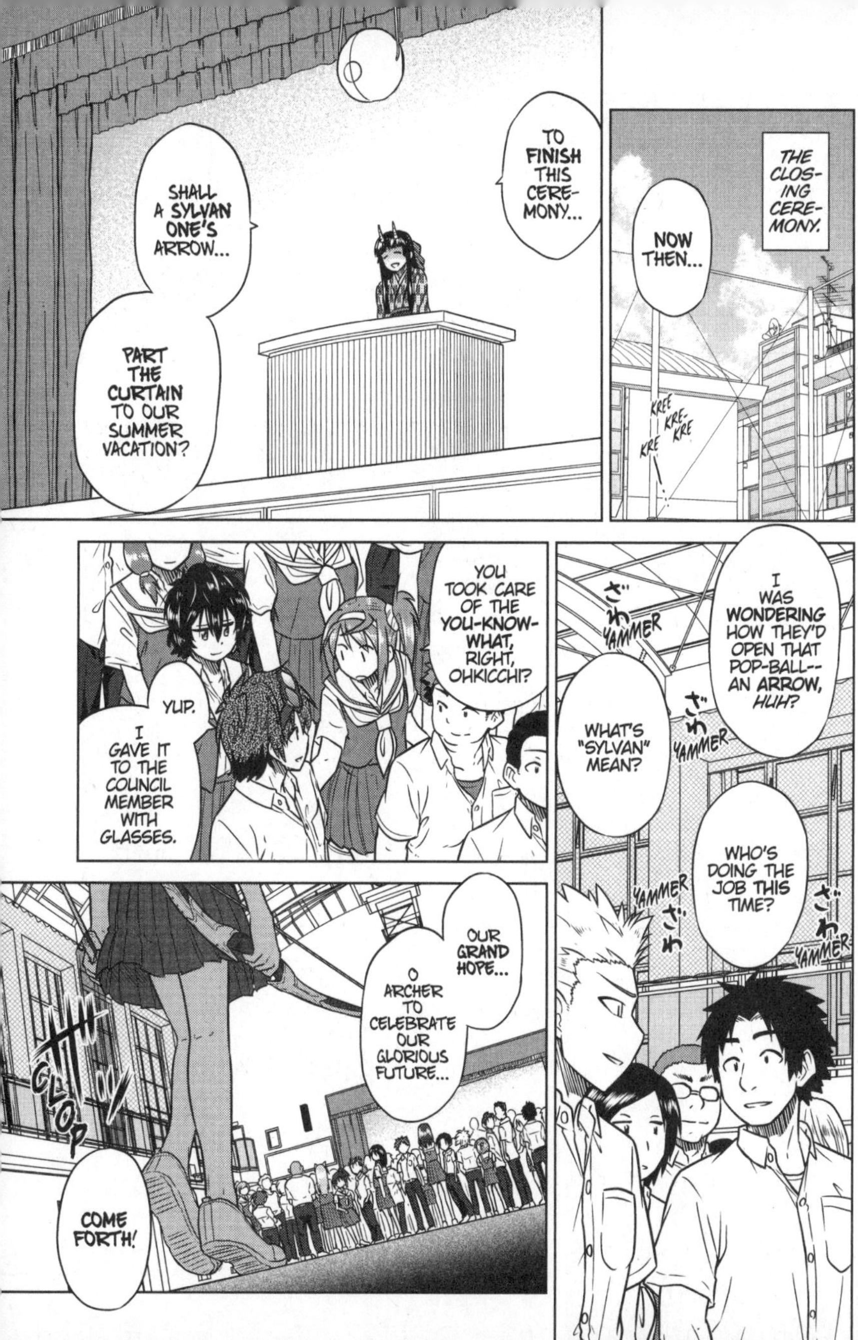
THE CLOSING CEREMONY.
NOW THEN...
KRE KRE- KRE- KRE
TO FINISH THIS CEREMONY...
SHALL A SYLVAN ONE'S ARROW...
PART THE CURTAIN TO OUR SUMMER VACATION?
I WAS WONDERING HOW THEY'D OPEN THAT POP-BALL-- AN ARROW, HUH?
ざわ YAMMER
WHAT'S "SYLVAN" MEAN?
ざわ YAMMER
WHO'S DOING THE JOB THIS TIME?
YAMMER ざわ
ざわ YAMMER
YOU TOOK CARE OF THE YOU-KNOW-WHAT, RIGHT, OHKICCHI?
YUP.
I GAVE IT TO THE COUNCIL MEMBER WITH GLASSES.
OUR GRAND HOPE...
O ARCHER TO CELEBRATE OUR GLORIOUS FUTURE...
CLOP
COME FORTH!

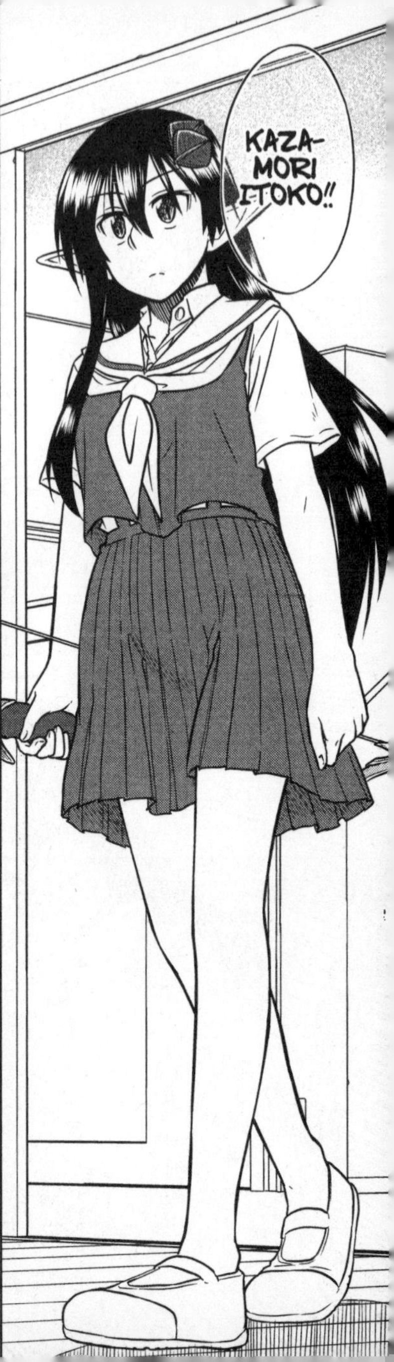
KAZAMORI ITOKO!!
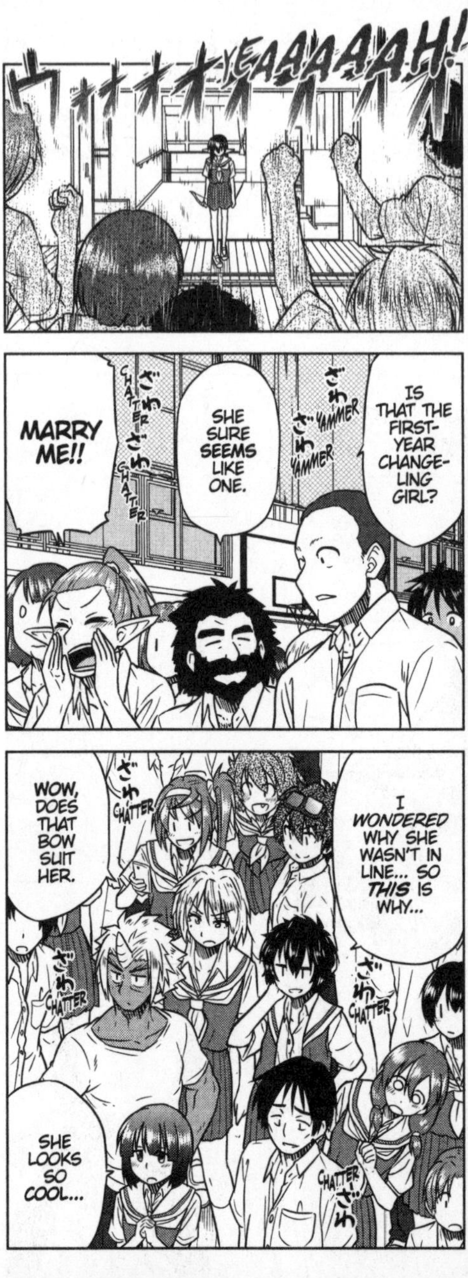
ウォォォォォ YEAAAAAH!
IS THAT THE FIRST-YEAR CHANGELING GIRL?
ざわ ざわ YAMMER YAMMER
SHE SURE SEEMS LIKE ONE.
ざわ ざわ CHATTER CHATTER
MARRY ME!!
I WONDERED WHY SHE WASN'T IN LINE... SO THIS IS WHY...
ざわ CHATTER
WOW, DOES THAT BOW SUIT HER.
ざわ CHATTER
ざわ CHATTER
SHE LOOKS SO COOL...
ざわ CHATTER

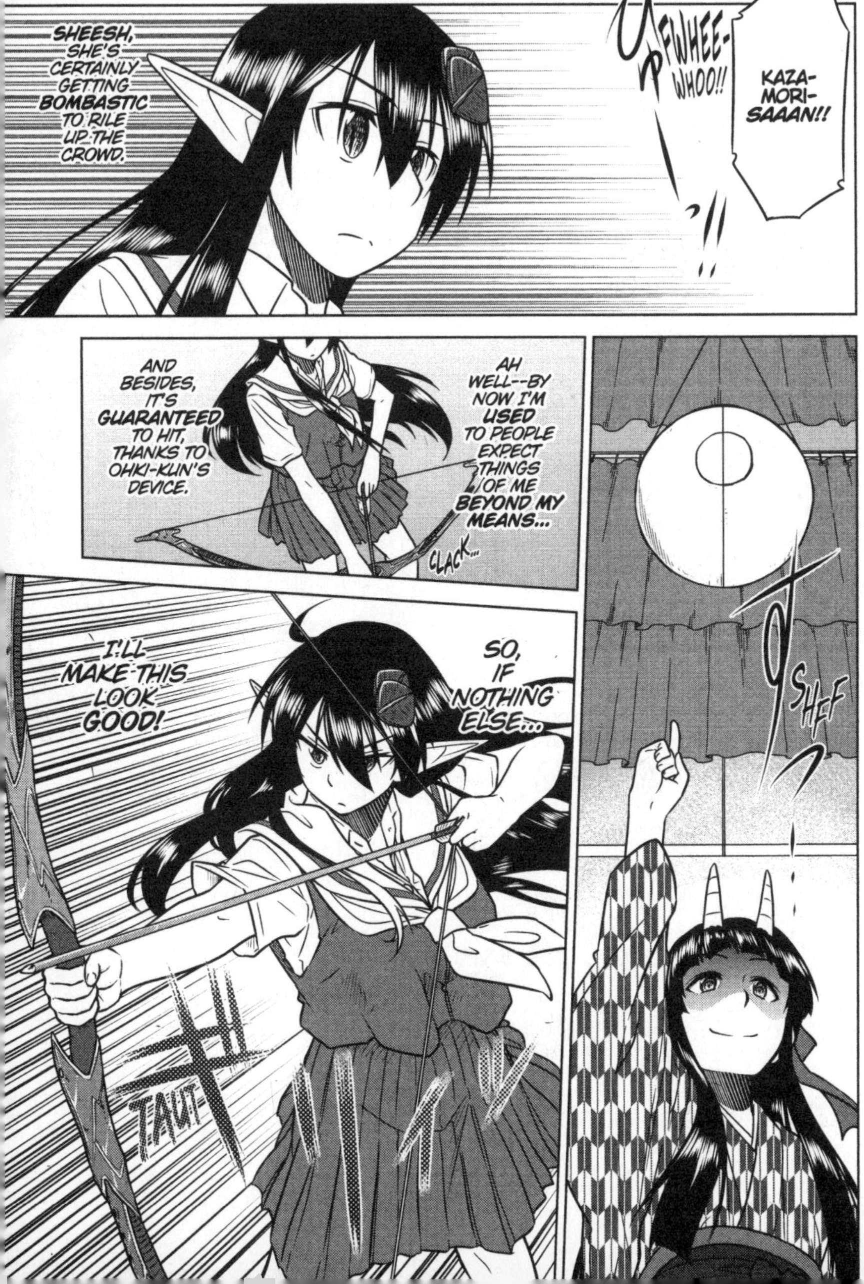
KAZAMORI-SAAAN!!
UP FWHEE-WHOO!!
SHEESH, SHE'S CERTAINLY GETTING BOMBASTIC TO RILE UP THE CROWD.
SHFF
AH WELL--BY NOW I'M USED TO PEOPLE EXPECT THINGS OF ME BEYOND MY MEANS...
AND BESIDES, IT'S GUARANTEED TO HIT, THANKS TO OHKI-KUN'S DEVICE.
CLACK...
SO, IF NOTHING ELSE...
I'LL MAKE THIS LOOK GOOD!
TAUT

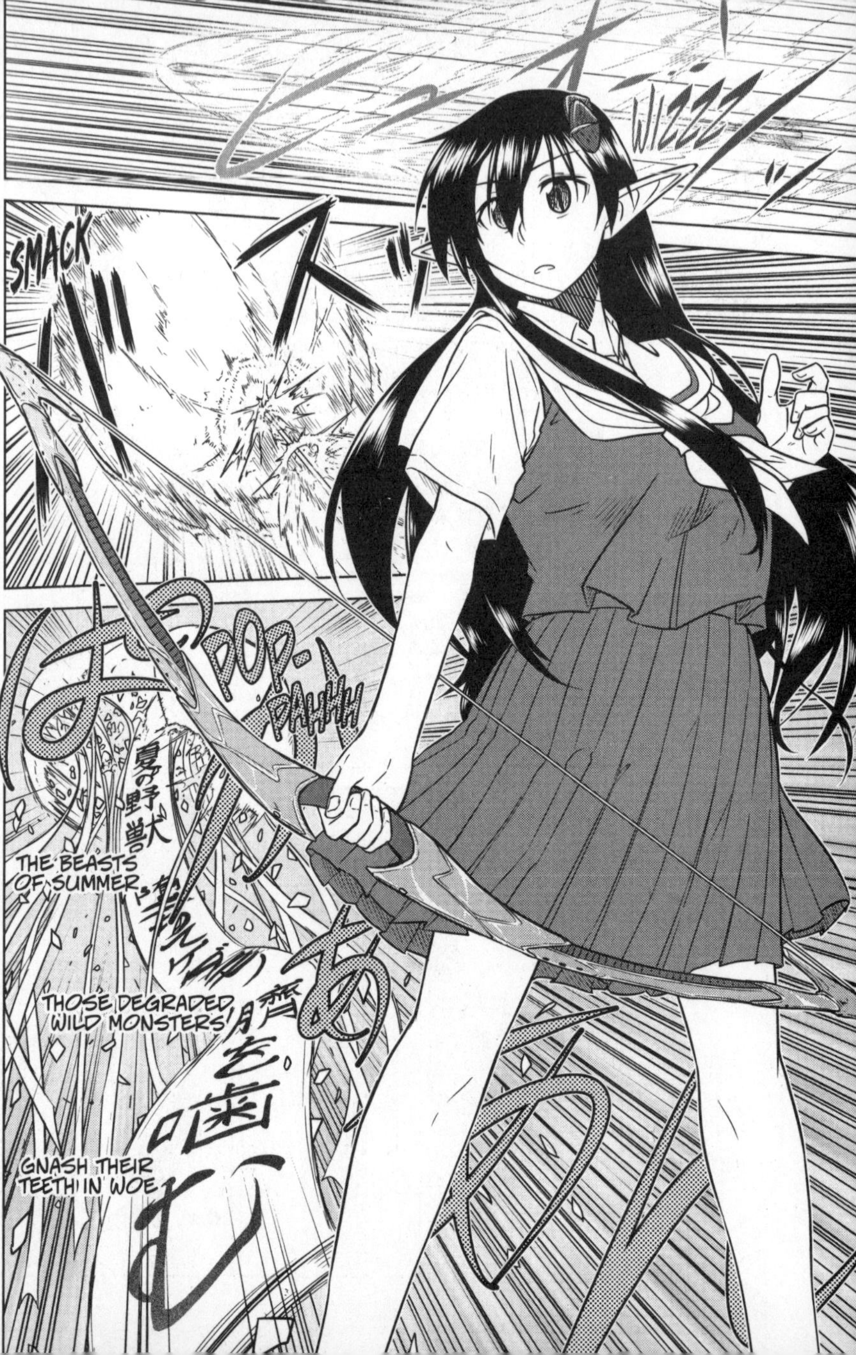
WIZZZZ
SMACK
POP-PAHHH
THE BEASTS OF SUMMER
THOSE DEGRADED WILD MONSTERS
GNASH THEIR TEETH IN WOE

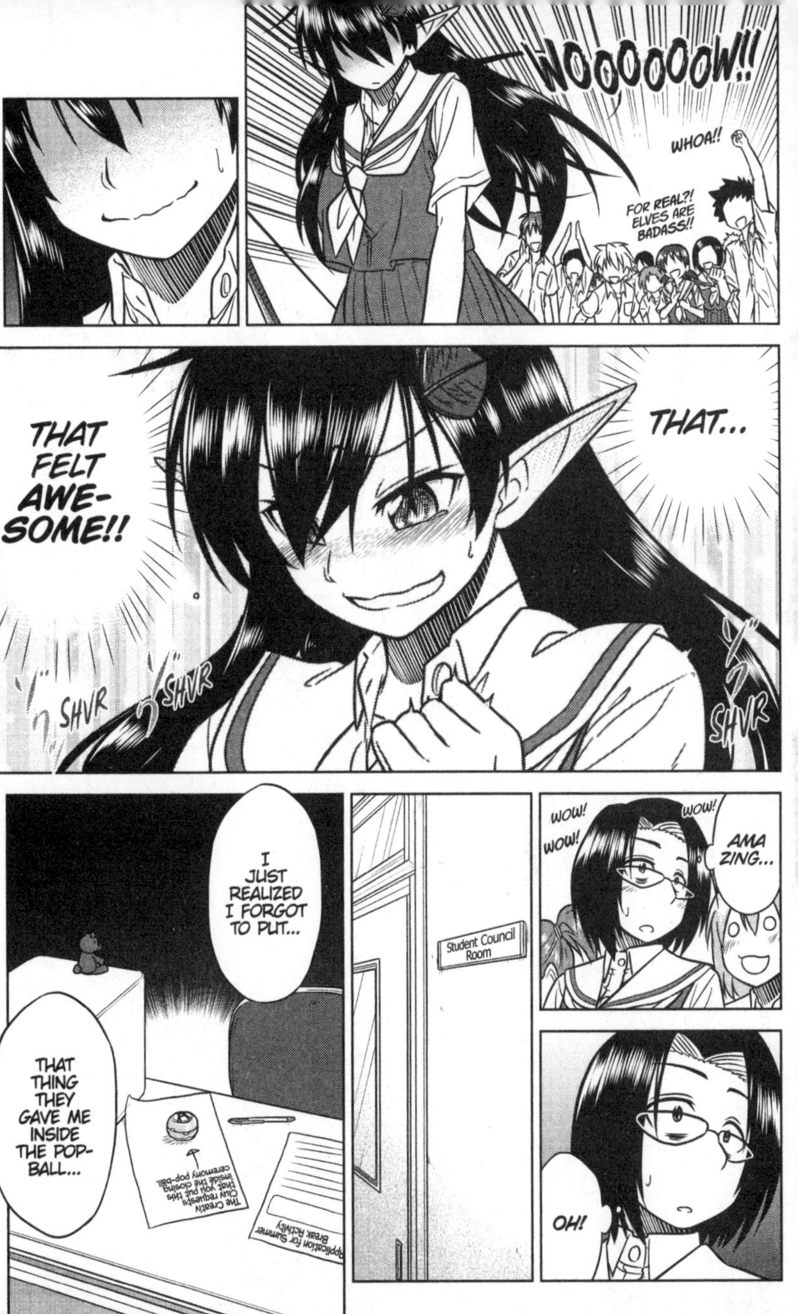
WOOOOOW!!
WHOA!!
FOR REAL?! ELVES ARE BADASS!!
THAT...
THAT FELT AWESOME!!
SHVR
SHVR
SHVR
WOW!
WOW!
WOW!
AMAZING...
OH!
Student Council Room
I JUST REALIZED I FORGOT TO PUT...
THAT THING THEY GAVE ME INSIDE THE POP-BALL...
The Creativ Club requests that you put this inside the closing ceremony pop-ball.
Application for Summer Break Activity

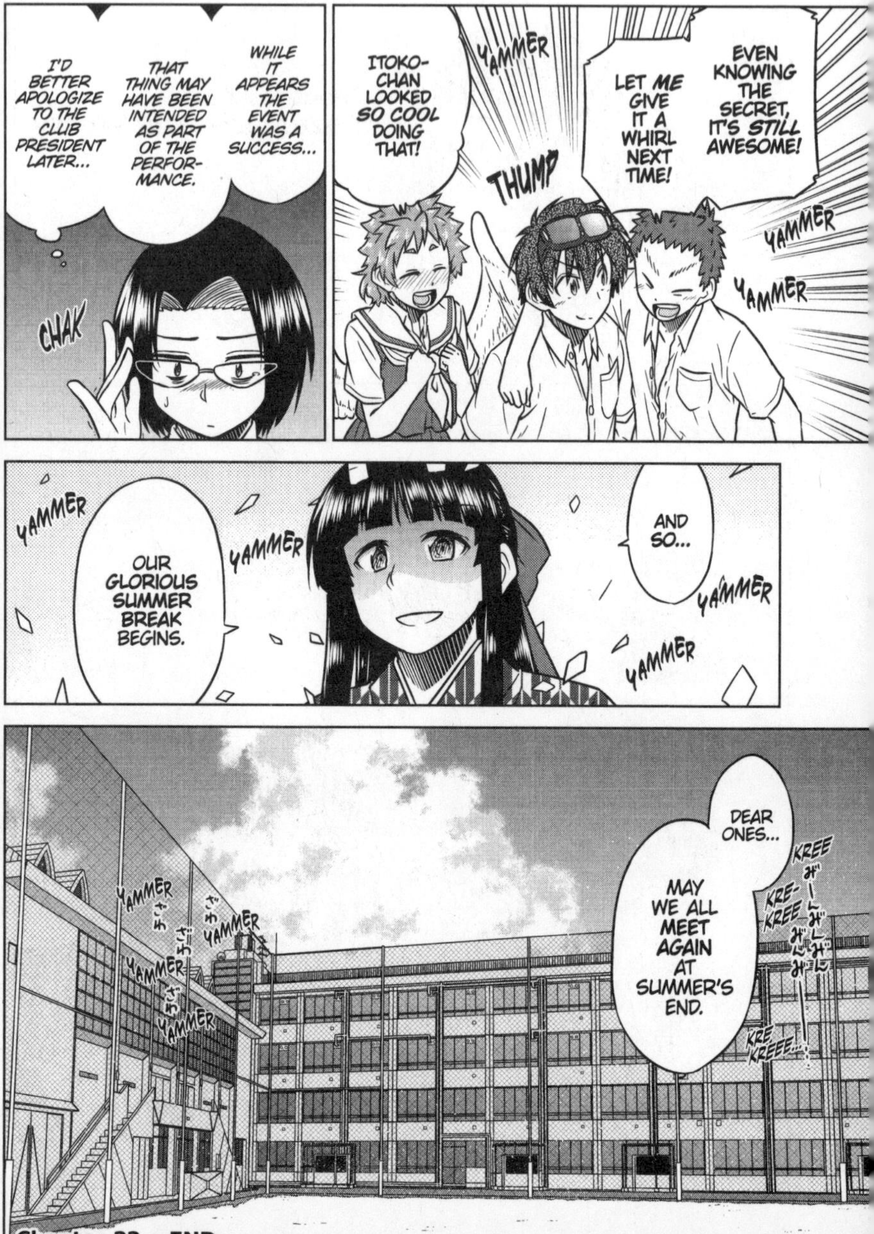
EVEN KNOWING THE SECRET, IT'S STILL AWESOME!
LET ME GIVE IT A WHIRL NEXT TIME!
YAMMER
YAMMER
THUMP
YAMMER
ITOKO-CHAN LOOKED SO COOL DOING THAT!
WHILE IT APPEARS THE EVENT WAS A SUCCESS...
THAT THING MAY HAVE BEEN INTENDED AS PART OF THE PERFORMANCE.
I'D BETTER APOLOGIZE TO THE CLUB PRESIDENT LATER...
CHAK
AND SO...
YAMMER
YAMMER
YAMMER
OUR GLORIOUS SUMMER BREAK BEGINS.
YAMMER
DEAR ONES...
MAY WE ALL MEET AGAIN AT SUMMER'S END.
KREE
KRE-KREE
KRE KREEE...
YAMMER
YAMMER
YAMMER
YAMMER

Chapter 22 • END

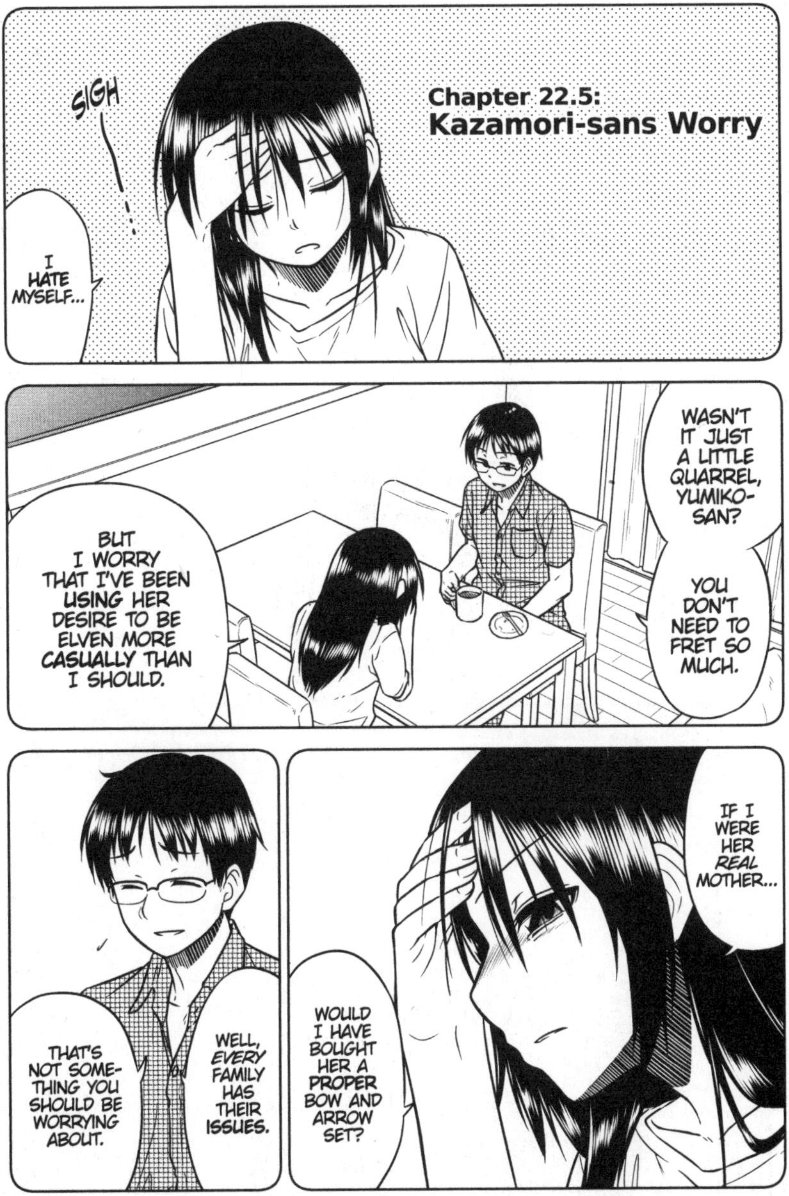
Chapter 22.5: Kazamori-sans Worry
SIGH
I HATE MYSELF...
WASN'T IT JUST A LITTLE QUARREL, YUMIKO-SAN?
YOU DON'T NEED TO FRET SO MUCH.
BUT I WORRY THAT I'VE BEEN USING HER DESIRE TO BE ELVEN MORE CASUALLY THAN I SHOULD.
IF I WERE HER REAL MOTHER...
WOULD I HAVE BOUGHT HER A PROPER BOW AND ARROW SET?
WELL, EVERY FAMILY HAS THEIR ISSUES.
THAT'S NOT SOME-THING YOU SHOULD BE WORRYING ABOUT.

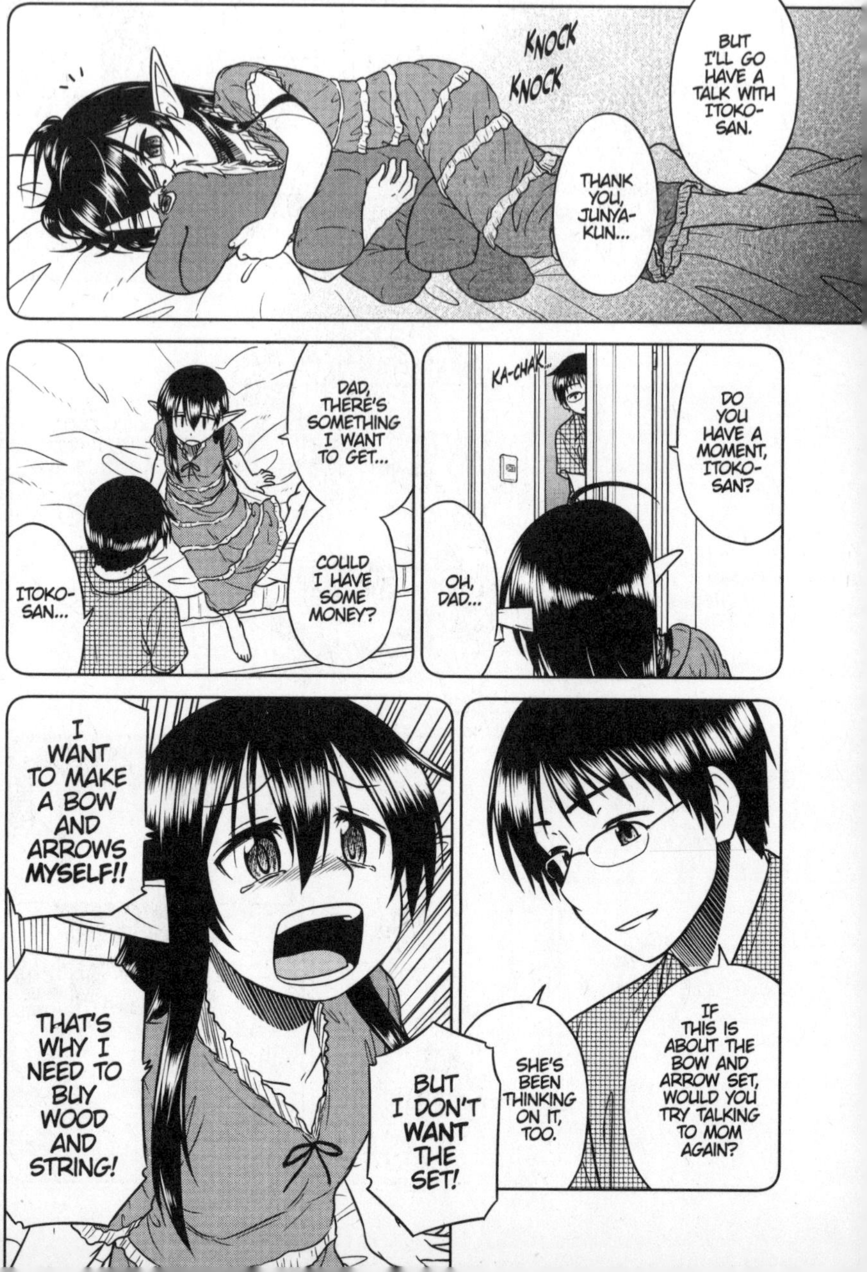
BUT I'LL GO HAVE A TALK WITH ITOKO-SAN.
THANK YOU, JUNYA-KUN...
KNOCK KNOCK
KA-CHAK..
DO YOU HAVE A MOMENT, ITOKO-SAN?
OH, DAD...
DAD, THERE'S SOMETHING I WANT TO GET...
COULD I HAVE SOME MONEY?
ITOKO-SAN...
IF THIS IS ABOUT THE BOW AND ARROW SET, WOULD YOU TRY TALKING TO MOM AGAIN?
SHE'S BEEN THINKING ON IT, TOO.
BUT I DON'T WANT THE SET!
I WANT TO MAKE A BOW AND ARROWS MYSELF!!
THAT'S WHY I NEED TO BUY WOOD AND STRING!

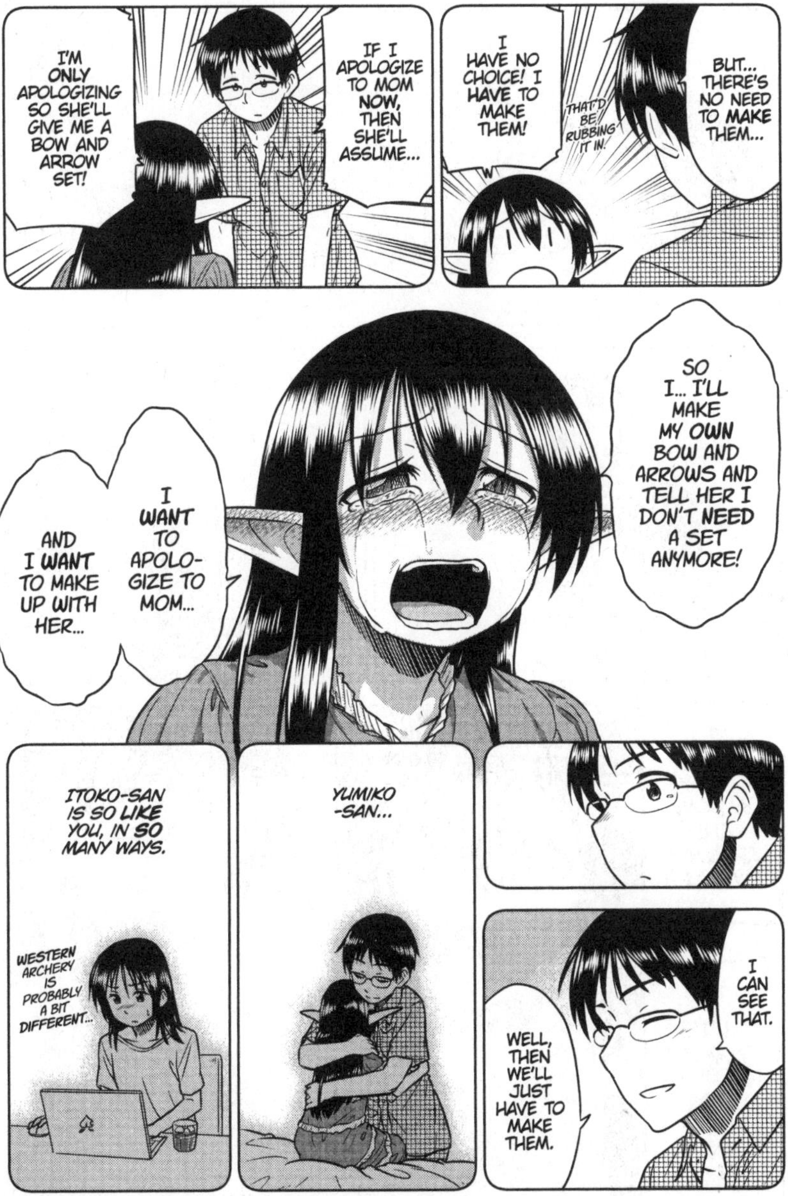
BUT... THERE'S NO NEED TO MAKE THEM...
THAT'D BE RUBBING IT IN.
I HAVE NO CHOICE! I HAVE TO MAKE THEM!
IF I APOLOGIZE TO MOM NOW, THEN SHE'LL ASSUME...
I'M ONLY APOLOGIZING SO SHE'LL GIVE ME A BOW AND ARROW SET!
SO I... I'LL MAKE MY OWN BOW AND ARROWS AND TELL HER I DON'T NEED A SET ANYMORE!
I WANT TO APOLOGIZE TO MOM...
AND I WANT TO MAKE UP WITH HER...
I CAN SEE THAT.
WELL, THEN WE'LL JUST HAVE TO MAKE THEM.
YUMIKO-SAN...
ITOKO-SAN IS SO LIKE YOU, IN SO MANY WAYS.
WESTERN ARCHERY IS PROBABLY A BIT DIFFERENT...

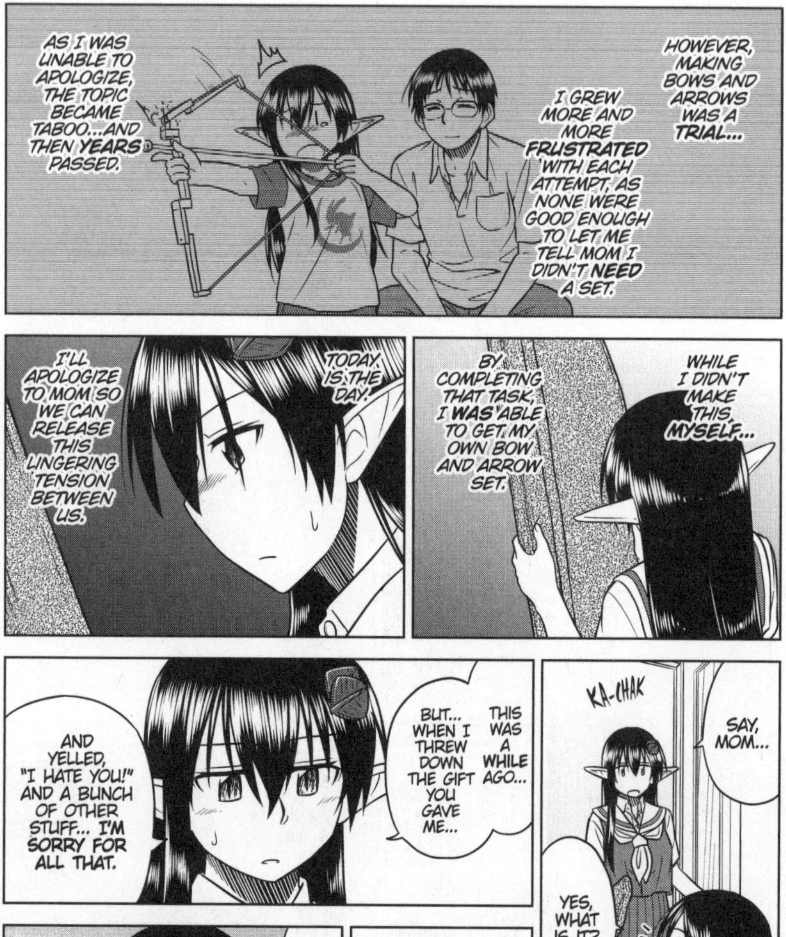
HOWEVER, MAKING BOWS AND ARROWS WAS A TRIAL...
I GREW MORE AND MORE FRUSTRATED WITH EACH ATTEMPT, AS NONE WERE GOOD ENOUGH TO LET ME TELL MOM I DIDN'T NEED A SET.
AS I WAS UNABLE TO APOLOGIZE, THE TOPIC BECAME TABOO...AND THEN YEARS PASSED.
WHILE I DIDN'T MAKE THIS, MYSELF...
BY COMPLETING THAT TASK, I WAS ABLE TO GET MY OWN BOW AND ARROW SET.
TODAY IS THE DAY.
I'LL APOLOGIZE TO MOM SO WE CAN RELEASE THIS LINGERING TENSION BETWEEN US.
KA-CHAK
SAY, MOM...
YES, WHAT IS IT?
THIS WAS A WHILE AGO...
BUT... WHEN I THREW DOWN THE GIFT YOU GAVE ME...
AND YELLED, "I HATE YOU!" AND A BUNCH OF OTHER STUFF... I'M SORRY FOR ALL THAT.
HEE HEE HEE.
TOOK YOU A PRETTY LONG TIME TO MAKE THEM, HUH?

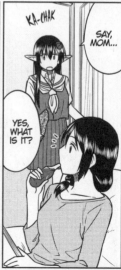

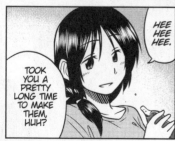

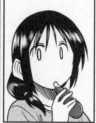

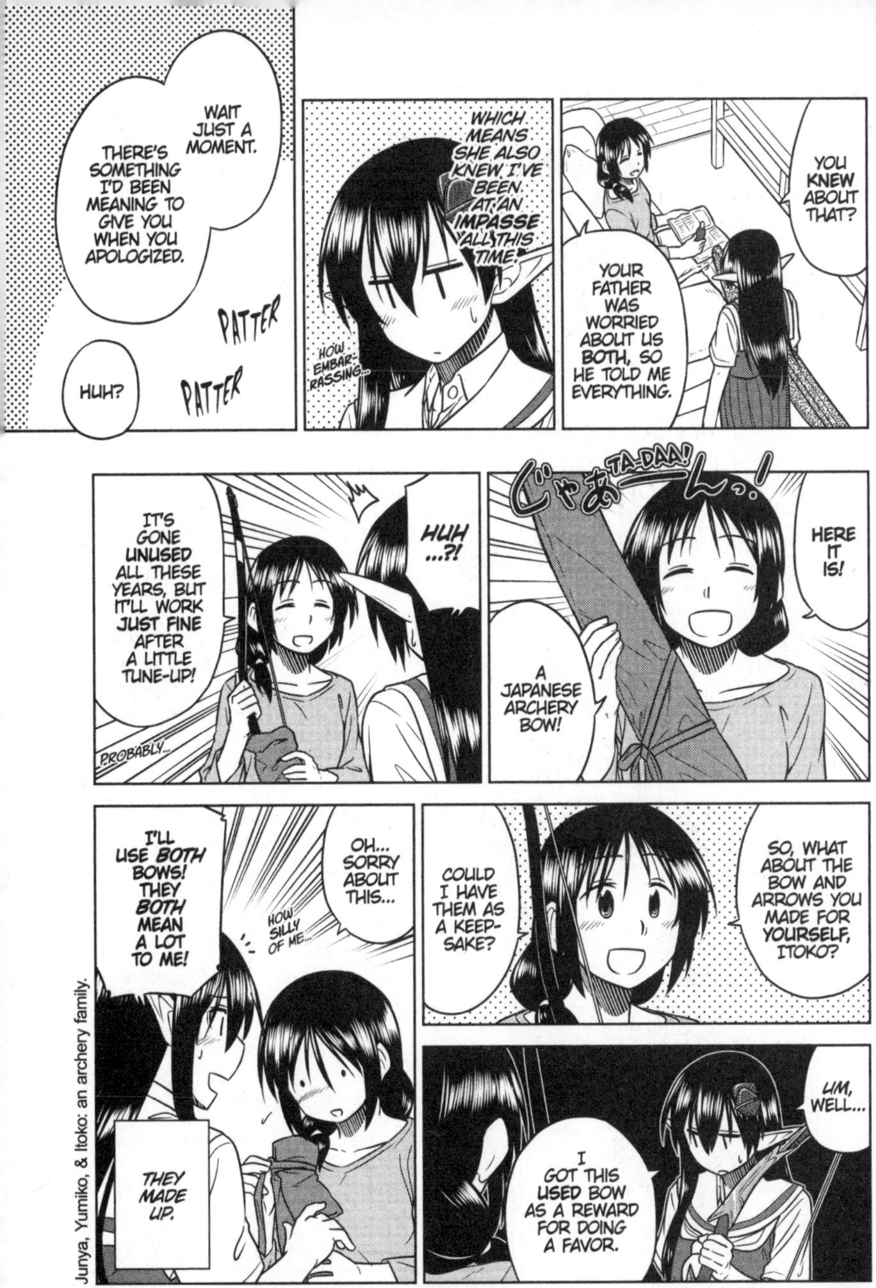
YOU KNEW ABOUT THAT?
YOUR FATHER WAS WORRIED ABOUT US BOTH, SO HE TOLD ME EVERYTHING.
WHICH MEANS SHE ALSO KNEW I'VE BEEN AT AN IMPASSE ALL THIS TIME.
HOW EMBARRASSING...
WAIT JUST A MOMENT.
THERE'S SOMETHING I'D BEEN MEANING TO GIVE YOU WHEN YOU APOLOGIZED.
PATTER
PATTER
HUH?
じゃあ〜ん
TA-DAA!
HERE IT IS!
A JAPANESE ARCHERY BOW!
HUH ...?!
IT'S GONE UNUSED ALL THESE YEARS, BUT IT'LL WORK JUST FINE AFTER A LITTLE TUNE-UP!
PROBABLY...
SO, WHAT ABOUT THE BOW AND ARROWS YOU MADE FOR YOURSELF, ITOKO?
COULD I HAVE THEM AS A KEEP-SAKE?
UM, WELL...
I GOT THIS USED BOW AS A REWARD FOR DOING A FAVOR.
OH... SORRY ABOUT THIS...
HOW SILLY OF ME...
I'LL USE BOTH BOWS! THEY BOTH MEAN A LOT TO ME!
THEY MADE UP.

Junya, Yumiko, & Itoko: an archery family.

Species Domain Volume 3 / The End

Chapter 22.5 • END

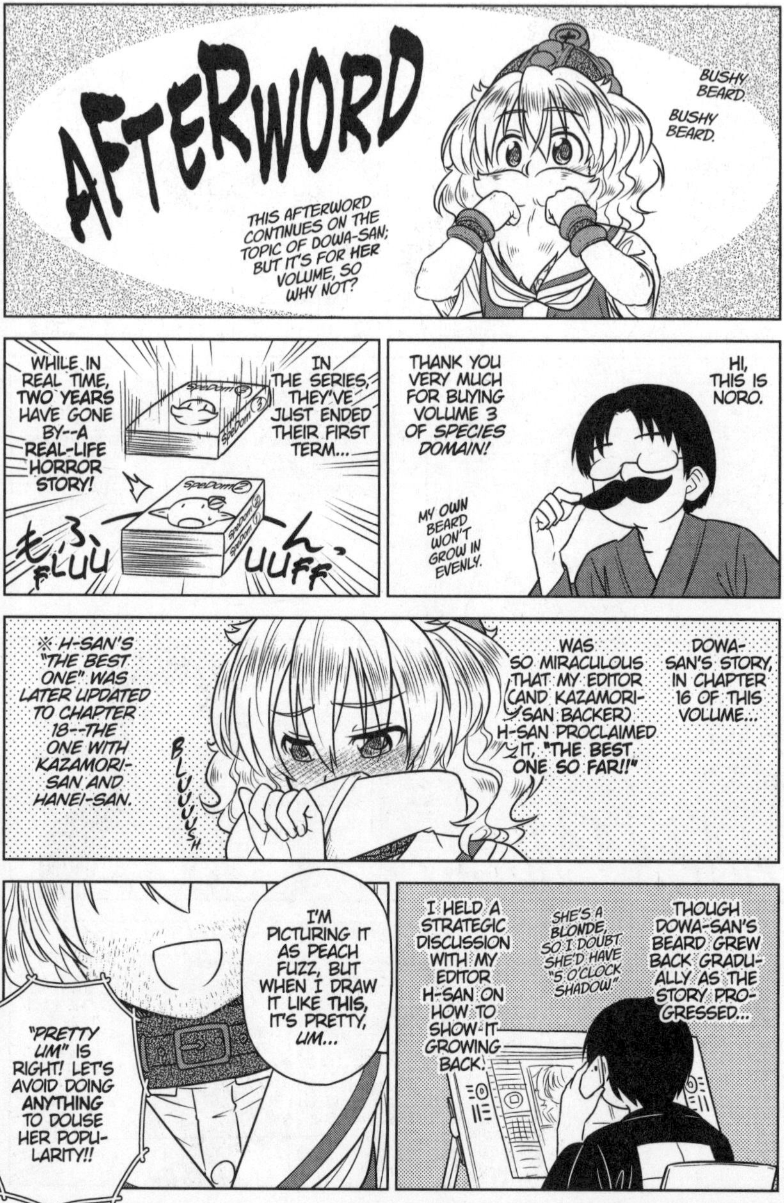
BUSHY BEARD.
BUSHY BEARD.
AFTERWORD
THIS AFTERWORD CONTINUES ON THE TOPIC OF DOWA-SAN; BUT IT'S FOR HER VOLUME, SO WHY NOT?
HI, THIS IS NORO.
THANK YOU VERY MUCH FOR BUYING VOLUME 3 OF *SPECIES DOMAIN*!
MY OWN BEARD WON'T GROW IN EVENLY.
IN THE SERIES, THEY'VE JUST ENDED THEIR FIRST TERM...
WHILE IN REAL TIME, TWO YEARS HAVE GONE BY--A REAL-LIFE HORROR STORY!
もふ FLUU
ん UUFF
DOWA-SAN'S STORY, IN CHAPTER 16 OF THIS VOLUME...
WAS SO MIRACULOUS THAT MY EDITOR (AND KAZAMORI-SAN BACKER) H-SAN PROCLAIMED IT, "THE BEST ONE SO FAR!!"
BLUUUUSH
※ H-SAN'S "THE BEST ONE" WAS LATER UPDATED TO CHAPTER 18--THE ONE WITH KAZAMORI-SAN AND HANEI-SAN.
THOUGH DOWA-SAN'S BEARD GREW BACK GRADUALLY AS THE STORY PROGRESSED...
SHE'S A BLONDE, SO I DOUBT SHE'D HAVE "5 O'CLOCK SHADOW."
I HELD A STRATEGIC DISCUSSION WITH MY EDITOR H-SAN ON HOW TO SHOW IT GROWING BACK.
I'M PICTURING IT AS PEACH FUZZ, BUT WHEN I DRAW IT LIKE THIS, IT'S PRETTY, UM...
"PRETTY UM" IS RIGHT! LET'S AVOID DOING ANYTHING TO DOUSE HER POPULARITY!!

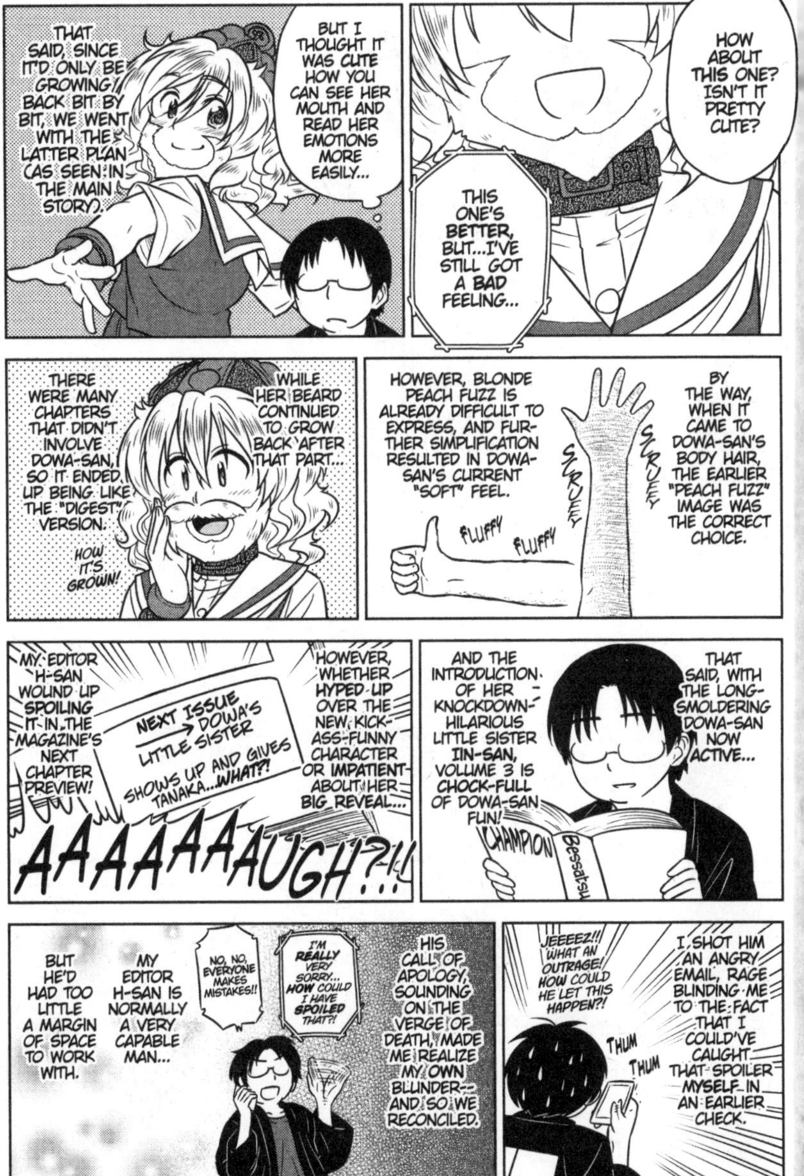

HOW ABOUT THIS ONE? ISN'T IT PRETTY CUTE?
THIS ONE'S BETTER, BUT...I'VE STILL GOT A BAD FEELING...
BUT I THOUGHT IT WAS CUTE HOW YOU CAN SEE HER MOUTH AND READ HER EMOTIONS MORE EASILY...
THAT SAID, SINCE IT'D ONLY BE GROWING BACK BIT BY BIT, WE WENT WITH THE LATTER PLAN (AS SEEN IN THE MAIN STORY).
BY THE WAY, WHEN IT CAME TO DOWA-SAN'S BODY HAIR, THE EARLIER "PEACH FUZZ" IMAGE WAS THE CORRECT CHOICE.
SCRUFFY
SCRUFFY
HOWEVER, BLONDE PEACH FUZZ IS ALREADY DIFFICULT TO EXPRESS, AND FURTHER SIMPLIFICATION RESULTED IN DOWA-SAN'S CURRENT "SOFT" FEEL.
FLUFFY
FLUFFY
WHILE HER BEARD CONTINUED TO GROW BACK AFTER THAT PART...
THERE WERE MANY CHAPTERS THAT DIDN'T INVOLVE DOWA-SAN, SO IT ENDED UP BEING LIKE THE "DIGEST" VERSION.
HOW IT'S GROWN!
THAT SAID, WITH THE LONG-SMOLDERING DOWA-SAN NOW ACTIVE...
AND THE INTRODUCTION OF HER KNOCKDOWN-HILARIOUS LITTLE SISTER IIN-SAN, VOLUME 3 IS CHOCK-FULL OF DOWA-SAN FUN!
CHAMPION
Bessatsu
HOWEVER, WHETHER HYPED-UP OVER THE NEW, KICK-ASS-FUNNY CHARACTER OR IMPATIENT ABOUT HER BIG REVEAL...
NEXT ISSUE DOWA'S LITTLE SISTER SHOWS UP AND GIVES TANAKA...WHAT?!
MY EDITOR H-SAN WOUND UP SPOILING IT IN THE MAGAZINE'S NEXT CHAPTER PREVIEW!
AAAAAAAAUGH?!!
I SHOT HIM AN ANGRY EMAIL, RAGE BLINDING ME TO THE FACT THAT I COULD'VE CAUGHT THAT SPOILER MYSELF IN AN EARLIER CHECK.
JEEEEZ!! WHAT AN OUTRAGE! HOW COULD HE LET THIS HAPPEN?!
THUM
THUM
HIS CALL OF APOLOGY, SOUNDING ON THE VERGE OF DEATH, MADE ME REALIZE MY OWN BLUNDER-- AND SO WE RECONCILED.
I'M REALLY VERY SORRY... HOW COULD I HAVE SPOILED THAT?!
NO, NO, EVERYONE MAKES MISTAKES!!
MY EDITOR H-SAN IS NORMALLY A VERY CAPABLE MAN...
BUT HE'D HAD TOO LITTLE A MARGIN OF SPACE TO WORK WITH.

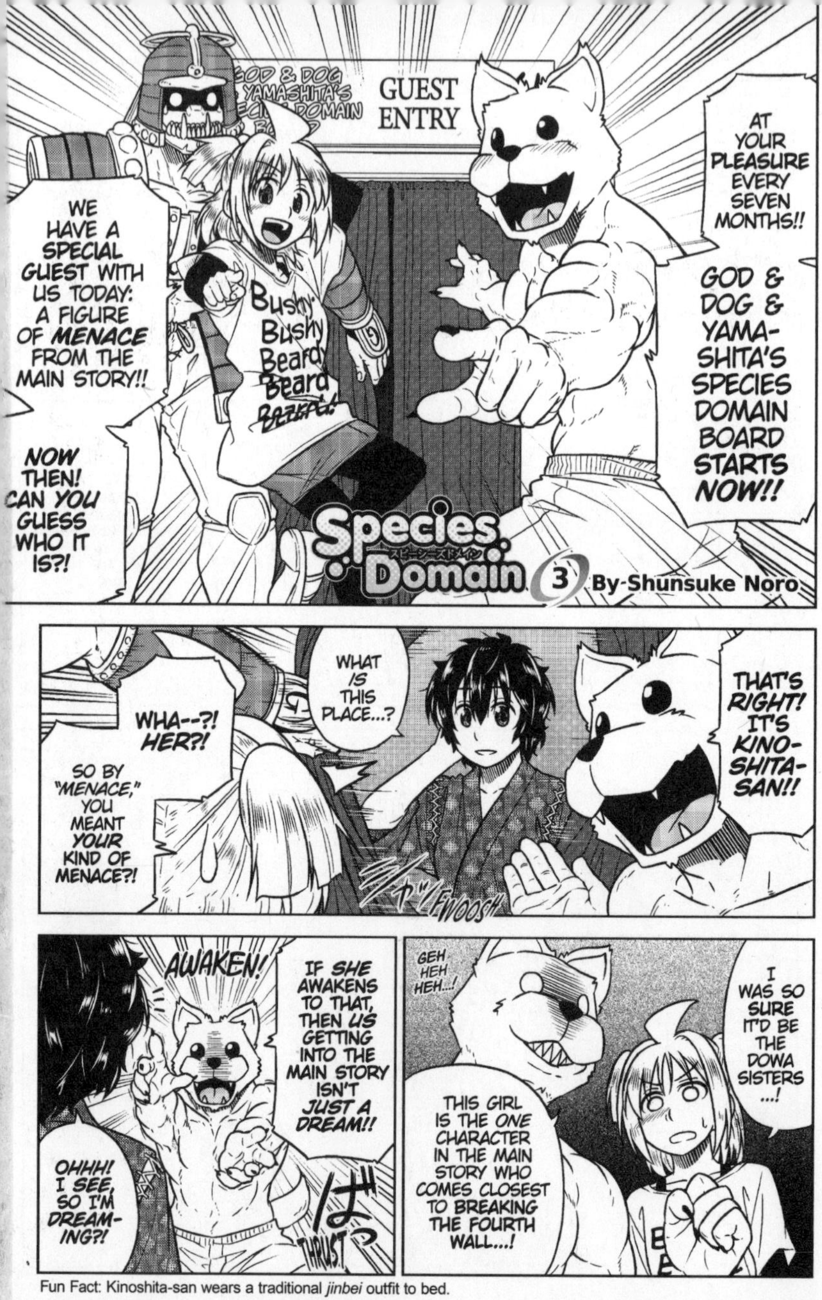
AT YOUR PLEASURE EVERY SEVEN MONTHS!!
GOD & DOG & YAMA-SHITA'S SPECIES DOMAIN BOARD STARTS NOW!!
GUEST ENTRY
WE HAVE A SPECIAL GUEST WITH US TODAY: A FIGURE OF MENACE FROM THE MAIN STORY!!
NOW THEN! CAN YOU GUESS WHO IT IS?!
Species Domain 3
By Shunsuke Noro
THAT'S RIGHT! IT'S KINO-SHITA-SAN!!
WHAT IS THIS PLACE...?
WHA--?! HER?!
SO BY "MENACE," YOU MEANT YOUR KIND OF MENACE?!
FWOOSH
I WAS SO SURE IT'D BE THE DOWA SISTERS ...!
GEH HEH HEH...!
THIS GIRL IS THE ONE CHARACTER IN THE MAIN STORY WHO COMES CLOSEST TO BREAKING THE FOURTH WALL...!
IF SHE AWAKENS TO THAT, THEN US GETTING INTO THE MAIN STORY ISN'T JUST A DREAM!!
AWAKEN!
OHHH! I SEE, SO I'M DREAM-ING?!
THRUST

Fun Fact: Kinoshita-san wears a traditional *jinbei* outfit to bed.